HUMAN RIGHTS

IN NATIONAL AND INTERNATIONAL LAW

*The Proceedings of the Second International
Conference on the European Convention on
Human Rights held in Vienna under the auspices
of the Council of Europe and the University
of Vienna, 18–20 October 1965*

EDITED BY

A. H. ROBERTSON

MANCHESTER UNIVERSITY PRESS
OCEANA PUBLICATIONS, INC.

© 1968 MANCHESTER UNIVERSITY PRESS

Published by the University of Manchester at
THE UNIVERSITY PRESS
316–324 Oxford Road, Manchester M13 9NR
Reprinted 1970

U.S.A.
OCEANA PUBLICATIONS, INC.
75 Main Street, Dobbs Ferry, N. Y. 10522

Library of Congress Catalog Card No. LC 67-24124
G.B.SBN 7190 0296 6

distributed in India by
N.M. Tripathi Private Ltd.,
Booksellers & Publishers,
Princess Street, Bombay-2

These Proceedings are also published in a German edition,
under the title *Menschenrechte im Staatsrecht und im Völkerrecht*, by Verlag C. F. Müller, Karlsruhe, and in French,
under the title *La Convention européenne des Droits de
l'Homme devant le droit national et international*, by Presses
universitaires de Bruxelles, A.S.B.L., Brussels

Printed in Great Britain by Butler & Tanner Ltd, Frome and London

Under the patronage of

Chairmen of the Sessions

Organising Committee

Chairmen

PROFESSOR FRITZ SCHWIND, *Dean of the Faculty of Law of the University of Vienna*

M. POLYS MODINOS, *Deputy Secretary-General of the Council of Europe*

Members

DR HERIBERT GOLSONG, *Registrar of the European Court of Human Rights*

DR WILLFRIED GREDLER, *Permanent Representative of the Federal Republic of Austria to the Council of Europe*

DR RUDOLF KIRSCHLÄGER, *Deputy Secretary-General of the Ministry of Foreign Affairs of the Federal Republic of Austria*

DR EDWIN LOEBENSTEIN, *Director-General of the Constitutional Service of the Chancellery of the Federal Republic of Austria*

MR A. B. MCNULTY, *Secretary of the European Commission of Human Rights*

DR A. H. ROBERTSON, *Head of the Directorate of Human Rights of the Council of Europe*

PROFESSOR HANS SCHIMA, *Vice-Dean of the Faculty of Law of the University of Vienna*

DR CH. VILLGRATTNER, *Head of the Office of International Law, Ministry of Foreign Affairs of the Federal Republic of Austria*

Secretariat

PROFESSOR FELIX ERMACORA, *Professor at the Vienna Law Faculty, Member of the European Commission of Human Rights*

DR WILLIBALD PAHR, *Member of the Constitutional Service of the Chancellery of the Federal Republic of Austria, Austrian Member of the Committee of Experts on Human Rights of the Council of Europe*

M. KAREL VASAK, *Principal Administrator, Directorate of Human Rights of the Council of Europe*

Contents*

		page
PREFACE		xi
INTRODUCTION		1
The opening ceremony:		
Josef Klaus		1
Peter Smithers		3
Günther Winkler, *Dean of the Faculty of Law and Political Science, University of Vienna*		6

I OBLIGATIONS OF A STATE PARTY TO A TREATY
  AS REGARDS ITS MUNICIPAL LAW — 11

Max Sørensen, *Professor in the University of Aarhus; member of the European Commission of Human Rights* — 11
Written Communications:
  Karl Doehring, *Honorary Professor, Member of the Max-Planck-Institut für ausländisches öffentliches und Völkerrecht, Heidelberg* — 31
  Helfried Pfeifer, *Professor in the University of Vienna* — 34
  René Marcic, *Professor in the University of Salzburg* — 38
Summary of the discussion:
  W. J. Ganshof van der Meersch, *Professor in the University of Brussels* — 41
  I. Seidl-Hohenveldern, *Professor in the University of Cologne* — 42
  Francesco Capotorti, *Professor in the University of Bari* — 42
  Karl Zemanek, *Professor in the University of Vienna* — 43
  Felix Ermacora — 44
  Jacques Velu, *Procureur du Roi, Brussels* — 44
Summing up by Max Sørensen — 46

II STATUS OF THE EUROPEAN CONVENTION IN THE
   HIERARCHY OF RULES OF LAW — 47

Alfred Verdross, *Emeritus Professor, University of Vienna; Judge, European Court of Human Rights* — 47
Written Communications:
  Heinz Guradze, *Honorary Professor in the University of Cologne* — 56
  Hans Beck, *Attorney, Vienna* — 59
  Alfred Kobzina, *Parlamentsrat, Vienna* — 61

*The titles of contributors whose names appear in the list of Patrons or the Organising Committee are not repeated in the Contents, and those of contributors of more than one paper or entry in the discussion are given once only. A complete list of participants the Conference is given in an Appendix.

vii

page

Summary of the discussion:
  H. Golsong   64
  Michel Virally, *Professor at the Institut des Hautes Etudes Internationales, Geneva*   65
  ✗ Seán MacBride,   66
  H. Miehsler, *Lecturer in the University of Vienna*   66
  André Vanwelkenhuyzen, *Director, Centre of Public Law, University of Brussels*   67
  Hans Spanner, *Professor in the University of Munich*   68
  Hans Weiler, *Counsellor, Austrian Federal Chancellery*   69
  Karl Doehring   70
Summing up by Alfred Verdross   70

III POSSIBILITIES OF CONFLICT IN NATIONAL LEGAL SYSTEMS BETWEEN THE EUROPEAN CONVENTION AND OTHER INTERNATIONAL AGREEMENTS   72

Francesco Capotorti, *Professor in the University of Bari*   72
Summary of the discussion:
  Karl Zemanek   93
  Louis B. Sohn, *Professor in the Harvard Law School*   93
  Michel Waelbroeck, *Director of Legal Research in the Institute of European Studies, University of Brussels*   94
  Felix Ermacora   95

IV DOES THE CONVENTION HAVE THE FORCE OF 'ORDRE PUBLIC' IN MUNICIPAL LAW?   97

W. J. Ganshof van der Meersch   97
Summary of the discussion:
  Egon Schwelb, *Yale Law School*   144
  Charles van Reepinghen, *Professor in the University of Louvain; member of the Royal Commission on Law Reform*   147
  M. H. van Hoogstraten, *Secretary-General, Hague Conference on Private International Law*   147
  Felix Ermacora   148
  André Vanwelkenhuyzen   149
  W. F. Prins, *Professor in the University of Utrecht*   149
  B. N. Esen, *Professor in the University of Ankara*   149
  Gustaf Petrén, *Judge; Swedish Secretary-General of the Nordic Council*   150

V COMPARISON OF THE JURISPRUDENCE OF NATIONAL COURTS WITH THAT OF THE ORGANS OF THE CONVENTION AS REGARDS THE RIGHTS OF THE INDIVIDUAL IN COURT PROCEEDINGS   151

Thomas Buergenthal, *Associate Professor in the State University of New York*   151

page

Written Communication:
   Nicola Picardi, *Professor; Judge, Ministry of Justice, Rome*   200
Summary of the discussion:
   W. J. Ganshof van der Meersch   204
   M. J. van Emde Boas, *Lecturer in the University of Leyden*   206
   V. Liebscher, *Public Attorney, Vienna*   206
   F. Capotorti   207
   Hans Weiler   208
   Karl Doehring   208
   I. Seidl-Hohenveldern   209
   Peter Benenson, *President, Amnesty International*   210
Summing up by Thomas Buergenthal   211

VI COMPARISON OF THE JURISPRUDENCE OF NATIONAL
   COURTS WITH THAT OF THE ORGANS OF THE
   CONVENTION AS REGARDS OTHER RIGHTS   214
Ulrich Scheuner, *Professor in the University of Bonn*   214
Summary of the discussion:
   J. Unger, *Professor in the University of Birmingham*   266
   Felix Ermacora   267
   H. Pfeifer   267
   Karl Doehring   269
   H. Golsong   269
   T. Mayer-Maly, *Professor in the University of Cologne*   270
   K. Vasak   270
Summing up by Ulrich Scheuner   273

VII CONSEQUENCES OF THE APPLICATION OF THE CON-
   VENTION IN MUNICIPAL AND INTERNATIONAL
   LAW   275
Roger Pinto, *Professor in the University of Paris*   275
Written Communication:
   A. H. Robertson   282
Summary of the discussion:
   Seán MacBride   286
   Jacqueline Rochette, *Avocat, Cour de Paris*   286
   Michel Gaudet, *Director-General of the Legal Service,*
      European Communities   286
   Louis B. Sohn   287
   C.-A. Fleischhauer, *Ministry of Foreign Affairs, Bonn*   287

VIII THE PROTECTION OF HUMAN RIGHTS ON A
   UNIVERSAL BASIS: RECENT EXPERIENCE AND
   PROPOSALS   289
J. E. S. Fawcett, *Fellow of All Souls' College, Oxford; member*
   of the European Commission of Human Rights   289

page

Written Communications:
János Tóth, *International Commission of Jurists*   299
Egon Schwelb   307
Summary of the discussion:
Andrew Martin, Q.C.; *Member, Law Commission, U.K.*   317
Paul Weis, *Legal Director, Office of the U.N. High Com-
missioner for Refugees*   319
Georges Aronstein, *Secretary-General, Ligue Belge pour la
Défense des Droits de l'Homme*   321
I. C. MacGibbon, *Professor in the University of Edinburgh* 322
Felix Ermacora   323
J. J. Cremona, *Professor; Judge, European Court of Human
Rights*   325
Peter Benenson   326
Father M. B. Crowe, *National University of Ireland*   327
G. O. Warburg, *European Representative of B'nai B'rith* 327
Gordon L. Weil, *Assistant Spokesman for the Commission
of the European Economic Community*   327
Summing up by Andrew Martin   328

IX THE PROTECTION OF HUMAN RIGHTS WITHIN THE
FRAMEWORK OF EXISTING REGIONAL ORGANI-
ZATIONS   330

Jean-Flavien Lalive, *member of the Geneva Bar; former
Secretary-General, International Commission of Jurists*   330
Written Communications:
Gordon L. Weil   342
Paul Weis   346
Louis B. Sohn   353
Summary of the discussion:
Egon Schwelb   355
Louis B. Sohn   356
János Tóth   357
B. N. Esen   358
C. W. van Santen, *member of the Committee of Experts on
Human Rights*   358
Paul Weis   359
Pierre Mertens, *Research Assistant, University of Brussels* 361
Summing up by Jean-Flavien Lalive   361

X CONCLUSIONS AND FUTURE PROSPECTS   363

Speeches by:
Polys Modinos   363
F. Schwind   380

APPENDIX: List of participants   383

INDEX   389

Preface

The Second International Conference about the European Convention on Human Rights was held in Vienna from 18 to 20 October 1965, organised jointly by the Law Faculty of the University of Vienna and the Council of Europe, with the support of the Austrian Government. It was one of the ceremonies which marked the sixth centenary of the University of Vienna. The importance of the occasion and its wider political implications are emphasised in the three speeches which constitute the Introduction to this book.

This Conference was the successor to the first of its kind, which was held in Strasbourg in November 1960 under arrangements made by the Strasbourg Law Faculty and the Council of Europe. The Proceedings on that occasion were published (in French only) under the title of *La Protection Internationale des Droits de l'Homme dans le cadre Européen*. The Proceedings of the Vienna Conference are being published in three languages. This is the English edition.

The European Convention on Human Rights, signed in Rome on 4 November 1950, not only constitutes the most important single achievement of the Council of Europe; it also marks a significant step in the development of international law. Under its terms the Contracting Parties undertake to secure to everyone within their jurisdiction a series of rights and freedoms taken from the Universal Declaration of the United Nations; in addition, they have set up a European Commission and Court of Human Rights 'to ensure the observance of the engagements undertaken by the High Contracting Parties in the present Convention'. Not only may States refer alleged violations to the Commission; individuals may bring complaints even against their own governments, provided that the latter have agreed to this novel procedure.

This 'right of individual petition' first became effective in 1955, when six Contracting Parties had agreed to its exercise. Eleven European governments have now done so, with the result that this remedy is available to at least 150 million persons within the jurisdiction of the High Contracting Parties. Many new problems arise out of the operation of this procedure; some of them were discussed at the Vienna Conference and are reflected in this book.

In a number of European countries an international treaty, once ratified, has the force of law in the internal legal system and can be directly applied by the national courts. In these countries, therefore, the European Convention has a double value. Not only does it provide an international remedy for the individual whose rights are denied; it may also be invoked to obtain a national remedy by reason of the fact that its provisions are directly binding on the national judge. It is evidently preferable in the general interest that the rights of the citizen should be effectively secured by the national courts under domestic law, rather than that violations should occur at the national level and international machinery be invoked by way of redress. The direct application of the Convention at the domestic level is therefore to be warmly welcomed.

But the application of international rules in national law gives rise to many problems. These were the main subject of discussion at the Vienna Conference. What obligations does a State assume in respect of its municipal law? Generally speaking, there is agreement that it must make its municipal law conform to its undertakings under a treaty. Must it do so by enacting domestic legislation transforming the international obligations into rules of internal law? Or is the better system that of making the treaty as such an integral part of domestic law? Even if the latter system is adopted, it remains to be seen whether all the rules of the treaty are capable of direct application at the national level; other problems of interpretation, moreover, are likely to arise, particularly if the treaty is not drafted in the national language, as is likely to be the case for many of the Parties to a multilateral convention. Are additional clauses of implementation then necessary?

In the legal systems of many countries there exists a 'hierarchy' of rules of law. A written constitution normally takes precedence, in case of conflict, over simple or ordinary rules of law. But certain laws of particular importance passed subsequently to the adoption of the constitution may, if the necessary formalities are complied with, be accorded the rank of 'constitutional laws' and thus achieve the same status in the 'hierarchy' as the constitution itself. When the Convention on Human Rights is directly incorporated into internal law, and when it deals in large measure with the very matters that normally form the object of constitutional guarantees, what is its place in the hierarchy of the rules of law? The answer, no doubt, will vary from country to country, but a comparative study is both necessary and instructive; it will show that in one country, at least, a treaty duly ratified 'outranks' even the national constitution and will take precedence in case of conflict.

But if the Convention on Human Rights is accorded the force of law in the domestic legal system by reason of the fact that it is a duly-ratified international treaty, it may well be that it is not the only treaty relevant to a particular matter to which this consideration applies. In this age of international legislation, when the United Nations Treaty Series contains more than five hundred volumes of international agreements concluded since the war, a given State may well be bound by several separate obligations in similar or related fields. These obligations may be identical, similar or divergent; they may have been assumed towards the same or a different group of partners. Here, then, it is necessary to study the situation which may result from possible conflicts between different international obligations, particularly in the case of those European countries which have assumed such far-reaching commitments under the treaties establishing the European Communities.

One subject that was discussed in Vienna is of particular importance to continental lawyers but unfamiliar to their brethren trained in the common law. This relates to the notion of *ordre public*. This expression has been deliberately kept in French, because its connotation is so much wider than that of 'public policy' (the nearest English equivalent), while the English expression 'public order' is in no way comparable. *Ordre public* has been defined as 'that body of institutions and rules designed to ensure, in a given country, the satisfactory functioning of the public services, security and morality of transactions between individuals, who may not exclude their application in private agreements'.[1] Its purpose is to ensure 'the supremacy of society over the individual' and its effect is to restrict the unfettered will of the parties to an agreement.[2]

Many rules of domestic law are held to be rules of *ordre public* and are therefore binding on individual litigants whether they will or no. Is this the case with the rules laid down by the Convention on Human Rights, once it has been incorporated into domestic law? Most people would agree that this is so for certain provisions of the Convention; for example the right to life and the prohibition of torture cannot be waived by private agreement. For other rights the position may be different; thus the right to a 'fair and public hearing . . . by an independent and impartial tribunal established by law' may be waived by the parties to an arbitration agreement, and the right to marry may be suspended by enrolment in certain forms of the public service. But the question of characterisation of the rules laid down by the Convention does not only affect the question of waiver; it also has procedural implications of considerable importance. Rules of *ordre public* must be invoked *ex officio* by the judge in proceedings before a national court. Does this apply equally to the Convention on Human Rights? Must the national judge apply its rules on his own initiative even if the parties to the case before him have not invoked them? If he fails to do so, can that failure constitute the basis

[1] Definition of Henri Capitant, quoted by Professor Ganshof van der Meersch in Chapter IV.
[2] Ibid.

of an application to the Commission alleging a violation of the Convention? It will be seen that the answers to these questions can have great practical importance both for national tribunals and for the Commission of Human Rights itself, particularly when it is considering the application of the rule of exhaustion of domestic remedies.

One of the most striking results of the direct application of the Convention in internal law is the growing volume of case-law. The jurisprudence relating to the Convention (in the continental sense of the term 'jurisprudence', which is coming to be used to an increasing extent in the English texts) is assuming considerable proportions. The Commission of Human Rights has taken about two thousand decisions, the more important of which are published in the *Yearbook of the European Convention on Human Rights*; about two hundred decisions of national courts interpreting, or referring to, the Convention have been collected and published in summary form by the Directorate of Human Rights of the Council of Europe. This volume of case-law is constantly growing, and provides much material for analysis and comparative study.

Two sessions of the Conference were devoted to this subject. One of them considered the rights of the individual in court proceedings —principally, the rights guaranteed to a person deprived of his liberty, the right to a fair trial and the right to an effective remedy, which might all be included in the notion of 'due process of law'. The second such session discussed the other rights secured by the Convention and its First Protocol, of which the number is greater (twelve) though the volume of jurisprudence is less extensive.

A series of interesting problems arise in the analysis of this case-law. First, as regards the decisions of the Commission: is its approach to alleged violations constant or has there been, as some people think, an evolution with the passage of time, perhaps as a result of changes in membership? Similarly, are the decisions of national courts consistent, both within a given country and between different countries? Again, are the interpretations given to particular provisions of the Convention by national courts the same as those of the Commission; if not, what are the divergencies? Is it true, as some scholars believe, that national courts have been more liberal in their interpretation than the international organs set up by the Convention? Moreover, if there are divergencies of interpretation, does this matter? Should some procedure be established to secure uniformity of interpretation, comparable to that set up by Article 177 of the Common Market treaty, perhaps by empowering the Court of Human Rights to give authoritative rulings that would be binding on national courts? The Vienna Conference undertook the most detailed study of these questions that has been published to date.

It is generally recognised that the system for the protection of human rights established by the European Convention is, though far from perfect, the most effective yet devised. But this is not the only attempt to secure international action in this field. The United Nations was, of course, the pioneer; and much has been done by the Organisation of American States, whose 'American Declaration on the Rights and Duties of Man', adopted at Bogota in April 1948, even ante-dates the Universal Declaration. Moreover, in recent years a number of proposals have been made for international action on a regional basis in other parts of the world.

The last day of the Conference was therefore devoted to the protection of human rights on a universal basis and within the framework of other regional organisations. This involved consideration of various techniques other than that of the European Convention. What has been the effect of the Universal Declaration? What is the value of other methods used by the United Nations and the Specialised Agencies, such as declarations (sometimes thought to be vested with more authority than simple resolutions since they are supposed to be declaratory of international law), publicity measures, reporting systems and complaint procedures? Is the proposal for a United Nations High Commissioner for Human Rights likely to provide an effective safeguard? What may be hoped from the UN draft Covenants?

At the regional level, one is led to enquire whether there are prospects for effective international action in other continents, while a major problem both of method and of principle is also posed: is it desirable to encourage regional action in other parts of the world, on the ground that it can be more readily achieved or is likely to be more effective as between neighbouring countries with similar political and legal systems; or is it to be deplored as a threat to the principle of universality which endangers the global solutions attempted in the framework of the United Nations?

The reader of this Preface will readily understand that there was ample material for discussion at the Vienna Conference on Human Rights. He will not find in this book the answers to all the questions posed; but he will find interesting and stimulating discussion of them by an outstanding body of specialists. A final chapter seeks to draw conclusions from the Conference and expresses certain ideas as to the future prospects for international co-operation in the protection of human rights.

A final word of thanks must be said to all those who have participated in the preparation of this publication containing the Proceedings of the Conference. There have been too many for them to be mentioned individually. But since it has been produced in three languages, a particular word of gratitude is due to the Translation Department of the Council of Europe, which provided the texts in English and French, and to a number of individuals who lent their good offices to make possible the German edition.

Strasbourg
  30 September 1966

Introduction

THE OPENING CEREMONY

JOSEF KLAUS

It is a happy coincidence that in the very year in which we have just celebrated the 600th anniversary of our venerable University of Vienna, an international organisation as important as the Council of Europe, represented by a group of highly qualified experts, should be studying, in concert with the Faculty of Law and Political Science of our University, problems in which man is the central concern.

It is opportune, in this fifteenth year of the existence of the European Convention on Human Rights, that specialists should discuss questions arising from the application of the Convention by national and international courts and should consider whether the objectives which the Contracting Parties wished to achieve by means of this highly important instrument can be achieved and whether they are sufficient to ensure the protection of human rights and fundamental freedoms.

In the preamble to the Convention it is rightly stated, among other things, that the maintenance and further realisation of human rights and fundamental freedoms is one of the methods of achieving greater unity between the Member States and that these fundamental freedoms are the foundation of justice and peace in the world.

Thus is affirmed one of the essential aims pursued by the States in co-operation, which illustrates the ultimate purpose of their endeavours.

It is not by chance that this deeply significant affirmation appears at the beginning of this politically important document. It serves, as it were, as a means to resist the pressure to which man is exposed today from all sides, as a consequence of the discoveries and practical application of science and of the authority exercised by the powers that be.

At a time when space exploration has become possible and when scientific research, notably in the fields of technology, chemistry and physics, foreshadows further discoveries which might well cause fundamental upheavals in the social order, we are fully justified in asking ourselves whether these new discoveries, when put into practice, will really benefit humanity or whether they may not, on the contrary, lead to its destruction.

We read with disquiet that the time may not be far off when we shall be able to determine the sex of our children at will, when it will be possible to influence the processes of procreation and birth, and thus of man himself. We cannot but ask ourselves whether this is still the same man whom our General Civil Code described 150 years ago, in rather poetical language, as having self-evident, inalienable rights which entitle him to be considered by the State as a person—and not therefore as the creature of the State.

We feel bound by this conception of man which forms the basis of our Civil Code and of the rules of law of many other States; it should be the constant concern of jurists, legislators, courts and administrations everywhere. Man must be enabled to develop his personality and order his own life. We must guarantee respect for human dignity and see that small communities are safeguarded. Man, as a natural and rational being, has not yet disappeared from the face of the earth. Jurists must provide legislators with a scientific instrument for determining the limits to be set to interference by the State and other agencies in man's private life. The State must, in its turn, through its legislation, courts and administrative authorities, give legal force to the findings of jurists.

The *societas perfecta* cannot be achieved by acknowledging human rights and fundamental freedoms in fine-sounding words in the Constitution, yet failing to apply them in legislation and legal practice in a manner permitting man, as a rational being, freely to develop personality and exercise his right to order his own life.

This is a vital problem in our present highly diversified society, in which the value attached to the individual is often rather doubtful. It is a problem which States must tackle in their relations with one another.

Let me enlarge on some further aspects of these relations and of the tasks devolving on States in this age in which we hear so much about co-existence.

We are very grateful to the Council of Europe and to its energetic Secretary-General, Mr Smithers, for choosing Vienna as the setting for this Conference. This choice reflects, I think, certain aspects of foreign policy which are important both for Austria and for the Council of Europe.

Austria's traditional role in Europe, conditioned by its history, has undergone a perceptible regeneration, I might even say, a timely transformation, since Austria's independence was restored by the signing of the State Treaty and its neutrality solemnly proclaimed. Occupying, as it does, a key position in present-day European events, from the geographical as well as the historical viewpoint—our country's situation, as one glance at the map will confirm, makes it a turntable for the whole of Europe—Austria can claim to be particularly qualified for this new role. The events, familiar to all of you, which have taken place in neighbouring countries have lent political significance to these historical and geographical factors. Austria's position over the past twenty years has been determined by the clash of two ideologies. As long as the hermetical sealing off of the two worlds, as a result of the so-called 'cold war', was the dominant feature of East–West relations, Austria could not conceive or define its role in Europe as other than that of an impassable boundary. However, since events in the Eastern world have taken a new turn, we Austrians are trying to look upon our country's situation as that of a link between two worlds which, overlooking their ideological differences, have begun a dialogue which raises new hopes. The purpose of such a link is, of course, to hold together two divergent, perhaps antagonistic elements; from this simile, Gentlemen, you will see that a new political role has devolved on Austria.

We consider it particularly important that we have succeeded, in the past ten years, in restoring normal relations with our neighbours in the East and South-East and that we have thereby contributed to stabilising European policy. In your discussions on the European Human Rights Convention, Gentlemen, there is one fact which you will not, cannot, forget: Vienna is the window on the Eastern world and everything you say here will be heard across the frontier.

But I think that the choice of Vienna as a meeting place is of significance for the Council of Europe too. In January of this year, when addressing the Consultative Assembly of the Council of Europe, I pleaded for co-operation on a 'Greater Europe' scale. When Austrians speak of Europe, they have in mind a Europe of continental dimensions. The Council of Europe itself declared in one of its Recommendations that it was its duty 'to contribute at the same time towards the unification of a free and democratic Europe and the easing of tension which has begun between East and West'.[1] You may rest assured that that part of Europe which you wish to interest in your activities will not fail to note that you are holding your Conference within the walls of this city. Your efforts will already have achieved some measure of success if our neighbours regard the choice of Vienna not merely as a courteous gesture on your part towards Austria, but also as a friendly invitation to them to accord to your activities the attention which they deserve.

I trust that, in this respect, your meeting will be crowned with success.

PETER SMITHERS

I am sure that you would wish me at the outset of our proceedings to offer your thanks to the Austrian Government, in the distinguished

[1] *Recommendation 389* on East–West Relations of 23 April 1964.

person of the Federal Chancellor, for the hospitality of the Austrian State and people, and to the University of Vienna and particularly to its Law Faculty, headed by its very distinguished Dean, Dr Winkler, who has organised our meeting. Vienna is, of course, a most seductive place to the tourist, particularly to the tourist with a highly developed intellectual and aesthetic sensibility, which of course we all are. But in the realms of international thought it needs, perhaps, an international official, a connoisseur in such matters, to sense and relish fully the bracing atmosphere which pervades this capital. It is not only the great imperial monuments which are here preserved. The acute political perception of the outside world, the sense of international common interest, which made possible a great empire, have their modern development in a city which is at the heart and centre of Europe politically as well as geographically. It will therefore come as no surprise to you if I now thank the Chancellor and his government colleagues, and the Austrian Parliament, for the contribution which they both make to the work of the Council of Europe, a contribution whose richness is matched not to the relatively modest physical resources of the Austrian state, but to the wealth of experience and tradition of the Austrian people gathered over many centuries.

Man has indeed travelled a long and difficult road from the days when he lived in the primitive society of the tribe, down to the present time when he is part of a social structure of immense and growing complexity. Today the development of modern technology has made him a member not only of the social structure of his state but also of a wider social structure which is international in character. As more and more problems of an economic or technical nature compel us to deal with them by international action, man himself becomes directly concerned with their solutions and therefore a part of an international social structure.

Ever since the beginning of civilised society down to the present time the position of man in society has been conceived as a balance of rights and obligations: what he was entitled to expect of his fellow men organised in society, and what they were entitled to expect of him. As society becomes organised not merely nationally, but also internationally, by the rapidly increasing numbers of conventions and agreements coming into force to regulate the details of daily life, man himself finds that his rights and obligations, which used to change as he crossed national frontiers, now to an increasing degree travel with him as part of his baggage.

The Council of Europe is the classical instrument in our continent for handling juridical and technical problems between governments by way of negotiating conventions, and over fifty such are now in force with many others to follow. It is now engaged in drawing up a comprehensive programme of work which conceives of man as a member of a European society and which seeks to deal with the problems which thus confront him in various walks of life: his economic, social, and hygienic requirements as a European, his education as such, his cultural and aesthetic environment, and in particular the European legal structure within which he lives. All this is an outgrowth of the Statute of the Council of Europe, a legal instrument which was conceived by those who drew it up in such a way as to permit the institution governed by it to grow and develop with the times.

Written into our Statute is the fundamental concept of respect for the rule of law, and, in Article 3, the concept of international guarantees for the rights of man in society. Both concepts are fundamental to the definition of the role of the Council as a means of promoting peace and co-operation between peoples, and both are basic to its national composition. Founded upon the concept of Human Rights expressed in the Statute, which in turn derives from the 'Universal Declaration' of the United Nations, is the daring international experiment of the European Convention on Human Rights. To put it in crude terms of politics, through this Convention man turns to the European society of which he is now a member, to seek added protection for certain basic rights assured to him by the Convention within the State in which he lives.

How important is this problem? Is it real or only theoretical? The fact is that every month that passes sees some new scientific discovery of importance which will in due time find its application through technology in the daily affairs of mankind. And as the control of man over his physical environment thus daily becomes more absolute, so governments are obliged to prescribe ever more complex rules to control the actions of man. It is clearly foreseeable that the State will be obliged in the future, as it has been in the past, but in a greatly increased degree, to lay down the duties of man towards a modern technological society, so that he may enjoy its benefits, and indeed to prevent him from destroying himself by abuse of the powers which modern technology has conferred upon him. It is against the background of this inevitable increase in the control over man's actions by the State, that the protection of his basic human rights against the State is a real and an important problem. It is with this problem that the European Convention on Human Rights is concerned. After 15 years of existence, is this instrument developing as our times require, and if not, what action is required of us? Hidden perhaps beneath phrases of juridical formulation, perplexing to the layman, to be found in your programme, here is the grand question which is posed to this eminent gathering.

In such company it would be impertinent for me to try to make any contribution to the legal substance of what you have to do. But I would like to venture a couple of thoughts upon the wider setting of our work as I see it from my desk in Strasbourg. We in Europe have certain fairly well-defined concepts of the rights of man. They find one of their expressions in our Convention. They find other expression in a different political system in the States of Eastern Europe. But the concept of the Rights of Man is basic to both and indeed to every civilisation whatever its ideology. If, therefore, we in Europe, taking the basic United Nations Declaration as our starting point, have sought to establish international machinery to protect these rights, that machinery ought in theory to be of great interest in other parts of the world and in other and different political systems, in spite of the fact that the rights it seeks to enforce might be differently defined. I can tell you that this is in reality the case, and that what we are doing, and particularly the work of the Court and the Commission, is arousing the greatest interest in the Americas, North as well as South, in Africa and in Asia. I hardly know how to comply with the requests coming to me for our learned staff to lecture and attend meetings on Human Rights problems in distant parts of the world, while still carrying on the basic work which they must do for the organs operating under the Convention. I think you will agree that this is a development which offers fascinating prospects of establishing at least a basis of comparison and discussion for men living in different kinds of society within the general framework of the United Nations.

The world is full, perhaps over-full, of international conferences, and I sometimes doubt the real utility of some of them. But this is a conference with real and important work to do and from which substantial results which will be of great practical importance are expected. Its purpose is to draw from the immense concourse of learning and experience here gathered together, a review of the working of the European Convention on Human Rights, with authoritative views as to how it should be developed now and in the future. These conclusions will find their application in our Europe, the Europe of the Convention; but they will find a place in the thinking and will thus affect the actions of men and women everywhere.

GÜNTHER WINKLER

The formation of human communities derives from a social need to which modern States owe their existence and growth. Today, it is true, we know little of the process by which larger communities developed out of the family. But it is possible to trace back to the earliest records of the development of the human race the continuous striving of small communities and States to grow in size and strength. One of the most striking examples of this is the Roman Empire. And yet none of the important political communities in history enjoyed any permanency.

Why was this? Possibly because human communities lose their inner vitality and finally die as they are absorbed by larger ones; possibly also because in the past the formation of larger communities was the result of compulsion rather than of peaceful union.

Perhaps in this sense we may rightly say that we live in a fortunate age. An inhuman war has shown us that the only real road to the future lies in the direction of peace and understanding among the nations. Our method is not compulsion, but moral and political consent under the rule of law. And it would seem that the example of the modern federations of states, such as the United States of America, Switzerland, the Federal Republic of Germany, and Austria is increasingly influential in urging present-day Europe towards the creation of a large community. This is apparent not only in cultural, social and economic alliances; national states and their peoples have entered into relations aimed at wider union. Neither the EEC nor EFTA contradicts this assertion. Rather do they appear to be intermediate and transitional stages on the way to a wider development which will one day include all Europe—and consequently also the Eastern European States—and present a worthy example for the rest of the world to follow.

Signs that the European States intend to enter into a wider association, particularly on the cultural plane, are already apparent. The various countries are opening up their frontiers increasingly and not only symbolically. They are joining European organisations and becoming parties to treaties which provide the legal and institutional basis for the creation of a community and will finally determine its legal character. Probably the most important step in this direction today is the European Convention for the Protection of Human Rights and Fundamental Freedoms, a Convention which sees and recognises man as a free individual. Indeed the Convention may be described as the motive force in the movement for European union. States are lowering their barriers in order to create a larger community for the sake of human freedom and their inhabitants are contributing as best they can. In all European countries signatories to the Convention the individual's territorial ties have largely disappeared and their place has been taken by something in the nature of a common citizenship. To a great extent aliens now have the same rights and duties as nationals. Freedom of circulation within States and between States, made possible by more flexible passport and currency regulations, is guaranteed by law and is being enjoyed to an extent far greater than ever before. Man is achieving an increasingly wide field of activity in a larger community, breaking out of his isolation within the territorial confines of the State. Moreover, data and facts concerning the social process of the creation of a European community in accordance with law and order and by peaceful means are available and can be empirically understood. This is something we cannot and dare not ignore.

But this occasion of the Conference on the European Convention for the Protection of Human Rights and Fundamental Freedoms—to which I am privileged to welcome you on behalf of our Faculty—while encouraging us to form a clear picture of the future, is a solemn one; it brings our belief in the necessity and possibility of forming a great European community down to the modest problem of the legal and political order inherent in these developments. It would be flying in the face of experience and would be quite wrong to suppose that the European States, having entered a larger community, should then be forced to relinquish or lose their sovereignty. Political history and political science both show that the extreme alternative, namely the merger of small communities in a larger one, leads to a loss of substance and to a situation in which the permanency of the greater community cannot be guaranteed, even by resorting to compulsion. Modern States are not mere associations or groupings. They are federatively constructed, down to their smallest ramifications, including the territorial groupings and the decentralised bodies of the State, on the one hand, and, on the other, the great number of political, economic, social and cultural associations. In the last resort, all these are based on the individual. Human beings form the basis of all these groupings in the community; man is deeply involved in them and, moreover, his involvement in one implies involvement in another. He thus plays a part in the shaping of society as a member of a political group, a group drawn together by common interests and with a territorial basis. None of these criteria excludes the others. On the contrary, one necessitates the other and leaves room for the other. However, the justification for their existence and functions lies in their having emerged as social and legal communities in accordance with the vital principle of subsidiary growth and the ancient laws governing the formation of human communities.

The problem of freedom, therefore, is not merely the freedom of man in the abstract, but of his freedom within organised national communities and their ramifications. Its 'subsidiary' nature, which gives the small community latitude to develop within the larger one, while preserving its identity, is therefore always in opposition to the larger community, which has to establish certain limits both to its functions and to its institutions, and which may not therefore suddenly release the individual from the ties of a subsidiary group. But a community of States under international law is bound by this principle still more strongly than is a State in relation to its own social groups. For it is still the States which guarantee individual existence and freedom. The wider community must, therefore, in its organisation, provide only a framework and establish principles that take full account of individual groups, and, within them, of individual human beings. Experience shows that the development of the individual and the community require more latitude within large social units than would appear consistent with a strictly organised society. International law teachings accordingly still quite properly assert the right of the State to constitutional autonomy *vis-à-vis* public international law, the latter's function being a very restricted one which can only indirectly affect State legal systems. Considerable reticence is still shown in allowing State constitutions to be affected directly by international law. Before it has the force of municipal law, international law must go through a process of transformation at national level. States quite rightly give undertakings in treaties subject to reservations and conditions. And the conviction is growing that it is essentially by indirect application that treaties are enforceable at national level, thus constituting an acceptable basis for larger unions of States.

It is owing to the legal and political innovation constituted by the European Convention on Human Rights and Fundamental Freedoms that this view has crystallised. If rules of international law, valid also for individuals, are directly applicable, the existence and effectiveness of national legal systems are threatened. State systems have developed heterogeneously and cannot therefore with impunity be treated uniformly by public international law. The fixing of general principles and aims in the rules which bind the State legislatures allows States the latitude which—by virtue of the 'subsidiary' principle—must not be denied them even in favour of international law. We know from experience of national constitutional law that constitutions too marked by casuistry tend to produce atrophy of national political life or rebellion against the Constitution. The same is surely true of international law in relation to national legal systems.

The short time during which the Convention on Human Rights has been in force has already shown that fundamental principles of our State, such as the separation of powers, are being threatened without valid reason or justification. Moreover, the direct application of the Convention—which derives largely from foreign national legal concepts—gives rise inevitably to legal uncertainty, due not merely to legal terminology, but also to the need, occasioned by innumerable derogations, to bring the Convention and national legal systems into line with one another. Though the purpose of the Convention may be to guarantee the freedom of man, its effect has quite obviously been to engender legal doubts at national level. This does not serve the cause of freedom. On the contrary. Freedom now faces a new danger due to the fact that at international level certain limits have been exceeded in an attempt to establish a new political order. There is an indissoluble link between the existence and organisational function of communities and the freedom of the individual. What freedom is to the individual as a member of the community and in relation to the community as a whole, constitutional self-determination is to the smaller communities in relation to the larger ones; indeed, to the national community in relation to the international community. It is necessary to consider this if we would understand what is to be gained, but may also be lost, by the formation of a larger community.

I certainly do not intend to deny the value and epoch-making significance of the European Convention on Human Rights and Fundamental Freedoms. Because of its noble aims which are to serve the dignity and freedom of man, it deserves the highest recognition and respect. However, it shows us more clearly than other international treaties hitherto that man's faith and his optimistic search for freedom which lead him towards a wider community cannot solve the concrete problems facing us; it also shows that the way to broader union can only be found through understanding and experience. Our watchword must not be the replacement of the existing order. Rather must we endeavour cautiously to build on the old order a new one which will allow States the independence to which they are entitled.

Those are the ideas I would like to submit at the outset for the critical consideration of this Conference on Human Rights, which, on behalf of the Faculty of Law and Political Science of the University of Vienna, I have the pleasure to open.

CHAPTER I

Obligations of a State Party to a Treaty as regards its municipal law

REPORT BY

MAX SØRENSEN

I. INTRODUCTION

This is a facet of the classic question of the relation between international law and national legal systems. Generations of jurists have lavished on it gifts of analysis as well as of imagination and synthesis which, looked at in retrospect, cannot but earn our admiration. Few are the international law students even today who are not fired with enthusiasm by the great controversy between the monist and the dualist theories.

And yet the debate now seems to be at an end. Nothing new has been said in the last twenty years in spite of the important works devoted to it during that time. Generally speaking research and study have turned into other channels, perhaps owing to the profound changes that we have seen and are still seeing come about in the substance of international law. These changes are characterised in the first place by the increasing importance of conventional law at the expense of customary law and then by the number of subjects regulated by international conventions. On a hitherto unprecedented scale international conventional law is becoming concerned with relations between individuals or other subjects of municipal law, as well as with relations between individuals and the public authorities. In short, matters which were once the traditional province of municipal law are today being governed more and more by international rules.

This trend raises many problems, some of which go to the heart of our national legal traditions. Others, while no less important or less interesting, are on the purely technical plane. Indeed the perfecting of legal institutions from the technical point of view is one of the essential conditions of progress towards a more perfect international legal order.

It is from this angle that the relation between international law and municipal law must be regarded. It is a question of determining what are the most appropriate juridical means of achieving, in State legal

11

systems, the aims and intentions lying behind the rules established by international law. And that is the angle, too, from which our present subject will be treated. The obligations imposed on a State by international law with a view to ensuring the implementation, in municipal law, of the terms of an international treaty to which the said State is a party, are the means of guaranteeing harmony and material agreement between the two legal orders.

II. THE ESTABLISHED PRINCIPLE IN TRADITIONAL INTERNATIONAL LAW

Our starting-point is a clear and unambiguous principle. In an advisory opinion of 21 February 1925, the Permanent Court of International Justice recognised 'a principle which is self-evident, according to which a State which has contracted valid international obligations is bound to make in its legislation such modifications as may be necessary to ensure the fulfilment of the obligations undertaken'. An explicit provision to this effect in Article 18 of the Lausanne Convention of 3 January 1923 on the exchange of Greek and Turkish populations thus had no independent effect but was justified, in the eyes of the Court, by the special nature of the Convention 'which closely affects matters regulated by national legislation and lays down principles which conflict with certain rights generally recognised as belonging to individuals'.[1]

In pursuance of this principle, the Court asserted that a State could not rely on municipal law as a reason for not executing the terms of a treaty. The Court noted that 'it is a generally accepted principle of international law that in the relations between Powers who are contracting Parties to a treaty the provisions of municipal law cannot prevail over those of the treaty'.[2] The same is true of a Constitution: '. . . A State cannot adduce, as against another State, its own Constitution with a view to evading obligations incumbent upon it under international law or treaties in force'.[3]

Thus, generally speaking, it is established that a State has an obligation to make its municipal law conform to its undertakings under treaties to which it is a party. That, however, is a rather elementary statement of fact and it may be asked whether international law imposes any more specific obligations concerning the procedure to be followed or the techniques to be adopted.

[1] *P.C.I.J.*, Series B, No. 10, pp. 20–1, Exchange of Greek and Turkish populations.

[2] *P.C.I.J.*, Series B, No. 17, p. 32, The Greco-Bulgarian 'Communities'.

[3] *P.C.I.J.*, Series A/B, No. 44, p. 24, Treatment of Polish Nationals in the Danzig territory.

For a better understanding of the significance of this question, we must first consider the various possible courses of action in this respect and, secondly, the various types of obligations, classified according to the measures they require for their execution in municipal law.

III. METHODS OF INCORPORATING INTERNATIONAL TREATIES INTO NATIONAL LEGAL SYSTEMS[1]

1. A method which reflects a clear separation between international conventional law and municipal law is that of the *transformation*, in the proper sense of the term, of an international treaty into an internal law or administrative regulation. Under this method the international rules, which are addressed to the Contracting States, serve as the basis for a corresponding set of rules issued in the country concerned and addressed to individuals, public authorities or other subjects of municipal law. Although the two sets of rules, international and national, are directed towards bringing about the same legal situation, they are, strictly speaking, independent of one another. The national rules may even precede the conclusion of the treaty, either because they were introduced before the treaty or because they have no connection with the treaty, which has created an international obligation conforming to a pre-existing legal situation.

The national rules may be substituted at any level in the hierarchy of internal laws and regulations, either at constitutional level (if there is a written constitution superior to the other laws), at legislative level or at administrative level. It may even belong to unwritten law, customary or otherwise. The legal distinction between the two sets of rules has certain consequences for their entry into force and their repeal. From the national point of view the national rules alone count, even if the treaty is not yet or is no longer in force in national territory. With regard to interpretation, however, it is a principle generally recognised in national legal systems that, in the event of doubt, the national rule is to be interpreted in accordance with the State's international obligations. Subject to that qualification, the

---

[1] A thorough study of the subject was undertaken recently under the auspices of the Deutsche Gesellschaft für Völkerrecht. See the report of Karl Josef Partsch, *Die Anwendung des Völkerrechts im innerstaatlichen Recht*, Karlsruhe, 1964. See also Ignaz Seidl-Hohenveldern, 'Transformation or Adoption of International Law into Municipal Law', *Int. and Comp. Law Quarterly*, vol. 12, 1963, pp. 88–124, and Thomas Buergenthal, 'The Effect of the European Convention on Human Rights on the Internal Law of member States', *The European Convention on Human Rights*, British Institute of International and Comparative Law, 1965, pp. 79–106.

language question is settled by giving preference to the national language in which the internal laws are couched, without regard to the language that is authoritative for the Contracting States.

Such is the system adopted, if not in all its details, at least in the main, by Great Britain, Ireland and the Scandinavian countries.

2. Another technique which is, in a way, at the opposite pole from the first, consists of regarding the treaty, once validly concluded at international level, as forming an integral part of municipal law. It follows that the administrative and judicial authorities are bound to apply the terms of the treaty as soon as and inasmuch as the State is bound by it. It remains to be seen whether all the clauses of the treaty lend themselves to such immediate application at national level and certain other questions arise, namely in regard to interpretation, when the treaty has not been drawn up (only) in the national language.

For our present purpose there is no need to dwell on the fact that the legal basis of this system in the countries which adopt it is provided for by a clause in the Constitution. In the last analysis it thus rests on a national rule of a general character conferring on future treaties the status of internal rules. This is a phenomenon whose significance cannot escape those who study the theoretical and doctrinal aspects of our present subject. It is this phenomenon, too, which explains the terms often used to designate this method. We speak of the *general transformation* of the international rules into municipal law. In this context the term transformation refers to the effect deriving from the constitutional clause and relates in particular to the incorporation of the clauses of the treaty into municipal law. It is not as well chosen as it might be, however, in the sense that this technique does not involve any alteration or reframing of the text of the treaty. The essential point is that the provisions of the treaty, in so far as their wording permits, will be applied in the same way as national laws and regulations, because the Constitution so prescribes.

Thus reduced to its simplest expression, this technique is rarely adopted. Apart from the need to use a translation into the national language or languages if the authoritative text of the treaty is not drawn up in that or those languages, most national constitutional systems which appear to have adopted this method nevertheless require, in addition, a special instrument for each treaty, *ordering its application in municipal law*. In most cases all that is required is the publication of the treaty in the Official Gazette. The fact that the treaty has been properly concluded from the point of view of international law is rarely sufficient, even if it has been approved by Parliament, to make it applicable in internal law.

One of the few countries where publication is not essential is the United States. A treaty ratified by the President with the consent of a two-thirds majority of the Senate and which has come into force internationally, must be applied by the national courts even in the absence of an official 'proclamation' such as is made in the case of Federal laws.[1]

In other countries, such as Austria, France and the Netherlands, where the system at first sight seems the same, the publication of the treaty is obligatory by reason of express constitutional provisions to that effect. A validly concluded treaty which has come into force in international law is not applicable in municipal law unless it has been published officially.

In addition, some countries adopting this practice, and others too which do not adopt it, have Parliament's approval or ratification of the treaty expressed in the form of an Act. Such an Act fulfils a two-fold function: it authorises the Government to commit the State internationally and it incorporates the terms of the treaty into municipal law. In order to produce these effects the Act must be published in accordance with the relevant constitution and legislative provisions.

Another important feature of this method is that the national Constitution, by providing for the treaty to take effect in municipal law, settles, implicitly or explicitly, the treaty's status in the hierarchy of rules of internal law.

In a Federal State, in the first place, the question arises whether the treaty is to take precedence over the laws of the federated States. The United States Constitution expressly describes treaties as 'supreme law of the land' taking precedence over the constitutions and laws of the States of the Federation. Similarly the Constitutions of Austria and the Federal Republic of Germany rank treaties with Federal laws.

In addition, in a Federal State as in any other State, the Constitution may rank treaties with the Constitution, with other laws or in between the two. As revised in 1964, the Austrian Constitution provides for the possibility of the *Nationalrat* approving the ratification of treaties, conferring on them constitutional status with all its attendant consequences in regard to precedence over ordinary laws, past or future, amendment procedure and the competence of the Constitutional Court.[2]

[1] Erades and Gould, *The relation between International Law and Municipal Law in the Netherlands and in the United States*, 1961, pp. 305–7.
[2] Marianne von Grüningen, 'Die österreichische Verfassungsnovelle über Staatsverträge vom 4. März 1964', *Zeitschrift für ausländisches öffentliches Recht und Völkerrecht*, Bd. 25, 1965, pp. 76–99, contains references to the discussion of the question in Austrian legal literature.

The Netherlands Constitution also provides for a special approval procedure (by a two-thirds majority) for treaties departing from the terms of the Constitution, which implies that, once approved in this way, a treaty is supposed to take precedence over the provisions of the Constitution. As the question of the constitutionality of laws is not a matter for the judiciary in the Netherlands, the problem does not arise whether such a treaty has the force of a constitutional provision. In any case a treaty which is applicable in municipal law takes precedence over all laws, even future laws; a treaty, whatever the procedure for its approval by parliament, is thus above all laws in the legal hierarchy. In relation to the Constitution, however, even a treaty approved by a two-thirds majority does not seem to take precedence over constitutional provisions adopted subsequently.

Similarly, the French Constitution specifies that treaties validly concluded have a greater force than laws, that is to say than past laws and future laws, although it does not rank them with the Constitution itself.

In Luxembourg, the jurisprudence of the Supreme Court of Justice is based on an interpretation of the Constitution in the above sense.

If, on the other hand, treaties are ranked with laws without any other qualification, the principle of *lex posterior derogat legi priori* applies to their relation to ordinary laws. In other words, in municipal law a new law could derogate from the treaty even though the latter remained fully in force at international level. This seems to be the position in the Federal Republic of Germany, whose Constitution ranks treaties with Federal laws without giving them precedence over subsequent laws. In Turkey, too, the Constitution gives treaties that have duly entered into force the status of laws.

3. A third method, which is adopted by a number of countries, such as Belgium, Greece, Italy and Switzerland, is rather similar to the preceding one. It resembles the latter in that it consists in authorising the ratification of a treaty and ordering its application in municipal law by means of a special Act of Parliament. However, unlike the method described above, the effects and validity thus acquired by the treaty do not derive from a clause of the Constitution but simply from the special law passed in respect of it. Those who speak of 'general transformation' in regard to the second method described, call this method 'special transformation'. As has been pointed out, however, it is not strictly a case of transformation, but of the incorporation of the treaty, without any change in its text, into municipal law.

The absence of constitutional provisions relating to the method to be adopted leaves the legislature free to suit it to the requirements of each case. Thus, the treaty may be incorporated in part or in whole. The legislature may single out the clauses of the treaty susceptible of internal application and omit the others. Or the law may simply specify that the treaty is to be applied in municipal law 'inasmuch as it concerns questions within the competence of the legislature' or again this method may be combined with transformation in the strict sense.

4. On the fringe of the procedures and methods already described, others may be conceived, if not as being capable of general application at least as special techniques to which the legislature can have recourse in certain circumstances. For example, a law may refer to the terms of existing or future treaties, thus giving them force of law. If, for instance, the law reserves certain rights to nationals but provides for their extension to aliens in conditions to be determined by treaty, the provisions of the treaties concluded will be incorporated into municipal law by the effect of the reference. Since, in such a case, future treaties may also be involved, this procedure is sometimes called 'advance transformation', though it should be realised that in this case there is no more question of real transformation than in the other cases described.

Of course such special techniques also raise problems to which a solution must be found in each legal system. Thus, the question arises whether the conclusion of the treaty in international law suffices in itself or whether the text must be published officially in the country before it is applicable in municipal law.

IV. DOES THE CHOICE BETWEEN THESE VARIOUS METHODS DEPEND SOLELY ON MUNICIPAL LAW?

The brief outline given above of methods of incorporating treaties into the municipal law of the Contracting States is not intended as a study in comparative constitutional law. However, it brings out clearly the well-known fact that the methods and principles differ from one country to another. Studies and exchanges of views at international level on the advantages and disadvantages of the various methods might well be valuable in paving the way to reform in different countries.

It is of interest to enquire, in this connection, to what extent each of the methods described meets present international needs. One must assume that in principle States have a common interest in seeing that their mutual undertakings are fulfilled without fail, even when the subject of those undertakings is a matter belonging essentially and traditionally to the internal life of national communities. The more international obligations are reflected in the

c

actual text of rules of internal law, the better the method used corresponds to the common interest of Contracting States. But, however sound that reasoning may be, it is not inevitably followed in the light of international law as it is today.

Here the question is to discover whether there exists a rule of international law whereby the choice of States between the various methods is restricted and, in particular, whether States are bound to adopt one of the methods favouring the integration of treaties into national legal systems. Such a rule could of course only arise out of international custom. The different practices in various countries show plainly that no such customary rule exists at present. The obvious conclusion is that there is freedom of choice between the various methods. States which transform treaties into internal laws worded differently from the treaties are fulfilling their international obligations just as much as those which incorporate the text of the treaty into their municipal law by a single instrument ordering its implementation.

But there is more to it than that. The Contracting States, among their obligations under the treaty, may have undertaken to incorporate the text of the treaty into their municipal law and to give it a specific status in the national legal hierarchy, ranking it as an ordinary law, as superior to ordinary laws or on a level with the Constitution. That is why it has to be asked, with regard to any given treaty, whether the Contracting States have given such an undertaking, either expressly in a special clause or by a common intention whose existence may be observed in some other way.

Such an enquiry in the case of the major European treaties is by no means purely academic. There is one case of the first importance where the problem has arisen in practice, namely in connection with the treaties setting up the European Communities.

The debate, which has been in progress for several years now and is likely to continue for many more, on the subject of the relation between Community law and national law has at least clarified the major aspects of the problem. From being at first a matter of doctrine, the problem became a practical one recently when certain decisions of courts in the member States and also of the Luxembourg Court were directly concerned with it.[1]

There is no need to retrace the course of this debate nor to analyse the arguments and ideas of the authors who have taken part. For our present purpose it is enough to note the opinion given by the Luxembourg Court on 15 July 1964 in a preliminary decision requested

---

[1] See the study by H. P. Ipsen, published in English translation under the title 'The Relationship between the Law of the European Communities and National Law', *Common Market Law Review*, vol. II, 1965, pp. 379–402.

by an Italian Court. The Court states 'that unlike ordinary international treaties, the EEC Treaty instituted a legal order of its own which was integrated into the legal systems of member States when the Treaty came into force and by which their courts must abide'. The Court goes on to state that this integration and, more generally, the terms and spirit of the Treaty have as their corollary that member States are not entitled to give a subsequent unilateral measure precedence over Community law. If the law deriving from the Treaty, says the Court, were to find itself overridden by any provision of national law whatsoever, the result would be to undermine the whole legal basis of the Community.[1]

Since the special feature of the treaties setting up the European Communities is the power they confer on the Community organs not only to establish rules of a more or less general character by way of regulations, but also to take concrete decisions, Community law embraces, in addition to the treaties, all the secondary rules issued by the competent bodies and deriving their force from the treaty. And so the Court, in the passage quoted above, recognises the precedence over the national law of member States not only of the treaties themselves but also of all Community law, including secondary rules.

A Report recently presented to the European Parliament by Professor Fernand Dehousse on behalf of the Legal Committee supports the Court's opinion in this matter. The Legal Committee asks the European Parliament to adopt a resolution 'endorsing the conclusions of the Report . . . which upholds the principle of the precedence of Community law over the municipal law of member States'.[2]

In this way a coherent idea of the relationship between Community law and national law is beginning to crystallise. True, its doctrinal basis is still disputed and certain decisions of national courts are still based on arguments that depart to a greater or lesser degree from that concept. Nevertheless there is a distinct inclination towards the opinion that member States are bound, under the system set up by the treaties, to apply the terms of the treaties, together with all the regulations issued under them in their municipal law, giving them not only force of law but precedence over national laws, past and future.

Does the Convention with which we are specially concerned, namely the European Convention on Human Rights, carry similar obligations for the Contracting Parties?

In the first place this question needs to be distinguished from the

---

[1] Decision of 15 July 1964 in the case *Flaminio Costa* v. *E.N.E.L.*, No. 6/64, *Recueil de la Jurisprudence de la Cour*, vol. x, 1964, pp. 1158–60.

[2] European Parliament, *Documents de Séance* 1965–66, Doc. 43, 25 May 1965.

other question as to whether the terms of the Convention are immediately applicable or 'self-executing' in the law of States which recognise conventions as a source of municipal law. That point will be discussed under the next heading below. Too often, however, jurists studying the position of the Convention in the municipal law of the Contracting States are inclined to confuse the above question with the one that interests us here, namely whether the Convention lays an obligation upon member States to adopt a given method to give effect to the Convention in their municipal law, although this obligation is not one which normally derives from international law.

Now, if we look at the Convention on Human Rights from this angle we note certain doubtful points. On the one hand the Convention contains clauses whose wording and origin incline us to the conclusion that States are bound to incorporate the actual text of the Convention, or of Section I at least, into their own law.[1] Article 1 has been quoted in support of this argument. According to the French text the Contracting Parties 'reconnaissent à toute personne relevant de leur juridiction les droits et libertés définis au Titre I de la présente Convention' and although the English text is less clear ('The High Contracting Parties shall secure to everyone within their jurisdiction' . . .) it is argued that the Convention therefore confers immediately 'subjective rights' on individuals and that not solely by the intermediary of national legislation. This view is upheld by a comparison of the final text of Article 1 with an earlier version whereby the Contracting States 'shall undertake to ensure' to everybody the rights and freedoms guaranteed. Such an undertaking would have been purely between States and an individual would not have been able to rely on it in a national court.

In support of the same theory Article 13 is also invoked. It states that 'everyone whose rights and freedoms as set forth in this Convention are violated shall have an effective remedy before a national authority . . .'. This, it is claimed, presupposes that the Convention is a part of municipal law.

The theory is further strengthened by a declaration made at a certain point in the drafting of the Convention. The Conference of Senior Officials which was appointed in June 1950 to prepare the Ministers' decisions on the texts to be adopted discussed whether the Convention ought to contain a solemn declaration to the effect that legislation in the States concerned would give full effect to the terms of the Convention. The Conference was unanimous in believing such

[1] Among the authors who have most clearly and soundly developed this theory is Heribert Golsong, 'Die europäische Konvention zum Schutze der Menschenrechte und Grundfreiheiten', *Jahrbuch des öffentlichen Rechts*, Bd. 10, 1961, pp. 123–57, in particular pp. 128–9.

a clause to be unnecessary. The report explained this attitude as follows: 'Indeed, in the absence of any provision to the contrary, every signatory State is presumed to give full effect to the provisions of the Convention from the moment that State has given its adherence.'[1]

However, this statement does not seem to be incompatible with the system whereby it is national law—constitution, ordinary laws or other rules of internal law—which gives effect to the Convention as soon as it has come into force. Otherwise it could scarcely have won the unanimous approval of the Conference, including that of Representatives of countries which, traditionally, have adopted the method of transformation in a strict sense.

Speaking more generally, none of the provisions cited above seems incompatible with this method. The rights and freedoms defined in the Convention can be incorporated in municipal law in their substance, without necessarily keeping to the text of the Convention. Substance and form are not identical and the same content may be put into words in different ways without its legal substance being affected thereby.

Moreover it is not without relevance for the interpretation of the Convention to observe how it has been applied in Contracting States. It will be seen that none of the States which traditionally adopt the transformation method, abandoned it in ratifying and giving effect to the Convention on Human Rights. The other Contracting Parties have never drawn attention to this fact and it would hardly be realistic to conclude that the six States in question had failed to fulfil their obligations under the Convention merely because they had not incorporated it into their municipal law.[2]

To conclude thus that the Convention on Human Rights does not interfere with the right of States to choose their own methods, is not in any way to prejudge the relative value of the various methods from the point of view of their efficiency and usefulness in ensuring respect for the rights and freedoms guaranteed by the Convention. In this connection it is remarkable that an author who occupies a most distinguished post in one of the countries which has ratified the Convention without conferring on it the status of municipal law, recently advocated that individuals should be able to invoke the terms of the Convention in national courts.[3] If it is possible, even in countries where legislation does not recognise the Convention as a source of

[1] Doc. CM/WP 4 (50) 19, para. 7.
[2] See also Karel Vasak, *La Convention Européenne des Droits de l'Homme*, 1964, pp. 234–5.
[3] 'Terje Wold: Den europaeiske menneskerettskonvensjon og Norge', *Legal Essay in honour of Frede Castberg*, 1963, pp. 353–74, in particular pp. 357–9.

municipal law, to have it recognised as such in case-law, considerable progress will have been made.

V. HAS THE CHARACTER OF THE PROVISIONS OF A TREATY ANY SIGNIFICANCE FOR THEIR EFFECTS IN MUNICIPAL LAW?

This question does not arise unless a Contracting State, either by virtue of an obligation under a treaty or in the exercise of the choice left to it by general international law as to the method to be adopted, incorporates the actual text into its municipal law. It will be seen that even in this case one cannot ignore the nature of the provisions of a treaty in determining their effects in national law.

1. In the first place there are treaties whose purpose and substance is outside the sphere of national law. A treaty of alliance, a treaty on the supply of armaments by one Government to another, a treaty on the peaceful settlement of international disputes, etc., are by their purpose and substance above the legal systems of the Contracting Parties. The question of their internal effects does not arise.

2. There are other treaties which take effect in the administrative sphere and concern rules governing the rights and duties of administrative authorities and other public bodies in relation to one another without reference to the rights of individuals. A treaty on the standardisation of statistics or medical nomenclature, on the exchange of publications or official documents, on mutual assistance in cases of shipwreck, etc., may have the same effect in municipal law as instructions from a superior to an inferior authority. However, it does not seek to produce legal effects in regard to private individuals or other subjects of private law and the problem of its execution does not arise in the courts.

3. To a third, much larger group belong treaties dealing with relations between public authorities and individuals. The classic example is the trade treaty which gives nationals of one country certain rights *vis-à-vis* the authorities as regards establishment or engaging in a trade or profession in another country. More recently, as a further stage in contemporary development, other aspects of the treatment of aliens have been regulated by treaty. A growing number of treaties tend to define the citizen's rights and duties in relation to the State of which he is a national or the relations between the individual and the State without regard to nationality. These relations are sometimes closely bound up with aspects of international relations, such as the legal and administrative rules governing international trade, but often they have only an indirect effect on international relations.

It is in the nature of these treaties that they seek to produce effects in the legal systems of the contracting States. Whether the provisions are concerned with restricting or extending the freedom of action of the public authorities in regard to individuals, their execution is a matter for municipal law under the control of the national judiciary.

4. There is a fourth and last group which comprises treaties which, in the last analysis, are concerned solely with relations between individuals or other subjects of private law. These are chiefly treaties on the unification of private law, such as those governing sea, air, road or rail transport, and treaties on conflict of laws in matters of private law. The aim and object of such treaties is to unify the internal law of the contracting States, which are accordingly obliged to incorporate the substance of the treaties into their own law.

The above classification of treaties is of interest because the technique for adapting them into municipal law is different in each case.

While the problem of their incorporation into municipal law is negligible for the first group, and for the second group only affects the mutual relations of the public authorities, for the last two groups the technique depends on the actual text of the treaties. Treaties in the last group are usually worded so as to lend themselves to immediate application in national legal systems, while the same is true to a limited extent only in the case of the third group.

Here the concept of a 'self-executing' treaty arises. International law doctrine has made great play with this term, not always without ambiguity. Sometimes it is used in connection with systems of law in which a treaty once ratified has force of law. It is said of such systems that treaties are 'self-executing'. This, however, is not the original meaning of the term and for the sake of clarity it should be avoided since, under such a system, a treaty may not be, or may be only partially 'self-executing' in the true sense of the term.

The term originated, of course, in the constitutional law of the United States and the words of Chief Justice Marshall in the case of *Foster and Elain* v. *Neilson* in 1829 are often quoted:

Our constitution declares a treaty to be the law of the land. It is, consequently, to be regarded in courts of justice as equivalent to an act of the legislature, whenever it operates of itself without the aid of any legislative provision. But when the terms of the stipulation import a contract, when either of the parties engages to perform a particular act, the treaty addresses itself to the political, not to the judicial department, and the legislature must execute the contract before it can become a rule for the Court.[1]

These words bring out the crucial point: the drafting of the provision in question. If the provision is so worded that it can be

---

[1] Quoted from Erades and Gould, op. cit., p. 329.

regarded as addressing itself not only to the contracting States but also to subjects of municipal law, it is ready to be applied immediately by national courts and may accordingly be called 'self-executing'. If, on the other hand it is so worded that it addresses itself to the contracting States as subjects of international law and requires them to introduce laws and regulations to give it effect in municipal law, then the courts cannot make use of it in determining an individual's rights and obligations and it cannot be called 'self-executing'. Furthermore, this applies to each provision of the treaty separately and not to the treaty as a whole. It is quite conceivable that certain clauses of a treaty may be 'self-executing' and others not.

In these circumstances it would be useless to endeavour to classify treaties according to the criterion under consideration. At best, to distinguish certain types of provision might help us to clarify the problem. In this respect the European Convention on Human Rights offers a wide variety of examples.

One type of provision is the 'obligation to refrain'. If the prohibited action is one affecting individuals, this restriction of the freedom of action of the public authorities may manifest itself in international and in municipal law simultaneously. Some examples, among many, are the clauses providing that 'No one shall be subjected to torture or to inhuman or degrading treatment or punishment' (Art. 3), that 'no one shall be required to perform forced or compulsory labour' (Art. 4 (2)) and that 'no one shall be deprived of his liberty save in the following cases. . . .' (Art. 5 (1)).

Let us look again from this angle at the Treaty setting up the European Economic Community, whose Article 12 reads:

Member States shall refrain from introducing, as between themselves, any new customs duties on importation or exportation, or charges with equivalent effect, and from increasing such duties or charges as they apply in their commercial relations with each other.

The Court of Justice of the European Communities has decided that this article is 'self-executing', basing its decision on arguments that are highly pertinent to our present problem. The following passages from the reasons given for the decision concerned will serve to illustrate the problem:

Whereas Article 12 constitutes a clear and unconditional prohibition, imposing an obligation to refrain and not an obligation to perform; . . . Whereas this prohibition is eminently of a nature to produce direct effects in legal relations between member States and the subjects of their jurisdiction; Whereas the execution of Article 12 calls for no legislative action on the part of States; Whereas the fact that in this Article it is the member

States which are designated as being under the obligation to refrain does not imply that their nationals may not derive benefit therefrom; . . .[1]

This point, though made in connection with a case that arose in the particular circumstances of the European Communities, is just as valid for any treaty about which a question arises as to its immediate application in the legal systems of the contracting States.

To return to the Convention on Human Rights, it will be seen that other provisions oblige the public authorities to take certain action in certain circumstances. That obligation may be so worded that there is no doubt as to the possibility of giving it immediate effect. That is the case, for example, with Article 5 (2): 'Everyone who is arrested shall be informed promptly, in a language which he understands, of the reasons for his arrest and of any charge against him'. Of the same type is Article 5 (5) which provides that 'Everyone who has been the victim of arrest or detention in contravention of the provisions of this Article shall have an enforceable right to compensation'. On the other hand, a clause which is manifestly incapable of immediate application is to be found in Article 3 of the Protocol, in which 'the High Contracting Parties undertake to hold free elections at reasonable intervals by secret ballot, under conditions which will ensure the free expression of the opinion of the people in the choice of the legislature'. The situation is similar in the case of provisions which, while enunciating individual rights, are concerned with matters which presuppose that the relevant laws or regulations have been introduced by the State. Such, for example, are the clauses designed to guarantee to the individual a judicial or administrative means of challenging the legality of measures which affect him (Art. 5 (3) and (4), Art. 13). Such legal remedies require the existence of competent bodies, a definition of their jurisdiction and the introduction of a certain procedure, none of which can be brought about by the terms of the Convention alone.

Then again certain provisions authorise the public authorities to take certain action which they would not otherwise be entitled to take. Here the question arises whether a treaty provision of this kind is an adequate basis for an administrative or judicial act whereby the public authorities intervene in the private affairs of individuals. In Western countries it is a basic principle that any interference of the kind must have a basis in law. Is a clause of a treaty equivalent to a legislative provision for the sole reason that the treaty in question has force of law?

In some cases the answer to this question depends on the terms of

[1] Decision of 5 February 1963 in case No. 26/62, *van Gend and Loos, Recueil de la Jurisprudence de la Cour*, vol. IX, 1963, p. 24.

the treaty. If its clauses authorise measures only on condition that they are introduced 'in accordance with a procedure prescribed by law' (Art. 5, (1)) or that they are 'in accordance with the law' (2nd paragraph of Articles 8, 9, 10, 11) it is clear that a basis in national law is required independently of, and in addition to, the permissive clause of the treaty. If, on the other hand, the treaty makes no reference to national law, the answer is less certain. It depends to some extent on judicial tradition in the State concerned. Some clauses, however, would not give rise to doubt in any national legal system. For example it can be said that no legal basis that would satisfy the requirements of national constitutional and administrative law could be found in Article 4 (3) which defines certain civic duties, such as national service, that are not regarded as 'forced or compulsory labour' for the purpose of the article. Nor could one be found in the second sentence of Article 10 (1) which states that freedom of expression as defined in the article 'shall not prevent States from requiring the licensing of broadcasting, television or cinema enterprises'. The same could probably be said of Article 15 which, in certain circumstances, authorises the High Contracting Parties to take measures derogating from their obligations under the Convention.

Continuing our review of the various types of conventional clause we come to those which, in the interests of the individual and in order to guarantee him effective protection, establish a certain division of powers between different public authorities. There are provisions, for example, which make the courts competent to decide, to the exclusion of the administrative authorities, in matters of individual rights. Thus, Article 5 (3) and (4) require judicial control in the case of individuals who are deprived of their liberty and Article 6 makes the courts competent to decide when civic rights or obligations are in dispute and when a criminal charge is preferred. Even in a State where the Convention has the force of municipal law such provisions are scarcely sufficient in themselves to establish immediately the jurisdiction of a given court. At most they might have the effect of excluding the competence of any non-judicial authority.

Lastly, the purpose of certain provisions is to regulate the procedure which the judicial authorities are to follow in the exercise of their functions. It is chiefly Article 6 of the Convention which contains provisions of that kind. On certain points the wording is sufficiently specific to make possible the immediate application of the provisions in question even in a national system in which judicial procedure is laid down in detail. However, in the face of a detailed and exhaustive code of judicial procedure forming a coherent whole, it would sometimes be difficult to allow that the elementary provisions of the Convention should be applicable without new legislation. This is the case in particular when the Convention refers in vague terms, open to varying interpretations, to such concepts as the fair hearing required under Article 6.

Thus the question whether a provision of a treaty is 'self-executing' or not, cannot be reduced to a plain, straightforward formula. Not only must the wording of the provision be analysed but the special nature of the national judicial system in which the treaty is to be applied is also a factor to be considered, according to the circumstances. It is quite possible, for instance, for the same provision to be immediately applicable in one State system and not in another. The contrary is true only in cases like that of the Community treaties where it is incumbent upon member States under the treaty to incorporate its actual text into their municipal law. In that case, the logical result would be that the same clauses of the treaty would be immediately and equally applicable in all member States.

VI. THE UNIFORMITY OF INTERPRETATION OF THE TREATY AS AN INTERNATIONAL RULE AND AS A RULE OF MUNICIPAL LAW

As we have already seen, a State may not evade its international obligations by invoking municipal law. Even less can it find an excuse for not complying with the terms of a treaty to which it is a party in the mere fact that the national courts interpret the treaty differently from the interpretation that must be placed on it in international law.

The problem becomes more complex, however, if the treaty, as is often the case, gives rise to legitimate doubts as to its interpretation and if it has no clause establishing a compulsory form of procedure, open to all the parties, for settling differences of opinion as to its interpretation. It is not enough, in order to smooth out all the difficulties, for the treaty to contain the traditional clause concerning the judicial settlement of disputes between the contracting parties. Very often differences of interpretation arising in municipal law do not give rise to disputes at diplomatic level and only the governments of the contracting States may refer cases to the International Court. It is well known that efforts to unify private law are sometimes hampered by the fact that national courts interpret the texts differently and there is no adequate means of co-ordinating their case-law.

However, the treaty itself may establish a procedure and impose obligations with a view to remedying these defects and ensuring greater uniformity and coherence. Article 177 of the Treaty setting up the European Economic Community makes the Court of Justice of the Communities competent to make preliminary decisions concerning the interpretation of the treaty and national courts may, and in some cases must, refer to the Court of Justice any question involving the treaty that is raised in cases brought before them.

The obligations deriving from this article exceed the purely procedural context in which it is placed. It is clear that the interpretation placed by the Court on the article will have repercussions in the law of the State concerned. In the first place the national court which has referred the matter to the Court of Justice for a preliminary decision is bound to abide by that decision in its judgment of the case. In addition, the Court's interpretation is binding for other courts in other member States whenever a similar point is raised. It is true that these other courts are entitled to refer the matter again to the Court in connection with another case and the Court would not refuse to give a decision, but if the point raised is identical with the earlier one the Court simply refers to its previous decision.[1]

However, the system of the European Communities is unique in this respect also. No other international control system carries the same consequences in internal law. The Convention on Human Rights, while it represents a considerable advance on the classic methods and procedure of international law, does not carry legal integration as far as that. In the first place, the Convention has no procedure for preliminary decisions. There is already a considerable body of case-law on the interpretation of the Convention in the various contracting States but the Convention makes no provision for a procedure to unify the interpretations given by national courts. It is possible for differences to exist indefinitely. Furthermore, if a case is taken to the European Court of Human Rights, that Court's decision does not necessarily have the force of law in the legal systems of the contracting States. Article 50 of the Convention provides specifically for cases in which the Court's decision is incompatible with a decision or a measure taken by a national judicial or other authority, and in such a case it is not the international decision which prevails. If the law of the State concerned allows only partial reparation to be made for the consequences of the decision or measure in question, then the Court may accord just compensation to the injured party. This is of course the normal solution in international law as established by the arbitration treaties of the years between the two wars. It is true that the State is obliged to fulfil its international obligations even in its municipal law, but those obligations do not include granting a decision by an international court any formal precedence over a final decision in municipal law.[2]

---

[1] See the decision of 27 March 1963 in the cases which had been joined, Nos. 28 to 30/62, *Da Costa et al.* v. *Netherlands Taxation Authorities*, *Recueil de Jurisprudence*, vol. IX, 1963, pp. 59–78.

[2] For a more detailed study of this point see Buergenthal, loc. cit., pp. 94–105.

VII. OBLIGATIONS RELATING TO INTERNATIONAL
PROCEDURE LAID DOWN IN A TREATY

We have already seen that the classic procedure for the judicial settlement or arbitration of international disputes raises no difficulty in international law unless the execution of the decision is found to be incompatible with a decision or rule of internal law.

However, the control measures provided for in certain important modern international conventions raise new problems in connection with their operation. The procedures prescribed cannot run their course in a legal vacuum. Although they are international, they have to be placed for practical purposes in a national context. They must of necessity be partly integrated into national legal systems and States which have accepted the procedures and recognised them as compulsory, find themselves obliged to modify certain features of their municipal law in consequence.

Here too the European Convention on Human Rights offers illustrations of the new problems raised. For the most part they are problems whose detailed solution has been left in suspense, so that the precise nature of the obligations accepted by the contracting States can be determined progressively, as the practice of the competent organs grows up and becomes established.

A general and vaguely-worded obligation is imposed by Article 25 of the Convention on those contracting States which have accepted the competence of the Commission to examine applications received from individuals. Those States have undertaken not to hinder 'in any way' the effective exercise of this right of individual petition. This is an obligation which, in spite of its negative form, is more than an obligation to refrain. Experience has shown that this obligation, in particular where prisoners are concerned, involves providing certain facilities to ensure that they are able to correspond freely with the Commission. Indeed certain countries have introduced administrative measures amending their prison regulation under municipal law. On the other hand, a State could scarcely be obliged to allow a prisoner to appear in person before the Commission, particularly as the Commission has no legal powers or practical facilities for guarding prisoners.

Another question in connection with Article 25 is whether States are bound to allow the exercise of the right of individual petition to the Commission to have a suspensive effect. It is clear that the immediate execution of a measure taken in violation of the rights guaranteed by the Convention might in certain circumstances make any appeal to the Commission vain. On the other hand, a general obligation to suspend the execution of a measure taken under municipal law would need to be worded more specifically than the sentence in Article 25.

A similar obligation exists under Article 28 in cases where the Commission is investigating the facts in connection with an application that has been declared admissible. For the efficient conduct of such an investigation the States concerned 'shall furnish all the necessary facilities'. It was in application of this article and of Article 59 of the Convention that under an Act of 8 January 1958, the British authorities in Cyprus issued certain regulations concerning the privileges and immunities of the members of the Commission and members of staff accompanying them in their investigation.[1]

In this connection, we might point to the more general problem of the immunities of members of the Court and the Commission and their staff in respect of their official acts. Special agreements have been concluded on the subject by States parties to the Convention and an example of their application in municipal law is afforded by the case of *Zoernsch* v. *Waldock and McNulty* in Great Britain[2] in which an applicant whose application had been declared inadmissible took proceedings against the former President and the Secretary of the Commission.

One last problem that the texts in force seem to overlook, but which is being studied by the competent Council of Europe bodies, is that of punishment for perjury and similar offences committed before the Court or the Commission. It is clear that neither the Court nor the Commission have any means of reacting effectively against such conduct on the part of the persons who appear before them. It is the States which, under their own law, must take steps to protect international courts by punishing persons guilty of impeding justice in such cases.

On this note we may conclude our brief remarks. Without the support of national legal systems, international procedures remain imperfect. Logically, a State which has accepted the procedure concerned is bound to remedy its imperfections by means of its internal law.

VIII. CONCLUSION

It will be seen from the above that the obligations of contracting States in the sphere of municipal law appear in a different light since the recent developments in public international law in Europe. The point of departure in the classic doctrine of international law, according to which the said obligations were almost negligible, has not been

[1] *Yearbook of the Convention on Human Rights*, vol. II, 1958–9, pp. 198–9.
[2] 1964, 2 All E.R. 256.

entirely abandoned. On the other hand, new needs arising out of international control, at once more extensive and more intensive than those of international law as it was known hitherto, have brought about important changes in the traditional situation. It is in the nature of things that a close bond must subsist between the substance of an international control by convention and the nature of the obligations it imposes on the contracting States in their internal law. The more that questions affecting the internal life of a national community are regulated by international law, the more need there is for effective means of preventing any incompatibility between a State's international obligations and its municipal law.

Today we are half-way between the point of departure and the goal. The new principles, established by the European Communities, point the way. Present-day needs, arising out of European co-operation even outside the framework of the Six, encourage us to go ahead. In the end there will be no half-measures. No doubt national tradition and the well-known conservatism of lawyers will slow down our progress, but the integration of national legal systems into a coherent European system is the only practical way of achieving the aims of the great European conventions.

WRITTEN COMMUNICATION BY
KARL DOEHRING

Did the signature of the Convention directly establish individual rights under international law, or can the individual avail himself of the rights set forth in Part I of the Convention only in so far as municipal law has assimilated these rights or ensured their application? Clearly there are still two schools of thought among the theorists. The recognition of individual rights conferred directly by the conclusion of the Convention as an international instrument could only be based upon the express will of the Contracting Parties. It is in keeping with the traditional conception of the effect of international treaties that the recognition of individual rights should only be based upon municipal law.

The notion that the conclusion of the Convention confers rights directly upon the individual would appear to be untenable for the following reason: the Convention does not contain an explicit provision to that effect. Such a provision would, however, be required, since, according to traditional theory, renunciation of sovereignty cannot be implied (restrictive interpretation) but can only be assumed to the extent that it is clearly established by the Treaty itself. It might be argued that in the case of a law-making treaty this rule does not always apply. But the Convention on Human Rights with its tendency to defend individual rights against States in fact constitutes an innovation in the field of international law to which the parties concerned have only responded somewhat cautiously—as experience has shown. An extensive interpretation would go beyond the limits which the member States have in any case already found it difficult to accept (e.g. in relations between the State and its own nationals).

Article 1 of the Convention, which is sometimes quoted to prove the existence of direct rights of the individual, does not constitute a valid argument either. Many traditional commercial and establishment treaties under which the parties have undertaken to recognise individual rights are formulated in the same way, but it has not been argued that they directly conferred rights on individuals.

According to the argument put forward here, it must be insisted that where there is no proof of a contrary intention of the parties, the conclusion and the entry into force of the Convention have not by themselves created individual rights. It is through the intermediary of municipal law that the individual acquires the rights mentioned in the Convention. Hence, if a member State has not fulfilled an obligation contracted under international law to confer rights on individuals either by assimilation or by some implementing enactment under municipal law, the individual cannot immediately claim these rights, since there is not only no practical possibility of his enforcing them but they have indeed no material existence for him. Naturally, any State may, as a Party to the Convention, demand that the obligations be carried out and thus indirectly contribute to the recognition of individual rights.

It might be objected that this conclusion is incompatible with Article 25 of the Convention, which makes it legally possible for the individual to apply to the Commission in the event of violation of his individual rights. Now, if the individual had not substantive rights, then in the event of non-execution of a treaty by the State in question, i.e. in the event of the latter not assimilating its municipal law to the Convention, he could not allege violation of a right. This argument appears convincing, but it neglects the fact that accession to the Convention does not in itself mean simultaneous acceptance of the right of individual petition provided for in Article 25. Accession and recognition of the right of individual petition constitute distinct and separate legal acts, so that a distinction must be drawn between the existing legal situation of accession without acceptance of the right of individual petition provided for under Article 25 and accession accompanied by recognition of that right. Certain States have not accepted these provisions, i.e. they have not recognised the competence of the Commission to give decisions on individual rights, whereas other States have done so. Consequently, it is not permissible for States in the former category to draw any inferences whatsoever from Article 25 regarding their other obligations. The reason why certain States have not recognised the competence of the Commission is precisely that they were not, or were not yet, ready to accept individual rights arising directly from the Convention in the field of international law.

We may therefore conclude that, without recognition of the competence of the Commission as defined in Article 25, the Convention is an international treaty which, although it obliges the State to apply its provisions, does not confer on individuals rights which they can claim against a State not recognising the competence of the Commission, so long as that State has not conferred these rights in some way or other through its own municipal law. The declaration provided for under Article 25 established the Commission's competence, which in turn implies its right to investigate whether in any particular case an individual has or has not been treated in accordance with the provisions of the Convention. By accepting this right of investigation, the State which makes the declaration in question necessarily recognises *uno actu* that individuals claiming to be victims of a violation of a right shall be able to invoke directly the rights prescribed by the Convention, for the mere fact of recognising the competence of the Commission would be completely meaningless if the declaration did not contain a further implicit recognition of the direct rights of individuals. Bearing in mind international practice and the particular legal situation in each case, it is wise, on the other hand, to consider that the declaration provided for under Article 25 implies acceptance both of the competence of the Commission and the fact that direct rights are conferred on individuals within the framework of the Convention in international law, rights which become effective immediately.

It might be objected that this inference cannot be drawn directly but only—if we follow the reasoning given above—by implication from the text of Article 25. But it cannot be said that this interpretation unduly extends the rights of the individual and curtails the rights of States. For if we consider the over-all significance of the Convention, the principles of restrictive interpretation referred to above are safeguarded. Only those rights are recognised which are indispensable for the implementation of the substantive law established by the Convention and its protective system.

It should be emphasised once more that the novelty of the Convention does not reside in the principles of the substantive law it embodies but in the means it supplies for their enforcement. It is only

D

when these means become effective, i.e. when they are recognised by means of a special declaration, that a new conception of the relation between substantive and adjective law becomes necessary and, perhaps, admissible. Essential though it is in questions of international customary law to make a strict distinction between substantive law and adjective law or their implementation, there can be no objection in international treaty law to considering that competence to implement the provisions of the treaty simultaneously confers those very substantive rights on whose sole account that competence was granted in the first place.

This view of the Convention in relation to the municipal law of member States does not correspond with the Commission's conception as shown in its decisions to date. However, that should not prevent us from considering seriously whether the approach suggested is not the best way of arriving at a logical theory of interpretation.

WRITTEN COMMUNICATION BY
HELFRIED PFEIFER

As far as Austria is concerned, the problem of the Convention on Human Rights is as follows: On 13 December 1957 Austria signed the Convention and First Protocol; the National Council unanimously approved them on 10 July 1958 as an *international treaty amending the Constitution* in accordance with prevailing constitutional law doctrine[1] and in accordance with the practice customary since 1920 (increased quorum and two-thirds majority without special requirements); on 5 August 1958 the Federal President ratified the Convention thus approved in accordance with the Constitution; on 3 September 1958 the instrument of ratification was deposited, and on 24 September 1958 the Convention and Protocol were published in the *Bundesgesetzblatt* (Federal Gazette).

In my view there were two stages: on 3 September 1958 the Convention became binding on Austria in international law, but it entered into force in municipal law only on 25 September 1958 as a constitutional law with its various orders and prohibitions concerning all those who are affected by it or to whom it is addressed, i.e. the State organs and the residents of Austria. This is only logical, moreover, since a law cannot be applied before it has been published.

Whereas I personally have always maintained, together with the National Council of which I was a member and in all my subsequent

[1] Cf. Kelsen-Froelich-Merkl, *Die Bundesverfassung*, p. 187; Adamovich-Spanner, *Handbuch des österreichischen Verfassungsrechts*, p. 330, n. 1.

writings[1], that the Convention always had constitutional status, the Constitutional Court gave a negative ruling on technical grounds, contrary to prevailing constitutional law doctrine and current practice, on the ground of failure to designate the international Convention as 'amending the Constitution' in the decision ratifying the Convention.[2] However, the legislative authority finally confirmed the constitutional status of the Convention and First Protocol in Article II of the Federal Constitutional Law of 4.3.1964 (BGBl. No. 59) with effect from the date of assimilation (*Transformation*) (25 September 1958) by means of an authoritative ruling and thus invalidated the contrary opinion of the Constitutional Court. This Federal Constitutional Law (B.VG) of 4 March 1964 not only authorised general assimilation in Article I, but also provided for the possibility of special assimilation by means of a future law or order. Article I laid down for the first time that international conventions amending the Constitution, or such provisions contained in international conventions, should be designated expressly as 'amending the Constitution' ('verfassungsändernd'). Until that time, only constitutional laws or constitutional provisions in individual laws were to be so designated expressly.[3]

It should be remembered that Austria made three reservations at the time of ratification to the effect that:

1. The provisions of Article 5 of the Convention shall be so applied that there shall be no interference with the measures for the deprivation of liberty prescribed in the laws on administrative procedure, BGBl No. 172/1950, subject to review by the Administrative Court or the Constitutional Court.

2. With regard to Article 6, civil and penal proceedings shall be conducted orally and in public before the competent Court as laid down in Article 90 B.VG, but specific derogations from this principle may be permitted by ordinary law.

3. Article 1 of the Protocol shall be so applied that there shall be *no interference* with the provisions relating to property in the Austrian State Treaty of 15 May 1955.

---

[1] See *inter alia*, *Die Menschenrechtskonvention. Europäischer Rechtsschutz der Staatsbürger*, 11 Jg. (1958), 15. u. 16. Folge; 'Die Bedeutung der Europäischen Menschenrechtskonvention für Österreich', *Festschrift für Karl Gottfried Hugelmann* (1959) Bd. I, 399–452; 'Die parlamentarische Genehmigung von Staatsverträgen in Österreich. Ihre innerstaatliche Wirksamkeit', *Österreichische Zeitschrift für öffentliches Recht*, (1962) Bd. xii, 1–70; 'Der Verfassungsrang von Staatsverträgen', *Österreichische Juristenzeitung*, 1962,29 ff. ; 'Der Verfassungsgerichtshof zu Art. 6 der Menschenrechtskonvention'. *Jur. Blätter*, 1961, 527 ff.; *Handbuch der Grundfreiheiten und Menschenrechte von Ermacora*. Eine Buch- und Lagebesprechung. *Deutsches Verwaltungsblatt*, 1965, 107 ff.

[2] Decision of 27.7.1960, no. 3767 and Decision of 14.10.1961, no. 4049.

[3] Article 44, paragraph 1 of the Federal Constitutional Law.

Since the constitutional status of the Convention on Human Rights and Protocol was placed beyond dispute, three other problems have continued to give rise to controversy:

1. Do the Convention and Protocol take precedence over older sources of law which may be in conflict with them and which have a different status in the hierarchy of rules of law?

I would immediately say that they do if the provisions of the Convention are more favourable to the individual (Article 60 of the Convention on Human Rights). The Constitutional Court however considers that the provisions of the Convention which are not directly applicable cannot derogate from directly applicable legal rules.[1] I cannot subscribe to this too general view of the Constitutional Court, for it does not take into account the contradictions existing between certain new rights deriving from the Convention and the old legal system, which necessarily lead to derogations from older legal principles.[2] In my opinion it cannot be affirmed with certainty that the provisions of the Convention would not modify older contradictory rules of law unless it were expressly stipulated in the decision of the National Council approving the Convention or in a constitutional law that the Convention on Human Rights and first Protocol would not take effect until after a certain date and that, in the meanwhile, the provisions of the Constitution and the ordinary laws should be adapted to the new provisions on human rights and fundamental freedoms. Such postponement of the entry into force of the Convention on Human Rights in municipal law would have been possible under Article 49 B.VG, but no action was taken under this Article.

A committee of experts meeting in the Federal Chancellery is at present discussing a new catalogue of fundamental rights, taking into account the existence of the Convention on Human Rights and Protocol.

2. Are the provisions of the Convention on Human Rights and Protocol directly applicable in Austria?

We agree with Professor Sørensen that the reply to this question depends entirely on the special provisions peculiar to each Article. Generally speaking, as I wrote in my article 'Die Bedeutung der Europäischen Menschenrechtskonvention für Österreich' ('The significance of the European Convention on Human Rights for Austria'), the provisions of the Convention are also applicable even if the Convention uses indefinite or extensive concepts, because such in-

[1] Decision of 14 October 1961, no. 4049.
[2] Cf. p. 46 *et seq.* of my article, 'Die Parlamentarische Genehmigung . . .' mentioned above.

pefinite concepts also occur in municipal law and are self-executing. Article 5, paragraphs 3 and 4, are generally applicable in Austria, especially since in this country very precise provisions exist regarding the hearing of prisoners, and their appearance before the competent authorities (para. 36 of the Administrative Penal Law, para. 4 of the Law on the Safeguarding of Personal Freedom, etc.). Some supplementary provisions are necessary, however, in regard to arrest by administrative authorities, as for example in the case of arrest with a view to expulsion.

Article 13 contains one of the rare provisions which are not directly applicable. It is true that the violation of a fundamental right guaranteed by a constitutional law may constitute a ground for appeal to the Constitutional Court, in so far as this fundamental right is not subject to a reservation in favour of ordinary legislation. But this applies only if the violation results from an administrative decision or an official act. But if a private individual is a victim of the violation of a right recognised in the Convention, either as a result of a sentence or through the effect of a general rule, he has no remedy before the Constitutional Court. The right of appeal must be extended in this respect too in favour of the individual victim of a violation.

3. The problem of reservations.

The European Commission of Human Rights considers itself to be the sole authority entitled to interpret reservations. But there is a risk of erroneous interpretation, so that the individual applicant and the State concerned should be able to have recourse to the European Court of Human Rights.

To take an example: whereas the Austrian reservation to Article 1 of the Protocol states that the provisions of the State Treaty of 15 May 1955 relating to property shall not be affected by Article 1, a complaint against the application of a provision of the State Treaty relating to property which is incompatible with Article 1 of the Protocol may be rejected because that is in accordance with the meaning of the reservation. If, on the other hand, an individual complains against a decision because the latter violates a provision of the State Treaty which is not affected by the reservation and is completely compatible with Article 1 of the Protocol, in my opinion the application should not be rejected. For, in that case, the non-fulfilment of the provision of the State Treaty not affected by the reservation is also a violation of Article 1 of the Protocol. For example, in Article 27 (2) of the State Treaty, Austria concedes to Yugoslavia the right to confiscate Austrian property in Yugoslavia, and, at the same time, undertakes in the place of Yugoslavia to compensate Austrian nationals who are victims of this measure; the obligation assumed by Austria is in no way affected by the reservation in regard to Article 1 of the Protocol. Consequently, the Commission of Human Rights should admit such an application since the fact of Austria's not respecting the undertaking constitutes a violation of Article 1 of the Protocol. Unfortunately, as far as I know, the Commission of Human Rights has not accepted such justifiable and admissible complaints, although they are perfectly compatible with the provisions of the reservation and of the Convention.

The success or failure of the Convention depends on its being applied according to the letter and the spirit of the Convention and in accordance with its provisions on individual petitions (Article 25 et seq.) and reservations (Article 64). If the European authorities fail to act, the Convention is meaningless. I therefore believe that in such cases it should be possible to apply for a remedy to the European Court, which may be expected to judge on a strictly impartial basis without concerning itself with the wishes of the States concerned. Indeed, it is the individual victim of a violation who must be protected and not the States responsible for violation.

WRITTEN COMMUNICATION BY
RENÉ MARCIC

Since my duties unfortunately prevent me from attending the Conference, I should like to submit in writing the following brief statement, which is divided into three parts:

(1) For the reasons given below I consider that the European Convention on Human Rights should give first place *expressis verbis* to the dignity of the human person as the basic concept which is at the origin of human rights and fundamental freedoms. In order not to quote myself, I would refer to Ulrich Scheuner, for whom a system of human rights and fundamental freedoms is neither conceivable nor applicable unless mention is made of the 'central value' which supports the whole structure. A system of human rights and fundamental freedoms that does not refer to the dignity of the human person is like a circle without any centre.

To my mind the first Article should be conceived as follows: 'Human rights and fundamental freedoms are the necessary consequence of the dignity of the human person'. The expression 'dignity of the human person' is synonymous with the *terminus technicus* 'nature of man'.

I think, however, that some precision should be given regarding the content of this basic concept, the dignity of the human person. Article 1 (1) of the German Basic Law merely mentions two material factors: the inviolability of human dignity (*status negativus* or *negatorius*) and the inalienable and absolute right of man to the protection of that inviolability by the public authorities (*status positivus*). But a third factor necessarily and directly derives from this basic value, the dignity of the human person: the *status activus* in the wider sense of the term, that is to say, man's right to co-operate in achieving the positive legal order which protects him, in maintaining and developing, transforming and suppressing that order. This co-operation is manifested not only by the vote or by other forms of *status activus* in the narrower sense of the term; it is most effectively exercised in the control of law by the judicial authorities. To sum up, the basic and absolute legal value of the dignity of the human person:

(*a*) prohibits any State or any other political community from ever depriving man of his status as a subject of the law and reducing him to the state of a pure object (means, instrument) of the community;

(*b*) requires the State or any other political community to provide man with the legal means by which he may implement the social system that will protect his dignity and his rights;

(*c*) requires the State or any other political community to provide man with the legal possibility of co-operating in the achievement, transformation or suppression of the system whose norms concern him as a human being.[1]

(2) The time has come to ensure that the *control of the law by the judicial authorities*, which protects human rights, fundamental freedoms and the Convention, is effectively established: in future an individual applicant should be legally entitled to approach the Court directly without going through the Commission. The present solution is a half-measure. The sooner we take this step forward, the sooner we shall be in tune with the spirit of our time.

(3) The present epoch is characterised by the fact that the unity of mankind, whether we conceive it according to the doctrine of monogenism or polygenism, has deeply penetrated the awareness of all men. Humanity is beginning to consider itself as a single community of rights and values as regards the dignity or nature of man. The recent trend of theories and studies on this subject throughout the world, including the Communist world and particularly the People's Republic of China, shows that 'the dignity of man' or 'the nature of man' has become a universal and single formula understood by all: everyone is careful of his dignity and of the rights deriving therefrom. It is undoubtedly the western philosophy of law which throughout the centuries and millennia has slowly and painfully worked out and

---

[1] For further details see my contribution to the publication in honour of Ernst von Hippel: *Ein neuer Aspekt der Menschenwürde*.

settled the formula which is spread abroad today. No one, then, is surprised that Europe should be the first continent to act on the United Nations Declaration of 10 December 1948 by concluding a Convention for the Protection of Human Rights and Fundamental Freedoms, which comprises guarantees that are partly effective. This model, however, should be followed throughout the world by similar institutions.

Once natural law is accepted as the common foundation and link of human law, the concepts and spiritual endeavours which inspire the various theories and institutions should no longer be sought only in the western tradition, but also equally among the thinkers and social and political institutions of the great civilisations of the East and of the New World, for example those of Central America. If these infinitely varied concepts could be collected, stored and set in order, we would appreciate in all their richness the multiple possibilities and aspects of human nature.

What should be done is to establish an international research centre independent of the University which would bring together on an international and scientific basis collaborators from all countries. The innumerable conceptions of human rights evolved by all nations of the world should be scanned in the clearly defined field of vision of science. Once collected, the various conceptions of human rights should be harmonised and brought into relation with one another in the field of jurisprudence, sociology and political science. Any gaps would be filled in. If natural law is in fact the common foundation and link of mankind, a unified doctrine of natural law will inevitably be found.

Sound preparatory work is necessary for this. Although it is Europe which has established their form, the human rights and fundamental values which constitute the dignity and the nature of man are known in substance to all the peoples of the earth, whatever natural circle they belong to.

Once this work has been achieved, the non-European peoples will have acquired the feeling that the dignity of the human person, that basic value, is no foreign concept that has been imposed upon them, but is their own, has always belonged to them and is quite familiar to them. Then will come the time when the Universal Declaration of Human Rights may be exalted into a world law which is strictly binding from a legal point of view. To ensure its implementation, an international court with compulsory jurisdiction should be planned and established, as is proposed by Hans Kelsen, Alfred Verdross and myself.

SUMMARY OF THE DISCUSSION

W. J. Ganshof van der Meersch drew attention to the reference by Professor Sørensen, in the last paragraph of Section IV of his report, to a development in the case-law in certain countries where the Constitution does not provide that rules of international law should take precedence over rules of internal law but where the courts have nevertheless recognised the Convention as a source of binding rules.

In the Belgian legal system, in order that an international convention should have the force of internal law, it is necessary that a legislative act should provide for it to be given 'full and complete effect'. The *Cour de Cassation*, which is only competent to take a decision on a point of the law, has on many occasions applied the provisions of the European Convention on Human Rights, which has been incorporated into the internal legal system by the law authorising ratification. One can see from its case-law that the Court has recognised that a number of the provisions of the Convention are immediately applicable in internal law. Nevertheless, the Court has not so declared *expressis verbis*.

When there is a conflict between a treaty and a provision of internal law, the Belgian *Cour de Cassation* seems to be going in the direction of recognising that the rule of international law should take precedence, provided that it is directly applicable.

A constitutional amendment is under consideration after two earlier procedures were found to be unsuccessful. There is reason to believe that the precedence of the conventional rule of international law over the rule of internal law will now be established. That is the direction in which we are going. The reasoning which the current jurisprudence tends to adopt is that it is by no means necessary that the principle of international law should be expressly asserted.

The Constitution of the Grand Duchy of Luxembourg, as revised in 1956, equally does not expressly affirm the precedence of international law over national law; Luxembourg has also adopted the method of judicial interpretation to find a solution to the problem of conflict between a treaty and a rule of internal law. But Luxembourg is taking a more progressive line than Belgium: the precedence of the rule of international law is not limited to cases in which a rule is immediately applicable; the precedence of a conventional rule of international law, even over a later rule of internal law, is deduced from the intrinsic nature of the former rule—this is said to be of a superior character to a rule which is only due to the 'will of an internal organ'.

It is interesting to note that the Netherlands, by means of constitutional amendments in 1953 and 1956, are following a line which corresponds closely to that which the Belgian *Cour de Cassation* seems to be adopting: the internal law will not be applied if such application would be incompatible with a provision of an international convention 'which is binding on individuals'. This limitation results in making a distinction in Dutch law, by virtue of Articles 65 and 66 of the Constitution, between two types of provisions in international conventions: those which apply directly to individuals and take priority over rules of internal law, whether they are earlier or later in date, and other provisions which do not have this character and therefore do not have the same effect.

I. Seidl-Hohenveldern discussed the question whether, in a State which has a written Constitution and has undertaken under international law to comply with the Convention, but in which, for one reason or another, the Convention is not or is not yet operative under municipal law, a judge who is bound by that Constitution or that law can nevertheless apply the Convention.

In addition to Professor Ganshof van der Meersch's remarks regarding the welcome tendency in Belgium to 'reverse the burden of proof', it might be added that there is still another way of ensuring the applicability of the Convention, a 'second line of defence' as it were. The human rights provided for in municipal law should be interpreted wherever possible in the light of international obligations, even if these have not yet acquired validity under municipal law. This raises a general problem as regards conventions which are not self-executing and have been ratified (e.g. in the case of Austria, obligations under international labour conventions). When applying (or interpreting) the Convention, the Court should give preference, in such cases, to the meaning which is consistent with the Convention.

Francesco Capotorti: Italy has incorporated the Convention in its municipal law (without altering the text) by means of an implementing Act to which the text of the Convention is annexed. This has two consequences: in respect of form, the international Convention, as a source of law, has the same status as the implementing Act; in regard to substance, it is necessary to effect a 'transformation'. When applying the Convention, the Court must take into account the place it occupies in the hierarchy of the legal order. Other laws may, moreover, derogate from or reinforce the implementing Act.

The Convention belongs essentially to constitutional law. Where the Constitution guarantees the same rights as the Convention, the Court can render a decision pursuant to the Constitution; where the Constitution does not embody a provision governing fundamental rights or where it lays down different rules, the Court cannot give preference to the Convention. In such circumstances it would be desirable for a State which incorporates international treaties into its municipal law in this way, to transform the Convention by means of a constitutional law. This would be the only means of preventing subsequent amendment by an ordinary law.

It would be useful to publish the relevant decisions of all domestic courts, for the interpretation of the courts is of special importance. This would establish the necessary conditions for the most uniform possible administration of justice.

Karl Zemanek: The decision of the Court of Justice of the European Communities of 15 July 1964, referred to by the Rapporteur, which has a distinctly federal character, would not appear to be automatically applicable to other communities which do not possess the necessary institutional structure. For example, the conditions prevailing in the European Communities do not all subsist throughout the area covered by the Convention.

The 'self-executing' theory contains a serious danger. It came into being in the United States where, because of the character of the Common Law, the courts are accustomed to apply very widely accepted rules and principles. Experience has shown that Continental European courts and administrative authorities are disinclined to adopt this empirical approach, being accustomed, under their own legal systems, to a work essentially of classification; they will, therefore, often assume a too guarded attitude to the question of 'self-executing'. Moreover, as each judicial body will have to decide this matter for itself, at least initially before a case is referred to a higher court, there will be divergent decisions even within one and the same legal system.

But the solution adopted by the European Communities, to which Mr Sørensen refers, is also unsatisfactory. Whether a treaty clause is self-executing does not depend only on its wording: it can also depend on the structure of the legal system within which it is to be applied. If an international body renders a decision on the self-executing character of a provision which has force of law within several legal systems, this second aspect can be taken into consideration only to a limited extent. The absurd situation may therefore arise where an international body declares a provision to be self-executing, although within one of the legal systems concerned it cannot be so in practice, owing to the absence of the machinery of execution which exists in other legal systems. In other words: even a decision by an international body that a provision is self-executing does not necessarily make it so within a given legal system. This contradiction shows clearly that jurisprudence has not yet adequately clarified the matter.

The Austrian solution, namely the *Bundesverfassungsgesetz* (Federal Constitutional Act) of 3 April 1964, may provide a useful answer; under this Act, the legislature is empowered to decide that a treaty clause is not self-executing. It must, however, draw the consequences and introduce an implementing Act—a step which is unfortunately not always taken.

Felix Ermacora stated that the question whether or not treaties are self-executing is influenced by the relevant constitutional law doctrine (e.g. by provisions governing the legality of the administration) as well as by the wording of the Convention (e.g. whether the Convention embodies concepts similar to those embodied in national laws and regulations) and by any reservations made to the Convention. For such reservations the national text is, as is known, regarded as the authentic one. Thus it will be necessary, particularly when a similar legal situation exists in States which have made reservations to the Convention, to compare these reservations, for this will also shed light on the question of the self-executing nature of the Convention. There now exists an original text of the Convention and several national texts which are not authentic. The Convention is noncommittal, for it does not specify whether its provisions should be interpreted uniformly or whether such interpretation should be a matter for national courts. Meanwhile States are left to make their own individual and frequently divergent interpretations.[1] For this reason the proposal was made that the European Court should be empowered to give authoritative interpretations by means of advisory opinions; but the Committee of Ministers has not followed up this proposal. Thus the Convention continues to lead an independent existence in the individual legal systems of the Contracting States, which is by no means a satisfactory situation.

Jacques Velu remarked that the Rapporteur had defended the theory whereby States parties to the Convention have discretionary powers in respect of the choice of method of incorporating the Convention into their domestic law.

There was (he said) no general rule of international law which obliged States to adopt one method rather than another of incorporating the Convention into their legislation. The real question was whether Contracting States were not in any event bound to take some appropriate action, having regard to the obligations they assumed by virtue of the Convention. In his view, no such obligation was implied. Did that view correspond with the facts stated in the 'travaux préparatoires' of the Convention?

Two distinct stages could be noted in the 'travaux préparatoires' relating to this particular problem.

During the first stage, up to mid-June 1950, it had not been disputed that States would have discretionary powers in the choice of the

[1] Cf. e.g. Article 6: civil rights and obligations.

method of incorporating the Convention into their law. Proof of this could be seen in the statements made on 12 June 1950 by MM. Perassi (Italy), Hoare (United Kingdom), Chaumont (France), Muuls (Belgium) and Vergin (Turkey) at the Conference of Senior Officials.[1]

A change in that attitude has become apparent from 24 June 1950. On that date, the Assembly Committee on Legal and Administrative Questions, following an intervention by Professor Rolin, had decided to avoid any ambiguity with respect to the legal effect of the Convention, that the High Contracting Parties, in accepting the Convention, should 'recognise' the rights and liberties listed in Section I, instead of 'undertaking to recognise them', which would seem to call for action on their part separate from and additional to the acceptance of the Convention.[2]

This had been clearly stated by Sir David Maxwell-Fyfe, Chairman of the Assembly Committee on Legal and Administrative Questions, in a letter of the same date, which he had sent to the Chairman of the Committee of Ministers.[3]

Following a proposal for an amendment, the Sub-Committee on Human Rights had met on 4 August 1950 and replaced the words 'undertake to secure' by 'shall secure' in Article 1.[4]

The revised draft had been approved by the Committee of Ministers on 7 August 1950.[5]

Professor Rolin had subsequently commented on the scope of his amendment before the Consultative Assembly on two occasions. On the first occasion, at the sitting of 25 August 1950, he had stated:

According to the new text of the Committee of Ministers, the High Contracting Parties shall not undertake to recognise, they *shall* recognise— so that once it is ratified by the States, the text, as at present worded, will no longer be the subject of subsequent amendments to our constitutions, or to our respective legislations. It will be incorporated bodily, of its own right, into the legislation of our 15 countries.[6]

On the second occasion, at the sitting of 18 September 1953, Mr Rolin had interpreted his amendment as follows:

The special thing about our Convention is that it is, as the British say, 'self-executing'. It incorporates these rights in our domestic laws direct without the need for any intermediary law.

By virtue of the first Article, for instance—and this at the suggestion of our own Committee—the countries do not 'undertake to recognise' these rights

---

[1] Collected Edition of the 'Travaux préparatoires', vol. III, pp. 589–90.

[2] Minutes of the Sitting on the morning of 24 June 1950; Doc. AS/JA (50) PV 2 of 5 August 1950; ibid. vol. III, p. 694.

[3] Ibid., vol. III, pp. 698 and 703.   [4] Ibid., vol. III, p. 733.

[5] Doc. A 1937 of 7 August 1950; ibid., vol III, p. 774.

[6] Ibid., vol. IV, p. 927.

in their laws. They have already recognised them. That is the big difference. Once this Convention has been approved by our Parliaments, and ratified, our Courts of Law will be fully within their rights, without waiting for any further legislation, in implementing the terms of this Convention.[1]

It was therefore obvious, Mr Velu concluded, that the authors of the Convention consider that it should be automatically incorporated into the domestic legislation of the Contracting States.

SUMMING UP BY

MAX SØRENSEN

1. It is interesting to note that in ratifying the Convention many countries simply brought their legislation into line with it in the usual way and did not give the force of law to the Convention as such. According to Mr Velu, this is contrary to the undertaking they gave to incorporate the Convention into their municipal law. If it is admitted that a treaty is to be interpreted in the light of its application by the Contracting States, it must be concluded that the Convention gives States a choice between various methods.

2. Mr Velu's contentions regarding the Iversen case are based on a doubtful interpretation of the judgment rendered by the Supreme Court of Norway which, indeed, left open the question whether or not the Convention formed part of Norwegian municipal law.

3. Professor Seidl-Hohenveldern's 'second line of defence' is a real and important consideration. Even in countries where the Convention does not form part of municipal law, judges may take account of it in order to avoid, as far as possible, conflict between the international commitments of the State and municipal law.

4. It must be admitted that the conclusions of the report, inasmuch as they relate to the European Communities, do not all apply necessarily to the field embraced by the Convention. The same can be said of the 'self-executing' question, to which the Community countries can find answers to suit themselves. As regards the Convention, the question whether its clauses are self-executing or not has always to be decided with reference to the text and to the national legal system concerned. As a result, certain clauses may be held to be self-executing in one contracting State and not in another. That is a weakness in the Convention from the point of view of European integration. One function of the Vienna Conference was precisely to point out such defects, to discuss them and, where possible, to remedy them in a European spirit.

[1] Official report of the sitting of the Consultative Assembly on 18 September 1953, p. 341.

CHAPTER II

Status of the European Convention in the hierarchy of rules of law

REPORT BY

ALFRED VERDROSS

I. BASIS IN THEORY

A few preliminary remarks on legal theory are necessary before we can discuss this question.

Various theories exist regarding the relationship between international and municipal law. The earliest of these, the dualistic or pluralist theory, established by Heinrich Triepel[1] and Dionisio Anzilotti[2] but still supported today by most Italian professors of international law,[3] holds that international law and municipal law are two completely separate and independent legal systems. This doctrine is based on the following considerations: the rules of international law are created in the course of mutual dealings between nations and are founded on international customary law and international treaty law. Municipal law, by contrast, has its origin in a specific national constitution, which is its prime source. Moreover, according to this theory, international law and municipal law are applicable to different persons or bodies: while the former applies solely to national states and other sovereign entities, such as the Holy See, the latter attributes rights and duties only to individuals or bodies (State authorities and private persons), national corporate bodies (provinces, municipalities) and legal persons. Lastly the dualistic theory points out that municipal laws which are contrary to international law are also legally binding, hence the autonomy and independence of municipal law *vis-à-vis* international law.

The dualistic theory was severely shaken by the fact that various rules of international law, e.g. the articles of war, and certain State treaties, ascribe rights and duties directly to private persons, and by the fact that numerous State constitutions recognise State

---

[1] *Völkerrecht und Landesrecht*, 1899.

[2] *Corso di diritto internazionale*, 4th edition 1955.

[3] Perassi, *Lezioni di diritto internazionale*, 4th edition 1939; Morelli, *Nozioni di diritto internazionale*, 3rd edition 1951; Balladore Pallieri, *Diritto internazionale pubblico*, 8th edition 1962. Exceptions are: Rolando Quadri, *Diritto internazionale pubblico*, 3rd edition 1960, and Piero Ziccardi, 'Diritto internazionale in generale', in *Enciclopedia del diritto*, 1964, p. 988 et seq.

treaties and international customary law as additional sources of municipal law. The bottom was finally knocked out of the dualistic theory when it was perceived that its premise was self-contradictory. The contradiction lies in the fact that while the dualistic theory admits that international law ascribes rights and obligations to States, it claims at the same time that municipal law is independent of international law. Now, since States are only communities of human beings, founded on a certain constitutional order which groups them together to form a legal unit, they cannot be disassociated from their legal systems. Consequently, if States are subject to international law, it follows that their legal order is likewise. Hence the dualistic theory must be replaced by a monistic theory which combines international and municipal law in a single legal system. But there are different types of monistic theory. A distinction must first be drawn between the monistic theory based on the primacy of municipal law and that based on the primacy of international law.[1] Thus according to Kelsen, for example, Article 9 of the Austrian Federal Constitution acknowledges the primacy of municipal law, since it declares the generally recognised rules of international law to be integral parts of Federal law.[2] But it is clear from the genesis of Article 4 of the 1919 Weimar Constitution, on which Article 9 of the Austrian Federal Constitution is modelled, that it was by no means the intention of the said Article 4 to infer the validity of international law from municipal law. Its intention was merely to recognise general international law as being *an additional* source of municipal law. It consequently does not state that international law is *solely* a source of municipal law but that it is *also* a source of municipal law.[3] The same applies to other State constitutions which contain similar provisions. Thus, for instance, Article 10 of the Italian National Constitution of 1st February 1948 says that the Italian legal order 'conforms' to the general rules of international law—in other words, it does not establish their validity, but presupposes it. Since there is little support nowadays for the theory of the primacy of municipal law,[4] we need not go into it any further here.

---

[1] Kelsen, *Das Problem der Souveränität und die Theorie des Völkerrechtes*, 1920, and latterly in *Principles of International Law*, 1952; Verdross, *Die Einheit des rechtlichen Weltbildes*, 1923, p. 159 et seq., *Die Verfassung der Völkerrechtsgemeinschaft*, 1926, p. 34 et seq., and latterly in *Völkerrecht*, 5th edition 1964, p. 111 et seq.

[2] The constitutional law of the Austrian Republic, 5th part, 1922, p. 75.

[3] Verdross, *Völkerrecht*, 5th edition 1964, p. 115 et seq.

[4] Kelsen is an exception in that he considers both the primacy of international law and the primacy of municipal law as arguable. See his *Principles of International Law*, 1952, p. 403 et seq.

By far the most widely held theory today is the monistic theory based on the primacy of international law. But this theory, too, is sub-divided into *radical* and *moderate* monism. The former asserts that municipal laws which are contrary to international law are invalid.[1] Moderate monism, on the other hand, which I was the first to defend, admits that State organs—being organs of a specific national legal order and consequently owing obedience to it—are, in principle, bound to apply also laws which are contrary to international law. But that does not preclude international law from taking precedence over municipal law, since State organs may also be, and as a rule are, bound by the State constitution to apply all duly promulgated laws, even if their promulgation was contrary to the State constitution. Nevertheless, it is an undisputed fact that the State constitution takes precedence over ordinary laws, particularly when a procedure exists whereby anti-constitutional laws can be amended or repealed. Similarly, the obligation of domestic courts to enforce laws which are contrary to international law is not inconsistent with the primacy of international law, since any national regulations which are incompatible with international law must be repealed or amended at the request of the State concerned. Thus we see that domestic procedure is subject to international law. Domestic law can, therefore, operate unchallenged only within a sphere delimited by international law.

Even the constitutional autonomy of States and the fundamental autonomy of their legal order are based on international law, since the latter is a decentralised order which recognises and safeguards a field of action reserved exclusively to States.[2]

Thus international law prohibits intervention in the internal affairs of States. Article 2 (7) of the United Nations Charter, also, forbids the organs of that Institution to interfere in matters which are essentially within the domestic jurisdiction of States. But it is *international law* that determines *which* matters are within the domestic jurisdiction (*vorbehaltener Wirkungskreis, domaine réservé*) of States. It can therefore restrict or extend this jurisdiction by means of new rules of international law, although the tendency is in the main to restrict it gradually.

For these reasons it is generally recognised in present-day literature and legal practice that States, and consequently their constitutions also, are subject to international law. This holds true both for international customary law and for international treaty law.[3]

---

[1] Thus Kelsen, earlier: *Das Problem der Souveränität und die Theorie des Völkerrechts*, 1920, p. 146 et seq.

[2] Quadri, op. cit., p. 49 et seq.

[3] For example, in the report of the Swiss Political Department of 18 December

E

The principle as stated does not, however, imply that international law, as such, automatically forms part of the legal order of a State as radical monism formerly asserted.[1] It merely means that States are under an obligation to enact, within their own sphere of jurisdiction, the laws and regulations required to implement the rules of international law.[2] In principle, however, international law leaves States free to determine how those rules shall be implemented.[3] They may, therefore, at their discretion, either implement each individual rule of international law or a given set of rules by means of national regulations, as is the case in Great Britain and Ireland, or provide for the application of international law by means of one or more general clauses. Thus we find in various Council of Europe countries, and in the Federal Constitutional Law of the Austrian Republic in particular, not only the aforesaid provision to the effect that the general rules of international law form part of the country's municipal law, but also the rule that international treaties concluded in conformity with the constitution and duly published, constitute a source of municipal law. We speak in the first case of a special conversion and, in the second, of a general conversion of international law into municipal law, although it is not properly speaking a matter of 'converting' international law, but simply of implementing it by means of national rules.[4]

Even when the second alternative, the so-called general conversion is chosen, this does not mean that all international treaty rules (which alone concern us here) can be applied directly by the courts or administrative authorities of the States concerned. That is possible only when the rules are self-executing, that is to say, when their content is such that they can be applied without any further regulations. But that is not peculiar to the relationship between international

---

1956, *Jurisprudence of the administrative authorities of the Confederation*, No. 29, p. 9 et seq.

[1] Georges Scelle, 'General Principles of the Law of Peace' in the *Collection of lectures of the Hague Academy of International Law*, vol. 46, 1933, IV, p. 353.

[2] Advisory Opinion of the Permanent Court of International Justice on the Greek–Turkish exchange of population, Series A/B, No. 12, p. 20.

[3] The Constitutional Amendment (*Bundesverfassungsnovelle*) of 4 March 1964, BGBl, No. 59, made it possible for the first time in the field of Austrian Constitutional law to depart, exceptionally, from the principle of the general transformation of State treaties.

[4] Taken from the Advisory Opinion mentioned in note 3 above; 'A State which has validly contracted international obligations is bound to make the necessary amendments to its legislation in order to ensure their fulfilment.' ['Un Etat qui a valablement contracté des obligations internationales est tenu d'apporter à sa législation les modifications nécessaires pour assurer l'éxecution des engagements pris.']

and municipal law, for there also exist, in domestic legal systems, laws simply laying down principles and which cannot be applied by courts or administrative authorities until regulations have been issued under them.

Although, in principle, States are free to determine how an international treaty shall be implemented, such a treaty may itself prescribe the manner in which it is to be implemented. Attention is called, in this connection, to Article 13 of the European Convention on Human Rights, according to which States undertake to ensure that anyone alleging infringement of the rights guaranteed to him in the Convention shall have an effective remedy before a national authority. The right to such a remedy presupposes, however, that the individual provisions of the Convention have become an integral part of municipal law, for otherwise they cannot be applied by the authority competent to give a decision. Article 13 therefore indirectly enjoins Contracting States to incorporate the various provisions of the Convention into their municipal law in such a way that they can be applied directly by domestic courts and administrative authorities and, consequently, also by the supervisory authority provided for in Article 13.

However, the guiding principle of the superiority of international law over municipal law, stated above, implies not only an obligation on the part of States to apply the rules of international law within their respective spheres of jurisdiction by issuing the necessary regulations, but also an obligation on the part of all international authorities to apply the rules of international law directly. No State, by pleading its own domestic law, can evade an obligation under international law. Consequently, when a body such as the International Court of Justice or an organ of the Council of Europe, has to judge a case, it must base its decision directly on international law.[1]

From the foregoing we may draw the following conclusions for our purpose:

1. The European Convention on Human Rights takes precedence over the municipal law of the Contracting States.

2. The Contracting States are accordingly under an obligation to make their municipal law conform to the provisions of the European Convention.

3. Furthermore, the organs of the Council of Europe (the Commission of Human Rights, the Court of Human Rights and the Committee of Ministers) must, within the limits of their jurisdiction, apply the Human Rights Convention directly, regardless of whether

[1] See various judgments cited in the 5th edition of my *Völkerrecht*, 1964, p. 114 et seq.

or not the State concerned has incorporated the provisions of the Convention into its domestic legislation.

II. THE PRIMACY OF THE HUMAN RIGHTS CONVENTION WITHIN THE SPHERE OF JURISDICTION OF THE EUROPEAN ORGANS

Since the legal pre-eminence of the European Convention on Human Rights is most clearly revealed in the last-mentioned principle, we shall consider this question first and note straightaway that the indisputable legal pre-eminence of the Convention[1] is, of course, fully effective only if the State concerned has recognised both the competence of the Commission to receive individual petitions (Article 25 of the Convention) and the jurisdiction of the European Court (Art. 46). For in these circumstances, the human rights set forth in the Convention can be enforced even if the State concerned has still not incorporated them into its domestic legislation, since the Commission can receive a petition from any private person alleging an infringement of his human rights and can institute conciliation proceedings, in pursuance of Article 28 (b), in an effort to secure respect for the human rights guaranteed by the Convention. Furthermore, under Article 48 (b) and (d) of the Convention, a case may be brought before the Court either by the Commission, or by the State against which a complaint is directed, or by the Contracting State of which the person seeking redress is a national. In this way, States can obtain a decision as to whether or not the legal opinion expressed by the Commission in its report drawn up in pursuance of Article 31 of the Convention is in conformity with the Convention.

Thus a Contracting State which, at the time when the petition was lodged, had not yet incorporated the provisions of the Convention, or some of them, into its municipal law, can be compelled through the conciliation proceedings of the Commission or by judgment of the Court to amend or amplify its domestic legislation. Thus, in the De Becker case for instance, Belgium amended its legislation on the ground of the legal opinion expressed in the Commission's report without waiting for a decision of the Court— to which the Commission had referred the case—as to whether or not it shared the Commission's legal opinion. The Court consequently

---

[1] The following abbreviations are used in the text: 'The Commission' for 'The European Commission of Human Rights'; 'The Court' for 'The European Court of Human Rights'; 'The Convention' for 'The European Convention for the Protection of Human Rights and Fundamental Freedoms'; 'human rights' for 'human rights and fundamental freedoms'.

stopped its proceedings at the request of the State concerned and with the Commission's assent. The Austrian Republic also amended its legislation in the light of the legal opinion given by the Commission, in the Pataki/Dunshirn and Ofner/Hopfinger cases. Hence Article 1 of the Convention, under the terms of which the Contracting States undertake to secure for everyone within their jurisdiction the human rights defined in the Convention, is also fully effective if the State concerned has recognised the competence of the Commission to receive individual petitions and the jurisdiction of the Court, even when it has not immediately brought its legislation into line with the Convention.

If, on the other hand, a Contracting State recognises the Commission's competence to receive individual petitions, but not the jurisdiction of the Court, then the Commission must endeavour to secure respect for the threatened human rights. If no settlement is reached with the State concerned, then the Committee of Ministers alone can take a decision on the case. But since the Committee of Ministers is a political organ, there is no guarantee that the human rights safeguarded in the Convention can be enforced in this way. On the other hand, even if a Contracting State accepts the Commission's legal opinion, this does not rule out the possibility that the Court may adopt a different legal opinion in another similar case. It is therefore very unwise, where doubtful legal issues are involved, to follow the Commission blindly and avoid the Court.

The Convention is even less effective when the Commission's competence to receive individual petitions has not been recognised, for then the Commission may be seized only by a Contracting State under Article 24 of the Convention. Such use of the Convention is exceptional, however, and will occur only when it is in the interests of a State to protect a particular group of people.

It can be seen from the foregoing that, while the Convention always takes precedence over the municipal law of the Contracting States, the degree of effectiveness of that precedence can vary greatly.

III. THE PRIMACY OF THE CONVENTION ON HUMAN RIGHTS IN THE NATIONAL SPHERE

For the reason just stated, those countries which have not recognised the competence of the Commission to receive individual petitions must fulfil their obligation, under the Convention, of making their domestic legislation compatible with the provisions of the Convention in order to ensure that they will be applied at least in that way. This obligation derives not only from the leading principle of international law singled out here as being of first importance, but also from Article 57 of the Convention, under which Contracting States undertake to furnish the Secretary-General of the Council of Europe, at his request, with information concerning the measures they have taken to implement the Convention. In its report of 9 June 1958 on the De Becker case, the Commission also rightly drew attention to the obligation laid upon Contracting States to bring their domestic legislation into line with the provisions of the Convention.[1]

This obligation is also laid upon Contracting States by Article 13 of the Convention already mentioned, which prescribes that Contracting States shall ensure that any person alleging violation of the human rights guaranteed by the Convention shall have an effective remedy before a national authority. But an effective remedy can be assured only if the provisions of the Convention have been made an integral part of the municipal law to be applied by the authority competent to render a decision.

There are, however, various circumstances which make it difficult for Contracting States to bring their domestic legislation into line with the provisions of the Convention. In the first place, according to its final clause, only the English and French texts of the Convention are authentic. Moreover, these two authentic texts are not always quite concordant, and so it must sometimes be doubtful whether the substance of the provisions is adequately rendered by a mere official, literal translation of one or other of the authentic texts into another language.

Furthermore, all the Council of Europe countries already had in their own legislation, prior to the conclusion of the Convention, either a list of human rights, or isolated provisions in the matter, which are frequently worded differently from those in the Convention. Moreover, these national basic rights are the subject of a case-law occasionally extending back over several decades and have achieved thereby, and by commentaries thereon, a significance frequently far removed from the mere words in which they are expressed. It will consequently often be difficult to define the relationship between the two sets of rules.

Added to this is the fact that, under the terms of Article 60 of the Convention, none of its provisions must be construed as limiting or derogating from any of the human rights and fundamental freedoms which may be ensured under the laws of any High Contracting Party or under any other agreement to which it is a Party. This principle makes it even more difficult to define simply the legal situation resulting from the co-existence of national provisions on human rights with those embodied in the Convention.

[1] *Yearbook* II, p. 234. Cf. K. Vasak, *La Convention européenne des droits de l'homme*, 1964, p. 230.

Thus we see that even in those States which have incorporated into their own legislation all the provisions of the Convention granting specific human rights, there is still no guarantee that the Convention will be applied *effectively*. For this, additional implementing clauses are necessary to help clarify the doubtful issues described above and thus make possible the perfect establishment by courts and administrative authorities of the legal situation provided for in the Convention.

All these difficulties do not, however, relieve Contracting States of their obligation to bring their legislation into line with the Convention. Admittedly, they are not obliged, in principle, to set the provisions of the Convention on a par with a constitutional law, since not all the Contracting States make a distinction between constitutional and other laws. However, in cases where municipal legislation does distinguish between constitutional and other laws, the provisions of the Convention must, in any event, be accorded the status of a constitutional law in order to preclude their amendment by an ordinary law. But that is still not sufficient, since even the embodiment in a constitutional law (with any necessary implementing regulations) of those provisions of the Convention which are more favourable than the corresponding national provisions does not constitute full implementation of the Convention. For constitutional laws, too, can be amended. The provisions of the Convention can be given full effect only if a provision is included in the legislation of all Contracting States to the effect that the clauses of the Convention have become an integral part of municipal law and may be amended only if the Convention itself is amended or denounced (in pursuance of Article 65).

I have considered the position of the Human Rights Convention purely from the point of view of international law and must leave it to comparative political science to examine, on the basis of the constitutional law of member States, the place actually accorded it in the hierarchy of national legal systems. The constitutional law of member States varies widely on this point. In Austria, the Human Rights Convention has unquestionably the status of a constitutional law.[1] In most other States which regard the Human Rights Convention as an integral part of their municipal law, the Convention has the status of an ordinary law. In a number of Contracting States, the position of the Convention in the hierarchy of domestic law is still controversial.[2] In general, member States have not yet accorded to the internal implementation of the Human Rights Convention the

[1] The initial doubts are cleared up in Art. II of the Federal Constitutional Law (*Bundesverfassungsgesetz*), BGBl. No. 59/1964.

[2] Cf. Vasak, op. cit., p. 236 *et seq.*

importance to which it is entitled from the point of view of international law, having regard, in particular, to its Article 13. It will be interesting, in this connection, to see what results are produced by the request recently addressed for the first time by the Secretary General of the Council of Europe, in pursuance of Article 57 of the Convention, to all States parties to the Convention.

Even if a Contracting State has made its laws fully compatible with the Convention, but has not recognised the competence of the Commission to receive individual petitions or the jurisdiction of the Court, there is a danger that national authorities will interpret these provisions differently from the Commission and the Court, with the result that in course of time, the divergent legal practice of national and European organs may lead to a diversified system of protection of human rights in Council of Europe countries and so foil the Convention's supreme aim, which is to establish a unified system, or, in other words, a European Charter of Human Rights. Every effort must therefore be made to induce all Contracting States to recognise the Commission's competence to receive individual petitions and to accept the jurisdiction of the Court. Only in this way can the legally undisputed pre-eminence of the Convention over national law be made fully effective.

WRITTEN COMMUNICATION BY
HEINZ GURADZE[1]

In the Federal Republic of Germany, according to predominant theory and practice, the Convention is self-executing. However, court decisions and the doctrine most widely followed do not give it any higher rank than statute law. In other words, the Convention takes precedence over earlier laws which run counter to it, but may be amended by subsequent statute law. This argument is based—if at all—on the fact that the 'Incorporation Act' itself ranks only as an ordinary law. This view is founded on the traditional doctrine of 'incorporation'.[2] It had already been pointed out by Erich Kaufmann that this theory was inspired by an outmoded positivism.[3] Incidentally, this writer finds support in the courts of the United Kingdom, Ireland and Iceland, where the Convention is not applied because it has not been incorporated in municipal law by Act of Parliament. In the Federal Republic of Germany, the 'incorporation' theory was

---

[1] For reasons of space the bibliographical notes have been kept to a minimum. This contribution is an extract from a longer work which has not yet been published.

[2] See Federal Constitutional Court, vol. I, 410 et seq, vol. 6, 294.

[3] *Collected Works*, I, 600; II, 476 et seq.

recently dealt a decisive blow by a group of specialists in public international law, who hold that the domestic validity of an international treaty no longer rests upon an Incorporation Act.[1]

Several attempts have already been made to elevate the human rights provisions of Section I of the Convention to a status above that of statute law. It is to these clauses that the following observations apply, since it is only with regard to them that the question of the place of the Convention in the hierarchy is important. We may leave aside here the problem whether they have potential constitutional status, are situated midway between ordinary laws and the Constitution or even rank above the Constitution. The main issue is to decide whether in fact they have the status of laws.

1. Echterhölter[2] cites Article 1 (2) of the Basic Law (*Grundgesetz*) as a ground for giving the human rights clauses of the Convention a rank higher than that of ordinary laws. The Article in question accords general recognition to 'inviolable and inalienable human rights', but its third paragraph justifies granting constitutional status only to the rights set forth in Part I of the Basic Law itself. Echterhölter's opinion has found no support.

2. Many writers and courts base the primacy of the Convention on the rule *pacta sunt servanda*. Under this reasoning every international treaty would be accorded a rank higher than that of ordinary laws, a theory to which no-one subscribes. The rule *pacta sunt servanda* obliges the State to respect the treaty, but says nothing about the latter's value in internal law nor about its place in the hierarchy of national legislation.

3. Meyer-Lindenberg has endeavoured to confer constitutional status on the human rights clauses of the Convention by making them into general principles of law within the meaning of Article 38 (1) (c) of the Statute of the International Court of Justice and assimilating them to the general rules of international law in the sense of Article 25 of the Basic Law. Thus regarded, these clauses would take precedence over laws.[3] To this the objection is made that, according to the most widely-held opinion, the general rules of law are already part and parcel of national law in the form of the quasi-public law of States and do not therefore need to be incorporated by virtue of Article 25 of the Basic Law.[4] This is a form, moreover, in which the list of human rights is not recognised by the majority of civilised nations, as is required by Article 38, para. 1 (c) of the Statute of the International Court. Lastly, it is disputed, and, as a rule, denied that

---

[1] Report of the 'Deutsche Gesellschaft für Völkerrecht', H.6, 1964.
[2] *Juristen-Zeitung* 1955, 689, 691.
[3] Report of the 'Deutsche Gesellschaft für Völkerrecht', 1961, p. 105.
[4] Friedrich Klein, *JIR* 11 (1962), 172, etc.

the general principles of law (Article 38, para. 1 (c)) are general rules within the meaning of Article 25 of the Basic Law.

4. It may be wondered, however, whether Article 25 of the Basic Law is not directly applicable to the human rights clauses of the Convention. Formerly I held that it was so applicable, though only for clauses embodying principles and not for the detailed and limiting provisions which render the general rules applicable only in particular cases.[1] For the detailed clauses, I recommended the application, by analogy, of Article 25 of the Basic Law. My view did not prevail. I argued from the premise that the detailed clauses could not be general rules within the meaning of that Article, because the adjective 'general' referred to the substance of the rule. I have since ceased to uphold this argument (see (d) below).

(a) It should first be noted that general rules in the sense of Article 25 of the Basic Law, although the reference is primarily to customary law, may also be codified in international treaties.[2]

(b) International treaties may also create general rules. Some writers, however, (Echterhölter, Pigorsch) admit this principle only where a large number of States are signatories of the treaty in question.

(c) But within a group of States forming a closed legal system, a certain majority should suffice to create general rules by virtue of a treaty. Some writers doubt whether special international law is sufficient, but today most agree that it is.[3] As long ago as 1956 I contended that the Council of Europe constituted a closed legal system;[4] at the time the view was contested in some quarters. Since then, Klein[5] and others have come round to my way of thinking. It may be felt that 15 out of 18 States (only France, Switzerland and Malta are lacking) are sufficient, on the understanding that the reference is to international law and not to validity in the sphere of municipal law.

(d) I no longer maintain that only the general rules and not the detailed and limiting provisions on human rights in the Convention can be qualified as 'general' within the meaning of Article 25 of the Basic Law. Klein[6] now agrees with me. The origin of the said Article 25, which is Article 4 of the Weimar Constitution, shows that the term 'general' refers not to the substance but to the territorial scope of the rule's application. Similarly, the general rules and the detailed (limiting) clauses form an applicable whole only when taken together.

---

[1] Guradze, *Der Stand der Menschenrechte im Völkerrecht*, Göttingen, 1965 172 et seq.

[2] Guradze, loc. cit.; Klein, loc. cit., 169.

[3] Klein, loc. cit., 166. [4] Loc. cit., 173.

[5] Loc. cit., 174. [6] Loc. cit., 175.

The result is that the application, by analogy, of Article 25 of the Basic Law is pointless.

5. The resulting conclusion, namely that the human rights clauses of the Convention are general rules of international law in the sense of Article 25 of the Basic Law, and have primacy over laws, i.e. are binding on the legislator, is still open to the following objections, which I have already pointed out[1] and which have also been admitted by Klein:[2] reservations (Article 64 of the Convention) and denunciation (Art. 65) are voided of their content if this conclusion is accepted. But this is true only of the Federal Republic of Germany and of those States which have a constitutional clause corresponding to Article 25 of the Basic Law. It is also true only of the human rights clauses and not of the institutional provisions.

The argument submitted here for the law of the Federal Republic of Germany was worked out in 1961 by Wäsche.[3] It should be noted that it does not represent the dominant opinion. It scarcely goes further than the views of Klein and, by means of a different train of reasoning, arrives at the same conclusion as Meyer-Lindenberg.

WRITTEN COMMUNICATION BY
HANS BECK

With regard to the controversial question of how far the provisions of the Human Rights Convention are immediately applicable within States, i.e. the extent to which they are self-executing, para. 2 of Article 15 of the Convention and Articles 2, 3, 4 (para. 1) and 7 referred to therein are of particular significance.

Whereas under para. 1 of Article 15 all other rights proclaimed in the Convention may be restricted in the event of war or other state of national emergency under specific conditions, and may even be temporarily suspended, the basic rights listed in the second paragraph of Article 15 may not be suspended in any circumstances ('No derogation from Article 2, . . . etc. shall be made').

Hence, the Convention contains the following inalienable rights: the elementary right to life, in the sense that 'life is sacred', which is guaranteed under Article 2; the elementary right to humane treatment in Article 3; and finally, the basic right of the individual person not to be held in slavery or servitude *vide* the explicit prohibition in Article 4 para. 1. No human being may be treated as a 'thing'. It may be of interest to note that the same basic provision was

---

[1] Loc. cit., 174.   [2] Loc. cit., 175.

[3] *Die innerstaatliche Bindung des deutschen Gesetzgebers an die europäische Menschenrechtskonvention*, Kölner Dissertation 1961.

included in the Austrian General Civil Code (*ABGB*) published in 1811, Section 16 of which states:

Every human being has innate, self-evident rights and shall therefore be considered as a person. Slavery and servitude and the subjection of others to such status shall not be permitted in these lands.

The provisions listed in the second paragraph of Article 15 of the Convention also include mention of Article 7, which Liebscher[1] calls 'the heart of the Convention and the key to its meaning and juristic interpretation'.

Whereas the first paragraph of this Article lays down the basic principle of the non-retroactive effect of penal laws, the second paragraph mentions the exceptions to this principle and deals with acts and omissions which, without being expressly liable to punishment under either municipal or international law, were criminal at the time when they were committed, according to the general principles of law recognised by civilised nations.

But the significance of this so-called 'Nuremberg Clause'[2] goes far beyond what was originally intended. For in this instance the existence of a pre-positive penal law is acknowledged, which is independent of written conventions and imposes an obligation upon everyone simply because he is a human being.

Everyone, therefore, has not only basic rights but also basic obligations[3] which are based upon moral law. It is precisely for that reason that human beings have 'dignity'.

The basic rights and obligations form the elements underlying the basic concept on which the Convention on Human Rights and the United Nations Declaration were built, namely, the image of man as an indestructibly 'free moral personality'[4] both in his substance and in his dignity.

Although opinions may differ as to whether one particular provision or another of the Convention on Human Rights may be self-executing in national law or only indirectly binding through international law, there is no doubt fundamentally that the image of man's moral personality implicit in the Convention, and derived from his essential nature, must be incorporated in national legal systems as an inalienable, absolute basic value or substantive fundamental

---

[1] Liebscher, *Die Grundzüge eines Völkerstrafrechts in der österreichischen Rechtsordnung*, *JBl*, 1959, p. 394.

[2] Liebscher, op. cit., p. 387, n. 17.

[3] Cf. Article 2, para, 1 of the Bonn Basic Law.

[4] Liebholz, *Verfassungsrechtliche Strukturprobleme im neuen deutschen Verfassungsrecht*, *Deutsche Sektion der Internationalen Juristenkommission, Vorträge*, 1963, p. 20.

standard (*materielle Grundnorm*)[1]—and is thus, in this sense, directly applicable.

WRITTEN COMMUNICATION BY
ALFRED KOBZINA

On this first day of the International Conference on the European Human Rights Convention, it is tempting to cast a glance at the historical background to these talks. The picture shows a world-wide movement: a gradual integration of the community of nations, preceded by the increasing surrender of the sovereign rights of States to institutions whose structure is that of a world State.

Such a transfer of sovereign rights can have significance for those schooled in the orderly thinking of jurists only if the supranational organs based on obligations assumed under international law are successfully equipped with a legal order of their own—a task which still rests with the future. But although the objective is set, it must not mislead us into demolishing the structure of our national legal systems; rather should it strengthen our resolve to go on improving them, until their place can be taken by a trans-national legal system which is equal to them in birth and rank for the security it affords. For whatever the normative values of such trans-national law, they will in the first place be taken over from the existing body of national laws. An example is already provided in the shape of the European Convention on Human Rights.

I feel therefore that the organisers of this second conference are deserving of high praise in that they decided to start our proceedings here with a debate on the place of the Convention in the hierarchy of laws, because this is a theme reflecting those reciprocal influences which are proof positive that the law of a community of States can be built only on the achievements of the national legal systems. It is also, I think, a fortunate circumstance that our basic report on this question has been presented by a jurist of such high repute as Professor Verdross-Drossberg, the doyen of international law in Austria.

May I now, in the short time available, submit a few specific remarks:

First, in Austria—unlike the Federal Republic of Germany—the Convention has, by virtue of a Constitutional ordinance,[2] been

---

[1] Ermacora, *Handbuch der Grundfreiheiten und der Menschenrechte*, p. 60.

[2] Cf. Bundesverfassungsgesetz (Federal Constitutional Law), BGBl. No. 59/1964 and comments thereon by H. Klecatsky. Bundesverfassungsnovelle (Protocol to the Constitution) of 4 March 1964 on State Treaties, JBl. 1964, p. 349 et seq.

placed on the legislative level of a constitutional rule. Nevertheless—again in contrast to the practice followed in our neighbouring Republic—it has been adjudged by authoritative opinion not to be self-executing.

Accordingly, as long ago as 1959 the Austrian Government introduced a constitutional Bill, drafted by the Head of its Constitutional Department, Dr Loebenstein, designed to make the necessary provisions for the implementation of the Convention, which had already been incorporated in municipal law.

The view that the Convention is not self-executing has admittedly been contested in some quarters.[1] This dispute between the 'schoolmen', however, has had no practical effect on the Austrian legal order, nor has the failure to vote on the Government Bill introducing a so-called 'gap-filling' Act (*Aufstockungsgesetz*): these are facts which bear witness to the worthy traditions and exemplary body of legal prescripts in regard to basic rights and freedoms in Austria, where the law in many cases grants rights that go beyond those defined in the Convention and first Protocol.

A few words now on the procedural aspects of this problem: on the legal protection afforded, which has always been the yardstick by which to measure the effectiveness of any legal system.

Article 13 of the Convention, which guarantees that everyone whose rights and freedoms are violated shall have an 'effective remedy', i.e. a legal remedy as such, 'before a national authority', allows of a multiplicity of procedural arrangements.[2]

The pattern of the Austrian legal order in this respect is as follows:

The nature of the Convention as a constitutional norm elevates the rights guaranteed therein to the status of constitutional rights, jointly protected by the Constitutional Court in its capacity as a special Administrative Court.

Legal protection is afforded within the meaning of Article 13, but also in cases where the rights and freedoms guaranteed by the Convention are violated through the incorrect application of an ordinary law. The legal channel leads to the Administrative Court, which acts indeed as a Court of Cassation, but whose ruling is binding on the administrative authorities, who must, in consequence, as it were, take a decision in their capacity as an extension of the powers of the Court.

At the same time, considerable protection is also provided in the admittedly rare cases where the applicant's rights have been violated

---

[1] H. Pfeifer, 'Die parlamentarische Genehmigung von Staatsverträgen in Oesterreich.' op. cit. (Parliamentary approval of State Treaties in Austria). *OZöffR.* 1962, p. 59 et seq.

[2] VfGH., Erk. B 58/64.

as a result of an incorrect finding of the authorities as to the facts.[1] Although the Administrative Court must examine the disputed decision on the basis of the facts as accepted by the authority concerned, it is in no way bound to base its investigation into the substance of such decision on an illogical view of the facts which is at variance with the documents in the case, or which has resulted from incomplete enquiries and may therefore well be incorrect. It is much more likely to quash the decision as illegal on the ground that it constitutes a breach of procedural provisions, and so be led to investigate the basis for the assessment of the evidence by the administrative authority.[2]

Allow me to conclude with a few remarks on Article 9B of the Constitutional Law (VG), to which reference is made in the special report before us. The purport of this article is to make the generally recognised principles of international law an integral part of Austrian Federal Law.

Research into the normative content of Article 9B–VG starts from the assumption that this article has the effect of continuous incorporation of the principles of international law which are generally recognised at any given time. This premise, initially propounded by Kelsen,[3] has not so far been proved, since the wording of the Article itself, with due regard for the rules of grammar and particularly of linguistic usage, should rather be interpreted as meaning that the framers of the Constitution intended to provide only for incorporation of those principles of international law which were recognised at the time when the Constitution was promulgated. This would be the more understandable in that the problem of incorporating certain legal provisions in the new legal order arose when the basic reform of constitutional law took place in 1920.

On the other hand, there can be no justification for interpreting the law to mean that there will be automatic assimilation of future international laws whose content and effects are still completely uncertain, even if reference is made to the model of the Weimar Constitution (Art. 4),[4] for that would be setting the seal of formal

---

[1] L. Werner, *Menschenrechtskonvention gegen Verwaltungsgerichtsbarkeit* (Human Rights Convention versus Administrative Courts), 'Der Staatsbürger', Series 10/1965; W. Rosenzweig, *Lücken der Rechtsstaatlichkeit* (Gaps in the constitutional character of States), Der Staatsbürger', Series 12/1965.

[2] K. Ringhofer, *Der Verwaltungsgerichtshof* (The Administrative Court), Graz, Vienna-Cologne, 1955, p. 224.

[3] Federal Constitution of 1 October 1920, p. 75: 'What is meant here is the incorporation of existing and future international law . . .'

[4] How little awareness there has been of the implications of this clause of the Weimar Constitution, and how vague and divergent were the views held on it may be seen from Verdross, op. cit., p. 67: 'This idea was at first *misunderstood*

approval on a 'legislative incorporation' which as such would include all the dangers of 'formal legislative procedure' and might lead to wholesale amendment of the Federal Constitution and the overthrow of the domestic legal order. It is clear that the arguments advanced against formal delegation of legislative powers must apply with even greater force to incorporation of international law by the same method, since it may well involve the sacrifice of the legal order in its most direct form.

SUMMARY OF THE DISCUSSION[1]

H. Golsong:

1. Mr Velu rightly drew attention to the obligation devolving on States under the Convention to recognise the substantive provisions of the Convention as self-executing under national law.

The wording of Article 1 of the Convention is of particular significance in this regard. The words 'the High Contracting Parties shall secure to everyone within their jurisdiction' the rights defined in the Convention mean—as the relevant documents show—more than merely 'undertake to recognise . . . .' The particular significance of this phraseology is brought out by the practice of the Council of Europe in the drafting of Conventions other than the Human Rights Convention. The wording 'shall secure to everyone' is not used in the later Conventions since rights are not granted directly to the individual in any of them. Thus the significance of Article 1 of the Human Rights Convention, accurately interpreted by Mr Velu, is also evidenced by subsequent practice.

When the Human Rights Convention was being drafted, a few, at least, of the States took it for granted that they were being required to apply the Convention in their national law. Such States considered that the Convention should entail more than mere international obligations. As constitutional situations differ from State to State, this view could naturally not lead automatically to the incorporation into all the national legal systems of the rights defined in the Convention. Nevertheless, the question remains whether the Convention does not impose an obligation on all Contracting States to incorporate the rights defined in the Convention into their national law.

---

by the German Constitutional Committee, which at the first reading therefore adopted the resolution previously mentioned, which related only to the international and not to the domestic validity of international law. *However, after I had drawn the Committee's attention to the error of its ways, it not only adopted the Government Bill, but stated through its Chairman D. Haussmann that it desired to make international law equally binding both internally and externally.*' (My italics).

[1] The written communications in Chapter I by Professor Doehring and Professor Pfeifer also relate to the subject of this chapter.

2. I can only partially support Professor Doehring's opinion regarding the significance of the declaration provided for in Article 25 of the Convention. There is hardly justification for asserting that recognition of the right of individual petition under Article 25 establishes personal rights under *national* law. The said declaration can have legal consequences only in the international sphere—it certainly cannot establish real rights under national law, unless (as in the case of pleas of nullity in Austria) an express ruling has been issued to that end. On the other hand, Professor Doehring is perfectly right when he says that by virtue of the declaration provided for in Article 25 an individual was for the first time recognised as having a personal right under international law.

3. Professor Seidl-Hohenveldern has already mentioned the principle according to which, even in countries in which an obligation under an international agreement is not made an integral part of national law, a judge is expected to interpret his country's law in the spirit of the provisions of the agreement.

Should it not be possible to say, in regard to the Convention, that, conversely, judges in countries in which the Convention is an integral part of national law should interpret the provisions of the Convention with due regard to their own country's legal traditions? This is certainly true as regards the application of Article 5 (5) of the Convention, which provides for compulsory compensation in the event of unlawful arrest or detention, but undoubtedly requires to be supplemented by reference to national legal conceptions. In other words, Article 5 (5) is a legal rule which is self-executing but requires to be supplemented, for example, as regards the problem of statutory limitation, and other matters of that sort.

Michel Virally: the question of the relationship between international and national law and, consequently, of the place of the Convention in the legal hierarchy is traditionally associated with that of the basis of international law. This association is, however, artificial and meaningless.

If it is acknowledged at the outset that international law governs relations between States, then it necessarily follows that it occupies a position above the States and consequently above their national law. Hence its supremacy derives from its inherent nature, whatever the basis assigned to it. However, the inferences which may be drawn from this are extremely diverse: they depend on the structure of the legal systems concerned.

Each legal system has its law-making and law-enforcing institutions which control each other in such a way as to constitute a closed system. For example, national courts normally apply only the law established or recognised by the national legislature. By contrast,

F

although international law has its own sources, it has no implementing machinery of its own. It relies for its application on national institutions, which carry out this function only to the extent to which the political authorities of the State permit them to do so.

The European Convention on Human Rights did not change this system by requiring its signatories to respect the rights defined therein. Nor do the words 'shall secure' (Fr. *reconnaissent*) in Article 1 of the Convention change it. Their significance is purely moral and political. The rules of national law relating to the acceptance of international law, rules made by the individual States themselves, are not affected thereby.

The Convention changed the relationship between international and national law only in so far as it set up its own implementing machinery, namely the Commission and the Court of Human Rights.

Seán MacBride: in its Preamble, the Hague Convention of 1907 contains what could be described as a broad convenient definition of customary international law in respect to human rights. It refers to:

The principles of the law of nations, derived from the usages established among civilised peoples, from the laws of humanity, and from the dictates of the public conscience.

Has the time not arrived, by the application of this broad conventional definition, to treat parts, at least, of the Universal Declaration of Human Rights as forming part of the law of nations and of customary international law? While not having the binding force of an international convention, the Universal Declaration surely represents 'the usages established among civilised peoples', 'the laws of humanity' and 'the dictates of the public conscience'. It was adopted by the nations of the world who composed the UN in 1948; it has been subscribed to by the nations which have since become members of the UN. Practically every international convention which deals with Human Rights adopted since 1948 refers to the Universal Declaration. Many new States have incorporated articles of the Declaration in their Constitutions. In some jurisdictions the Courts have had regard to the provisions of the Universal Declaration.

H. Miehsler (Article 1 of the Convention is the 'referential rule' (*Delegationsnorm*) for Section I of the Convention): there can be no doubt as to the intention of the Contracting States to establish personal rights for individuals by means of the Convention, despite the fact that the Convention does not state whether special national legislation is also necessary.

The Convention appropriately omits any mention of the legal processes whereby the individual acquires these rights, for, considering the diversity of national legal systems within which it is to be applied, no general formula is conceivable.

These processes depend rather on the legal system of each State. If a Constitution provides, for instance, for the transformation of an international agreement by means of a national implementing law, the agreement cannot be interpreted as bestowing personal rights. It is different with Article 25 of the Convention, which is not applied in the context of a national legal system. Its acceptance by the Contracting State is sufficient to create a personal right. In this case there is no reference to national law; indeed, it would be super-fluous, since the provisions of Sections II to V are not applied in the framework of a national legal system. Nor does the question of precedence arise here. Hence we can agree with Mr Doehring.

What is the position as regards the enforceability of Section I at national level? Here again Article 1 must be taken into consideration. The effectiveness of the individual rights depends also on whether the State institutions can apply them directly or whether their application must be deferred pending the issue of national implementing regulations. This can be decided only in the light of the national legal system, as the practice followed by the Contracting States seems to confirm. Hence, for example, the divergent views held by the Federal Republic of Germany and Austria regarding the self-executing character of the provisions of Section I.

The referential rule (Art. 1—see above), like the rules in Section I, undoubtedly takes precedence over national legal rules. It is, how-ever, left to each Contracting State to decide what rank these pro-visions shall hold in the national legal system. But whilst it rests with public law specialists to determine the position of Section I of the Convention in the internal hierarchy, it is, nevertheless, the duty of the international law specialist to insist that at least as high a value be attached, at national level, to the human rights contained in the Convention as to the fundamental rights listed in most Constitutions.

André Vanwelkenhuyzen (Objection, deriving from Article 13 of the Human Rights Convention, to the theory of 'moderate monism'): A defender of 'moderate monism', Professor Verdross considers that treaties should have pre-eminence over the internal legal system though rules of national law should, in principle, take precedence over those of international law before national authorities. This theory has the merit of justifying the practice followed by the judicial and administrative authorities of numerous countries, including Austria and Belgium.

However, where the European Convention for the Protection of Human Rights is concerned, this theory appears to come up against an objection deriving from Article 13 of the Convention. This

Article stipulates that everyone is entitled to an *effective* remedy before a *national* authority. If the national authority were to apply, in a given case and by virtue of the theory of moderate monism, a rule of internal law which is incompatible with the provisions of the Convention, that authority would, in a way, be making itself an accessory to the violation of a right guaranteed by the Convention. How, in these circumstances, could it still be maintained that the violated right is guaranteed by an effective remedy before a national authority?

If the theory of moderate monism is accepted, Article 13 is drained of its substance, for when the Convention is violated by internal law, there can be no effective remedy before a national authority.

Professor Verdross resolves the contradiction between the principle of the sovereignty of international law and the obligation on the part of national courts to apply internal law which is contrary thereto, by referring to the fact that these national decisions will be 'rescinded or altered' at the request of the State concerned. Is this not exaggerating the scope of the supervision exercised by the international authorities?

Article 50 of the Convention authorises the Court to afford just satisfaction to the injured party where, under the relevant national law, only partial reparation can be made for the consequences of an act violating one of the rights guaranteed. But it cannot declare the said act null and void under internal law, as is shown by the *Boeckmans case*.

Therefore, the intervention of the institutions of the Convention does not always restore harmony between the internal and the international legal order.

Hans Spanner (Pre-eminence of the Human Rights Convention in international law):

1. Efforts are being made in various States to obtain constitutional status for the Convention. But the value of constitutional status must not be exaggerated. The mere fact of granting such status will not necessarily be a guarantee of permanence. An important factor in this regard is whether these constitutional rules are easy or difficult to change and whether they are effectively applied. In Austria, for example, where there are well over a hundred accessory constitutional laws in addition to the Constitutional Charter, the granting of constitutional status is of no particular value where the permanence of the Convention is concerned. But it does mean the recognition of a special competence, namely that of the Constitutional Court. As for ensuring the permanence of the Convention, I share Professor Verdross's view that the Convention cannot be properly implemented under national law unless States are authorised by their own legislation to amend the Convention only if it has been amended or

denounced by the Contracting Parties through an act of international law. In this way alone can the permanence of the Convention be effectively guaranteed.

2. Uniformity of judicial practice in applying the Convention must be the goal, at both national and international level. A special court empowered to superintend the implementation of the Convention should be set up in every State in which one does not already exist. In Austria, for example, the way should be cleared for an appeal to the Constitutional Court from a decision by any other court.

3. A further difficulty arises when a State has omitted to enact laws of application. This raises the question of the self-executing character of an agreement. Vague legal concepts in international agreements must not simply be treated like vague legal concepts in national laws. Rather must they be considered non-self-executing because, according to the general interpretation rule, limitations on sovereignty must, in cases of doubt, be interpreted restrictively. Unlike Professor Seidl-Hohenveldern, who spoke merely of a 'back-door' method of applying the Convention under municipal law, one could, by analogy with the theory of interpretation in conformity with the Constitution, go so far as to say that laws must be interpreted and applied in conformity with the Convention.

Hans Weiler (Significance, in national law, of the authenticity of the English and French texts of the Convention): the final clause of the Convention states that the English and French texts, signed in Rome, are the authentic ones ('equally authentic'). What is the significance of this provision in national law, and particularly in those States in which English and French are not official languages?

Austria published the Convention in the two authentic versions and also in German, the national language, in its Federal Law Gazette. However, the Austrian Constitutional Court recently expressed the view that, by virtue of the authenticity clause, the French and English texts of the Convention were legally binding, while the German text was not. Departing from its earlier rulings, it also took the view that Article 6 was self-executing. These views cause surprise for, taken together, they imply that even legal rules written in a language which is incomprehensible to the vast majority of the population can be valid national law.

The authenticity clause is embodied in the last paragraph of the text, in a form customary in international agreements. This circumstance alone seems to indicate that the clause concerns only international law relations and imposes no obligation on States to make the English and French versions—and not the national language version—of the Convention operative in national territory.

Were it otherwise, States which do not recognise the principle of general transformation would have to incorporate the English and French texts into their national legislation. The traditional position and content of the authenticity clause do not suggest any intention to interfere with national constitutional law to this extent. Last but not least, if only the English and French texts are to be considered legally binding, it would be more difficult to familiarize the general public with the contents of the Convention. This is sufficient reason for giving preference to the view that the authenticity clause applies solely to the sphere of international law. Only when its content has become the common property of all Europeans will the Convention be able to carry out its function to the full.

Karl Doehring (Place of the Convention in national law): there is really nothing to add to Mr Miehsler's intervention, but one point might perhaps be emphasised. But for the possibility of protecting human rights through the procedure set out in Article 25 and the establishment of the Court, there would have been no departure from traditional international law. The Convention would be an international treaty like any other. It is Article 25 which introduces the innovation. By virtue of this Article, an individual was for the first time recognised as having a personal right, even under international law, as a result of the recognition by States of the right of individual petition. The distinction between dualism and moderate monism leads to no other practical result. It is left to States to settle the questions of the rank and self-executing character of a rule of law. The recognition of Article 25 as a means of protecting the rights of the individual makes the quarrel between dualism and monism superfluous so far as the Convention is concerned. In any event, a State which has recognised the right of individual petition can no longer claim that the individual does not possess material rights.

SUMMING UP BY

A. VERDROSS

I agree with MM. Golsong, Spanner and Weiler but wish to make the following comment on Mr MacBride's statement. The rights laid down in the Universal Declaration have unfortunately not yet become international customary law because the Declaration constitutes an instance of limited international agreement, and the rules embodied in it have thus not yet been recognised by all civilised nations.

I would like to reply to MM. Virally, Miehsler and Vanwelkenhuyzen that I have always distinguished between national and international protection of human rights. There can be no question of merging the two forms of legal remedy as they are not wholly compatible. Domestic remedies have their own machinery. As for my criticism of the system of rigid dualism, I would refer to the written text of my paper.

In regard to Mr Vanwelkenhuyzen's objection, I would like to point out that, notwithstanding Article 13, domestic courts are bound to apply municipal law even when it conflicts with the Human Rights Convention. However, Article 13 obliges States to assure to the individual a procedure for enforcing the rights laid down in the Convention. On the principle of *bona fides*, therefore, States must 'transform' the Convention in such a way that it can also be applied internally. This is borne out by the fact that, under Article 50, the European Court is not empowered to declare decisions which conflict with the Convention void, but only to enjoin States to make reparation. States are moreover under an obligation so to amend their legislation as to preclude decisions which conflict with the Convention from being rendered *in the future*.

The acceptance of the right of individual application and of the jurisdiction of the Court is an indispensable prerequisite for the effectiveness of the European Convention on Human Rights and its uniform application.

CHAPTER III

Possibilities of conflict in national legal systems between the European Convention and other international agreements

REPORT BY
FRANCESCO CAPOTORTI

1. Something must first of all be said about two general questions: what are the probabilities of conflict between different international agreements, and the consequences of such conflict in international law; and, secondly, what are the effects of such phenomena in the field of municipal law. Consideration of these problems will provide the necessary criteria for appreciating the subject of this Report.

Two agreements may be said to conflict when they have at least one subjective point of contact and one objective: subjective in the sense that one or more States are parties to both agreements; objective in the sense that a single matter or related matters are governed by one or more provisions of both Agreements. A situation of this kind arises in the case of conflict between mandatory clauses stipulated separately by the same party: i.e. when a State, in two agreements with different Contracting Parties, assumes obligations that are mutually incompatible so that fulfilment of the one entails violation of the other. I should like immediately to stress that the notion of conflict of agreements, as briefly indicated above, goes far beyond this example. It is wider than the notion of a conflict of mandatory clauses, and covers various types of subjective connection.

In fact, from a subjective point of view, it may occur: (*a*) that all the parties to one agreement may conclude a second agreement which can conflict with the first; they may conclude it between themselves alone or in conjunction with other States; or (*b*) that a single one of the contracting parties to an agreement may conclude a new agreement with one or more other States which can conflict with the earlier one; or (*c*) that several of the parties to a multilateral agreement may conclude a later agreement—between themselves or in conjunction with third States—which can conflict with the first.

So far as objective connection is concerned, we must consider not only the possibility of two absolutely incompatible agreements which impose courses of action that are conflicting or at least necessarily alternative. It more frequently happens that two successive agreements on the same subject make provisions that are not radically conflicting but different, and this difference may be total—amounting to incompatibility—or partial, with a greater or lesser margin of compatibility. Finally, we regard the concept of conflicting agreements as covering also those cases in which one agreement is complementary to another or provides for conduct or a situation in which another agreement must be applied.

The combination of these forms of subjective connection with each of the possible objective connections makes the overall picture not only varied but complex. It should be added that the nature of the norms prescribed by the agreements concerned has an influence, as we shall see, on the phenomena of overlapping. From this point of view a distinction must above all be made between those norms that impose on one party obligations that are strictly related to the rights of a specific second party; those which within the framework of a multilateral convention prescribe conduct which is of immediate concern to all contracting parties or is of general and absolute interest (we may speak of 'interdependent' and 'integral' obligations respectively); and finally those which govern the functioning of international organisations.

The consequences of the phenomena we are discussing may, to some degree, be studied from the point of view of the provisions themselves—i.e. with regard to the validity and effect of the agreements concerned—and also from the point of view of the responsibility of States (whether, and to what extent, the conclusion or implementation of the second agreement constitutes an illicit act, to the detriment of the earlier one). For the purposes of this report this aspect of the provisions will be particularly considered, because of their repercussions on municipal law.

We should observe, finally, that the parties to an agreement may make provision for certain cases of conflict with previous and subsequent agreements by means of appropriate clauses. More will be said of this later; first of all, let us consider what happens in the absence of any such clauses.

2. Analysis of the phenomena of overlapping between agreements may be approached from various angles; the simplest seems to us to be the subjective. We shall therefore begin by considering the case in which all the parties to one agreement conclude a second agreement between themselves, or with other States as well, and we shall attempt to determine what are the consequences in three cases: when the new agreement contains provisions that are incompatible, or merely different, or complementary in relation to the earlier provisions.

There is no doubt that incompatibility between earlier and subsequent provisions entails, from the subjective point of view, the tacit abrogation of the earlier ones. It is generally agreed that the same result is obtained even if the later provisions settle *ex novo* the whole subject of the earlier agreement: it is not necessary, then, for the content of the second agreement to be in conflict with that of the previous one, but it is sufficient for it to be different (provided, of course, that its scope is equal or greater). In the draft articles on the Law of Treaties, prepared by the International Law Commission of the United Nations, the accent has been laid on the declared intention of the parties to regulate a particular subject by their new agreement, termination of the earlier agreement depending upon this (Article 41 of the Draft).[1] We are not convinced that it is necessary for the intention of the parties to be indicated in the agreement; what is certain is the decisive force of establishing the intention of the contracting parties for purposes of determining whether there has been tacit abrogation of the earlier pacts. In fact, particularly when the content of the earlier rules is more restricted and specific than that of the subsequent provisions, the former may continue to exist as special rules. Another possibility is that the earlier agreement is merely modified by the subsequent one; this obviously occurs when the difference in content is only partial.

If, then, the two agreements are complementary or at least fully compatible, they may both be applied: their effects, one might say, are cumulative. In principle it may be observed that differences (in structure, premisses, or scope) between two successive agreements governing the same subject and pursuing the same aims do not mean automatically that the second supersedes or modifies the first; it must rather be assumed that the first remains effective, until it is proved that the parties wished the more recent agreement to supersede the earlier one, or that the more recent one modified the previous provisions. Two agreements are complementary if they share the function of governing the same subject or interdependent aspects of the same subject, and are in complete harmony (we might suppose, as an example, a convention guaranteeing individual freedom of movement followed by another that ensures for everyone the freedom to leave his own State and return to it). A similar case is that in which one of two agreements creates a situation that is among those provided for by the other agreement (one might imagine a treaty establishing an international judiciary body accessible to individuals, in relation to another agreement between the same parties guaranteeing certain fundamental rights of individuals in judicial proceedings). It is super-

---

[1] See Report of the ILC on the work of its 15th Session, UN, New York, 1963, p. 16.

fluous to add that the criterion of integration of the effects of two complementary agreements does not by any means exclude the possibility that certain points of the earlier agreement may be changed by the later one.

We suggested in the first case that other States might participate in the second agreement, in addition to all the contracting parties to the first. In such a case the combined effect of the two conventions—whether this amounts to amendment or completion of the earlier agreement—is limited to the contracting parties to the first agreement, while relations between these and the States which only participated in the second agreement are obviously governed only by the latter. This is a first example of the co-existence of two agreements within subjective fields that only partly coincide.

3. When only one of the contracting parties concludes a new treaty with one or more other States which may overlap with the first *ratione materiae*, the solution is inevitable and follows from the respective content of the two agreements: they co-exist in separate subjective fields of effectiveness.

It is easy to understand why there is no possibility of integration, modification or abrogation between two conventions that have only one point of subjective contact, i.e. a single contracting party in common: it is common knowledge that the field of effectiveness of any agreement is limited to the parties thereto, i.e. to a minimum of two States, and that an agreement can complete or annul the effects of a previous agreement only if their respective fields of effectiveness coincide.

If the two agreements which have only one contracting party in common lay down provisions that are different, but compatible or complementary (on the same subject or related subjects) there is no problem; each agreement will undoubtedly be valid and effective within its own subjective field, and there will be nothing to prevent the implementation of both of them. The problem arises, however, when the provisions of the two agreements are incompatible; in this case, there may be some doubt as to the validity of the second agreement, if it is held that international law makes the capacity of States to conclude an agreement dependent on the absence of any previous incompatible obligations.

The theory that an agreement which conflicts with a previous agreement is invalid, has in fact some supporters in doctrine.[1] But the current view, and in our opinion the correct one, is that two conflicting agreements concluded in different subjective fields are both valid and effective in their own particular fields; inasmuch as the pre-existence of an obligation entered into under an earlier agreement

[1] See particularly Oppenheim–Lauterpacht, *International Law*, London.

with another State by one of the contracting parties to the second agreement entails only the illegality of conduct contrary to the obligation imposed by the second agreement. In substance, any State bound by two treaty obligations which conflict with each other may choose between carrying out the one or the other, nor are there any criteria of priority to guide such a choice; the fact that one of the two obligations will be violated will render that State responsible towards its partner in the agreement that has not been respected. In this connection it should be observed that the moment of responsibility is the actual moment of implementation: there is nothing illegal in the mere conclusion of an incompatible agreement, since at that time it is still not apparent which of the two obligations will be fulfilled. It may sometimes happen that the contracting party's freedom to interpret and implement each agreement is sufficient to enable him to respect both the obligations entered into.

This view is based on the elementary principle that every agreement binds the parties thereto—and only those parties—in their reciprocal relations; this principle is valid independently of the content of the agreements, inasmuch as it is not shown that international law restricts the capacity of States to conclude agreements which conflict with earlier agreements. Oppenheim's theory referred to above has rightly been criticised and rejected by Fitzmaurice.[1] It is significant that the United Nations International Law Commission in the aforementioned draft Articles on the Law of Treaties has authoritatively accepted the view that incompatible provisions of two Conventions may both be applied; in fact, according to Article 63 (4) of the Draft, in cases of incompatibility between the provisions of two treaties it is the earlier one that applies as between a State party to both treaties and a State party only to the earlier one, while the later treaty as between a State party to both treaties and a State party only to the later treaty.[2]

4. It remains to be seen what happens when several of the contracting parties to a multilateral agreement conclude a new agreement between themselves, with or without other States as well. If the two agreements are complementary, or at all events compatible, there is nothing to prevent the effects of their respective clauses from being cumulative in respect of those who are parties to both agreements (obviously it is only the earlier agreement that will be binding on those countries in their relations with States not parties to the later). But even if the two agreements are different or actually in-

---

[1] *Yearbook of the International Law Commission*, 1958, II, UN, New York, 1958, pp. 43–4.

[2] See Report of the ILC on the work of its 16th Session, UN, New York, 1964, p. 13.

compatible, the basic criterion is the same: the second agreement, that is to say, modifies or entirely supersedes the first, as between contracting parties who subscribe to both, while the earlier agreement continues to be binding on the States in their relationships with countries that did not accede to the later agreement. The phenomenon may, therefore, be described as a partial modification or abrogation of the original treaty—or rather as a derogation or abrogation agreed upon by some of the contracting parties—accompanied by the continuance of the treaty itself in respect of those relationships that are not affected by the derogation.

This naturally does not mean that the attitude of the parties to the second treaty when it comes to be put into force can always be regarded as lawful. On the contrary: observation of the new provisions will constitute violation of the first agreement—and vice versa—whenever the later agreement prescribes lines of conduct alternative or absolutely contradictory to those laid down in the previous provisions, particularly when such lines of conduct do not strictly correspond to any bilateral agreement between the contracting parties. On the other hand, if either of these two conditions does not exist, it becomes possible to give effect to both treaties, each of them in its own subjective field of influence. In this sense, Article 67 of the Draft Articles on the Law of Treaties prepared by the United Nations International Law Commission rightly admits modification of earlier provisions restricted to a group of the contracting parties, provided this is not prohibited by the first treaty, if the other parties to that treaty remain able to enjoy their rights and perform their obligations, and if there is no hindrance to the execution of the original purposes of the treaty.[1]

It should also be remembered that some theories maintain the invalidity of any new pacts between contracting parties to a multilateral agreement, if the provisions of that agreement have certain specific characteristics. In particular it has been said that 'normative dualism'—the simultaneous validity of two conflicting treaties—is not admissible when the first treaty institutes a territorial system.[2] The opinion has also been expressed that the later agreement is null if the earlier agreement prohibits the conclusion of incompatible treaties, or contains 'interdependent' or 'integral' obligations (examples quoted are respectively those of a convention on disarmament and another on human rights), or if the second treaty[3] necessarily

---

[1] See Report of the ILC, 1964, op. cit., p. 25.
[2] See Rousseau, *Principes généraux du droit international public*, Paris, 1944, p. 511.
[3] See Fitzmaurice, 3rd Report on the Law of Treaties, in the ILC *Yearbook*, op. cit., p. 28.

requires the parties to act in violation of their obligations under the earlier treaty.

These views are without foundation. In the case of treaties making territorial arrangements, everything depends on whether a group of contracting parties is or is not in a position, through its own behaviour, to change the territorial situation, which may already have become established as a fact that can no longer be altered by the attitude of a few States. In other words: if the initial agreement has been implemented and has thereby fulfilled its function, there is no longer any question of modifying that agreement, but rather of altering the *de facto* situation which has been established. As to the other presumed cases of nullity, there is no doubt that the conclusion of a more restrictive treaty is *illicit* under the conditions suggested; but no international norm stigmatises such an agreement as *invalid*. The reasoning and conclusion are the same as in the case of conflicting agreements concluded by a single State with two different contracting parties: the position of the International Law Commission was unanimous after careful examination of Fitzmaurice's view.[1]

5. One question that should be briefly mentioned is that of a conflict between a norm set out in a convention and a peremptory international norm. It is notoriously very debatable whether norms of this kind exist in international law; moreover, they must be general norms, so that no conflict should arise between two norms originating in conventions. However, if the existence of an international *jus cogens* is admitted, it cannot be excluded that norms of such a kind may appear in a treaty, the parties desiring to reaffirm them and include them in the context of the agreed clauses. Supposing such a situation arises, it is certain that any rule that departs from the *jus cogens* must be regarded as null, whatever its relationship in time with that peremptory norm.

It should be noted that, according to the United Nations International Law Commission, an agreement containing clauses contrary to an earlier peremptory norm would be entirely null, whereas, in the case of a *jus cogens* which comes into force subsequently, nullity—or rather abrogation—would affect only the incompatible clauses (Articles 37 and 45 of the Draft Articles on the Law of Treaties).[2] This distinction does not seem to us to be justified: it seems necessary rather to distinguish between provisions closely connected with the offending one and independent provisions, and to determine whether the agreement retains its purpose even if its content is reduced to the latter.

6. It was mentioned above that in some cases questions of the

[1] See Report, 1964, op. cit., p. 13 et seq.
[2] Ibid., p. 11 et seq., and p. 23.

overlapping of conventions are covered by specific clauses in the conventions themselves.

Clauses of this kind may be divided into four groups: some provide that the agreement in which they appear takes precedence over a previous agreement, the total or partial abrogation or modification of which is provided for; others declare that the earlier agreement shall not be impaired, or reaffirm its applicability, so that they sanction the co-existence of the two treaties; others prohibit the conclusion of further agreements (between some of the parties or with third States) on the same subject, or declare that the present agreement will take precedence over any future incompatible agreements; others, finally, declare the admissibility of specific future agreements.

Clauses in the second and fourth classes are always effective: there is nothing to prevent the parties to any treaty from providing that it is compatible with other past or future agreements, thus preventing any possible modification, derogation or abrogation of previous treaties, or the possible illegality of a position held by one or more parties as a result of earlier or later agreements. In Article 63, already referred to, of the Draft Articles on the Law of Treaties, the United Nations International Law Commission maintained that 'when a treaty provides that it is subject to, or is not inconsistent with, an earlier or a later treaty, the provisions of that other treaty shall prevail.[1] This is understood to mean that the provisions of the agreement referred to in the compatibility clause shall not in any way be impaired as a result of overlapping with the agreement in which that clause is contained.

Our conclusions as regards what we might call incompatibility clauses must be different. In fact a stipulation regarding abrogation or modification is effective only if the parties to both agreements are the same, or at most it is effective in derogating from the earlier multilateral agreement as between the parties to the new agreement (depending on the legality or otherwise of such derogation). As for the prohibition of future agreements or the declaration that they must yield to the agreement containing the clause, these will have no significance if all the parties of the earlier agreement are also parties to the subsequent one—since one agreement can always modify an earlier one in the same subjective field; if, on the other hand, the later agreement is concluded between only some of the parties to the earlier one, or between one of these and a third State, the result of the clause will be to make illicit the conclusion or implementation of the new agreement, but it will remain effective within its own field.

7. We must now determine what are the repercussions in international law of overlapping agreements. For this purpose it seems to

[1] See Report, op. cit., p. 13.

us necessary to recall briefly a few principles regarding the ways in which agreements become effective within the internal order and the limits of this phenomenon; we do not claim to discuss the complex theoretical aspects and numerous implications of such an important problem.

The first point that must be stressed is: not all agreements are intended to have effect, or at least not the same kind of effect, in the municipal law of the contracting States. Some agreements, indeed, govern situations or attitudes which have nothing to do at all with internal order (e.g. an agreement deferring an international dispute to the decision of an arbitrator and laying down the procedure); others deal only with the conduct of national bodies in the field of external relations (e.g. a treaty of alliance); and, finally, others aim at influencing the attitude of individuals or establishing rules for the treatment of individuals or of individual interests by State bodies. In view of the subject of this Report, it is obviously the last group of treaties that concerns us most closely. A distinction between the possible effects of agreements within the system of each of the parties may be made on the basis of a different criterion: i.e. according to whether the provisions of an agreement call for some change of the municipal law previously in force, or whether they are applicable without any alteration at all in the framework of the previous regulations (e.g. when the organs of a State are already competent or obliged to take the action provided for in the agreement). Conventions on the treatment of individuals tend as a rule to modify municipal law, because even if that law has already made partial provision, the rules established at the international level almost always introduce something new in the way of formulation and system.

A second point to be made clear is that not all agreements that tend to modify municipal law are so framed as to be able at once to take their place alongside the Acts of the State. There are no doubt some treaties which are so framed as to make it possible to apply their provisions to State bodies and individuals without any need for domestic measures of implementation (in our opinion the Convention belongs to this category); there are others, however, for whose application provisions of this kind are essential.

In the third place, it may be remembered that the introduction of an agreement into the domestic law of the parties is not everywhere effected by the same machinery. It may be that in virtue of an explicit or implicit constitutional principle, an agreement that is duly ratified (after parliamentary authorisation, where necessary) is automatically regarded as being capable of producing effects in the internal legal system. At other times, this effectiveness is subject to some further formality, such as the publication of the agreement in the official collection of laws and decrees. On other occasions, it is necessary to promulgate special implementing measures, which, with due reference to the agreement, create internal provisions in conformity with the international provisions. Lastly, implementation may be provided for by a normal legislative act, formally independent of the agreement.

There is certainly no occasion here to allude to the theoretical premisses—'monist' or 'dualist'—which have influenced the constitutional tradition of each country and thus the choice of one or other of the types of machinery described; it is more important to point out some of the consequences of the various attitudes of the different States on this subject.

First of all, it is clear that in the systems in which the agreement automatically becomes effective in internal law, its immediate inclusion in the State order is assured, whereas in other cases this direct or indirect inclusion (including its timing) is dependent on the diligence of the body responsible for publication, for the implementing measures or for the ordinary legislative act. The first two methods also guarantee a permanent position for the agreement among the internal sources of law—a position either superior to the ordinary law, as is provided in some systems, or equal to the ordinary law; the method of transformation into internal norms by means of implementing measures or an ordinary legislative act leaves room for the possibility that this transformation may sometimes be completed by an act having the force of law and at other times by an act of lesser force (a regulation) or of greater force (constitutional law) according to the views of the responsible body (which in turn is guided by formal considerations of domestic law). On the other hand, when the transformation into internal rules is effected by means of an ordinary source of law without reference to the text of the Treaty, it is that source which counts even from the point of view of its content, and not the provisions of the Treaty, which influence the domestic system only through the filter of the new municipal normative instrument.

When, on the other hand, transformation is effected by means of an act referring to the text of the Treaty, it is for the domestic interpreter—the judge in particular—to extract from the international provisions those provisions which are applicable within the State; the practical result frequently is that interpretation of the agreement is guided rather by the principles and requirements of the domestic system than by those of international law.

8. Let us suppose that the succession in time of two agreements likely to overlap has given rise in the field of international relations

G

to one of the results described in the foregoing pages. Let us further suppose that both agreements are intended to have effect within the municipal law of the contracting States, both influencing previous norms, and that the following conditions are fulfilled: (a) provision was made, if necessary, as regards both agreements, for the action required for their incorporation into internal law (publication or issue of the implementing measures); (b) this inclusion was not effected by an ordinary method, independent from the Treaty; (c) in the case of the implementing measures, that both were framed in the same way, that is to say both of them were given effect by instruments having the same force; (d) there was no need for any further domestic procedure.

Under these circumstances, it may be considered that the international phenomenon of overlapping between agreements has a direct repercussion within the municipal order of the parties.

If we wish to determine what such repercussion consists of, we must once again distinguish overlapping within the same subjective field, overlapping between a multilateral and a more restricted agreement, and that between two agreements which have only a single contracting party in common. The first case is the simplest: abrogation, modification or integration of the earlier agreement will be effective also in the municipal law of each of the parties. (From the point of view of the incorporation of the agreements into the municipal law it will be said that the domestic norms corresponding to those of the original agreement will be abrogated, modified or integrated under the influence of the corresponding norms of the new agreement). The second and third cases must obviously be considered on the basis of the systems of that State or those States which are parties to both agreements; otherwise the phenomenon of overlapping can have no effect. Now, corresponding to what happens on the level of international relations, the municipal law of a State which accedes to an agreement which supplements or derogates from a previous and wider multilateral convention will take account of the integration or derogation in so far as it is effective: it will, therefore, accept the norms of the first agreement as completed, or abrogated or modified by those of the second, in its relations with States that are contracting parties to the new agreement, retaining unchanged the norms of the first agreement in its relations with the other original contracting parties.

All this, of course, presupposes that the provisions of the two agreements are compatible in the sphere of municipal law, or to be more precise, that the obligations imposed by each of these provisions on the organs of the State or on individuals can both be fulfilled. If it is a matter of provisions that protect the interests of specific States, their compatibility will depend on each provision being capable of application or relation to different situations (e.g. in relation to treatment guaranteed by the first agreement simultaneously to the citizens of several States, a new agreement may make a distinction between the treatment in the same matter guaranteed to citizens of some of those States). The legality or otherwise of the second agreement or its implementation under international law will have no influence: for inclusion in domestic law all that is required is that an agreement should be valid and effective. If, however, the provisions of the two agreements are incompatible for the purposes of domestic law, because they contain alternative or contradictory positions—as in the case of two successive absolute or 'integral' obligations which conflict with each other—one of them must take precedence from the point of view of the State legal order. This order in fact is not divided into distinct subjective spheres, as is international law deriving from conventions, and therefore it does not tolerate normative dualism that results in a conflict of rules: any conflict of this kind must be settled according to the principles of the unity of the legal order and of reciprocal coherence between norms. If, then, it is quite impossible to harmonise the provisions of the two agreements by interpretation, in our opinion the more recent rule must take precedence, abrogating the earlier rule that is incompatible with it; it will be of no importance that the first agreement is wider and remains internationally effective. The State in concluding the second agreement has indicated its wish to derogate from the first, even if this means violating its obligations towards the other parties to the original convention, and the result of this wish—by the inclusion of the new agreement in the domestic legal order—is that the earlier provisions cease to be effective.

Similar considerations apply to the case of two agreements that have a single contracting party in common. In the domestic order of that party, the provisions of both agreements co-exist if they are compatible. If, however, they are incompatible, the provisions of the later agreement will prevail.

In the foregoing pages we have considered the possibility of agreements that conflict with the peremptory norms of international law (presuming the existence of such norms). It is clear that such peremptory norms should prevail in municipal law as well; the latter should therefore take into account the nullity or abrogation of any agreements—subsequent or previous—which conflict with such norms.

Certain circumstances relating to the inclusion of the agreement in State law might alter the conclusions hitherto reached. In particular, if in the case of one of the two agreements provision is not made for the domestic instrument of implementation, the phenomenon of overlapping does not occur from the point of view of the State legal system. The same thing happens if the inclusion of one of the two agreements is made by an ordinary method, independent of the treaty even as to its content. If again the implementing measures—normative instruments referring to the text of the agreement—are different in force, so that one of them formally takes precedence over the other (if, for example, one agreement is implemented by a constitutional law and another by an ordinary law) this formal precedence prevents the usual effects of overlapping. Finally, if the first agreement required a certain domestic procedure for its incorporation into internal law, not only the overlapping of the new agreement with the earlier one must be taken into account, but also its repercussion on this procedure; while if it is the second agreement which calls for such procedure, this may correct the normal effects of overlapping.

9. At this point the problem of overlapping between the European Convention on Human Rights and other international agreements in the field of municipal law may be considered in the light of the criteria which the foregoing arguments have enabled us to establish. It seems to us necessary first of all to mention those characteristics of the Convention which are the most important for this purpose.

The Convention is, of course, a multilateral agreement. As such it may come into any of the subjective relationships mentioned above (that is to say that it may overlap with other agreements, previous or subsequent, concluded between all or some of the same parties—with or without the inclusion of third States—or between one of those parties and a third State). In view of the subject of the Convention, again, there may be overlapping not only with other agreements relating to human rights and fundamental freedoms, but, more generally, with any agreement governing the treatment of individuals which may have a bearing on human rights or be related to this matter (even in the sense of giving occasion for the application of these rights). Regarding the object of the Convention, its principal rules of conduct—that is to say those in Section I, which define the rights and freedoms protected—impose on the contracting parties absolute or integral obligations according to the terminology previously used: that is to say obligations the fulfilment of which may be demanded by any one of the contracting parties and which call for identical behaviour towards all persons who in any way are subject to the jurisdiction of the parties. The same Convention, of course, contains provisions of a different character; it suffices to recall that Sections II, III and IV deal with the establishment and functioning of the two organs which are the special instruments securing the rights guaranteed to individuals, i.e. the European Commission and Court of Human Rights. The presence of such provisions certainly does not mean that overlapping may not occur with respect to one or more of the provisions of Section I; the universal nature of the rules regarding human rights is, however, accentuated, and this goes to show that any possible derogations in more restricted spheres must be regarded as internationally illegal.

One aspect to which attention must be drawn is that of clauses which may have an influence on overlapping with other agreements. According to Article 17 of the Convention, none of its provisions may be interpreted 'as implying for any State, group or person any right to engage in any activity or perform any act aimed at the destruction of the rights and freedoms set forth herein, or at their limitation to a greater extent than is provided for in the Convention'. According to Article 60: 'Nothing in this Convention shall be construed as limiting or derogating from any of the human rights and fundamental freedoms which may be ensured under the laws of any High Contracting Party or under any other agreement to which it is a Party'.

The first of these provisions prohibits any act by any State which would deny or restrict the rights and freedoms protected; from this may be deduced the determination of the parties that the Convention should prevail over any previous agreements that have such an effect and that the conclusion of future agreements with such aims should be regarded as illegal. The second provision in substance declares that previous or subsequent agreements entered into by one of the parties with any other State shall not in any way be prejudiced in so far as they recognise human rights and fundamental freedoms.

Since these rights and freedoms can hardly be recognised without some restrictions being established, one may wonder whether any other agreement protecting human rights, apart from any restriction it contains, can be regarded as compatible with the Convention. The combination of the two Articles quoted suggests the answer that only the most favourable provisions of other agreements are definitely compatible; however, before it is considered that any provision that is less favourable (because accompanied by greater restrictions) is in conflict with the Convention, the whole system of the agreement that contains it must be considered, in as much as it is difficult to assess a single norm independently of its relations with others. As we shall see, this problem is of particular interest in view of possible relations between the European Convention and the two universal Covenants on Human Rights which have reached an advanced state of preparation in the United Nations.

10. We have said that, in principle, the Convention may overlap

with other agreements under any of the circumstances considered above. However, if we are to deal with the actual circumstances of the problem, we must take into account certain factors that in practice limit the extent of cases of existing or easily foreseeable overlapping. First of all, it is clear that cases of overlapping with other agreements in an identical subjective sphere will probably be linked with other initiatives of the Council of Europe itself (presuming that these receive the same wide ratification); apart from some initiative arising within that Organisation, it can scarcely be imagined that all the parties to the Convention and they alone would decide to conclude another agreement likely to affect the treatment of individuals. Consequently, one might reasonably expect that any new agreements on the subject between the same parties would be inspired by the same principles, and would therefore be compatible or even integrated with the Convention, and not totally different or incompatible (that is, of course, until it is decided to modify or even abrogate the Convention). One example of an integrated agreement between the same parties is the Protocol signed at Paris on 20 March 1952. Remembering, then, that the drafting of the Convention was one of the earliest activities of the Council of Europe, the question of relations between the Convention and previous agreements with the same scope may in practice be disregarded.

In this connection it should be recognised that the Convention and the Statute of the Council are complementary, since under Article 3 of the Statute every member of the Council recognises 'the principle ... of the enjoyment by all persons within its jurisdiction of human rights and fundamental freedoms'. But it must not be forgotten that the Statute has one Contracting Party more than has the Convention (France).

In general, then, it must be considered unlikely in the present state of international relations that there will be any agreements that are in direct conflict with the Convention.

Even if we do not accept the theory that some provisions of the Convention are a part of international *jus cogens* (for instance, the norm prohibiting slavery), it cannot be denied that the ideas on which the Convention is based are widely accepted in the community of States; this is shown by the fact that the Convention makes explicit reference to the Universal Declaration of Human Rights, and that the United Nations has of late years continued and developed its activities for the protection of human rights and fundamental freedoms (as it is obliged to do under Article 55 (C) of the Charter). Under these circumstances, the possibility of overlapping between the Convention and subsequent agreements entered into by only one of the parties with third States is of little account: it has been seen, in fact, that the criteria applicable to this type of overlapping is the co-existence of two agreements, each within its own sphere, and that the problem becomes delicate only in the case of conflict between the two agreements (particularly on the level of municipal law, if both agreements impose absolute or 'integral' obligations). As regards overlapping between the Convention and earlier agreements entered into by one of its Contracting Parties with third States, we consider that Articles 17 and 60 of the Convention itself, already quoted, ensure from the point of view of the domestic laws of the State which is a party to both agreements that the later provisions will take precedence over earlier less favourable provisions as regards human rights, and more favourable provisions will be maintained.

There remains the possibility of overlapping between the Convention and previous or later agreements entered into by some of the parties to it between themselves or with other States. These undoubtedly are the most important and common cases; it is sufficient to recall that many conventions which may have some influence on human rights or the treatment of individuals are concluded under the auspices of the United Nations and its Specialised Agencies, and thus within a subjective circle which normally includes a good number of the parties to the European Convention and also other States. The problem of overlapping between the Convention and the Community Treaties also comes into this category, and the same may be said of treaties concluded under the auspices of the Council of Europe which have not been ratified by all the Contracting Parties to the Convention on Human Rights (e.g., so far, the European Convention on Establishment). We should, therefore, consider analytically this kind of overlapping, not forgetting that the viewpoint that interests us here is that of municipal law.

There is no difficulty about relations between the Convention and an earlier agreement entered into by some of the parties thereto without any third State (e.g. a bilateral treaty on establishment determining the situation of citizens of the two States concerned). The criteria that are applicable are the same in the case of coincidence of the parties; the agreement will therefore be abrogated, modified or supplemented according to whether the new provisions are incompatible, partially incompatible or compatible with it. Abrogation of the more unfavourable provisions regarding human rights and maintenance of the more favourable provisions are ensured by Articles 17 and 60 of the Convention, already quoted. Apart from this, account is taken of the presumption that the two agreements are compatible to which we have already referred, and which must be accepted failing any definite evidence of a contrary intention on the part of the parties. Compatibility means supplementing the provisions of the earlier agreement; the rules of the Convention are added to, or rather take their place alongside, its provisions.

A similar case to that mentioned, so far as relations between the structure of the first and second agreements is concerned, seems to be that of a multilateral instrument subsequent to the Convention in which all its contracting parties participate along with other States. We might quote as an example the Convention relating to the Status of Refugees (signed on 28 July 1951, entered into force on 22 April 1954) of which Article 4 (Freedom of religious education) 15 (freedom of association) 16 (access to courts) and 22 (education and admission to studies) are closely connected with Articles 9, 11 and 6 of the European Convention and Article 2 of its Protocol. In this case the problem of co-ordination is settled by Article 5 of the Convention relating to the Status of Refugees, according to which 'nothing in this Convention shall be deemed to impair any rights and benefits granted by a Contracting State to Refugees apart from this Convention'. Apart from this, it may be observed in general that the existing clauses of the European Convention on cases of overlapping cannot operate in respect of a subsequent agreement in which all Contracting Parties to the Convention participate; they are in fact completely free to agree to an entirely new treatment of the matter (subject to the debatable limit of the *jus cogens*). Consequently, the problem must be settled on the basis of general principles alone, and these, as has been seen, permit the content of a new agreement to influence the earlier agreement by supplementing it, modifying it, or even terminating it. Moreover, the scope and importance of the subject dealt with by the Convention, and particularly the establishment of the machinery of guarantee, make it very problematical whether 'tacit' abrogation could be resorted to. (It would be necessary for new guarantee provisions to be made if the *entire subject* were to be settled on a different basis).

Let us now see what would be the result of the possible conclusion of a new agreement between some of the Parties to the Convention, without any outside State (e.g. a bilateral agreement affecting the treatment of individuals). If the new agreement is compatible with the Convention, there is no difficulty: the two groups of provisions have a cumulative effect in relations between the States which agreed to them and in their respective municipal law. If the new agreement amends the Convention favourably, it will supersede the earlier one (under Article 60 already quoted), of course in its own subjective sphere; the corresponding changes will be made in the municipal order of both parties. If, finally, the agreement limits the provisions of the Convention (or even provides that its application will cease between the Contracting Parties), it must according to the principles set forth above be regarded as illicit but also effective in its own sphere; the Convention at the same time will continue to be in force in relationships between States that remain outside the new agreement and in relations between these States and the contracting parties to that agreement. From the point of view of municipal law, however, presuming that the new agreement is implemented, those of its provisions which are incompatible with the Convention will prevail, for the reasons that we have already explained.

There is, therefore, the risk that the provisions of the Convention may be modified by means of an agreement between some of the contracting parties in such a way as to diminish the protection of human rights, and that a similar agreement, although illicit (confirmed by Article 17), may pass into municipal law, thus becoming fully effective. A similar risk, one might say, is that the legislative body in one State might make provisions that are more restrictive than, or even contrary to, those of the Convention and these would prevail in all systems that give legal force to an agreement enforced in internal law, and might also prevail in systems that provide for the precedence of the agreement over the ordinary law, if the legislative body makes constitutional provision for this. It must, however be repeated that on an international level the current trend is to extend, rather than restrict, the protection of human rights; thus there have hitherto been no actual cases of restricted agreements that are incompatible with the Convention.

An example of the restricted agreement that is compatible is provided by the Treaty on Friendship, Trade and Navigation between Italy and Germany, signed at Rome on 21 November 1957. Article 3 (1) of this Treaty guarantees to the citizens of each Contracting Party within the territory of the other 'full freedom of thought, conscience, worship, meeting and association, and of public worship, in accordance with the provisions of the Constitution of that Party'; it also provides for freedom to engage, even as a group, in any religious, scientific, benevolent, educational, cultural, recreative, sporting or social activity. The second paragraph of that same Article 3 recognises the principle of freedom of the press and of free exchange of information and deals with the collection, exchange and transmission of information. Article 4 (2) makes detailed stipulations regarding the treatment of a citizen of one of the parties who is arrested by the authorities of the other party. Article 6 provides for the protection of property and restricts cases of expropriation. Article 7 lays down that access to the courts should be open to citizens of the other party on an equal footing with the nationals of the first party.

These provisions obviously closely resemble those of Articles 9 (freedom of thought, conscience and religion), 11 (freedom of association), 10 (freedom of expression), 5 (right to liberty and security of person), 6 (right to a fair trial) of the European Convention, and Article 1 (protection of property) of the Protocol. Naturally there are not only resemblances but many differences, particularly in the formulation of the rules and their scope; but none of these differences in our opinion amounts to a modification of the provisions of the Convention. In both Italian and German law, therefore the provisions of both agreements may be simultaneously applied when necessary.

The conclusions reached regarding possible overlapping between the Convention and subsequent restricted agreements should logically apply also to the previous relationship between the Convention and agreements previously concluded between parties to the Convention and third States. (From the point of view of such agreements, in fact, the Convention would be a restricted agreement). The only difference is that Articles 17 and 60 of the Convention would be applicable in the sense of confirming the precedence of the Convention over more restrictive earlier agreements and the retention of the more favourable clauses of the earlier agreements. However, there are no agreements earlier and wider in scope than the Convention which could overlap with the Convention itself, if we except the Statute of the Council of Europe (Article 3) to which we have already referred.

There are, on the other hand, many agreements earlier than the Convention which overlap with it, concluded between some of the parties and third States; and, similarly, cases are becoming very frequent of agreements subsequent to the Convention that overlap with it in which participate some of its Contracting Parties and third States. An example of the first type is the Treaty of Peace with Italy, signed at Paris on 10 February 1947 (in which, among the States now bound by the Convention, Great Britain, Belgium and the Netherlands participated), and particularly its Article 15, by which Italy undertook 'to secure to all persons under Italian jurisdiction, without distinction as to race, sex, language or religion, the enjoyment of human rights and of fundamental freedoms including freedom of expression, of press and publication, of religious worship, of political opinion and of public meeting'. Examples of the second type are already quite numerous; we might mention the Convention on the Political Rights of Women of 1953 (to which among others, Denmark, Greece, Iceland, Norway, Sweden and Turkey are parties), in so far as it impinges on Article 3 of the Protocol and Article 14 of the European Convention; the Protocol amending the Slavery Convention of 1926, opened for the signature in December 1953, the supplementary Convention on the Abolition of Slavery, the Slave Trade and Institutions and Practices similar to Slavery of 1956, and the Convention concerning the Abolition of Forced Labour of 1957, all of which may be related to Article 4 of the European Convention; the Convention on the Status of Stateless Persons of 1954, whose Articles 4 (Freedom of religion), 15 (right of association), 16 (access to the courts), 22 (education) and 13 (protection of property) clearly overlap with Articles 9, 11 and 6 of the European Convention and with Articles 2 and 1 of the Protocol. (It may be observed, however, that the rights granted to stateless persons, apart from the 1954 Convention, are protected by Article 5, which is similar to Article 5 of the Convention relating to the Status of Refugees already referred to). Finally let us remember the Convention of 1960 on the Prevention of Discrimination in Education, because of the objective connection between its provisions and Article 2 of the Protocol to the European Convention and Article 14 of the Convention itself.

In the cases mentioned there can be no hesitation in asserting compatibility between the European Convention and the earlier or later agreements concluded between some of its Contracting Parties and other States. The consequence of this compatibility is integration of the clauses of the two international instruments which individually correspond; but obviously only as regards the parties to both agreements (and in their respective municipal laws). Any case of incompatibility, on the other hand, would be settled in the same way as described for overlapping between the Convention and subsequent agreements concluded by some of its Contracting Parties (or between the Convention and earlier wider agreements); what is significant is that only a group that is smaller than the subjective sphere of the earlier agreement takes part in the new agreement. Consequently, the new agreement always prevails from the point of view of the municipal law of those States that are parties to both conventions; this is not affected by the existence or otherwise on the international level of obligations of one of these States towards the other contracting parties to the old agreement. Only those provisions of an agreement earlier than the Convention that are more favourable to the protection of human rights than are the clauses of the Convention would remain in force, as provided by Article 60 of the Convention itself.

11. Two particular questions seem to us to call for at least brief mention: that of overlapping between the Convention and Agreements which set up international judicial bodies accessible to individuals or create organisations that can intervene on behalf of individuals and thus influence their treatment; and the question of possible relations between the Convention and the universal Covenants on Human Rights that the United Nations has been preparing for several years.

The first question may be expressed as follows: is the Convention applicable to the operation of the judicial bodies and organisations mentioned above? Mr H. Golsong's valuable communication to the 1960 Colloquy quoted several examples of judicial bodies accessible to individuals which some of the Contracting Parties to the Convention helped in setting up; from the Central Commission for the Navigation of the Rhine established by the Statute of 1868 to the Franco-German Mixed Court set up by the 1956 Treaty between France and Germany for the settlement of the Saar problem. Among the organisations which possess powers in relation to individuals, the most important are undoubtedly today the European Communities: the problem of relations between the Convention and Treaties concluded by the European Communities has been carefully studied.[1]

This problem cannot really be regarded as pertinent to the subject of the present report; in fact, problems of the functioning of an international judicial body or of the organs of an international union do not have anything to do with the municipal law of the States which established such organs. It may reasonably be asked, however, whether the principles set forth regarding possible overlapping between the European Convention and other agreements are applicable to overlapping with the constituent instruments of judicial bodies or unions of the type referred to. In our opinion, the answer can be in the affirmative only if these instruments have no parties other than the Contracting Parties to the Convention. In fact, if the conduct of an international body is to be influenced by a subsequent convention, that convention must be such as to supplement or amend the constituent instruments of the international body; this is fully possible only if all the parties to the instrument become parties to the Convention. On the other hand, an international body can accept as applicable to its own conduct only the rules of earlier conventions in which all parties to its own constituent instrument participated; and this naturally, provided that that instrument contains no different rules on the same subject. This is why we think that the European Convention cannot be applied to the activities in relation to individuals of the organs of the ESCS, EEC or EURATOM, since one of the member States of the three Communities, France, has not ratified the Convention.

The second point—relations between the Convention and the expected universal Covenants on Human Rights—need only be mentioned because such cases of overlapping would undoubtedly be of much greater importance than all those hitherto referred to. The

[1] Waelbroeck, 'La Convention européenne des droits de l'homme lie-t-elle les Communautés européennes?', communication to the 'Semaine de Bruges' in 1965.

drafts of the two Covenants (that on economic, social and cultural rights and that on civil and political rights) already approved by the Assembly with the exception only of those Articles referring to measures of implementation, enable us to say that these will be wider conventions than the European Convention.

Presuming, then, that all parties to the latter ratify both Covenants, is the European Convention to be regarded as tacitly abrogated or not? The reply in our opinion should be in the negative, for the reason already given: that is to say, the existence of specific guarantees for the European Convention—the machinery of the Commission and Court—for which these pacts could not 'tacitly' substitute the guarantee machinery, of a different type, which they may perhaps contain. In any case, Article 5 of both United Nations draft Covenants provides that the more favourable provisions of earlier agreements will continue to apply. Finally, it is superfluous to add that if not all Parties to the European Convention should become parties to the universal Covenants, the problem would be differently presented; here we need only refer to the criteria already set out above.

SUMMARY OF THE DISCUSSION

Karl Zemanek: in modern international law doctrine the principle of 'general transformation' is regarded as authorising the application of a rule of international law in the sphere of municipal law. It follows therefore that, even when applied internally, such a rule depends on its validity in international law, i.e. that it can only be applied in municipal law as long as it is valid in international law. The authorisation to apply it in municipal law implies, however, an obligation to apply it at a certain level of law in the context of which it has binding force.

Now, if a given State has concluded with other States two or more treaties whose content is conflicting, they can be simultaneously valid in international law because of their different spheres of application. But since in municipal law this difference in their spheres of application disappears, the rule that is later in time derogates from the earlier one. However, as rules of international law are applicable in municipal law as long as they continue to be valid in international law, in such a case derogation exists which is unjustified.

This contradiction has not yet been sufficiently studied by legal experts.

Louis B. Sohn (Relation between the European Convention on Human Rights and the United Nations' Covenants): the relation between the Convention and the Covenants is particularly important, especially as it is quite likely that several European States will ratify the Covenants. What will happen if the substantive or implementation provisions of these instruments should prove incompatible? In particular, how can one apply two different ways of enforcement?

Three types of difficulties are possible: (1) a conflict between the instruments themselves; (2) a conflict between the implementation procedures; and (3) interpretation problems. In case of conflict between the two instruments, which should prevail? Do the new instruments prevail over the older one? Do the more specific instruments prevail over the more general one? Or should the criterion be which instrument provides more protection of human rights in a particular case?

If in some cases the Covenants should be more favourable, what will happen to the Convention? Is the European Commission obliged to apply the Convention even if the Covenants should provide greater protection, or could the Commission apply the Covenants in such cases? Which remedies should be exhausted first? Should the applicant go first to the European Commission or to the United Nations? What should be the attitude of the domestic courts in case of a conflict?

As far as interpretation is concerned, the European institutions and national courts might benefit from the specificity of some United Nations documents, not only the Covenants but also the special conventions on racial discrimination, religious intolerance, etc. In interpreting the Convention, they might borrow from the more specific provisions of the other instruments. Reciprocally, in interpreting the Covenants, the United Nations might take advantage of the jurisprudence of the European institutions and the decisions of national tribunals interpreting the Convention.

Michel Waelbroeck (Is the European Convention on Human Rights binding on the European Communities?): the dynamic aspect should be considered as well as the static aspect on which the report dwells particularly; in other words, it is not sufficient to examine the conflicts resulting from the conclusion of two successive agreements, for the interpretation or application of the agreements can also give rise to conflicts which may not be apparent at the outset. The risk of conflict is all the greater when one of the agreements establishes an international organisation whose task is to complete the agreement and take measures to implement it. If this organisation is established by a subsequent agreement concluded between a number of the parties to the previous agreement, it must respect the interpretation rule that the rights of non-member States must not be prejudiced. The same applies when certain of the States which are parties to the second agreement have not ratified the first one.

To come to the question of the Communities, the fact that France, a member of the Economic Community, has not ratified the Convention does not prevent the Community organs—where there are several possible ways of interpreting or applying the Community Treaties—from being bound to choose the one which is also compatible with the Convention. Indeed, Article 234 of the EEC Treaty provides that earlier agreements 'shall not be affected by the provisions of this Treaty'.

Felix Ermacora (Solution of conflicts between the Convention and other international agreements): the essential preliminary question to the problem of interpretation is: How does the international or national organ see the world from the legal point of view? As homogeneous or dualistic? No hypotheses are necessary: it is the concrete cases of conflict that are important. The EEC Treaty is not included among these, since it makes no reference to the Convention. The following examples may be mentioned:

(a) The overlapping between Article 4 of the Convention and the ILO agreements on the abolition of forced labour;

(b) The relation between the Convention and the provisions on human rights in the Treaty of Versailles;

(c) The relation between the Convention and the Austrian State Treaty as regards provisions on the law of property.

The Convention may conflict:

1. as *lex posterior* with earlier agreements. Here there is the possibility of

(a) a reservation under Article 64, which will then take precedence over the Convention. This possibility is open to France, Switzerland and Malta. Austria is the only country to have made fairly detailed reservations. Where no reservations have been made, the Convention takes precedence.

(b) Article 60 of the Convention, with its clause protecting human rights guaranteed under existing laws, offers a further possible solution.

(c) Failing this, the problem of derogation arises. According to the Vienna School, the decision must rest with the authority which concluded the agreement.

2. with post-Convention agreements (e.g. United Nations agreements)

(a) The State organs, which are represented at the United Nations, must act with expert knowledge and bear in mind that the European States have special difficulties. It is not too late yet to insert special provisions; this will be one of the Council of Europe's principal tasks in its relations with the United Nations.

(b) For the European authorities the Convention alone is decisive. For the international organs, the other obligations of a Contracting

State, which can be called to account under the terms of the Convention, are legally irrelevant. The difficult problems of interpretation could be solved by empowering the European Court to give advisory opinions on the compatibility of a draft treaty with the Convention.

CHAPTER IV

Does the Convention have the force of 'ordre public' in municipal law?

REPORT BY

W. J. GANSHOF VAN DER MEERSCH[1]

A. INTRODUCTION

1. *'Ordre public' in municipal law*

The notion of *ordre public* may be considered in terms of its aim and its effects. Henri Capitant combines these two aspects in a frequently-quoted definition:

> that body of institutions and rules designed to ensure, in a given country, the satisfactory functioning of the public services, security and morality of transactions between individuals, who may not exclude their application in private agreements.[2]

In private law, the purpose of *ordre public* is to ensure 'the supremacy of society over the individual', and the effect is a restriction of the unfettered will.

Freedom of contract is likewise restricted by the principle of *boni mores*. But this is reflected in rules belonging to the moral order while *ordre public* covers the actual principles of political or social organisation and the guarantees of its stability.

The scope of *ordre public* has widened. In the nineteenth century it referred only to political organisation and good government. Today, it still governs public, administrative, fiscal and criminal law, but it also pervades social legislation, family law and professional rules.

Ordre public likewise influences procedural law; it enables a judge to bring up an argument *proprio motu*, to quash a decision without further examination, to substitute grounds; it may also require a judge to bring up a certain argument or quash a certain decision, and to conform to various provisions relating to judicial organisation and competence.

---

[1] The full text of this Report is published in the French edition of the Proceedings of the Conference. In the English edition, the first half of the Report is summarised under A. Introduction. The second half is given in full under B. The European Convention on Human Rights and 'Ordre Public' in municipal law.

[2] *Vocabulaire juridique*, v, Ordre public.

The mandatory nature of the institutions has many aspects and degrees. 'There is not an *ordre public*: there are merely matters of concern to *ordre public*.'[1]

The rules of *ordre public* determine the validity of juristic acts. Agreements contrary to *ordre public* are void. A matter of *ordre public* cannot be the subject of agreement, arrangement, arbitration, acquiescence, compromise or renunciation. Parties may in all circumstances avail themselves of the rules of *ordre public*; the '*ministère public*' is responsible for seeing that *ordre public* is observed and has the right to take action to this end; the courts must apply it, even on their own initiative.

But every rule of *ordre public* does not necessarily entail all these consequences simultaneously; the authority which the rule carries varies with the matter and its importance to the community in the mind of the legislator.

The principal source of *ordre public* is increasingly *the law*. The legislator may designate *any* matter as being of *ordre public* on grounds of political expediency.

A law of *ordre public* is mandatory by reason of its subject matter.

A mandatory law which enjoins or prohibits is a law of *ordre public* only if the injunction or prohibition is determined by the need to protect the public good.

There is also, however, a *judicial ordre public*, in other words, one accepted by the courts by reason of the subject matter. In the first place, the court may declare a law to be of *ordre public* when its mandatory or suppletory character is not, or is not adequately, indicated. Secondly, the court may find other mandatory rules based on the common good in the unwritten general principles of law.

This form of judicial *ordre public* has affinities with the common law concept of public policy, which applies to considerations of public interest which move English courts to derogate from the principle of freedom of contract. Under the rule of precedent, public policy has a permanent content according to the prevailing opinion. It nevertheless also reflects economic and social evolution.

2. *Ordre public in private international law*

'International *ordre public*' is a concept in private international law whose content varies from one country to another despite its name. It has greater force than in municipal law. It determines those cases a judge will refuse to refer to a foreign law, which according to the other rules of private international law he ought to apply, because the said law runs counter to accepted ideas in his country and its application would be socially disturbing.

[1] P. Malaurie, *L'ordre public et le contrat*, 1953.

3. *International ordre public in the sense of the law of nations*

International *ordre public* in the sense of the law of nations governs relations between States. It restricts the right to conclude international agreements for reasons connected with their objects.

Opinions are divided regarding the content of this *ordre public*. It is taken to include the rules essential to the maintenance of general peace and order, the essential rules of universal morality and respect for fundamental human rights.

Henri Ro in[1] described the progress made by the concept of international *ordre public* in the law of nations, citing in support Article 103 of the United Nations Charter, which states that the obligations embodied therein shall prevail over any other undertaking. He stressed that the provisions of the Charter, including those of Article 1, para. 3, which assigns to the United Nations the task of promoting and encouraging respect for human rights and fundamental freedoms, prevailed on account of their definite, if not explicit, character of *ordre public*.

The European Convention for the protection of Human Rights has opened up a new and decisive phase in international *ordre public*. It has established organs—the Commission and the Court—whose jurisdiction and operation are subject to rules in which the public interest is overriding. The remedy of an individual for violation of these rights serves higher interest than that of the individual or even that of the State as protector of its nationals. The Convention attaches new guarantees to international *ordre public*.

4. *International ordre public in the sense of the law of nations and respect for fundamental human rights*

Human rights are referred to seven times in the United Nations Charter. Article 56, in particular, places member States under a legal obligation to co-operate in promoting effective and universal respect for human rights. The question of human rights does not lie within a State's sovereign powers but in the domain of international law, where disputes must be settled according to the procedure established by the Charter for this purpose. As a result, respect for human rights has become 'a positive rule of international treaty law'.

The Universal Declaration of Human Rights is merely a declaration of principles, but most writers do not question its legal value. It is a restatement of certain general principles of law whose existence is to some extent reinforced as a consequence. It offers States guiding principles for carrying out the proposed and desired adjustment of their legislation.

---

[1] 'Vers un ordre public réellement international', in *Hommage d'une génération de juristes au Président Basdevent*, Paris, 1960, p. 441.

In United Nations practice, a declaration is technically a more portentous instrument than a mere recommendation. But it is particularly the purpose of the 1948 Declaration which gives it such a wide influence, affecting international *ordre public* in the sense of the law of nations: for 'there is a direct and close link between respect for rights of man in the society in which he lives and the establishment of a true international order'.[1]

In the preamble to the European Convention on Human Rights the High Contracting Parties declare 'their profound belief in those Fundamental Freedoms which are the foundation of justice and peace in the world'. This statement confirms that the subject is one on which order in the international society depends. Stress is thus laid on pre-eminence of the general interest, which is the basis of the concept of *ordre public* in the law of nations and in municipal law alike.

The Commission has itself had to decide whether the rights protected by the Convention partake of *ordre public*. Italy argued the inadmissibility of an application by Austria (No. 788/60) on the ground that, according to the principle of reciprocity, Austria could not rely on facts which dated from a time before the two countries had assumed obligations towards one another. The Commission rejected the application of the principle of reciprocity because 'the purpose of the High Contracting Parties in concluding the Convention was not to concede to each other reciprocal rights and obligations in pursuance of their individual national interests, but to realise the aims and ideals of the Council of Europe, as expressed in its Statute, and to establish a common[2] public order of the free democracies of Europe'.[3] The Commission stressed 'that a High Contracting Party when it refers an alleged breach of the Convention to the Commission under Article 24, is not to be regarded as exercising a right of action for the purpose of enforcing its own rights, but rather as bringing before the Commission an alleged violation of the public order of Europe'.[4] It points out that in pursuance of Article 24 of the Convention, any other State could, like Austria, have made the same application. The Commission thus stressed the international *ordre public* aspect which characterises both the rights protected and the machinery set up to protect them.

The European public order referred to by the Commission is a

---

[1] R. Cassin, *La Déclaration Universelle et la mise en oeuvre des droits de l'homme,* Recueil des cours de l'Académie de droit international, 1951, IV, p. 294.

[2] The term 'communautaire' in the French text has acquired a special meaning since the conclusion of the ECSC, EEC and Euratom Treaties and is not adequate here.

[3] Decision of 12 January 1961, *Yearbook*, IV, p. 138.   [4] Ibid., p. 140.

regional *ordre public*, something between international *ordre public* in the sense of the law of nations and domestic *ordre public*. It retains the characteristics of the former but limits its effects to the member States of the Council of Europe. It partakes of the latter through its purpose, which is to protect the essential interests of a society, in this case the European society.

5. *Application of the Convention in the internal juridical order*

The European Convention for the protection of Human Rights is self-executing; in other words, it is directly applicable by national courts. That was the intention of the High Contracting Parties when they declared, in Article 1 of the Convention, that they 'secure to everyone within their jurisdiction the rights and freedoms defined in Section I of (this) Convention'.[1]

The obligation imposed on all States by Article 57 of the Convention to furnish on receipt of a request from the Secretary General of the Council of Europe 'an explanation of the manner in which its internal law ensures the effective implementation of any of the provisions of this Convention' confirms that the authors of the Convention intended that it should be directly applicable in internal legal systems. Moreover, most of the provisions of the Convention recognise or confer subjective rights, define measures of defence or proclaim the invalidity of agreements or other juristic acts without the need for supplementary enforcement measures. Finally, the third feature which signifies that the normative provisions of the Convention and its Protocols are directly applicable in the internal legal system is that the majority of the rules are couched in specific terms and form a juridical system complete enough to be applicable without additional rules having to be drawn up by the national legislature.

However, some of the Convention's provisions, merely stating a principle or rule of conduct for the signatory States, are not directly applicable, such as, for example, Article 3 of the first Protocol according to which 'the High Contracting Parties *undertake to hold* free elections at reasonable intervals by secret ballot'. It also appears to be true of Article 13 of the Convention which states that 'everyone

[1] Mr Rolin who suggested substituting the expression 'shall recognise' for 'undertake to recognise' in the draft, gave the following reasons for his amendment: 'According to the new text of the Committee of Ministers the High Contracting Parties shall not undertake to recognise, they *shall* recognise—so that once this is ratified by the States, the text, as at present worded, will no longer be the subject of subsequent amendments in our Constitutions, or our respective legislation. It will be incorporated bodily, of its own right, into the legislation of our fifteen countries' (*Consultative Assembly Reports*, Sitting of 25 August 1950, Part III, p. 914).

whose rights and freedoms . . . are violated *shall have an effective remedy* before a national authority. . . .'[1]

In fact the *self-executing* rules will be applicable only in so far as the constitutional order of the States is not, in the court's view, opposed to their direct application. This is a problem of internal public law.

Where the constitutional system recognises the pre-eminence of the rule of international law over rules of municipal law—even constitutional rules—there is no obstacle to application of the Convention, even where it conflicts with municipal law.

If pre-eminence is accepted only in relation to laws and regulations and if the rights and freedoms protected by the Convention are the subject of a constitutional system in municipal law, the application of the Convention will encounter difficulties in so far as its system is inconsistent with that of the municipal law.

If international law is not recognised as superior to municipal law, either the State brings its legislation (and possibly its Constitution) into line with the Convention and its Protocols—as moreover it has undertaken to do—or the normative provisions of the Convention and of the first and fourth Protocols are accepted as being directly applicable in the internal order. In any event, those provisions of the treaty which are *self-executing* must be applied by the national court. This is the case in Belgian law, although the Belgian constitution is silent on this point.[2]

The refusal of national authorities to apply the self-executing rules of the Convention involves the responsibility in international law of the State to which these authorities are responsible, whether or not the Constitution of that State recognises international law as overriding and whether or not that Constitution has been adapted to conform to the Convention and its Protocols.

In Denmark, Iceland, Norway, Sweden and Turkey, the Convention and its Protocols do not have the force of law since no legislative act has given them that force. This is also the case in the United Kingdom and Ireland.

The Convention has acquired the force of law in the Federal Republic of Germany through parliamentary approval, followed by ratification and publication. It appears to have the status merely of an ordinary federal law.

The Austrian Constitutional Court decided that, following its approval by the National Council and its publication, the Convention was equivalent to a federal law. But it refused to recognise the

---

[1] See Hoge Raad, 24 February 1960, *N.J.* 1960, p. 1121.
[2] See R. Hayoit de Termicourt, 'Le conflit "*traité-loi interne*" ', *Journ. Trib.*, 1963, p. 481.

self-executing character of such detailed provisions as Articles 5 and 6 of the Convention on the grounds that these Articles were not sufficiently precise.[1] An Act of 4 March 1964 expressly recognised that the Convention had the status of *constitutional law*.

In Belgium and Italy the normative provisions of the Convention are treated as legal provisions.

Luxembourg judicial practice[2] recognises the primacy of treaty law over domestic law. As a result, the provisions of the Convention for the protection of Human Rights relating to the rights and freedoms protected can be applied immediately by national courts.[3]

Since 1956 the Constitution of the Netherlands has recognised the superiority of an international treaty over municipal law and even, if it has been approved by both Houses by a two-thirds majority of votes cast, over the Constitution. The European Convention on Human Rights is considered to be directly applicable by national courts in all cases where it is susceptible of immediate application.

B. THE EUROPEAN CONVENTION ON HUMAN RIGHTS AND 'ORDRE PUBLIC' IN MUNICIPAL LAW

1. *The nature of the rights safeguarded*

(*a*) The preamble to the Convention expresses the essential nature of its rules as regards order in the State and in society. A more categorical statement could not be made: ' . . . those Fundamental Freedoms which are the *foundation* of justice and peace in the world. . . .' Is this not the very notion of *ordre public*? That being so, need one be surprised at the mandatory nature of the stipulations relating to most of the rights guaranteed in the Convention and the First and Fourth Protocols?

The authors of the Convention regard human rights as the 'foundation of justice' and take care to make this clear at the beginning of the Convention, for this opening statement embodies the Convention's whole philosophy. This philosophy is also expressed at the beginning of the Statute of the Council of Europe, Article 1 (*b*) of which provides that the aim of the Council of Europe shall be pursued 'in the maintenance and further realisation of human rights and fundamental freedoms'.

(*b*) The fundamental nature of the rights stated in the Convention

---

[1] Verfassungsgerichtshof, 17 June 1960, B.469/59/12, Ann. III, p. 617; 13 October 1960, B. 102/60/13, Ann. III, p. 614; 14 October 1961, G.2/61/8, Ann. IV, p. 605.

[2] Cass. crim. 8 juin 1950, *Pasicrisie luxembourgeoise*, xv, p. 41, etc.

[3] *Contra*: Trib. arrondissement Luxembourg, 24.10.1960, Ann. IV, p. 623.

and the system there laid down for their protection were made strikingly clear in the debates to which the draft gave rise in the Consultative Assembly.

For instance Mr Harold MacMillan, after saying that none of the objectives of European Union could be attained 'without a real unity of purpose', declared that the Convention on Human Rights was 'the prior condition—the *condition préalable*—without which our society will fail. . . .'.[1] The Rapporteur, Mr P. H. Teitgen, was equally categorical: 'These rights and freedoms are the common denominator of our political institutions, the first triumph of democracy, but also the necessary condition under which it operates'.[2]

(*c*) The traditional rights and freedoms safeguarded by the Convention are proclaimed, and in general guaranteed, by most constitutions.[3] In general, too, infringements of such rights and freedoms are punished under municipal criminal law.[4]

(*d*) The predominance of *ordre public* is apparent not only from the actual rights guaranteed, but also from the international procedural system before the Court laid down in the Convention and from the nature of the parties' interest in taking action.

(*e*) The Constitutional Court of the Federal Republic of Germany has, it seems to us, recognised beyond any doubt the Convention's force as *ordre public* in the municipal law of the Federal Republic in a judgment of 10 May 1957,[5] when it decided that it was necessary to examine *ex officio* the question whether or not Articles 175 *et seq*. of the German Criminal Code were consistent with the Convention.

What the Court had to examine was, first, whether or not Articles 175 *et seq*. of the Criminal Code were compatible with the 'general principles of international law'. Under Article 25 of the Basic Law of the Federal Republic of Germany 'the general rules of public international law form part of the federal law. They take precedence over the laws and directly create rights and duties for the inhabitants of the federal territory'.

[1] Sitting of 17 August 1949, Reports, First Session, Part 1, sitting VI, p. 234.

[2] Sitting of 5 September 1949, Doc. 77, 1st Session, sitting 15, pp. 197–209. See also sitting of 8 September 1949, Reports 1st Session, Part IV, sitting 18, pp. 1164–1299; and sitting of 12 August 1949, Reports 1st Session, Part 1, sitting 3, pp. 72–3.

[3] It is not possible in this context to make an exhaustive study of comparative constitutional law.

[4] G. Janssen-Pevtschin, J. Velu, A. Van Welkenhuyzen: 'La Convention de sauvegarde des droits de l'homme et des libertés fondamentales et la fonctionnement des juridictions belges', *Chronique de politique étrangère*, Brussels, June 1962, no. 3, p. 226.

[5] Bundesverfassungsgericht, 10 May 1957, Entsch., 6, p. 389. An extract from this judgment is given in the *Yearbook of the European Convention on Human Rights*, 1958–9, p. 594.

The appellant argued that the normative provisions of the Convention for the Protection of Human Rights and Fundamental Freedoms signed at Rome on 4 November 1950 formed part of the 'general rules of public international law' referred to in Article 25 of the Basic Law. The Constitutional Court had decided in an earlier case,[1] and held again in the judgment referred to, that Article 25 of the Basic Law was not concerned with any fundamental rights and that consequently no appeal to the Constitutional Court could be based on a violation of it. Moreover, Article 25 only mentions 'general rules'. It does not cover international law based on conventions. Thus the question of precedence of international law over municipal law did not arise in this case.

The Convention, having been approved by an Act of the Parliament, had become part of the municipal law of the Federal Republic of Germany.

Examination *ex officio* by the Court of the question whether Articles 175 *et seq.* of the German Criminal Code were in accordance with the Convention would seem to lead inevitably to the conclusion that the Constitutional Court considers that the Convention has the force of *ordre public* in German municipal law.

(*f*) The Federal Court has also recognised that the Convention has the force of *ordre public* in the municipal law of the Federal Republic as a factor limiting the freedom of individuals in their relations with each other. This judgment, which also argues in favour of direct application of the Convention, deserves to be quoted.

To record a conversation on tape without the permission of the person concerned constitutes a violation of the individual rights guaranteed in Articles 1 and 2 of the Basic Law and Article 8 of the Convention. Articles 1 and 2 of the Basic Law are not binding solely on the State and its authorities; *they must also be observed by individuals in their relations between each other* (Privatrechtsverkehr). *This also holds good for Article 8.*[2]

2. *Cases brought by the Contracting Parties*

(*a*) A case may be brought before the Court 'by one of the High Contracting Parties concerned'. Under Article 48 of the Convention a Contracting Party 'concerned' is one 'whose national is alleged to be a victim', one which has 'referred the case to the Commission' or one 'against which the complaint has been lodged' by another Contracting Party. While in the first and last of these cases the State's interest is clear and rests on the traditional principles of international law, the situation is different in the second case. Here it is enough for

[1] Bundesverfassungsgericht, 13 November 1954, Entsch., 4, pp. 111 and 112.
[2] See judgment by the Bundesgerichtshof (Federal Court of Justice), 20 May 1958, *Entsch. des Bundesgerichtshof in Zivilsachen*, 27, p. 284.

the Contracting Party to have 'referred the case to the Commission'; its interest is thus the same as the interest which led it to bring the case before the Commission.

(*b*) As we have seen, a governmental application may be made to the Commission by *any* Contracting Party for *any* breach of the Convention, not merely for a breach affecting one of its own nationals. This is the very essence of the 'collective enforcement', which according to the Preamble of the Convention was the intention of the signatory Governments. A Contracting Party may take action in the case of a national of a State which is not a party to the Convention, a stateless person, a national of another Contracting Party or even a national of the State accused of the violation.[1]

(*c*) In his report to the Colloquy held in Strasbourg in November 1960 Mr H. Lannung showed the extent to which 'intervention by a Contracting Party on behalf of an individual other than one of its own nationals constitutes a break with traditional international law, under which a State may not present an application (to an international court) concerning an individual unless he is one of its own nationals'.[2] This innovation does indeed run counter to the traditional theory of diplomatic protection. One may, of course, share Mr Lannung's scepticism with regard to the use which a State will in fact make of this right and doubt whether it will avail itself of it for anyone but its own nationals, but the fact that the Convention confers the right on the Contracting Parties without this limitation seems to us to show once again the intrinsic fundamental public interest of respect for basic rights. In this case, as Mr Kiss pointed out at the same Colloquy, the State is exercising a right enjoyed by it as a party to the Treaty, not a right based on the principle of diplomatic protection.[3]

(*d*) A Government's interest may therefore in certain cases be to ensure respect for the rights of its nationals. But it will not necessarily be this interest which leads it to take action. And, even if it is, there

---

[1] See H. Rolin, 'Le rôle du requérant devant la Commission européenne des Droits de l'Homme' *Rev. hellénique de droit international*, 1956, p. 8.

[2] 'Quelques observations sur le problème de la mise en oeuvre des Droits de l'Homme', in *Strasbourg Colloquy*, p. 231, at p. 235. Cf. *Panevezys-Saldutiskis Case*, Permanent Court of International Justice, Series A/B, no. 67 (1939), p. 16.

[3] As Mr Kiss remarked, this distinction entails an important difference with regard to the *admissibility* of the application; there is no such difference as to the State's actual *right*. In the case of diplomatic protection there is also a right enjoyed by the State itself, 'its right to respect for international law in the persons of its nationals'. *Mavromatis Case, P.C.I.J.* Series A, no. 2, p. 12; *Serbian Loans Case, P.C.I.J.* Series A, no. 20–21, p. 17; Nottebohm Case, *ICJ*, 1955, p. 24, see A. C. Kiss, 'La Convention européene des Droits de l'Homme et le système de garantie du droit international public', *Strasbourg Colloquy*, p. 241, and n. 2.

will be a further interest, that of the Contracting Party in question, in seeing that the obligations relating to the rights guaranteed by the Convention are respected before the whole world. In other words, its interest will be identical with the general interest.[1]

The interest of the Contracting Parties here is that of ensuring that each State shall respect an undertaking relating to a rule of *ordre public*.

(*e*) This is not so much a right as a *competence* attributed to States parties to the Convention and to the Commission, 'a competence entailing rights to be exercised and duties to be performed in accordance with the objects for which it was conferred'.[2] Applicants are therefore fulfilling a real function,[3] that of setting in motion the system of enforcement laid down in the Convention and participating in it; the function of the Commission and Court is to ensure, once the matter has been referred to them, that the rights recognised in the Convention are effectively safeguarded.

(*f*) In its decision of 11 January 1961, in the case of Austria against Italy, the Commission gave expression to the idea that an applicant State should not be considered as acting to enforce its own right, but as submitting to the Commission a question of concern to European *ordre public*.[4]

(*g*) Mr Rolin sees in an application by the Contracting Parties the 'institution of (veritable) *public action*'.[5] This is a striking expression, and the comparison with municipal law is tempting. Of course there is no question of criminal proceedings, but an application by a Contracting Party has this in common with proceedings by the Director of Public Prosecutions, that in both cases action is taken in the interests of society—a wider society than the national community, one which comprises the whole community of those Member States of the Council of Europe that have signed and ratified the Convention. Essentially the application pursues aims of public interest which are at the very foundation of *ordre public*.

(*h*) The function of protecting a fundamental public interest— transcending any individual or private interest—which is fulfilled by the Contracting Parties may be compared, in the municipal law of countries which have the institution of a *ministère public*, to civil proceedings taken by it in matters of *ordre public*.[6]

---

[1] H. Rolin, loc. cit.
[2] A. C. Kiss, op. cit., p. 242, n. 2.
[3] R. J. Dupuy, 'La Commission européenne des Droits de l'Homme', *Annuaire Français*, 1957, p. 449, n. 2.
[4] See *Yearbook of the Convention*, vol. 4., p. 116, and particularly p. 140.
[5] H. Rolin, 'Le rôle du requérant ...', op. cit., p. 8.
[6] French law of 30 April 1810, article 46.

3. *Individual applications*

(*a*) The right to institute proceedings before the Commission is also enjoyed by 'any person, non-governmental organisation or group of individuals'. Of course a party 'claiming to be the victim of a violation' may, in submitting this application to the Commission, have the object of securing recognition of a subjective right which has been violated and compensation for damage suffered as a result of the violation.

(*b*) But under Article 25, par. 1, of the Convention, the Commission may not receive a petition from any person, non-governmental organisation or group of individuals that does not claim to be the *victim* of a violation of the rights set forth in the Convention.

(*c*) Thus the individual must have an *interest* in taking action. He may not complain of a violation of one of the rights set forth in the Convention unless it concerns him personally. This is rightly affirmed in the Commission's decisions and in theoretical writings on the subject.[1] Thus an Applicant cannot ask the Commission to consider *in abstracto* whether a law is in accordance with the Convention without maintaining that he himself has been a victim of its application. This was the Commission's ruling in two decisions given on 29 March 1960 (*X against Ireland*, No. 290/57)[2] and on 29 May 1961 (*X against Norway*, No. 867/60).[3]

In its decision of 29 May 1961 it rejected an application by a person who was contesting a resolution adopted by the Norwegian Parliament on 7 October 1960 in favour of an enactment authorising the termination of pregnancy in circumstances laid down therein. The Applicant claimed that his application was lodged 'on behalf of parents who without their own consent or knowledge, but with express consent of the Norwegian Authorities or under a law about to be presented to the Norwegian Parliament, have or will have their offspring taken away by *abortus provocatus*, and on behalf of those taken away by such operations—all unfit or unable to plead on their own behalf. . . .'[4]

The Commission recalled that it was 'not competent to examine *in abstracto* the question of the conformity of this Law with the provisions of the Convention'.[5] In a decision dated 28 July 1961 it

---

[1] Decision 28 July 1961 on application by *X against the Federal Republic of Germany*, No. 742/60, *Yearbook*, IV, p. 297. See in particular A. B. McNulty and M.-A. Eissen, 'The European Commission on Human Rights: Procedure and Jurisprudence', *Journal of the International Commission of Jurists*, Spring-Summer 1958, vol. 1, No. 2, p. 198; R. J. Dupuy, 'La Commission européenne . . .', op. cit., p. 458.

[2] *Yearbook*, III, p. 214. [3] *Yearbook*, IV, p. 270.
[4] Ibid., p. 274. [5] Ibid., p. 276.

rejected an application with the remark that 'in putting forward the allegation that a certain Professor A. wilfully killed by medical experiments at least five men *who were not apparently in any way connected with him*, the Applicant is not claiming to be himself the *victim* of a violation within the meaning of Article 25 of the Convention'.[1]

(d) Here too, then the Commission rightly draws attention to the wording used by the authors of the Convention in Article 25, referring to any party 'claiming to be the *victim* of a violation . . . of the rights set forth in (the) Convention'.

Under Article 25 (1) the Commission may only receive a petition from a person, non-governmental organisation or group of individuals provided they claim to be *victims* of a violation of the rights and freedoms set forth in the Convention.[2]

(e) But it will surely be admitted that if the Commission, in the exercise of its power to take a decision on an individual application, may, under Article 25, receive a petition 'from *any* person, non-governmental organisation or group of individuals claiming to be the victim of a violation by one of the High Contracting Parties of the rights set forth in (the) Convention', and not merely from nationals of States parties to the Convention, this is by reason of the fundamental public interest attaching to the protection of human rights. The fact that the right of individual application is not subject to any condition relating to the applicant's nationality[3] must surely be viewed in the light of Article 1 of the Convention, which provides that 'the High Contracting Parties shall secure to *everyone* within their jurisdiction the rights and freedoms defined in Section 1 of (the) Convention'.

(f) Mr Dupuy uses similar terms, when speaking of individual applications to the Commission, to those he employs in describing applications by the Contracting Parties. He writes, 'The individual applicant institutes a kind of popular action. . . .'[4] This view is of course too sweeping, since at the basis of an individual application is the claim to have been the victim of a violation of a right. But it is true that the setting in motion of the procedure on an individual application is more than a matter of securing respect for an individual right. There is a fundamental interest which goes further than the applicant's rights or even his person, and over which he has no control; this is the overriding interest of respect for 'the law', that is to say the protection of basic rights as laid down in the Convention.

[1] Ibid., p. 298.　　　　[2] *Yearbook*, I, p. 60.
[3] See H. Golsong, 'La défense des droits de l'homme en Europe', *Sciences humaines et intégration européenne*, 1960, pp. 210–11.
[4] R. J. Dupuy, op. cit., p. 457.

This interest, too, is identical with the general interest and is a matter of *ordre public*.

(*g*) Mr Rolin also points out that the idea of 'victim' is a very wide one, and 'even where the remedy is exercised by an individual victim, the injury on which the action rests may be an indirect and not an actual one; it may even be a mere contingency for the applicant or applicants'. He writes that in some cases 'relatives (of the actual victim) may feel threatened by the precedent, may be interested in taking action against it and may be entitled to consider themselves victims'. He points out that the very wide term 'non-governmental organisations and groups of individuals' would be superfluous if the only groups of individuals to come into question were those in which each member was affected by the act complained of.[1]

(*h*) It is true—as Mr Dupuy[2] and Mr Rolin[3] do not fail to point out—that the Commission gives a wide interpretation to this notion. A near relation of the victim (*stricto sensu*), or even a third party who has suffered damage and who has a personal interest, may refer a violation of the Convention to the Commission, especially if the victim himself is unable to act in defence of his rights.[4] The Commission will not declare inadmissible an application in which it is stated that all that is asked for is an examination *in abstracto* of the compatibility of a law with the Convention, if it appears that the applicant has *in fact* been a victim of the operation of the law complained of.[5] But unless at least one of these conditions is fulfilled the application will not be admissible, a fact which limits the possible framework of the 'public action' referred to.

(*i*) Here the Commission is in a delicate situation in relation to the Contracting States, which might be apprehensive about a broad interpretation of the Convention with regard to the acceptability of individual applications.

Its jurisprudence—which, as we have seen, is fairly liberal— shows that an applicant who claims to be a victim must invoke some

---

[1] 'Le rôle du requérant . . .', op. cit., pp. 8, 9.   [2] Loc. cit., p. 458.
[3] 'Le rôle du requérant . . .', op. cit., pp. 8, 9.
[4] See Commission's Jurisprudence: Application no. 113/55, *X against Fed. Rep. of Germany*, decision of 30 May 1956, *Yearbook*, I, pp. 161–2; no. 100/55, *X, Y and Z against Fed. Rep. of Germany*, decision of 31 May 1956, *Yearbook*, I, pp. 162–3; no. 155/156, X *against Fed. Rep. of Germany*, decision of 29 September 1956, *Yearbook*, I, pp. 163–4; no. 282/57, *X against Fed. Rep. of Germany*, decision of 16 December 1957, *Yearbook*, I, pp. 164–5; no. 290/57, *B. against Ireland, Yearbook*, II, p. 214; no. 898/60, *X against Austria*, decision of 14 December, 1961, *Collection of Decisions* no. 8, p. 136.
[5] See decision of 17 December 1955 on application *X against Fed. Rep. of Germany*, No. 99/55, *Yearbook*, I, p. 160. It thus appears that an applicant is not obliged to furnish proof of his interest in taking action.

interest other than the purely general interest of respect for the Convention. One therefore cannot subscribe unreservedly to the suggestion of our learned colleague 'that the idea of a victim yields to that of an interested party who intervenes not so much in defence of a subjective right as in order to protect freedom'.[1] For the expression 'public action' to be truly justified, the Commission would have to interpret its task even more broadly than it does.

4. Individual 'petitions'

Complaints may be lodged—and in fact are lodged—against States which have not made a declaration accepting the right of individual petition provided for in Article 25 of the Convention. Such complaints will not be 'applications' but individual 'petitions'.[2] Mr Vasak has pointed out that, paradoxically, while the Universal Declaration has no binding force, petitions sent to the United Nations are nevertheless communicated to the States concerned, whereas the Convention—which is binding on the States that have ratified it— contains no such provision; the Secretary General of the Council will inform petitioners that in present circumstances the Commission is not competent to examine the case and the Commission will declare the application inadmissible.[3] Several solutions have been proposed to 'facilitate the transformation of individual petitions into applications'.[4] The over-riding interest shown by the member States of the Council of Europe and the High Contracting Parties to

[1] R. J. Dupuy, op. cit., p. 458.

[2] In this context Mr Rolin points out the confusion that may arise from the fact that the English text of Articles 25, 27 and 28 uses the term 'petition'. There is no such confusion in Rules 40–4 and 45–7 of the Commission's Rules of Procedure, where the word 'application' is used. (H. Rolin, 'Le rôle du requérant . . .', op. cit., p. 5). For the procedure at the United Nations see G. A. Pordea, 'Remarques sur l'efficacité de la protection des droits de l'homme', *Revue de droit international, de sciences diplomatiques et politiques*, July-Sept. 1954 (p. 262 et seq.) and Oct.-Dec. 1954 (p. 385 et seq.); 'Les juridictions des droits de l'homme', *Les juridictions internationales*, International Union of Lawyers, D. et S., 1958, p. 76.

[3] See K. Vasak, *Strasbourg Colloquy*, pp. 262–6 and op. cit., pp. 103–4.

[4] K. Vasak, *Strasbourg Colloquy*, p. 271 and op. cit., p. 104. The following solutions have been contemplated:
   (i)   adoption of the United Nations procedure;
   (ii) transformation of petitions into State applications under Article 24 of the Convention (Mr Rolin's proposal);
   (iii) organisation of arrangements for collective reference to the Commission by the Contracting Parties, on the lines of the system of Committees of three members used by the League of Nations for the protection of minorities;
   (iv) *ad hoc* recognition of the Commission's competence by the State concerned.

the Convention in the protection of human rights makes it desirable to adopt one of them in order to complete the machinery for 'public action' set up under the Convention.

5. *Fundamental role of the Commission and Court: Article 19 of the Convention*

The Commission's status, the conditions under which it may hear cases, the rules governing its competence and even procedural principles are of course dealt with in Section III of the Convention, just as the fundamental rules governing the status of the Court, the bringing of cases before it, its competence and procedure are to be found in Section IV; but it is in Article 19 that we find a definition of the role common to both the Commission and the Court. This is not merely to settle disputes arising in respect of rights guaranteed by the Convention; as stated in that Article, it is 'to ensure the observance of the engagements undertaken by the High Contracting Parties in the . . . Convention'.[1] The function of the Commission and its role in proceedings before the Court also show this is a matter of *ordre public*. At this stage the Commission represents the public interest in the first place. As Mr Rolin has written;

Proceedings may go forward before the Court at the initiative of the State cited before the Commission by one of its nationals, without there being any opposing party, since the victim has no access to the Court as a party, and the Commission itself, assuming it sends a representative, cannot be considered equivalent to a party *but rather fulfils the role of the Ministère public*.[2]

Sir Humphrey Waldock, President of the Commission, when presenting the Lawless case to the Court on its behalf himself characterised the Commission's role. He pointed out repeatedly that the Commission's duty was to defend the public interest: 'The High Contracting Parties . . . established both the Commission and the Court to *serve the common public purpose* of all the member States of the Council of Europe'.[3] He also said in the course of the same hearing 'the Commission does not pursue any interest of its own (before the Court) but the *public interest* of all the countries of the Council of Europe in the maintenance of human rights and freedoms'.[4]

Lastly, still on the same occasion:

[1] H. Rolin, 'Vers un *ordre public* . . .', p. 462.   [2] Loc. cit., p. 461.
[3] Sir Humphrey Waldock, President of the Commission, at the Court hearing of the *Lawless case* on 3 October 1960. See *Publications of the European Court of Human Rights*, Series B, Pleadings, Oral Arguments, Documents, 1960–61, p. 244 (my italics).
[4] Ibid., p. 245 (my italics).

... if the Commission considers the rights of the individual to have been violated, it is the Commission's duty to say so, in its Report, and to present that opinion to the Court. The Commission, however, does not understand its function before the Court to be to defend the interests of the individual as such. The Commission's function is that stated in Article 19, namely to ensure the observance of the engagements undertaken by the Contracting Parties in the Convention. . . .[1]

The idea that the Commission 'appears before the Court *to represent the public interest* with regard to human rights' by lodging 'a kind of appeal in the interests of the law, in this case the Convention' was also stated by Mr M.-A. Eissen in connection with the *Lawless case*.[2] He illustrates this particularly well by pointing out that there is nothing to prevent the Court from 'considering the Commission as a *"public" party* defending not some individual interest but *the general interest in the safeguarding of human rights*'. He also stresses that the use of the term 'party', which is not applied to the Commission, may have created confusion or ambiguity and that when the Commission 'intends to bring a case before the Court' it lodges, with the Registry of the Court, not an application but a 'request' which, unlike 'applications' by the Contracting Parties need not necessarily have a specific 'object'. Mr Eissen also points out that the Commission's Rules of Procedure do not oblige it to make final submissions before judgment is given, and he closes by saying that 'the role of the Commission is akin to that of the *Ministère public*, the *Commissaire du Gouvernement* or the *"amicus curiae"* of municipal law'.

Elsewhere Mr Eissen gives an acute analysis of the nature of the Commission's task before the Court:

since its duty, like that of the Court, is to ensure that the Convention is observed, the Commission need not present any special argument; on the contrary, its task is to assist the Court in a completely impartial manner, giving it the benefit of its own close knowledge of the case. It will frequently happen that it abides by the opinion expressed in its Report; if it thinks necessary, it may also refute or, inversely, support the thesis of a Government—whether respondent or applicant—or even depart from that thesis on a particular point and support it on another.[3]

---

[1] Ibid., p. 261.
[2] Ibid., and M.-A. Eissen, 'Le premier arrêt de la Cour européenne des Droits de l'Homme, Affaire Lawless: exceptions préliminaires et questions de procédure', *Annuaire Français*, 1960, pp. 458–9.
In his dissenting opinion appended to the Court's judgment Mr Maridakis describes the Court as a 'high supervisory authority set up to guarantee the European order established by the Convention' (*Yearbook*, III, p. 520).
[3] M.-A. Eissen, 'La Cour européenne des Droits de l'Homme, de la Convention au règlement', *Annuaire Français*, 1959, p. 652.

This, too, is equivalent to saying that the Commission, far from being a spokesman of the parties before the Court, plays the same role as that exercised by the *Ministère public* in the municipal law of certain countries, in relation to *ordre public*.

6. *Human rights before the Commission and Court: powers exercised ex officio*

(*a*) Once a matter has been brought before them neither the Commission nor the Court may defer to the parties in the matter of evidence and factual and legal arguments that may be advanced in support of the application or, more generally, the outcome of the application.

(*b*) The Commission claims the power, once an application has been referred to it, to examine whether it should not *ex officio* give consideration to a violation that the applicant may have omitted to mention. Alternatively it will consider that *in general*[1] examination of the case as it has been submitted does not disclose any appearance of a violation of any of the rights recognised in the Convention.[2] Again, if of its own accord it notes certain facts which may possibly involve a violation of the rights laid down in the Convention, the Commission satisfies itself *proprio motu* that there is no violation: 'the Commission will carry out this examination *ex officio* in order to determine whether the subject of the complaint falls, by its nature, within the scope of the Convention, even if the applicant does not rely on a specific Article of the Convention'.[3] This is shown even more characteristically by a decision given on 7 July 1959:[4]

whereas . . . (the Commission) has noted *ex officio* . . . the aggravation of the sentence passed on the applicant by the imposition of 'sleeping hard'; whereas, however, this additional sentence, which is applied once

---

[1] My italics.
[2] See in particular: App. No. 1028/61, *X against Belgium*, decision of 18 September 1961, *Yearbook*, IV, p. 338; App. No. 606/59, *X against Austria*, decision of 19 September 1961, *Yearbook*, IV, p. 344; App. No. 1134/61, *X against Belgium*, decision of 19 December 1961, *Yearbook*, IV, p. 382; App. No. 722/60, *X against Fed. Rep. of Germany*, decision of 6 March 1962, *Yearbook*, V, p. 106; App. No. 1103/61, *X against Belgium*, decision of 12 March 1962, *Yearbook*, V, p. 188; App. No. 1094/61, *X against Netherlands*, decision of 4 October 1962, *Yearbook*, V, p. 220; App. No 1211/61, *X against Netherlands*, decision of 4 October 1962, *Yearbook*, V, p. 226; App. No. 1527/62, X *against Austria*, decision of 4 October 1962, *Yearbook*, V, p. 244; App. No. 1068/62, *X against Netherlands*, decision of 14 December 1962, *Yearbook*, V, p. 284; App. No. 1802/63, *X against F. R. G.*, decision of 26 March 1963, *Collection of Decisions* No. 10, p. 39; App. No. 1793/63, *X against Austria*, decision of 22 July 1963, *Collection* No. 11, p. 30.
[3] *Yearbook*, II, p. 488.
[4] App. No. 462/59, X *against Austria*, *Yearbook*, II, p. 382.

every three months, is not, in view of the circumstances in which the applicant serves it, inhuman or degrading within the meaning of Article 3 of the Convention . . . the Commission declares the application inadmissible. . . .[1]

The Commission was set up to ensure that the Contracting Parties respected their obligations under the Convention and Protocol. It interprets this task of safeguarding human rights as implying that it has authority, in cases properly referred to it, *to examine the whole file ex officio and independently of any arguments presented by the applicant.* This *ex officio* examination is one of the fundamental rules of its jurisprudence.[2]

It examines *proprio motu* whether or not, in the case before it, there is a violation of the Convention, in order to determine whether the object of the application is such as to bring it within the scope of the Convention.[3]

(c) The Court, too, is entitled to consider all aspects of a case referred to it. The parties may not restrict its power to judge the matter. It will itself raise all aspects *ex officio.*

Mr Rolin, again, pointed this out in the following terms when referring during the Strasbourg Colloquy to the drafting of the Rules of Court:

It struck us, when drafting the Rules of the European Court of Human Rights, that even in connection with Rule 25 we were not confronted with a dispute between States having opposing interests, the sole interest at stake being acknowledged as a common one, identical with that of individuals. The Court thought that, since it was responsible for ensuring respect for human rights, once a violation of the Convention was referred to it, it should clear the matter up; whether the complaint was made by an individual or a State, it still concerned the Court.[4]

Here, too, we have the characteristics of *ordre public.*

(d) Discontinuance of a case, even if accepted, does not terminate the Court's power to consider it.[5] The Court 'shall, after having obtained the opinion of the Commission, decide whether or not it is appropriate to approve the discontinuance and accordingly to strike the case out of its list'.[6] Article 19 of the Convention places on it

---

[1] Ibid., p. 385. See also App. No. 261/57, *X against Fed Rep. of Germany,* decision of 16 December 1957, *Yearbook,* I, pp. 255–8 and App. No. 1237/61, *X against Austria,* decision of 5 March 1962, *Yearbook,* v, p. 100.

[2] *Yearbook,* I, p. 255. See also Doc. H. (57) 1, pp. 31–2.

[3] Commission, decision 28 September 1956, App. No. 202/56, *Yearbook,* I, p. 190; decision 16 December 1957, App. No. 261/57, *Yearbook,* I, p. 255.

[4] *Strasbourg Colloquy,* p. 297.

[5] Cf. International Court of Justice, *Rules of Court,* Articles 68 and 69; Court of Justice of the European Communities, *Rules of Procedure,* Articles 77 and 78. See also Article 69 (4).

[6] *Rules of the European Court of Human Rights,* Rule 47 (1).

certain peculiar duties independent of its strictly jurisdictional function of settling disputes. This is explicitly stated in Rule 47 (2) of the Rules of Court:

The Chamber may, having regard to the responsibilities of the Court in pursuance of Article 19 of the Convention, decide that, notwithstanding the notice of discontinuance, it should proceed with the consideration of the case.

(e) These rules seem to us to be necessarily determined by the preeminent character of the rights guaranteed in international and municipal law by the Convention and First and Fourth Protocols. This pre-eminence is equivalent to *ordre public*.

(f) The proceedings in the De Becker case highlighted this situation. The conclusions of both the Commission and the respondent Party, although differently formulated, both asked that the case be struck off the list, although there had been no friendly settlement and no discontinuance, which can only be effected by the applicant.[1] The Court pointed out that De Becker's declaration was no more binding on it than on the Commission. In its judgment it satisfied itself 'as to whether there are any grounds, such as might . . . jeopardise the observance of the human rights set forth in the Convention, oppose the removal of the case from the list or oblige the Court to decide . . . *to proceed with the consideration of the case ex officio* notwithstanding the latest submissions of the Belgian Government and the Commission'.[2]

(g) Withdrawal of an application before the Commission is subject to the same principles.

In the case of *Greece against the United Kingdom* (App. No. 299/57) in which, following conclusion of the Zurich and London Agreements, both parties asked the Commission to terminate proceedings without taking a decision on the merits, the Commission replied that 'under Article 19 of the Convention it had been set up to ensure the observance of the engagements undertaken by the High Contracting Parties in the Convention'. This being so, the Commission added:

when an Application alleging a breach of the Convention had been referred to the Commission, the withdrawal of the Application was a matter which concerned the Commission as well as the Parties and Commission must satisfy itself that the termination of the proceedings was calculated to serve, and not to defeat, the purposes of the Convention.[3]

[1] *Rules of Court*, Rule 47.
[2] European Court of Human Rights, 27 March 1962, *Yearbook*, v, p. 332. K. Vasak points out that this solution, which is concerned with the Court's duty of supervision under Article 19, is in harmony with the spirit of the Convention; op. cit., No. 350, p. 184.
[3] Summary of decision, *Yearbook*, II, p. 178.

7. *The Committee of Ministers*

The Convention also provides for other jurisdictional arrangements: the competence exercised by the Committee of Ministers under Article 32.[1]

If a case is not referred to the Court, either by the Commission or by one of the High Contracting Parties, within the period stipulated in Article 32, it is for the Committee of Ministers to decide whether or not there has been a violation of the Convention. The consequences of such a decision are laid down in paragraphs 2 and 3 of Article 32. In paragraph 4 the Contracting Parties undertake to regard the Committee's decision as binding on them.

The fact that the decision is taken by the Committee of Ministers 'by a majority of two-thirds of the members entitled to sit on the Committee',[2] rather than by the Court after a reference to it under Article 48, does not in principle affect the nature, as part of *ordre public*, of the right protected by the Convention. But in fact we are bound to acknowledge that the Committee of Ministers, although it is in this case a jurisdictional organ, is by reason of its composition less independent of considerations of political expediency than is the Court. There are serious grounds for thinking that it was indeed with the aim of bringing into the system an additional element of political expediency that a jurisdictional organ with an essentially political composition, giving its decisions by qualified majority, was set up side by side with the Court. It encourages the taking of political decisions on questions which, forming part of *ordre public*, should in principle receive solutions dictated by legal considerations.

8. *Declarations of recognition of the Commission's competence to examine individual applications (Art. 25). Declarations recognising the compulsory jurisdiction of the Court* (Art. 46)

(*a*) But the fact that a rule is of the nature of *ordre public* is not sufficient to ensure that rights guaranteed in principle are effectively safeguarded always and in all circumstances; the consequences which in municipal law flow from rules of *ordre public*, as a result of their mandatory nature, do not occur here either generally or directly.

(*b*) This is because the question before us lies at the meeting-point of international and municipal public law. What we are considering is whether the legal rules laid down in the Convention have the force of *ordre public* in *municipal law*. Neither in municipal

---

[1] See the analysis of the system of settlement by the Committee of Ministers in K. Vasak, op. cit., No. 389–408, pp. 202 et seq.; see also H. Golsong 'Control Machinery of the European Convention', in "The European Convention on Human Rights", *Int. & Comp. Law Quarterly*, 1965, pp. 66 et seq.

[2] *Convention*, Article 32 (1).

law nor in private or public international law does *ordre public* at present encounter the same difficulties as regards the consequences that naturally follow from it.

(c) International agreements may alter, reduce or even do away with the consequences attaching in municipal law to rules of *ordre public*. This will occur to the extent to which conventional rules of international law withdraw the matter of *ordre public* from its normal consequences under municipal law. It is not enough that the Convention should have been ratified for the jurisdictional guarantees laid down in it to take effect. Its operation is subject to exceptions and reservations. This has direct repercussions on the consequences that flow in law from matters of *ordre public*. To some extent such consequences are prevented from taking effect in municipal law, despite the fact that a matter of *ordre public* is affected.

(d) For the Convention does not lay down any absolute system of protection. Since it was thought that not all the Contracting Parties were ready to submit to such a radical solution 'safety devices' were introduced. The consequences resulting from those rules for the protection of human rights that are directly applicable and enshrined in the Convention cannot occur unless the Contracting Parties have taken the initiative of making an express declaration.

(e) Article 25 provides that the Commission may not deal with individual applications unless 'the High Contracting Party against which the complaint has been lodged has declared that it recognises the competence of the Commission to receive such petitions'; if this condition is complied with, the Contracting Parties 'undertake not to hinder in any way the effective exercise of this right'.[1]

(f) Article 46 lays down a system of optional declarations by the High Contracting Parties accepting the Court's compulsory jurisdiction; they may be made unconditionally or on condition of reciprocity.[2]

9. *Reservations*

Lastly, the Convention allows the Contracting States to make reservations with regard to particular provisions of the Convention, based on some law in force in their own territory.[3] The States in question may thus escape the collective enforcement of human rights. The Commission's view is that a reservation covers legislative and administrative measures directly concerned with the matter.[4]

[1] *Convention*, Article 25 (1).
[2] *Convention*, Article 46 (1) and (2); see also Article 6 (2) of 4th Protocol.
[3] *Convention*, Art. 64.
[4] Application No. 473/59, Decision 29 August 1959, *Yearbook*, II, p. 400; Application No. 1047/61, Decision 15 December 1961, *Yearbook*, IV p. 356; both quoted by Vasak, op. cit., p. 69, n. 116.

10. *Consequences of the dual system of declarations and reservations*

Although, in principle, adoption of the Convention by the Contracting States means that they 'will not avail themselves of treaties, conventions or declarations in force between them for the purpose of submitting, *by way of petition*, a dispute arising out of the interpretation or application of (the) Convention to a means of settlement other than those provided for. . . .',[1] it follows that they still have three ways by which—admittedly in varying degrees and at different levels—they may avoid implementation of the system of collective enforcement set up by the Convention and prevent it from having the effects appropriate in municipal law to matters of *ordre public*.

11. *Exceptions to and restrictions on the system of protection of the rights laid down in the Convention and in its 1st and 4th Protocols*

(*a*) The Convention has also made provision for derogations from the system of guarantee which it establishes, based on the circumstances or conditions attending the actions or rights subject to protection.

(*b*) Most of the articles in Section 1 of the Convention are subject to very carefully worded exceptions or restrictions, which limit the field of operation for the guarantee of the rights stated.

(*c*) While no derogation is possible to the prohibition of 'torture' or 'inhuman or degrading treatment or punishment' (Convention, Art. 3) or of 'slavery' or 'servitude' (Convention, Art. 4 par. 1) *exceptions* are laid down in respect of the prohibition of 'forced or compulsory labour' (Art. 4 pars. 2 and 3). There are also exceptions to the prohibition of deprivation of liberty (Art. 5 par. 1 (*a*)–(*f*)), to the principle that offences and penalties may not be made retrospective (Art. 7) and to the 'peaceful enjoyment' of possessions (First Protocol, Art. 1).

(*d*) Other rights are accompanied by restrictive clauses.[2] This is true of Article 6 of the Convention concerning the public nature of civil and criminal proceedings; Article 8, concerning respect for private and family life, home and correspondence; Article 9, concerning freedom of thought, conscience and religion; Article 10, concerning freedom of expression; Article 11, concerning freedom of

---

[1] *Convention*, Article 62. This undertaking applies 'except by *special agreement*'. The Article thus leaves available to the High Contracting Parties the means of settlement under international law listed in Article 33 of the Charter of the *United Nations*. See further below and K. Vasak, op. cit., No. 392, p. 205.

[2] See M. Neumann, 'Les droits garantis par la Convention européenne des Droits de l'Homme, Etude des limitations de ces droits', *Strasbourg Colloquy*, pp. 143 et seq. The writer refers to the jurisprudence of the French *Conseil d'Etat* on *détournement de pouvoir*, the theory of special powers in war-time or in exceptional circumstances.

assembly and association; Article 2 of the 4th Protocol, concerning the right to liberty of movement and free choice of residence. Each of these restrictions invokes the idea of necessity. The restriction may not exceed what is considered 'strictly necessary in a democratic society' to achieve the aims of public concern clearly set out in each article.

These aims are: the public and general interest (1st Protocol, Art. 1); the interests of juveniles, the protection of private life and the interests of justice (Convention, Art. 6); territorial integrity (Convention, Art. 10); national security (Convention, Arts. 6, 8 and 10, 4th Protocol, Art. 2); public safety (Convention, Arts. 8, 9, 10, 11, 4th Protocol, Art. 2); the protection of health or morals (Convention, Arts. 6, 8, 9, 10, 11, 4th Protocol, Art. 2); the protection of the reputation, rights and freedoms of others (Convention, Arts. 8, 9, 10, 11, 4th Protocol, Art. 2); prevention of the disclosure of information received in confidence, maintenance of the authority and impartiality of the judiciary (Convention, Art. 10); and even that variable and imprecise concept: the economic well-being of the country (Convention, Art. 8).

(e) The system involves an examination of objectives on the part of the Commission and the Court. It does not entail any compromise on the right itself; the restrictions, like the exceptions, exclude the specific matter from the system of collective guarantee; their applicability depends on an element of intention. It therefore remains compatible with the character, as part of *ordre public*, of a rule protecting a right as determined both in the actual statement of it and in the qualifications such as might accompany it in municipal law.

(f) It is only within the fundamental limits laid down in the Convention and in the First and Fourth Protocols and in any reservations made by a High Contracting Party that the national court will deduce the consequences that should follow from the fact that a rule forms part of *ordre public*.

12. *War or other public emergencies threatening the life of the nation*

(a) Lastly, Article 15 of the Convention lays down a fairly general right of derogation from a State's obligations in time of 'war or other public emergency threatening the life of the nation . . . *to the extent strictly required by the exigencies of the situation*', provided that the measures taken by the State 'are not inconsistent with its other obligations under international law'.[1]

[1] Under Article 15 (2) no derogation may be made from the exercise of the rights laid down in 'Article 2, except in respect of deaths resulting from lawful acts of war, or from Articles 3, 4 (paragraph 1) and 7'.

(*b*) It is necessity that justifies derogation, just as it governs the restrictions that may be placed on Articles 8, 9, 10 and 11 of the Convention. The idea of 'exigency' or necessity is explicitly stated in each of those articles.

(*c*) Even in such exceptional circumstances, as Mr J. Velu has pointed out,[1] there is no *suspension* of the Convention. The State remains bound and subject to the supervision of the Commission, the Court and the Committee of Ministers. The fact of necessity in itself does not authorise the exercise of the right when there is a danger to the nation's *ordre public*. It is clear that 'measures derogating from the obligations laid down in the Convention must, under Article 15, comply with certain strict conditions'.[2]

(*d*) The *travaux préparatoires* show that the formulation of Article 15 is almost word for word that of the article in the draft International Covenant on Human Rights prepared by the United Nations Commission of Human Rights in 1949. It was adopted very quickly with hardly any discussion.[3]

(*e*) So far only three States have availed themselves of the right of derogation provided for in Article 15: The United Kingdom, which in 1953 extended the Convention to 42 territories, has informed the Secretary-General of the Council of Europe in various *notes verbales* that in certain of those territories it was taking measures derogating from its obligations under the Convention.[4] In July 1957 Ireland took measures of derogation which it revoked in March 1962.[5] The Turkish Government which came into power as a result of the revolutionary movement on 27 May 1960 took measures of derogation which it revoked in December 1961.[6] It gave notice of the measures adopted on 31 May 1963, which have since been extended.[7]

In every case the *note verbale* informing the Secretary-General of the Council of Europe of the measures taken in derogation of the Convention stressed that the reason for them was to guarantee 'public safety and the maintenance of public order'. On each occasion

[1] J. Velu, 'Le contrôle des organes prévus par la Convention de Sauvegarde sur les mesures d'exception y dérogeant', *Mélanges offerts à Henri Rolin*, 1964, pp. 462 et seq.

[2] K. Vasak, op. cit., p. 70.

[3] Statement by Mr Rolin on the occasion of the report presented by Sir David Maxwell Fyfe, on behalf of the Committee on Legal and Administrative Questions, on the draft Convention on the Protection of Human Rights and Fundamental Freedoms.

[4] See *Yearbook*, I, pp. 48–51; *Yearbook*, II, pp. 78–86; *Yearbook*, III, pp. 68–90; *Yearbook*, IV, pp. 38–54; *Yearbook*, V, pp. 8–10.

[5] See *Yearbook*, I; pp. 47–8; *Yearbook*, V, p. 6.   [6] *Yearbook*, IV, pp. 54–62.

[7] According to K. Vasak, op. cit., 1964, p. 70, the last extension was on 22 February 1964.

they were taken in a political context which was obviously and seriously disturbed.

(*f*) The right of derogation provided for in Article 15 was invoked in two important cases: the *Lawless Case* and one of the cases between Greece and the United Kingdom relating to Cyprus.[1]

In the *Lawless Case* the Court decided that the conditions laid down in Article 15 had been observed, that the Irish Government was justified in declaring that there was in fact a public emergency threatening *ordre public* in the nation, and that there had therefore been no violation of the Convention.[2] The terms in which it described the situation with regard to the derogation under Article 15 of the Convention are noteworthy.[3] They deserve to be quoted as part of the present reasoning:

Whereas, in the general context of Article 15 of the Convention, the natural and customary meaning of the words 'other public emergency threatening the life of the nation' is sufficiently clear; whereas they refer to an *exceptional situation of crisis or emergency which affects the whole population and constitutes a threat to the organised life of the community of which the State is composed.*

(*g*) Both the *travaux préparatoires* of the Convention and the jurisprudence of the Commission and Court show that Article 15 translates into international terms the 'state of necessity'[4] which is accepted in municipal public law as justifying suspension of the exercise of basic rights.[5] The element of *ordre public* in rules of law suspended during a period in which the operation of institutions is impaired or paralysed by reason of acts of war or other circumstances

---

[1] *Lawless Case*: See App. No. 332/57, *Lawless against Ireland*, Commission's decision of 30 August 1958, *Yearbook*, II, p. 308. In its Report adopted on 19 December 1960 the Commission expressed the view that the measures of admini strative internment taken against Lawless could be justified by reference to Article 15. *Greece against United Kingdom*: See App. No. 176/56, *Yearbook*, I, p. 128; summary of the Commission's decision of 2 June 1956, *Yearbook*, II, p. 174; text of the decision, pp. 182–6. Neither the Committee of Ministers nor the Court had to take a decision, since a political solution was found to the Cyprus case (see *Yearbook*, II, pp. 174–8).

[2] Judgment 1 July 1964, *Yearbook*, IV, p. 438; see especially pp. 472–4.

[3] See also App. No. 493/59, *X against Ireland*, Commission's decision of 27 July 1961, *Yearbook*, IV, p. 302 and *Collection of Decisions* No. 7, p. 85, and the references to Article 15 in the De Becker judgment, *Yearbook*, V, pp. 320 et seq., especially p. 326.

[4] On the state of necessity in public international law see P. Grapin, *Valeur internationale des principes généraux du droit*, Thèse, Paris, 1934, p. 118.

[5] See W. J. Ganshof van der Meersch, 'Les états d'exception et la Constitution belge', *Annales de droit et de science politique*, Louvain, t. XIII, 1953, pp. 49 et seq.; idem, 'Sécurité de l'État et Liberté individuelle en droit comparé', *Rapports Généraux, Congrès international droit comp.*, Brussels, 1960, pp. 593 et seq.

jeopardising the life of the nation is not affected by this exceptional situation. The criteria for such a situation being determined by *force majeure* which may impair the working of institutions, just as in private law it paralyses intentions,[1] are very strictly formulated.

13. *Friendly settlement*

(*a*) Article 28 of the Convention provides that 'in the event of the Commission accepting a petition referred to it . . . it shall place itself at the disposal of the Parties concerned with a view to securing a friendly settlement of the matter. . . .'.

The Court may only deal with a case after the Commission has acknowledged the failure of efforts for a friendly settlement.[2] The Commission is obliged to attempt to reach a settlement. Acknowledgement of the failure of its efforts is one condition of the admissibility of any application before the Court, whether submitted by the Commission or by one of the High Contracting Parties.

(*b*) If the attempt is successful, the Court can no longer properly deal with the case. The Sub-Commission, whose duty it is under Article 29 of the Convention to try to effect a friendly settlement, draws up a report on its efforts; the report is transmitted to the States concerned, the Committee of Ministers and the Secretary General.[3] This constitutes a 'settlement'. It is final. The case is closed as far as the Commission is concerned. It cannot be submitted to the Court.[4]

(*c*) In the case of failure of an attempt at a settlement, the Commission transmits to the Committee of Ministers a report, the purpose of which is defined in Article 31 of the Convention. The report is also transmitted to the States concerned, who are not at liberty to publish it. It appears that the intention was to give the Committee itself the opportunity to make a final effort at conciliation.[5]

---

[1] W. J. Ganshof van der Meersch, 'La sécurité de l'État et les libertés individuelles en droit belge', *Revue de droit international et de droit comparé*, 1958, p. 336.

[2] *Convention*, Art. 47.

[3] Article 2 of the 3rd Protocol, signed at Strasbourg on 6 May 1963, substitutes the Commission for the Sub-Commission in the performance of this duty. The Protocol will only come into force when all States parties to the Convention are parties to the Protocol, in accordance with its Article 4 (1).

[4] In theory does a friendly settlement deprive a person 'whose rights and freedoms are set forth in (the) Convention are violated' of 'an effective remedy before a national authority' as provided in Article 13 of the Convention? Not in our opinion. As we have said, Article 13 is not applicable directly. It is an obligation assumed by the High Contracting Parties; it is for them to establish the principle and procedure in their municipal legislation. But applicants, like respondent States, will be wise not to lose sight of the right embodied in Article 13 when they agree to a 'friendly settlement'.

[5] See Convention on Human Rights, *Manual*, published by the Council of

(d) There is no doubt, as Mr Vasak writes, that the authors of the Convention attached great importance[1] to this effort at a 'friendly settlement', with which several articles in the Convention are concerned.[2] In view of the place of the friendly settlement in the overall system of protection, the question arises what is the extent of the Sub-Commission's powers in this connection, and what is the nature of the decision which may be taken.

(e) One observation appears imperative: the philosophy underlying the Convention, which is not a mere declaration of rights but seeks to provide protection which should have the character of 'maintenance' and even of 'the further realisation' of 'those fundamental freedoms which are the foundation of justice and peace in the world',[3] provides no justification for a compromise, which by definition involves some measure of sacrificing the said rights and freedoms.

(f) The text of Article 28 (b) calls for a second observation: it strictly limits the nature of the settlement, which is of course to be 'friendly' but must be based on 'respect for human rights as defined in (the) Convention'. The object in view here is *respect* for the said rights. Such a settlement is irreconcilable with any compromise on the fundamental right itself. The Commission cannot associate itself with any compromise on the principle of a violation of one of the rights stated in the Convention.

(g) Of course reference has frequently been made to the Commission's task of *conciliation*,[4] but even if the term is to be accepted, agreement must still be reached on the object of the task.

In the case of an individual application more especially, if the applicant shows that a subjective right has been violated, the conciliation will bear on the question of compensation; the object of the attempt at a friendly settlement will be to fix damages. As Mr Dupuy writes, the matter in dispute will be the reparation.[5] It is true that the applicant's right to respect for objective legality may also be at stake. In this case, too, the applicant must be a 'victim' of

---

Europe, June 1963, p. 130. It should be noted, however, that neither the Convention nor the Rules of Procedure of the Commission contain any reference to a friendly settlement *by the Committee of Ministers*. The question also arises whether the Committee could validly 'effect' a settlement in this context that was not in accordance with the specific conditions laid down in Article 28 (b) of the Convention.

[1] Vasak, op. cit., p. 137. [2] *Convention*, Arts. 28, 29, 30, 31 and 47.
[3] *Preamble to the Convention*.
[4] E.g. Dupuy, op. cit., p. 751. At the Conference of Senior Officials, Professor Chaumont spoke on the nature of conciliation: 'Conciliation means any action not motivated by exclusively legal considerations'.
[5] Op. cit., p. 471.

the action, though not necessarily a direct one.[1] There are no grounds for thinking, either here or in an inter-State case, that 'conciliation' can relate to the right itself, that is to say to its substance.

(*h*) But is the question here even one of an attempt at conciliation in the strict sense? We do not think so. In the course of their preliminary work the Committee of Experts preferred to replace the French term *conciliation* by *règlement amiable*, since 'this first term is used primarily in the case of disputes between States, whereas the Commission is equally concerned with disputes between States and individuals'. Moreover, the procedure of 'international conciliation' has political aspects which are quite different from the procedure of friendly settlement provided for under Article 28 of the Convention.[2]

The scope of the 'friendly settlement' procedure was only mentioned and defined with any precision at the meeting of Senior Officials which followed that of the Committee of Experts. Moreover, it was not until that stage that the expression 'règlement amiable' gained acceptance in preference to 'conciliation' and 'solution amiable', which were rejected.[3]

(*i*) In its report to the Committee of Ministers in March 1950, the Committee of Experts noted that, in the opinion of some of its members:

the Convention provides for a minimum standard of protection of human rights. If the protection accorded by a State is found by the Commission to be below that standard, there is clearly a violation of the Convention. It seemed to them that, in such circumstances, it is inappropriate to introduce the notion of conciliation. A denial of the enjoyments of human rights could not be rectified by a process of compromise. The other experts considered, however, that even in the case of a violation of the Convention, it might be possible to effect a friendly settlement, even if it was only to determine the total of compensation to be accorded to the

---

[1] See Comm. 30 May 1956, *Yearbook*, I, No. 113; 31 May 1956, p. 162, No 100 29 September 1965, ibid., p. 163, No. 155; 16 December 1957, ibid., p. 164, No; 282. For the interpretation of the term 'victim', see above Section 3.

[2] On international conciliation see in particular H. Rolin, 'Une conciliation belgo-danoise', *Revue Générale de Droit International Public*, 1953, pp. 351–71; idem, 'L'heure de la conciliation comme mode de règlement pacifique des litiges', *European Yearbook*, vol. III, p. 3; A. Gros, 'Remarques sur la conciliation intergnatonale', *L'évolution du droit public, Études en l'honneur d'A. Mestre*, pp. 279–84.

[3] 'Reconciliation' by a 'Committee of enquiry' was proposed by H. Rolin at the first Session of the Consultative Assembly in September 1949. It appears that the object of his proposal was to set up a conciliation body of the traditional kind, especially since at that time he was stronly opposed to the establishment. of a European Court.

victim. These members therefore wished to maintain the provisions . . . if the European Court were not created.

Thus, at that stage, a friendly settlement procedure was advocated, free from any compromise on the right itself, and solely in case the Court was not established by the Convention.

It was clear to the Senior Officials that no compromise on the right itself was acceptable. A drafting Sub-committee prepared a draft article based on the text adopted by the United Nations Commission on Human Rights, laying down a similar procedure. Both texts provide that no 'friendly solution' can be adopted that is not 'based on respect for human rights', which clearly seems to exclude any compromise on the right itself.

The Commission cannot, without contravening the Convention and failing in its mission, give its agreement to any solution which would leave untouched a remediable but unremedied violation of one of the rights which it is the Convention's object to safeguard. *A friendly settlement can only be concerned with the reparation for the consequences of violation, more especially with compensation, not with the right itself.*[1]

(*j*) Any friendly settlement that may still be reached after the Commission has referred a case to the Court must be based on the same principle and remains subject to the same principle and remains subject to the same limitation. Under Rule 47 (3) of the Rules of Court the case *may* be struck off the Court's list only if the settlement satisfies the conditions of Article 28 of the Convention.[2] What has been said about discontinuance[3] also applies to a friendly settlement of this kind.

(*k*) Since a friendly settlement does not relate to the substance of the right itself, which it is the object of the Convention to protect, we see nothing in the principle embodied in Article 28 that conflicts with our view that this is a matter of *ordre public*.

(*l*) So far as we know, the Commission has so far only once brought about a friendly settlement. In the *Boeckmans case*[4] the Applicant concluded in his original application that Belgium should 'agree, be invited and, if necessary, obliged to afford the Applicant

---

[1] See also W. Vis, 'La réparation des violations de la Convention européenne des Droits de l'Homme' *Strasbourg Colloquy*, 1961, p. 280.

[2] K. Vasak writes that 'this solution to the action constitutes in fact a form of discontinuance brought about by the Commission' (op. cit., p. 182).

[3] See above Section 6; European Court of Human Rights, *De Becker case*, 27 March 1962, *Yearbook*, v, p. 332.

[4] App. No. 1727/62, *Yearbook*, vi, p. 370; see the Commission's decision on the admissibility of the application, 29 October 1962, *Collection of Decisions*, No. 12, April 1964, p. 29.

just satisfaction if (the) internal law (of Belgium) allows only partial reparation to be made for the consequences of decisions declared void'.[1] The Sub-Commission's report on the friendly settlement was adopted on the 17 February 1965. After noting that 'remarks made about the Applicant by the Presiding Judge of the 14th Chamber of the Court of Appeal of Brussels at the hearing on 24 February 1962 were such as to disturb the calm of the proceedings in a manner incompatible with the Convention and might have caused moral prejudice to the Applicant', but that *under Belgian municipal law the validity of the Applicant's conviction cannot be questioned, it having been final since rejection by the Court of Cassation on 6 June 1962 of his petition* against the judgment by his appeal of 24 March 1962',[2] the Sub-Commission approved a settlement involving the payment of damages on which the Applicant and the Respondent State had agreed. A sum of 65,000 Belgian francs was considered adequate compensation for the prejudice suffered.

There was not, nor could there be, any settlement with regard to the right itself.

The fact that the Sub-Commission noted, on the one hand, that the Belgian judicial authorities had acted 'in a manner incompatible with the Convention', but on the other that 'under Belgian municipal law the validity of the Applicant's conviction cannot be questioned', left the question of the merits of the right violated outside the settlement, which was concerned with the conditions and amount of compensation.

(*m*) The text of the friendly settlement adopted on 17 February 1965 shows how difficult it is to set a limit to the direct applicability of the Convention; it will be for the Court's jurisprudence to state such a limit. In the case in question the Commission—in our view rightly—accepted the fact that under Belgian law the rejection of the appeal to the Court of Cassation was final.

The Commission appears to have based itself on the principle stated in Article 50 of the Convention that:

if the Court finds that a decision or a measure taken by a legal authority ... of a High Contracting Party is completely or partially in conflict with the obligations arising from the ... Convention, and *if the internal law of the said Party allows only partial reparation to be made for the consequences of this decision or measure*, the decision of the Court shall, if necessary, afford just satisfaction to the injured party.

14. *Article 62 of the Convention*

(*a*) As we have seen, the Convention permits the High Contracting Parties in certain circumstances to adopt a different procedure for

[1] *Collection of Decisions*, No. 15, p. 65.   [2] Ibid., p. 66. My italics.

the purposes of settlement of a given dispute from the system of safeguards laid down in the Convention. Article 62 provides that the Contracting Parties 'will not avail themselves of treaties, conventions or declarations in force between them for the purpose of submitting, by way of petition, a dispute arising out of the interpretation or application of (the) Convention to a means of settlement other than those provided for in (the) Convention'; the Article however stipulates that exceptions may be made to this 'by special agreement', which leaves open to the Contracting Parties, the methods of general international law listed in Article 33 of the Charter of the United Nations, if an agreement between them to this effect was in force at the time the Convention was signed. These methods include mediation, conciliation and arbitration.

(b) Of course, when a State submits an application to the Commission, it expresses an intention and chooses a method of settlement, in the same way as when a case is referred to the Court, and from that moment a compromise can no longer enable the State to evade the consequences of its choice,[1] a fact which considerably reduces the possibilities of agreement. Nevertheless, one effect of Article 62 is that, as the result of a *special agreement*, the Contracting Parties may, if bound by an earlier treaty, convention or declaration, submit a specific dispute arising out of the interpretation or application of the Convention to a means of settlement different from that provided for in the Convention.

(c) It will be observed that the arrangements laid down in Article 62 do not entail abandonment of the right itself; existing agreements among the Contracting Parties—treaties, conventions, or declarations—may, within the limits described above, differ as to procedure from the system laid down in the Convention; they may also differ from it in respect of the *exercise* of the right.[2] The possibility of resorting to some other system for the settlement of a dispute arising out of the interpretation or application of the Convention, in the event of a special agreement as laid down in Article 62, does not in any circumstances make it possible to renounce the right itself. Any purported renunciation of one of the rights stated in and protected by the Convention would be unlawful.

'There are some qualities that are so inherent in the natural or legal personality of private citizens', writes Professor Dabin, 'that they cannot be renounced without considerable damage to that

---

[1] K. Vasak, op. cit., No. 392–4, pp. 204 and 205.

[2] For the distinction between renunciation of the right and renunciation of its exercise, see below Section 15 *in fine* and, more particularly, the last footnotes in that section.

personality'.[1] These 'qualities' are identical with fundamental human rights. It is not for the individual to dispose of them.

(*d*) The clause must enable the signatory States to observe the rule *pacta sunt servanda*, but one cannot escape the fact that the exception permitted is difficult to reconcile with the element of *ordre public* in the subject. Even if, in municipal law, the parties can validly renounce their prerogatives under a mandatory enactment intended to protect private interests, at least after it has become effective, they cannot abandon their rights under a mandatory law affecting *ordre public*.[2] But, as Professor Bakaert writes, 'when one looks for what is common to all varieties of *ordre public*, one finds that it is *the will of the legislative authority that it alone shall regulate a given situation*'.[3]

Does this not also mean that the legislative power, which remains supreme, can exempt a procedure of *ordre public* from all the consequences that normally follow from it, without thus vitiating its very character? It seems that we must admit this.

(*e*) The municipal law of several States has sometimes departed from the absolute character of the principles of *ordre public*.

This is the case where public action against certain offences—generally minor ones—can be avoided by immediate or deferred payment of a certain sum of money. Nevertheless, here as elsewhere, the taking of public action is indisputably governed by *ordre public*. There has been a considerable spread of the *oblation volontaire* and *amende de composition* in French criminal law.[4] A *décret-loi* of 28 December 1926, made under the Finance Act of 3 August 1926, which empowered the Government to make all desirable economies by decree, gave them a place in the legislation on traffic offences.

This measure was extended to other categories of offences.[5] There followed the *amende de composition* paid on proposal of the

[1] 'Autonomie de la volonté et lois impératives, ordre public et bonnes mœurs, sanction de la dérogation aux lois, en droit privé interne', *Annales de droit et de sciences politiques*, vol. VIII, no. 34, April 1940, p. 235.

[2] See note by G. Bacteman, on a judgment given by the Belgian Court of Cassation on 6 December 1956 (*Pasicrisie*, 1957, 1, p. 361) in *Revue critique de jurisprudence belge*, 1960, p. 160.

[3] H. Bakaert, *Introduction à l'étude du droit*, Brussels, 1964, p. 200.

[4] See R. Legeais, 'L'oblation volontaire et l'amende de composition', *Rev. int. dr. pénal*, 1962, p. 449.

[5] Railway offences, decree of 30 June 1934 and 30 October 1935; offences against the public transport regulations, decree of 30 October 1935; offences relating to navigable waterways and seaports, decree of 30 October 1935; offences against transport co-ordination, decree of 11 April 1936. See also *ordonnance* of 5 May 1945 and Act of 17 August 1950 on offences against the public passenger transport regulations and Article 27 of the Highway Code (*ordonnance* 15 December 1958).

K

court.[1] The practice has spread and has been incorporated into the Code of Criminal Procedure.[2]

The *oblation volontaire* procedure, like that of the *amende de composition*, contains an element of compromise; the offender must give his agreement to the decision. Article 1 of the Act of 7 August 1950 states this with the utmost clarity by providing that

> where notice of prosecution has been served in respect of an offence subject to a fine . . . the officer serving the notice and the offender may, *on the initiative* of one of them and provided that judgment has not been passed on the facts of the case . . . come to an *agreement* as provided in Article 2.[3]

The 'compromise' procedure was introduced into Belgian criminal law by the Criminal Code,[4] without its being confined to particular categories of offences.[5] It may be proposed and applied for any offence 'punishable by a fine, by a term of imprisonment not exceeding 1 month or by either of these sentences'.[6] An Act of 30 December 1957 extended the availability of this procedure, in particular, to 'all cases in which the maximum term of imprisonment provided by law does not exceed three months' where 'the offender has never received a criminal sentence or been sentenced unconditionally to a term of correctional imprisonment'.[7] An Act of 15 April 1964 amending the Haulage Act of 1st August 1899 enables certain officials and agents to receive a specified sum immediately, *subject to the agreement* of the person committing the offence; this has the effect of extinguishing the possibility of prosecution.[8]

A system of 'voluntary settlement' or 'composition' has been introduced in various forms in the criminal law of most States, either for relatively minor offences or for particular categories of offences.[9]

[1] *Ordonnance* of 2 November 1945.

[2] *Livre II*, titre troisième, Chapitre II, Articles 524–30. Article 528 (5) excludes certain subjects from its operation.

[3] With regard to the criminal law in the Netherlands see *Wetboek van Strafrecht*, Article 74.

[4] The Act of 26 August 1822 introduced it for prosecutions in customs and excise matters.

[5] *Code pénal*, Articles 166, 167, 168, 180 and 180 bis.

[6] See de Cant, 'La procédure "transactionnelle" en droit pénal belge', *Rev. int. dr. pén.*, 1962, p. 243.

[7] Act of 30 December 1957 amending Article 180 of the Criminal Code. The *Parquet* may propose the '*transaction*' procedure only in cases in which it sees fit to demand, and cannot legally demand more than, a fine or a fine with confiscation.

[8] Act of 15 April 1964, Art. 9, *Moniteur belge*, 15 May 1965.

[9] See *Rev. int. dr. pén.*, 1962, Nos. 3 and 4; for studies on the procedure under French and Belgian law mentioned in the above notes and also in the Federal Republic of Germany, Italy, the Netherlands, Poland, Sweden, Switzerland and

(*f*) In this way the individual will is by legislation left free to act in a matter which, however, is essentially a procedure of *ordre public*. Nevertheless, it would not occur to anyone to dispute that criminal prosecution was a matter of *ordre public*.

The Act in municipal law, like the treaty in international law—we have in mind here Article 62 of the Convention—thus derogates, though subject to very strict conditions, in favour of the individual will from the mandatory character which is generally inherent in proceedings affecting *ordre public*.

15. *Article 6, par. 1 of the Convention and arbitration clauses*

(*a*) The question of an agreement not to take advantage of the system laid down by the Convention has arisen outside the scope of Article 62. The Commission has had occasion to consider whether the provision of Article 6 para. 1, guaranteeing a public hearing by an independent tribunal is incompatible with an arbitration clause.

(*b*) This question was the subject of a decision on 5 March 1962[1] in which the Commission, after saying that it was not concerned to ensure observation of the municipal legislation of States (it was a question of labour legislation) except in so far as an infringement might involve a violation of the rights and freedoms protected by the Convention, added:

... *whereas the inclusion of an arbitration clause in an agreement between individuals amounts legally to partial renunciation of the exercise of those rights defined by Article 6* (2); whereas nothing in the text of that Article nor of any other Article of the Convention explicitly prohibits such renunciation; whereas the Commission is not entitled to assume that the Contracting States, in accepting the obligations arising under Article 6 (2), intended to prevent persons coming under their jurisdiction from entrusting the settlement of certain matters to arbitrators. . . .[2]

In this decision, which is, as may be seen, of considerable interest, three rules are stated:

(1) The Commission, which like the Court has the task of ensuring 'the observance of the engagements undertaken by the High Contracting Parties in the . . . Convention' (Art. 19), looks at the *legislation* of the States parties to the Convention; it is concerned to see that such legislation does not violate the rights and freedoms protected by the Convention and also that the infringement of the law does not involve any violation of those rights and freedoms.

(2) The Convention does not rule out the possibility that

---

the Federal Republic of Yugoslavia. See also the Luxembourg Act of 14 February 1955 and Order of 23 December 1955.

[1] *X. against Fed. Rep. of Germany*, No. 1197/61 *Yearbook*, v, p. 88 and *Collection of Decisions*, 8, p. 68.   [2] *Yearbook*, v, pp. 94–6.

certain disputes may be the subject of settlement by arbitration instead of being referred to a court.

(3) An arbitration settlement of this kind between private persons cannot, if it is to comply with the Convention, relate to the right itself; from the point of view of the rights of judicial organisation and procedure stated in Article 6, par. 1, such a settlement can only be considered from a legal point of view as a partial renunciation of the *exercise* of those rights.[1]

(c) In another decision, dated 4 August 1960,[2] the Commission confirmed its position, considering as valid an applicant's 'implicit renunciation . . . of his right of challenge' before a Court while continuing to take part in the hearing. Here too the question is merely one of the *exercise* of the right, not of the right itself.

The limits set by the Commission to the faculty of renunciation enjoyed by applicants are thus clearly stated in both cases.

(d) It seems doubtful to us whether, apart from the case stated in Article 62, the Convention allows any compromise with regard to the exercise of the rights stated in it, which are sources of municipal law. Certainly there is *no such general option* in respect of the rights guaranteed by the Convention.

Since such an option implies that of renunciation of the exercise of rights, why should it exist in the case of the rights of the defence laid down in Article 6, paragraph 1, which refers to rights before courts which are to determine 'civil rights and obligations or . . . any criminal charge'?

Is the protection of such rights, which may be called rights of the defence *lato sensu*, required any less imperatively in principle? Does such protection occupy a merely secondary place in the Convention? We do not think so.

(e) The Belgian Court of Cassation has decided that the right of defence is a general principle of law. The overriding character of the *general principles of law* recognised by the French *Conseil d'État* in three celebrated judgments, and on many occasions since, lies in the fact that they have their own intrinsic value. That means that they exist independently of any text, even of the text in which they are formulated.[3] A court, when enforcing respect for general prin-

---

[1] See above Section 14 and below Section 15 *in fine*.

[2] Application No. 556/59, *X against Austria*, *Yearbook*, III, p. 288.

[3] French *Conseil d'État*, 77726 and 78126, Belloir, 77728 and 78106, Mattei, *Rec. arr. C.E.*, 1945, pp. 213, 214 and 215; see the conclusions of Mr Odent, *Commissaire du gouvernement*, *S.*, 1946, III, 1 to 5, and *Études et Documents*, 1947, p. 48 et seq. See also the conclusions of Mr Chenot in the *Guieyesse case*, February 1944, *R.D.F.*, 1944, p. 169; those of Mr Letourneur in the *Aurore case*, 25 June 1948, *S.*, 1948, III, 69; C.E., 26 June 1959, Syndicat général des ingénieurs-conseils, *S.*, 1959, III, 202 and Professor Drago's note.

ciples, notes and confirms their existence. They are not created either by legislation or by jurisprudence.

They come into being independently of them, but once in existence they are *binding* on the court, which determines the conditions of their application. They have legislative force and the court is *obliged* to see that they are observed.[1]

The Belgian Court of Cassation has given rulings on this subject in two judgments. It has laid down that the right of the defence, which in Professor Cambier's expression 'is a matter of manifestation of fundamental human and civic rights',[2] is a general principle 'inseparable from any act of jurisdiction'.[3] A more forthright statement of the fundamental nature of the rights of the defence before the court would not be possible.

(*f*) If we think it doubtful whether there can be any renunciation of the *exercise* of defence rights before a court whose function it is to determine a person's 'civil rights and obligations' or 'any criminal charge'[4] we utterly reject the argument that an applicant can renounce the substance of a right whether it is one stated in Article 6 or some other personal right, which it is the Convention's object to protect and which are the sources of municipal law.[5]

---

[1] See J. Boulanger, 'Principes généraux du droit et droit positif', *Le droit privé français au milieu du XXème siècle. Études offertes à G. Ripert*, I, pp. 56 and 57; see also Del Vecchio 'Les principes généraux du droit', *Recueil d'études sur les sources de droit en l'honneur de Francois Geny*, t. 11, p. 72; P. Roubier, *Théorie générale du droit*, p. 8 et seq.; J. Rivero, 'Le juge administratif français: un juge qui gouverne?', *D.*, 1951, *Chronique*, VI, p. 21; J. Hamson, *Pouvoir discrétionnaire et contrôle juridictionnel de l'administration*, Paris, 1958, p. 179 et seq. Speech by Mr Bouffandeau on the occasion of the 150th anniversary of the French *Conseil d'État*, quoted in *Études et Documents*, 1951, p. 19; Letourneur, 'Les principes généraux du droit dans la jurisprudence du Conseil d'État', *Études et Documents*, 1951, especially p. 24 et seq.; R. Drago, 'The general Principles of Law in the Jurisprudence of the French Conseil d'État', *The American University Law Review*, 1962, vol. 11, no. 2, p. 126.

[2] C. Cambier, *La censure de l'excès de pouvoir par le Conseil d'État*, 1956, p. 59.

[3] Cass. Belg. 2 May 1961, *Pasicrisie* 1961, 1. 926 and 928. See B. Jeanneau, *Les principes généraux de droit dans la jurisprudence administrative*, 1954, p. 78 et seq., and the authorities quoted in that part of the work; see also W. J. Ganshof van der Meersch, 'Le droit de la défense, principe général de droit', *Mélanges en l'honneur de Jean Dabin*, 1963, p. 569 et seq.

[4] See K. Vasak, *L'application des droits de l'homme et des libertés fondamentales par les juridictions nationales*, Report to the symposium organised by the Collège d'Europe at Bruges in April 1965. This learned commentator on the Convention does not appear to us to have given all the attention it deserves to the distinction, which we think fundamental, between the *exercise* of a right and the right itself. This distinction exists with regard to the delegation of a right just as it does for its renunciation.

[5] In public international law a distinction is drawn between discontinuance, which has the import of a purely procedural act, and an act of renunciation of any

16. *Application of the Convention ex officio in municipal law*

(*a*) The Convention's character as *ordre public* is drawn from its object, the protection of fundamental human rights. As it represents a source of municipal law, subject to the conditions indicated, one is bound to ask what will be the attitude of a national court called on to settle a dispute relating to a right guaranteed by one of the directly applicable provisions of the Convention. What we have in mind is, of course, the case of a State which has ratified the Convention, thereby, or so it seems to us, manifesting its intention that those rights shall be considered to form part of its municipal *ordre public*.

(*b*) Having ratified the Convention, the Contracting State has, under Article 13, assumed an obligation to grant to every person within its jurisdiction an effective remedy before a national authority against violations of the rights and freedoms recognised in the Convention. On the basis of this undertaking alone, without either of the declarations provided for in Articles 25 and 46 of the Convention, the rights set out in the Convention will be guaranteed, though solely in national law, by virtue of constitutional or ordinary legislation; protection will be the result of the operation of the organs and procedures of internal public law. Thus it cannot be said that the Convention is a dead letter if neither of the optional declarations has been made relating to the compulsory jurisdiction of the Court and the competence of the Commission to examine individual applications. People whose rights have been violated will not benefit from the system of appeal laid down in the Convention, but they will have an *effective*[1] remedy before a *national* authority. Neither

---

right of action. I.C.J., *Barcelona Traction, Light and Power Co. Ltd. case*, 24 July 1964, especially p. 14 et seq. I.C.J., *Rules of Court*, Art. 69. In the law of judicial procedure a distinction is drawn between discontinuance of *action*, which makes further proceedings impossible, and discontinuance of a *suit*, which is a renunciation of proceedings in the form in which they were opened. On French Procedural law see: Garsonnet et César Bru, III, No. 852 and note 10, p. 667; R. Japiot, *Traité él. proc. civ. et com.* 1935, No. 884 et seq., p. 577 et seq. and No. 902, p. 587. For Belgian law see: *Cass.* 27 February 1958, *Pasicrisie*, 1958, 1. 712, and the conclusions of P. Leclercq, Procureur général, before the Court of Cassation 18 May 1933, *Pasicrisie*, 1938, 1. 234 et seq. especially p. 241.

[1] The term 'effective' is unfortunate, being both vague and ambiguous. Does it mean that the remedy must be 'efficacious' as, under Article 25 (1), should be the right of every person, non-governmental organisation or group of individuals to submit a petition to the Commission? Or does it mean that effect must be given to the remedy if it is well-founded? Or that it must be the same as the remedy provided by the Convention? This last interpretation seems doubtful; both in French and English any mention of a remedy before a national *court* has been avoided. The French text reads '... recours effectif devant une *instance* nationale...' and the English '... an effective remedy before a national *authority*...'

will they draw any benefit from the Court's competence to interpret the Convention.[1]

(*c*) It is not until a High Contracting Party has made the declarations provided for in Articles 25 and 46 that the system laid down in the Convention applies to it or that it submits fully to it, subject to any reservations it may make as provided in Article 64.[2] Only by these declarations can this *ordre public*, hitherto potential, take effect.

(*d*) Here we are faced with *ordre public* which seems to be of a special nature, at least in its effects; it must decide its own scope in municipal law, but is determined by an international convention, which has shaped it in a particular way, since it has different effects depending on whether the Contracting State has made one, both, or neither of the declarations provided for in the Convention.

While, as we have seen, the rights stated in the Convention are a matter of *ordre public*, the system for their protection has the unusual feature that its completeness depends on decisions and rules made, in accordance with procedures established under international law, by the actual Contracting Parties on whom this *ordre public* is to take effect. Declarations and reservations will also have direct repercussions on the scope and completeness of the protection extended to human freedom. The effects in municipal law of the nature as *ordre public* of the rights stated in the Convention must therefore be considered as special ones governed by particular rules.

(*e*) Does it follow from the nature of this matter as *ordre public* that a national court asked to ensure respect for the provisions of the Convention has the *option* of applying them *ex officio* or an obligation to do so?

---

[1] *Convention*, Article 45. The Court's competence does not extend to the interpretation of the Convention unless the High Contracting Party concerned is subject to its compulsory jurisdiction (Arts. 45, 46 and 48). It does not exist in regard to individual applications except in cases where the Contracting Party has declared its recognition of the Commission's competence (Art. 25 (1)). There are two ways in which attempts have been made to remedy divergent interpretation of the Convention by national courts. On the one hand, the Court itself has proposed that an Article 54 bis should be added to the Convention, enabling it to give a preliminary ruling on any question of interpretation that arises in connection with a case pending before a national court of the last instance; it will be seen that the system proposed is similar to that laid down in Article 177 of the EEC Treaty and Article 150 of the EURATOM Treaty. So far the proposal has met with no response (with regard to this interesting suggestion see Vasak, op. cit., no. 484, p. 249). Another proposal by the Consultative Assembly was adopted by the Committee of Ministers and culminated in the signature at Strasbourg on 6 May 1963 of the Second Protocol to the Convention, of which the proposal in question constitutes Articles 1–3; when this Protocol comes into force it will give the Court competence equivalent to the advisory competence of the International Court of Justice (*Statute*, Arts. 65–8; *Rules of Court*, Arts. 82–5).

[2] See Section 9 above; see also remarks on Art. 62 in Section 14 above.

(*f*) The question was put to the Commission indirectly in the case of *Austria against Italy*.[1] No complete answer was given. Indeed, the Commission could not have given any general reply, that is to say, a reply valid in municipal law in all States parties to the Convention. However, the procedure then followed points the way to an answer.

(1) In the case in question the Italian Government invoked the argument of non-exhaustion of domestic remedies by Austria;[2] it is therefore from that angle that the question was put to the Commission. According to the Italian Government, since the Convention forms an integral part of the Italian legal system, its provisions should have been invoked before Italian courts in the same way as any law,[3] the more so since—contrary to the statement of the Austrian Government—the principle that the criminal courts are bound *ex officio* to enquire into the truth was not applicable to the Court of Cassation, but only to the judges dealing with the merits.[4]

(2) Following this statement, the Commission put to the Parties, during the course of the proceedings, the following two questions, which deserve to be quoted:

Do the clauses in Article 6, paragraph (1), (2) and (3) (*d*) and in Article 14 of the Convention, invoked by the Austrian Government, coincide with the corresponding provisions of Italian law (Constitution, legislation, etc.) or are they wider or less extensive in scope?

Have the Italian criminal courts, by virtue of the principle 'jura novit curia', the *right* or the *duty* to ensure *ex officio* compliance with the clauses and provisions mentioned in the previous paragaph? If so, is the Court of Cassation different in this respect from the Court of First Instance and the Court of Appeal?[5]

(3) The Italian Government replied to the first question that the articles in question 'coincided with particular clauses of the Constitution . . . of the Penal Code . . . and of the Code of Criminal Procedure', but made it clear that 'this opinion was based on a particular interpretation of the Convention' and was not shared in full by the Austrian Government.[6] The way in which the question was put shows that the difficulty only arises where the Convention does not coincide with municipal law.

(4) The answer to the second question affects the solution of the problem before us even more, since it shows that the problem may differ from one State to another, and also from one court to another,

---

[1] Application No. 788/60, Decision 11 January 1961, *Yearbook*, IV, p. 116.

[2] *Convention*, Art. 26. With regard to the applicability of the rule to both State and individual applications, see *Yearbook*, IV, pp. 144–50.

[3] Ibid., p. 154. See also the publication of the Council of Europe containing the case of *Austria* v. *Italy*, 1963, p. 46.

[4] *Austria* v. *Italy*, p. 46.   [5] *Yearbook*, IV, p. 156.   [6] Ibid.

in the municipal law of a particular State. The Italian Government, the respondent, replied to this question that:

the decisions of the Courts of Appeal and Cassation under the Italian system, unlike the decision of the court of first instance, were subject to the 'principio dispositivo', whereby the *parties themselves by selecting their grounds for appeal* (*motivi d'impugnazione*) *restricted the aspects of the case of which the judge can take cognizance in either the Court of Appeal or the Court of Cassation.*

But it added immediately that, since this principle is not absolute, the Code of Criminal procedure has introduced exceptions to it and that the judge must, *at any stage of the proceedings, draw attention ex officio* to 'any reasons for which the accused should not be punished or any absolute grounds of nullity'.[1]

(5) The Commission did not rest content with this. It asked the Parties a still more specific question:

when a defendant submits a certain argument before the Court of Cassation in sufficient detail but *without expressly invoking* in its support the relevant provisions of Italian municipal law, including *the Convention, does the Court nevertheless have the right or the duty to ensure that the said provisions are complied with* or will it declare the appeal inadmissible . . .?[2]

According to the answer of the Italian Government, the Code of Criminal Procedure 'which stipulates that the grounds must be stated in detail *for an objection to be admissible, established a general rule which applied to any appeal*, including appeal to a Court of Cassation . . .' It follows, in the Italian Government's view, that ' . . . *the party concerned is under the absolute obligation*, in presenting the grounds for his appeal, *to indicate not only the provisions of the criminal law which are alleged not to have been observed* or to have been erroneously applied, *but also* any other relevant legal provisions, for example, the Convention . . .', which forms part of Italian municipal law. Subject to Articles 152 and 185 of the Code of Criminal Procedure, the Italian Court of Cassation *is not competent*, according to the Italian Government, '*to consider an argument specified de facto but not de jure*'.[3]

According to the Austrian Government, on the other hand, the Italian courts should have applied the provisions of the Convention *ex officio*, and in so far as Italian law did not make the fulfilment of this duty compulsory it was contrary to the Convention. The

[1] Ibid. (My italics).
[2] *Austria* v. *Italy*, p. 48 (my italics). The Commission put to the Parties other questions of less direct interest for the problem under discussion.
[3] Ibid., p. 49 (my italics).

Austrian Government maintained that ' . . . it was sufficient for the complaints in respect of which the Applicant alleged violation of Articles 6 and 14 of the Convention to have been brought *in substance* before the Italian courts'.[1]

(6) The Commission, for its part, referring to the generally recognised rules of international law[2] decided that, in order to determine whether or not domestic remedies had been properly exhausted, 'only the non-utilisation of an "essential" recourse for establishing the merits of a case before the municipal tribunals leads to non-admissibility of the international complaint'.[3] On the other hand, where invocation of the Convention is only a *supplementary argument*, it is not necessary to previous exhaustion of domestic remedies.[4]

(g) In a decision on 18 December 1963, the Commission ruled that, since the Convention was an integral part of Belgian municipal law, the Applicant 'could and should have invoked before the (said) Court (of Cassation), as he has before the Commission, those articles of the Convention . . . which he considers to have been violated to his detriment'. In the circumstances of that case it therefore seems that, in the Commission's view, the reference to the provisions of the Convention there constituted not a mere 'supplementary argument' but an essential ground for substantiating the claim.[5]

(h) These decisions illuminate the scope of the requirement with regard to exhaustion of domestic remedies under the Convention. They do not directly settle the question whether the national court

---

[1] *Austria* v. *Italy*, p. 52.

[2] See Resolution passed by the Institute of International Law at its Granada session on 18 April 1956, *Yearbook of the Institute*, vol. 46, p. 358; see also the preliminary statement by J. H. W. Verzyl, vol. 45, p. 1, the supplementary report, vol. 46, p. 1, and the discussions, vol. 46, p. 275 et seq.; Cavaré, *Droit international public positif*, 11, 1962, p. 360 et seq.; P. Reuter, *Droit international public*, 1958, pp. 169–72.

Ambatielos Case: Award of 6 March 1956, *International Law Reports*, ed. H. Lauterpacht, 1956, p. 306, *RSA*, XII, pp. 83–153, especially pp. 118–23; *Annuaire Français*, 1956, pp. 402–16; *Clunet*, 1957, p. 564 and note by R. Pinto; *International Law Reports*, 1956, p. 334. For the scope of the rule in the European Convention of Human Rights see H. Wiebringhaus, 'La règle de l'épuisement préalable des voies de recours internes dans la jurisprudence de la Commission européenne des Droits de l'Homme', *Annuaire Français*, 1959, p. 689 et seq.

[3] *Yearbook*, IV, p. 172.

[4] *Yearbook*, IV, p. 176; K. Vasak, op. cit., p. 249. See also App. No. 1661/62, decision 17 January 1963, *Collection of Decisions* No. 10. p. 20. In his dissenting opinion Professor Sperduti considered that in this case the Convention should have been invoked before the Italian courts (see *Austria* v. *Italy*, op. cit., Appendix II, p. 263 et seq.).

[5] Application No. 1488/62, *Collection of Decisions*, No. 13, p. 96.

is obliged to give consideration *ex officio to* a plea of violation of the Convention. But if we have so far been disappointed in our hope of finding the answer to the question in the Commission's jurisprudence, at least it reveals quite clearly an additional difficulty to that of the peculiar character of a system of *ordre public* whose effects in municipal law are determined by an international convention. The questions put to the Parties as well as the replies received and the Commission's decisions show that the problem is a complex one and cannot be solved in a way that is valid for all States parties to the Convention.

(*i*) The question whether the national court can or must apply the Convention *ex officio* depends to some extent on the municipal law of each State.

There is no doubt that the Convention, which constitutes a particular system of law to which the High Contracting Parties have subscribed, is, for the reasons stated, binding, *in respect of the rights guaranteed by it*, on national courts in the States parties to the Convention, and those provisions on rights and freedoms which are both complete and sufficiently precise are directly applicable in those States at the application of the parties concerned. But the *judicial organisation and procedure* of national courts are still governed by municipal law. In other words, it is the laws governing these matters which in each State determine on what conditions and before what court a rule applicable *ex officio* may be invoked.

It is therefore not enough to acknowledge that most of the rights and freedoms guaranteed in the Convention have the force of *ordre public* in municipal law, and that the majority of the provisions in which they are embodied are directly applicable, in order to deduce that, in all those States parties to the Convention that have made the two declarations already mentioned,[1] the courts—all courts—must or even may apply the Convention *ex officio* and that a plea of violation of the Convention in any matter may be invoked by the Parties for the first time before the Supreme Court.

As we have seen, when it is necessary to decide whether domestic remedies have been exhausted, the Commission necessarily refers to national law. It also defers to municipal law if it finds that, although there has been conduct of a kind 'incompatible with the Convention ... under ... municipal law the validity of the applicant's conviction cannot be questioned, it having been final since rejection by the Court of Cassation ... of his petition'.[2] After noting that rejection of the appeal constituted in municipal law an obstacle to the reopening of proceedings on a conviction brought about in

---

[1] See above Section 16.
[2] *Boeckmans case, Collection of Decisions*, No. 15, p. 66.

circumstances 'incompatible with the Convention', the Commission gave its support to the subsidiary remedy of the friendly settlement.

(*j*) The nature as *ordre public* of the subject matter of the Convention does not make it possible either to ignore the conditions on which appeals in municipal law may be brought or to disregard the time-limits for appeal to the Court of Appeal or to the Supreme Court.

In our view the laws of procedure to this extent limit the powers of the national court to apply the Convention *ex officio*.[1]

But in States where procedural law allows the Court to which a case has been referred to invoke grounds *ex officio* in the particular circumstances of the case, the argument of violation of the Convention *must* be invoked by the Court (or the *Ministère public*) if the Convention is more rigorous in the protection of fundamental rights than is municipal law.

(*k*) As far as we know, the question has only been decided once by a municipal court in one of the States parties to the Convention.

The Constitutional Court of the Federal Republic of Germany had to decide whether Articles 175 *et seq.* of the German Criminal Code were incompatible with the general rules of international law, thereby violating Article 26 of the Basic Law.[2]

The appellant thought the provisions of the Convention should be viewed as '*general* rules of international law'. The Constitutional Court rejected this claim, but adopted the following principle, which is in accordance with the opinion expressed here:

Irrespective of the Applicant's allegations *it is necessary for the Court to examine ex officio the question of whether Articles 175 et seq. of the Penal Code are or are not consistent with the Convention*, in view of the fact that after its ratification by an Act of 7 August 1952 (*Federal Official Journal*,

---

[1] It will be remembered that, in so far as municipal law is not in harmony with the system of enforcement laid down by the Convention, States are bound to bring their legislation into line with it. The Commission has recalled this general principle of international law, which is confirmed by the *travaux préparatoires* of the Convention: '. . . the Contracting Parties have undertaken . . . to ensure that their domestic legislation is compatible with the Convention and, if need be, to make any necessary adjustments to this end, since the Convention is binding on all the authorities of the Contracting Parties, including the legislative authority. . . .' (*De Becker case*, decision 9 June 1958, *Yearbook*, II, p. 234). See opinion of the Permanent Court on the exchange of Greek and Turkish populations, Series A/B, No. 12, p. 220. It will also be recalled that under Article 50 the Court affords just satisfaction to any Party injured by a decision or measure taken that is even partially in conflict with the obligations arising from the Convention.

[2] Basic Law, 23 May 1949, Art. 25: 'The general rules of public international law form part of the federal law. They take precedence over the laws and directly create rights and duties for the inhabitants of the Federal territory'.

vol. 11, pp. 685, 953) the said Convention entered into force in the Federal Republic on 3 September 1953.[1]

Indeed the Court examined *ex officio* the compatibility of Articles 175 *et seq.* of the Criminal Code successively, together with Articles 8 (par. 1), 13 and 14 of the Convention and then rejected the appeal on grounds which are not relevant here.

(*l*) The obligation to supervise *ex officio*, to the extent mentioned, application of the provisions of the Convention, which represent sources of municipal law, is also binding on the *Ministère public*, where such an institution exists and the *Parquet* is able to take civil action in matters of *ordre public*.[2]

(*m*) Mr Vasak writes that, if the Court were bound to supervise observance of the Convention *ex officio*, no application could be rejected for failure to exhaust domestic remedies.[3] We do not feel able to agree with the eminent commentator on the Convention with regard to this proposition. It leads us to study briefly the effect of the Court's obligation to supervise *ex officio* the application of the Convention, within the limits described on the rule of previous exhaustion of domestic remedies.

(1) Article 26 states that the rule of the previous exhaustion of domestic remedies must be interpreted 'according to the generally recognised rules of international law'.[4]

---

[1] *Entscheidungen des Bundesverfassungsgerichts*, vol. VI, p. 389; *Yearbook*, II, p. 594.

[2] E.g. French law of 20 April 1810, Article 46, applicable in Belgium.

[3] See K. Vasak, *L'application des Droits de L'Homme* ... p. 15; idem, *La Convention* ... no. 485, p. 249.

[4] Although, 'according to the generally recognised rules of international law' it is to the Courts of the respondent State that appeals must be addressed. It is not without interest to note that, before this happens, applications and complaints, if not actual appeals, may and generally are made to governmental authorities and departments. Mr H. Wiebringhaus rightly refers to the applicant's obligation to exhaust all ordinary remedies and, if necessary, to lodge requests or applications with *administrative authorities* (op. cit., p. 690). Such authorities, unlike the general rule applicable to courts of justice, do not need to have a matter referred to them in order to be able to act and take decisions. While courts of justice are as a rule 'passive', administrative authorities may always act *proprio motu* within the limits of the law, and the fact that they may do so in no way affects the obligation of the person concerned to take the initiative with a view to the redress of the right violated or claimed to have been violated. There is nothing new, from the point of view of customary law, in the conjunction of the Applicant's obligation to exhaust domestic remedies with the power of the administrative authority to apply the Convention *proprio motu*. The appeal to the Court is subsidiary, and we may say that, as a rule, it is residual. When the appeal is first made to the administrative authority, it is addressed to an authority which could at any time *proprio motu* remedy the illegal situation or give the Applicant just redress.

Thus the foundation and scope of the obligation must be sought in general international law, more particularly in international decisions. The appellant must exhaust all remedies open to him in the *jurisdictional* system of the respondent State.

(2) In States in which the courts are not bound to ensure application of the Convention *ex officio*, because the law of procedure gives them no power to invoke its provisions *proprio motu*, there is by definition no problem.

(3) In States in which the law of procedure only allows certain courts to invoke its provisions *proprio motu*, there is similarly no problem for those courts that have not this power.

(4) This leaves the case of the remedy which has to be exercised by the Applicant before a court which is bound *ex officio* to give him satisfaction if the right has been violated. Under article 26 of the Convention the obligation to exhaust domestic remedies lies on the applicant. It is in respect of him that the obligation exists and must be considered.[1]

(5) The obligation on the Applicant is to exhaust *all* remedies before the courts of the respondent State[2] which are available to him.[3]

This means *adequate* and *effective* remedies; they must be exercised in accordance with the judicial system of the respondent State and therefore by using such *legal channels* as may redress the grievance. The Commission has made clear the scope of the obligation by deciding that only non-utilisation of a remedy that is *essential*, in order to demonstrate to the domestic courts that the grievance is justified, makes a complaint inadmissible.[4]

What the appellant is obliged to do, in order to avoid having his application declared inadmissible, is not to omit to exercise a remedy

---

[1] A distinction must be drawn between an individual application submitted to the Commission and a State application submitted to the Commission or the Court. In the former case it is strictly the applicant's responsibility to exhaust all remedies. In the latter, domestic remedies may have been exercised by 'the representatives of the private interests' (see I.C.J., *Barcelona Traction, Light and Power Co. Ltd. case*, 24 July 1964, p. 6 et seq., especially p. 22). Here the 'representatives of the private interests' may be 'any person, non-governmental organisation or group of individuals claiming to be the victim of a violation by one of the High Contracting Parties of the rights set forth in the . . . Convention' (Art. 25 (1)).

[2] Courts of justice but also, where the violation is the work of an administrative authority, administrative Courts, if they exist under the law of the respondent State.

[3] 'The generally recognised rules of international law required the Applicant to exhaust not merely the remedies in the ordinary Courts *but the whole system of legal remedies available* in the Republic' (*Lawless case*, App. No. 332/57, *Yearbook*, II, p. 322).

[4] Cf. arbitral award in the *Ambatielos case*, 6 March 1956, mentioned above.

that is open to him or, in exercising the remedies available to him in municipal law, not to omit to invoke a ground such as would cause the appeal to be declared well-founded. But the action of the court that hears the appeal is beyond his power.

(6) The obligation on the Court is to apply the Convention *ex officio*, that is to say to invoke *ex officio* any arguments based on a violation of it. Thus a Supreme Court that establishes from the record of a criminal case that there has been a refusal to examine witnesses on the defendant's behalf 'under the same conditions as witnesses against him'[1] would be obliged to invoke this ground *ex officio* in a case in which an applicant who did not understand the language used at the hearing and had nevertheless been denied 'the free assistance of an interpreter'[2] would have invoked this plea successively before the Appeal Court and the Supreme Court.

(7) Why should the fact that the *court* itself is obliged to invoke *ex officio* all arguments based on violation of the Convention make it impossible to reject a petition if the *applicant* had not exhausted domestic remedies within the meaning of these terms as defined above? As we have seen, it is solely in respect of the Applicant that the obligation to exhaust domestic remedies is to be judged, whether or not the Court has verified *ex officio* the application of the Convention.[3]

(8) The rule of exhaustion of domestic remedies prior to submission of an international application is based on the principle that the respondent State should first have an opportunity to redress the alleged grievance by its own means within the framework of its own domestic legal system.[4] It is based on the generally recognised rules of international law. The obligation of the national court to apply the Convention *ex officio* is derived from the fact that human rights are a matter of *ordre public* and protection *must* be guaranteed. The two rules have absolutely different foundations.

---

[1] *Convention*, Article 6 (3) (*d*).
[2] *Convention*, Article 6 (4) (*e*).
[3] Might it be maintained that if the Court is obliged to invoke *ex officio* arguments based on a violation of the Convention, it is no longer in the power of the Applicant to *exhaust* domestic remedies? We do not find this acceptable. What Article 26 of the Convention requires is that the *applicant* should have exhausted the remedies, that is to say exercised all appeals and pleaded all well-founded arguments at his disposal. The fact that the Appeal Court should have the same arguments at its disposal and be *bound* to invoke them if this is not already being done, cannot mean that the Applicant is to be deprived of the benefits of having fulfilled the obligations placed on him by the Convention.
[4] I.C.J., *Interhandel case*, Reports, 1959, p. 27.

SUMMARY OF THE DISCUSSION

Egon Schwelb: in his admirable Report Professor Ganshof van der Meersch gives so comprehensive a picture of a variety of problems touching on the general task of the international protection of human rights that it is, perhaps, admissible to submit a few short comments on one or two questions which he has examined, even though these comments do not affect, and are not intended to affect, his conclusions on the principal subject of his report. My remarks are intended to supplement rather than to contradict Professor Ganshof van der Meersch's report, to supplement it with certain data derived from recent United Nations developments.

Ordre public—public order—public policy

Professor Ganshof van der Meersch points to the confusion which reigns in both European and United Nations texts in regard to the terms and concepts of *ordre public*—public order—public policy.

He refers to the European Convention on Establishment of 1955 which uses the term *ordre public* also in its English version. He also points to the Protocol to it, where it is expressly provided that the concept of *ordre public* is to be understood in the wide sense generally accepted in continental countries. This is a comparatively innocent use of the concept of *ordre public* in an international text, because it applies to the rights and facilities which the Convention grants to aliens, nationals of States parties. The second example given by Professor Ganshof van der Meersch, the Protocol No. 4 to the European Convention on Human Rights, is of a more serious nature because there the right to liberty of movement and to leave any country, including one's own, is open to restrictions which are necessary in a democratic society for the maintenance of *ordre public*. To subject the right of nationals and foreigners alike to *ordre public*, i.e. to public policy, is bad enough; the objectionable character is, however, somewhat mitigated by the reference to 'a democratic society' and, mainly, by the fact that the Protocol, when it enters into force, will apply in Western Europe. If it were not for the reference to 'a democratic society' the Republic of South Africa could very well become a party to a provision couched in these terms without having to change one *iota* of its policy of *apartheid*, because the separation of the races, the segregation of various groups in specific areas and restrictions on the right of the African population to travel abroad is part and parcel and the very heart of the public policy, of the *ordre public*, of South Africa.

I agree with Professor Ganshof van der Meersch when he points out that the use of *ordre public* in Article 6 (2) as the French rendering of *public order* is simply a mis-translation.

There can, of course, be no doubt that *ordre public* cannot be correctly rendered in English by 'public order', but only by 'public policy'. A recent corroboration of this can be found in the Convention on the Recognition and Enforcement of Foreign Arbitral Awards of 1958; Article V (2) thereof is to the effect that recognition and enforcement of an arbitral award may be refused in the country where recognition and enforcement is sought if 'the recognition or enforcement of the award would be contrary to the public policy of that country'. The French text says: 'Que la reconnaissance ou l'exécution de la sentence serait contraire à l'ordre public de ce pays'.

Now a few words about the same question as it has developed in the course of the consideration by the United Nations Commission on Human Rights, and by the General Assembly, of the draft Covenant on Civil and Political Rights. A series of rights set forth in the draft as prepared by the competent General Assembly Committee are subject to 'public order', the term *ordre public* being added in brackets in the English text. This is the case in regard to Article 12 (which corresponds to Article 2 of the Fourth Protocol to the European Convention and which deals with freedom of movement and freedom to leave one's country); Article 14 on the publicity of trials; Article 19 on freedom of expression; Article 20 on freedom of assembly; and Article 21 on freedom of association.

This, in my submission, is very serious indeed and it is still more serious that it was done *en pleine connaissance de cause*.

Over many years the Secretariat repeatedly drew the attention of the Commission on Human Rights, of the Economic and Social Council and of the General Assembly to the fact[1] that the English expression 'public order' was not equivalent to—and indeed was substantially different from—the French expression *l'ordre public* or the Spanish expression *orden público* and that the use of the expression *l'ordre public* in the limitations clauses would create uncertainty and might constitute a basis for far-reaching derogations from the rights guaranteed. However, the majority of the competent General Assembly Committee of the Whole insisted on using *l'ordre public* in both the French and English texts. There was clearly agreement that these 'far-reaching derogations' should be possible. Apparently, delegations using the English language did not wish to admit to their own public opinion that the draft was subjecting such fundamental rights as freedom of expression, freedom of assembly and freedom of association to the possibility of limitations for reasons of

[1] See e.g. doc. A/2929, p. 48.

L

public policy and the French term served therefore as a convenient *euphemism*. The French delegation, on the other hand, believed that as *ordre public* in French municipal law had a well defined, though wide, meaning, the term, even if applied in less developed jurisdictions, would not be open to abuse.

L'ordre public international within the meaning of the law of nations

Professor Ganshof van der Meersch gives a survey of the teachings of publicists on the question whether there are rules of Public International Law which constitute what one could call *un ordre public international*. His affirmative reply to this question is now corroborated by Article 37 of the draft Articles on the Law of Treaties which have been prepared by the International Law Commission at their 1962 to 1965 sessions. Draft article 37 deals with 'Treaties conflicting with a peremptory norm of general international law (*jus cogens*)'. It is to the effect that a treaty is void if it conflicts with a peremptory norm of general international law from which no derogation is permitted and which can be modified only by a subsequent norm of general international law having the same character. The American Law Institute's Restatement of the Foreign Relations Law of the United States (Proposed Official Draft, 1962) also accepts the concept and uses the term 'rules of international law incorporating basic standards of international conduct'.

The Universal Declaration of Human Rights

In conclusion I would like to add a few words to what Professor Ganshof van der Meersch says on the question of the legal status of the Universal Declaration of Human Rights. Here again, I find myself in full agreement with the learned Rapporteur and his presentation, at least as far as it goes. While Professor Ganshof van der Meersch to a large extent relies on the *travaux préparatoires* of the Declaration, i.e. on what Governments *said* in 1947 and 1948, I submit that it might be appropriate also to take account of what Governments *did* in the seventeen years that have elapsed since 10 December 1948, of their 'subsequent conduct' and, in general, of the use the international community has made of the Declaration: its use by international organs as a yardstick of the observance of human rights; its penetration into international conventional law on the universal and regional levels; its reflection in constitutions and municipal legislation; and its impact on international and national developments in general.

Relevant to our question is also the use made by the international community of the form of solemn declarations of international organs to state the law both in the field of human rights and in other sectors. In the course of a short intervention I can only mention, and not go into, these developments, landmarks of which have been, in addition to the Declaration of 1948, the Declaration against Colonialism of 1960, the Declaration on Permanent Sovereignty over Natural Resources of 1962, the Declaration of Legal Principles Governing the activities of States in the Use of Outer Space of 1963, and the United Nations Declaration on the Elimination of All Forms of Racial Discrimination of 1963. All these and the many draft instruments which are in preparation have, in my submission, contributed to the blurring of the traditional distinction between 'binding conventions' and 'non-binding' pronouncements. All this may necessitate a revision of the traditional doctrine of the sources of international law.

Charles van Reepinghen: the distinction between a right and its exercise, which is a common distinction in private law, should not be taken too far. For there are cases where renunciation of the exercise of a right may be accompanied by renunciation of the right itself. When, for example, a single authority is competent to give a ruling and the institution of proceedings before that authority is renounced, it is idle to claim that the right itself has not been renounced. In contracts in which decisions are entrusted to an arbitral tribunal, the parties renounce the right to go to law, and therefore the exercise of that right; as the arbitrator is not bound to base his ruling on rules of law, this implies renunciation of the right itself. On this point reference should be made to the *Boeckmans case*.

M. H. van Hoogstraten: the subject for this session appears to require some thought as, according to the Rapporteur, the ideas of *ordre public* and *ex officio* are not identical. The notion of *ex officio* is concerned with the application of a rule *proprio motu*, whereas in the realm of *ordre public* the Court must defend the interests of the State on its own initiative and must not, therefore, apply a given rule. In other words, everything belonging to the sphere of *ordre public* must be applied by the judge *ex officio* but the converse is not the case; there are provisions which the judge must apply *ex officio* although they are not based on *ordre public* or are not independent of the will of the parties.

This aspect is revealed clearly by the decision (quoted on page 39 of Document H (65) 7) by the *Bundesverwaltungsgericht* (Federal Administrative Court) on 22 February 1962 concerning the *Zölibatsklausel* (celibacy clause) and its relationship to Article 12. This gives rise to the question of the relationship between free will and human rights. The Rapporteur raises the question whether a distinction should be made whereby human rights would not all have the same weight or have the same importance for human life. One cannot, for example, allow that anyone may submit voluntarily to torture or slavery; all forms of torture and slavery are an objective violation of fundamental rights. Is it, however, possible to renounce fundamental rights relating to marriage and the family? The case of migrant workers throws light on this question: they are admitted to and employed in a foreign country, but without their families. Have these workers renounced their right voluntarily? And, what is more serious, were they free to renounce it?

Felix Ermacora: The French concept *ordre public* is known in German legal terminology too.[1] The concept has been examined repeatedly in Austrian legal theory and judicial practice (see, for example, the judgment of the Constitutional Court regarding Section 67 on the form of marriage of the Registration (births, deaths and marriages) Act (*Personenstandsgesetz*)).

A development towards a European standard of *ordre public* is discernible in the Convention and in the case-law based on the Convention: *ordre public européen* (Roman law once played a similar role in Europe). This has practical consequences:

(*a*) The Commission must examine *ex officio* cases brought to its notice.

(*b*) The withdrawal of an application can be left out of account although a distinction should, of course, be made between State applications and individual applications—for, on the withdrawal of an individual application, a case is stopped because the applicant no longer regards himself as a 'victim'.

(*c*) A State which accedes to the Convention later is entitled to bring an action against a State which acceded earlier (see the case of *Austria* v. *Italy*).

(*d*) The case-law of other national authorities must be taken into account wherever the factual circumstances are comparable and the legal situation is identical.

(*e*) The authorities—the Committee of Ministers, the Commission and the Court—competent to deliberate and give a decision on one and the same case, will, in certain circumstances, arrive at different interpretations of *ordre public* (such a possibility exists in the Belgian linguistic cases).

In connection with the interpretation of the Convention the question will arise whether it is *ordre public européen* or *ordre public interne* that is to be taken into consideration; such conflicts have already been foreshadowed.

State applications are lodged—as the Cyprus and Austrian-Italian examples show—when political tension already exists between the States concerned. Political aspects can dominate legal aspects in

[1] Cf. Article 63 of the Treaty of Saint Germain.

such cases. The solution—although, at present, this is still utopian—
would be to do away with State applications in future and appoint a
European Public Prosecutor, a European High Commissioner or a
European Ombudsman, who could safeguard rights regardless of
political considerations.

André Vanwelkenhuyzen: Professor Ganshof van der Meersch
considers that the possibility of a 'friendly settlement' provided for
in Article 28 of the Convention is not inconsistent with the idea that
the Convention relates to matters of *ordre public*, because the said
Article stipulates that the friendly settlement negotiated through the
intervention of the Commission of Human Rights must be based on
'respect for human rights as defined in this Convention'.

The main purpose of this friendly settlement will generally be to
determine the amount of compensation due to the applicant. The
conciliation proceedings will concern compensation for loss or
injury, not fundamental legal issues.

But the Commission's role can and must be wider. Wherever a
violation of the Convention is liable to continue to produce its
effects in the future, i.e. wherever a legal provision—law or regulation—violates a guaranteed right, the fact that the Convention
relates to matters of *ordre public* makes it essential that the Commission should endeavour, while a friendly settlement is being negotiated,
to secure the repeal or withdrawal of the provision which is incompatible with the Convention.

W. F. Prins: State treaties in the Netherlands do not enter into force
without the prior approval of the States-General, which may be
tacit or express in the form of a Law. A State treaty which amends
the Constitution can, however, be approved only by a law passed
by a two-thirds majority of the votes of both Houses of the States-
General. But even if this provision is disregarded and even if it
transpires later that a treaty departs from the Constitution in a
certain respect, that treaty is still valid law and its provisions must
be applied in so far as they are self-executing. Such provisions thus
take unconditional precedence over the provisions of national
constitutional legislation, especially such as were not adopted until
after the entry into force of the treaty.

B. N. Esen: the Turkish Constitutional Court had to deal with the
Convention in connection with a complaint lodged by the Labour
Party with a view to the repeal of certain provisions of the Penal
Code relating to the death penalty. This complaint was founded on
the constitutional guarantee of the inviolability of fundamental
rights. The Court decided that there was no cause to repeal the
provisions attacked, because the Human Rights Convention itself
(Article 2) did not exclude the possibility of the death penalty.

Consequently, the death penalty is not contrary to the spirit of European civilisation and it is in this sense that the relevant constitutional provision must be interpreted.[1]

With reference to the question of derogations[2] the Constitution stipulates that when the Turkish Parliament proclaims a state of war or siege, this state shall be temporary and shall automatically come to an end on the expiry of the period prescribed by the Constitution.

Gustaf Petrén: in the investigations into the USA–Panama dispute of 1964 by a Commission appointed, at the request of the parties, by the International Commission of Jurists, the parties accepted the United Nations Universal Declaration of Human Rights as a basis for the enquiry. In the report resulting from the enquiry, a violation of the Declaration was consequently treated as a violation of a treaty. The conclusions of the Commission were reached as an application of the articles of the Declaration in this specific case.

Although the Scandinavian countries recognise the principles of the Convention, the Convention has not been made an integral part of their municipal law: judges cannot apply it *ex officio*. Many concepts in the Convention are too vague and very difficult to handle in the domestic legal system. If, as proposed, the Court were empowered to give advisory opinions, these would contribute to solving doubtful issues, for instance, whether certain rules of municipal law comply with the articles of the Convention. Difficulties arise from the fact that the Convention is based on Continental and Anglo-Saxon legal concepts which do not always coincide with the Scandinavian concepts.

It is easier for individual citizens in the Scandinavian countries to apply to the national Ombudsman than to submit an application to Strasbourg, since this involves language difficulties and high costs and demands technical knowledge. It would be advisable to simplify the procedure for individual applications.

[1] See *Yearbook of the Convention*, vol. VI, 1963, p. 820.
[2] Discussed in Vasak, op. cit., p. 70.

CHAPTER V

Comparison of the jurisprudence of national courts with that of the organs of the Convention as regards the rights of the individual in court proceedings

REPORT BY

THOMAS BUERGENTHAL

I. INTRODUCTION

A comparison of the jurisprudence of the Convention Institutions relating to Articles 5, 6 and 13 of the Convention with that of national courts could be approached in at least two ways. The first would combine a discussion of analogous cases decided by the domestic and international tribunals. Such an analysis, however, presents certain difficulties. This is mainly because a large number of cases relating to Articles 5 and 6 that were adjudicated by the Convention Institutions were either decided by national courts without reference to these provisions or, if these courts dealt with them specifically, the judgments in question were apparently not reported. We thus do not have enough domestic decisions to enable us to compare them systematically with the jurisprudence of the Convention Institutions. Were we accordingly to limit our discussion only to analogous adjudications, we would not be able to evaluate adequately a large body of relevant case law emanating from the Convention Institutions, which throws considerable light on the problems these provisions present or will present for the domestic legislator and judiciary.

In the following paper I have accordingly approached my topic by choosing the other alternative. That is, I shall first attempt to present a systematic analysis of the jurisprudence of the Convention Institutions relating to Articles 5 and 6. It will in each case be followed by a discussion of the relevant domestic adjudications, which will then be compared to the standards enunciated by the Convention Institutions. However, an examination of decisions relating to Article 13, rendered by the Convention Institutions and the national courts can readily be combined without sacrificing a systematic analysis of this provision. Its discussion will accordingly follow this pattern.

Before embarking upon this task, it is perhaps in order to single out what I regard to be the most significant contributions made by the European Commission and the Court in interpreting Articles 5 and 6.[1] Two rulings that are bound to have a lasting impact on the interpretation and growth of the Convention stand out.

I have reference first to the decision of the Human Rights Court in the *Lawless case*.[2] Since the facts giving rise to this litigation are well known, one need only recall that Lawless had been arrested and detained for a number of months without a trial, pursuant to a law permitting the detention of persons certified by a government minister to be engaged in activities prejudicial to the security of the State. On the crucial question whether this detention violated Article 5, the relevant English text of the Convention, viewed in the light of the *travaux préparatoires*, was open to some doubt. Article 5 (1) (c) permits 'the lawful arrest or detention of a person effected for the purpose of bringing him before the competent legal authority on reasonable suspicion of having committed an offence or when it is reasonably considered necessary to prevent his committing an offence or fleeing after having done so'. The Irish Government asserted that this provision did not require 'that a person arrested or detained on preventive grounds shall be brought before a judicial authority'.[3] In its view, that requirement applied only to a person arrested on 'reasonable suspicion of having committed an offence', and not to detention effected for the purpose of preventing the commission of a crime, which in some States was not even a punishable offence. In its opinion, it accordingly followed that Article 5 (3), in requiring a person detained pursuant to Article 5 (1) (c) to be brought promptly before a judge and to be tried within a reasonable time, meant to accord that right only to those suspected of having committed a criminal act. Refusing to adopt this interpretation, the Court ruled that Article 5 (1) (c)

can be construed only if read in conjunction with paragraph (3) of the same Article . . . [which] plainly entails the obligation to bring everyone arrested or detained in any of the circumstances contemplated by the provisions of paragraph (1)(c) before a judge for the purpose of examining

---

[1] Valuable and comprehensive discussions of relevant case law can be found in the following studies: Vasak, *La convention européenne des droits de l'homme* (1964); Scheuner, 'Die Grundrechte der Europäischen Menschenrechts-Konvention in ihrer Anwendung durch die Organe der Konvention', in *Festschrift für Hermann Jahrreiss*, 355 (1964); Robertson, *Human Rights in Europe* (1963); Weil, *The European Convention on Human Rights* (1963); Pinto, *Les Organisations Européennes* (1963).

[2] *Lawless* v. *Ireland* (*Merits*), Judgment of the European Court of Human Rights of 1 July 1961, *Yearbook*, IV, 438.

[3] Ibid., 456.

the question of deprivation of liberty or for the purpose of deciding on the merits.[1]

As the Court rightly noted, a contrary construction of these provisions would have sanctioned the arrest and detention of any person 'suspected of harbouring an intent to commit an offence . . . for an unlimited period on the strength merely of an executive decision. . . .' By branding such a practice 'repugnant to the fundamental principles of the Convention',[2] the Court proclaimed freedom from arbitrary detention a basic principle of European public law.

The other decision that stands out was rendered by the European Commission on Human Rights in the *Nielsen case*.[3] Here the Commission was called upon to pass upon the allegation of a Danish national that he was denied a fair trial in a proceeding which resulted in his conviction for planning and instigating an attempted robbery leading to a homicide. Article 6 (1) of the Convention provides in part that 'in the determination of his civil rights and obligations or of any criminal charge against him, everyone is entitled to a fair and public hearing within a reasonable time by an independent and impartial tribunal established by law. . . .' Under Article 6 (2) 'everyone charged with a criminal offence shall be presumed innocent until proved guilty according to law', while Article 6 (3) accords the accused certain enumerated 'minimum rights'.[4] One of the questions that had to be decided in the *Nielsen case* was whether the notion of a 'fair trial [hearing]' in a criminal case expressed in Article 6 (1) was defined exclusively by reference to the rights guaranteed in Article 6 (2) and 6 (3) or whether it had a broader content. In adopting the latter construction, the Commission ruled that the six rights specifically enumerated in Article 6 (3) were not exhaustive, and that an individual's right to a 'fair trial' might be violated even if he was accorded the minimum rights guaranteed by Article 6 (3) and those

---

[1] Ibid., 464.   [2] Ibid., 466.

[3] *Nielsen* v. *Denmark* (*Merits*), App. No. 343/57, *Yearbook*, IV, 494.

[4] Article 6(3) of the Convention provides:

Everyone charged with a criminal offence has the following minimum rights:

(*a*) To be informed promptly, in a language which he understands and in detail, of the nature and cause of the accusation against him;

(*b*) To have adequate time and facilities for the preparation of his defence;

(*c*) To defend himself in person or through legal assistance of his own choosing or, if he has not sufficient means to pay for legal assistance, to be given it free when the interests of justice so require;

(*d*) To examine or have examined witnesses against him and to obtain the attendance and examination of witnesses on his behalf under the same conditions as witnesses against him.

(*e*) To have the free assistance of an interpreter if he cannot understand or speak the language used in court.

set forth in Article 6 (2).[1] This interpretation, while not strictly required by the language of the Convention, is of profound import-ance. It permits the Commission to develop an enlightened fair-trial standard in criminal cases unhampered by rigid rules limiting its authority and carries with it the power to scrutinise national criminal proceedings for violations of evolving European due process of law principles. It has already had a significant impact on the administra-tion of criminal justice in certain countries adhering to the Conven-tion; more profound consequences are readily foreseeable.

II. ARTICLE 5
Before the Convention Institutions

1. Permissible deprivation of liberty

Article 5 of the Convention in paragraph (1) provides that 'everyone has the right to liberty and security of person'. This right is qualified to the extent that the next sentence stipulates that 'no one shall be deprived of his liberty save in the following cases and in accordance with a procedure prescribed by law. . . .' As this language indicates, the Convention recognises as lawful a deprivation of liberty only if it was effected pursuant to a procedure prescribed by law,[2] and if it falls within one of the categories described in the six sub-paragraphs of Article 5 (1).[3]

The remaining provisions of Article 5 deal with the rights that must be accorded to an arrested or detained person. Pursuant to Article 5 (2) he must be informed promptly of the reasons thereof and of the charges against him. If arrested or detained in accordance

[1] *Neilsen v. Denmark, Yearbook*, IV, at p. 548.
[2] App. No. 892/60, *Yearbook*, IV, 240, 250.
[3] Article 5(1) sanctions:

(*a*) The lawful detention of a person after conviction by a competent court;

(*b*) The lawful arrest or detention of a person for non-compliance with the lawful order of a court or an order to secure the fulfilment of any obligation prescribed by law;

(*c*) The lawful arrest or detention of a person effected for the purpose of bringing him before the competent legal authority on reasonable suspicion of having committed an offence or when it is reasonably considered necessary to prevent his committing an offence or fleeing after having done so;

(*d*) The detention of a minor by lawful order for the purpose of educational supervision or his lawful detention for the purpose of bringing him before the competent legal authority;

(*e*) The lawful detention of persons for the prevention of the spreading of infectious diseases, of persons of unsound mind, alcoholics or drug addicts or vagrants;

(*f*) The lawful arrest or detention of a person to prevent his effecting an unauthorised entry into the country or of a person against whom action is being taken with a view to deportation or extradition.

with Article 5 (1) (c), he must, under Article 5 (3), be brought 'promptly' before a judicial officer. He is entitled to be tried 'within a reasonable time or to release pending trial'. The right to have the lawfulness of one's deprivation of liberty determined 'speedily by a court' is guaranteed by Article 5 (4). Finally, Article 5 (5) accords the victim of an arrest or detention which violates Article 5 'an enforceable right to compensation'.

The relative paucity of decisions involving charges of arbitrary arrest and detention might well be an indication that such practices are rather rare in those countries at least which recognise the right of individual petition to the Commission. The Convention Institutions have accordingly not had an opportunity to develop an extensive jurisprudence relating to Article 5. They have, however, provided us with some guidelines.

(a) Article 5 (1) (a)

Since Article 5 (1) (a) sanctions the detention of a person convicted by a 'competent court', two questions might be asked. First, is the determination as to what constitutes a 'competent court' made solely by reference to the domestic law of the country involved or does this term contemplate a Convention standard? This problem, which does not seem as yet to have been squarely considered by the Convention Institutions might arise, for example, in a case where the defendant has been forcibly abducted from the jurisdiction of one state to stand trial in another.[1] Here it might be crucial to know whether an international or a national standard of competence is applied. How the Convention Institutions will resolve this issue remains to be seen, although a recent Commission decision may provide us with at least a partial answer. The Commission was in this case called upon to decide the second question that presents itself in analysing the meaning of a 'competent court', namely, whether by 'competent court' the Convention contemplates only tribunals subject to the jurisdiction of the Member States? The Commission had to resolve this issue in passing on the complaint of a German national. He charged that his imprisonment in the Federal Republic in accordance with a law implementing an interzonal agreement for judicial assistance in criminal cases, under which a sentence imposed on him in East Germany was executed in the Federal Republic, violated Article 5 (1). In finding that this practice was not in contravention of the Convention, the Commission concluded that the notion of a 'competent court' in Article 5 (1) (a) was not limited to

[1] See De Schutter, 'Competence of the National Judiciary Power in Case the Accused has been Unlawfully Brought Within the National Frontiers', *Revue Belge de Droit International*, i, 89, 122–3 (1965).

judicial tribunals of Member States and that it neither expressly nor by implication prohibited the execution of a prison sentence imposed by a foreign state.[1] It then noted that it had no reason to believe that the East German tribunals that imposed the sentence lacked the requisite competence pursuant to their own legislation. But the Commission added that the guarantees contained in Article 5 prevented Member States from executing judgments in conflict with 'democratic principles', because the detention must be 'lawful' and in accordance with 'procedures prescribed by law', and must have been decreed by a 'competent court'.[2] In the instant case, the Commission was satisfied that the governing Federal law was expressly designed to assure compliance with these safeguards and did in fact do so.

This decision would seem to permit the assumption that as a general rule the determination whether a person is being detained 'lawfully' after conviction by a 'competent court' pursuant to a 'procedure prescribed by law', is made by reference to the national legislation involved. But since domestic laws must conform to the overriding 'democratic principles', it would seem that the definition of 'competence' is not one exclusively for the determination of national authorities, since it can be reviewed by the Convention Institutions.

In view of the fact that Article 5 (1) (a) permits the detention of an individual who has been duly convicted 'in accordance with a procedure prescribed by law', it might be interesting to ascertain what factors the Convention Institutions will look to in determining the regularity of a person's conviction. The Commission had to deal with this problem in a case involving an Applicant who had been convicted and sentenced by a German court in reliance on a law subsequently invalidated with retroactive effect by the Federal Constitutional Court. Since the same factual and legal findings were covered by another law that had not been challenged, the Applicant's conviction was subsequently 'revalidated' without a new trial and he was ordered to serve his sentence. The Applicant contended before the Commission that, since his conviction was based solely on a law held to be unconstitutional with retroactive effect, the entire basis for his conviction and sentence had disappeared. In rejecting this argument, the Commission concluded that the Applicant was duly convicted by a competent court within the meaning of Article 5 (1) (a).[3] In the Commission's view, the invalidation of the law here in question 'had the effect of vitiating the legal basis of the sentence . . .

---

[1] App. No. 1322/62, 13 *Collection of Decisions of the European Commission o, Human Rights* (hereafter cited as *Collection*) 55, 68 (1964).
[2] Ibid. [3] App. No. 2136/64, 13 *Collection* 116, 122 (1964).

but in no way affected the legal or factual basis of his conviction . . .'
under the other applicable legal provisions.[1] In thus deciding this
case, the Commission no doubt assumed that Article 5 (1) (a) does
not permit it to examine the validity of the substantive law under
which a person is convicted, but only the procedural regularity of
the conviction. This is, of course, an entirely valid interpretation of
Article 5 (1) (a).[2] It does not necessarily, however, dispose of the
instant case. If, as the Applicant alleged, he was in effect tried solely
under a law that was void *ad initio*, it is certainly arguable that he
was never duly convicted. His detention would, therefore, violate the
Convention. The 'lawful' detention of a convicted person surely
presumes the detention of an individual convicted for having violated the law under which he was tried, and not just any law that
may be on the books and under which he could be, but was not,
tried.

(b) *Article 5 (1) (b)*

Article 5 (1) (b) of the Convention authorises the arrest and detention of a person 'for non-compliance with the lawful order of a court
or in order to secure the fulfilment of any obligation prescribed by
law'. The first clause of this provision is, of course, self-explanatory.
The second is by no means clear. It was invoked by the Irish Government in the *Lawless case*, both in the proceedings before the Court
and the Commission, to justify the Government's detention of the
Applicant. In its report, the Commission rejected Ireland's defence
based on this clause. It held that this provision did not apply to
arrest or detention for the prevention of offences against the security
of the state. It was designed, in the Commission's view, to secure
'the execution of specific obligations imposed by law'.[3] While it is,
of course, true that the acceptance of the interpretation proffered
by Ireland would have sanctioned preventive detention, it is difficult
to see to what type of a case this provision, as interpreted by the
Commission, could apply. Would not imprisonment to secure 'the
execution of *specific* obligations imposed by law' always presume a
judicial determination of the existence of such an obligation, the
noncompliance with which gives rise to the detention? If so, it
follows that the detention has actually been effected in accordance

---

[1] Ibid., 121.

[2] See, in this connection, the decisions of the Commission that the indeterminate sentence that can be imposed under German penal law on habitual
criminals does not violate Article 5 (1) (a) since it is imposed by a court following
a conviction. App. No. 99/55, *Yearbook*, I, 160; App. No. 100/55, *Yearbook*, I,
162.

[3] *The Lawless Case*, Publications of the European Court of Human Rights,
Series B: Pleadings, Oral Arguments, Documents 1960–61, p. 64.

with the first clause of Article 5 (1) (*b*), that is, 'for non-compliance with the lawful order of a court'.[1] It is accordingly interesting to note that the Human Rights Court disposed of Ireland's reliance on Article 5 (1) (*b*) with the curt remark that this provision was 'irrelevant' in this case, because Lawless had not been detained 'for non-compliance with the . . . order of a court'.[2] It is, therefore, not unreasonable to conclude that the second clause of Article 5 (1) (*b*) has been effectively and, in my opinion, with good reason, read out of the Convention.

(c) *Article 5 (1) (c)*

In approaching a discussion of Article 5 (1) (*c*), we start with the proposition that the arrest or detention of a person suspected of having committed an offence, to prevent him from committing it or to forestall his escape after having done so, is lawful only if it was effected for the purpose of bringing him before a competent legal authority.[3] It is equally clear that, in assessing the reasonableness or necessity of any detention based on one of these grounds, the Commission will look 'to the circumstances of the case as they appeared at the time of the arrest and detention'.[4] In other words, the mere fact that it subsequently appears that these conclusions were unwarranted, does not mean that Article 5 (1) (*c*) has been violated, provided that at the time such preventive action was taken, it appeared reasonable or necessary. An examination of the cases indicates, furthermore, that in applying this test to cases involving persons detained on suspicion of having committed an offence, the Commission will be satisfied, if there was any evidence at all linking the individual to the crime.[5]

(d) *Article 5 (1) (d) and 5 (1) (e)*

Article 5 (1) (*d*) of the Convention, which permits the detention of minors under certain specified conditions, has, to my knowledge, not been invoked before the Convention Institutions. I have, further-

---

[1] I suppose it is possible to assert that by speaking of a 'specific' obligation the Commission in fact held that the imprisonment of a person 'to secure the fulfilment of any obligation prescribed by law' will only be sanctioned if such an obligation is sufficiently certain or concrete. In other words, that the obligation to be loyal to the State, which Ireland sought to enforce against Lawless by detaining him, was much too vague, i.e. not specific enough to be lawful.

[2] *Lawless* v. *Ireland* (Merits), Judgment of 1 July 1961, *Yearbook*, IV, 438, 464.

[3] Ibid.

[4] App. No. 1936/63, *Neumeister* v. *Austria* (Admissibility), 14 *Collection* 38, 49 (1964), App. No. 1602/62, *Stögmüller* v. *Austria* (Admissibility), 14 *Collection* 62, 73 (1964); App. No. 1216/61, 11 *Collection* 1, 5 (1963).

[5] See e.g. App. No. 297/57, *Yearbook*, II, 204.

more, been able to find only one case that dealt with Article 5 (1) (e). Under this provision an individual may be deprived of his liberty in order to prevent the spread of infectious diseases. It also permits the detention of persons of unsound mind, alcoholics, drug addicts and vagrants. Based on this provision, the Commission has rejected an Application in which the complainant asserted that he was detained in violation of the Convention because, in addition to being sentenced to six months imprisonment for vagrancy and begging, he was ordered to serve a four-year term in a workhouse for vagrants.[1] Here, the Applicant obviously misconceived his rights under the Convention. However, it might be worth noting that Article 5 (1) (e) neither requires the conviction of one so detained, nor does it define the term 'vagrant'. While its definition would, as a general rule, be matter for domestic law, it is certainly arguable that this is only true so long as national authorities give it the commonly recognised meaning and do not misuse arrests for vagrancy for purposes inconsistent with the Convention.[2] Accordingly, care must be taken in examining these cases, because in some countries—and I am thinking especially of the United States—the police have been known to arrest and detain people ostensibly as vagrants, in order to extract evidence justifying the issuance of arrest warrants on other charges.[3]

(e) Article 5 (1) (f)

In Article 5 (1) (f) the Convention permits a person's arrest or detention to prevent his illegal entry into the country. Under this provision, such action may also be taken to execute deportation or extradition orders. In determining the legality of such deprivations of liberty, the Commission has merely sought to verify whether the detention in question was effected under circumstances calling for the application of this provision and in reliance on applicable domestic law, that is, whether it was effected in accordance with 'a procedure prescribed by law'.[4] The Commission has not yet had to face the question whether the lengthy internment of an undesirable alien, who cannot be deported to any country, would be consistent

---

[1] App. No. 770/60, 6 *Collection* 1, 4 (1961).

[2] See Convention, Article 18. Presumably such arrests and detentions would also not be 'lawful' under Article 5 (1) (e).

[3] See Douglas, 'Vagrancy and Arrest on Suspicion', 70 *Yale L.J.* 1, 9–10 (1960–61); Foote, 'Vagrancy-type Law and its Administration', 104 *U. Pa. L. Rev.* 603 (1956). It would not be surprising to find such practices in those countries which, like the United States, impose a higher standard for lawful arrest than merely reasonable suspicion.

[4] App. No. 858/60, *Yearbook*, IV, 224, 236–8; App. No. 2143/64, 14 *Collection* 15, 23 (1965); App. No. 1465/62, *Yearbook*, V, 256; App. No. 1802/63, 10 *Collection* 26, 37 (1963).

with this provision.[1] It is certainly arguable that Article 5 (1) (*f*) only contemplates a detention for the purpose of achieving either one of two results: to prevent an unauthorised entry or to implement deportation or extradition orders. The internment of an alien served with a valid deportation order that cannot as a practical matter be executed would, in my opinion, therefore be inconsistent with Article 5 (1) (*f*).

2. *Rights of persons arrested or detained*

Under Article 5 any person who has been deprived of his liberty must be accorded certain rights. Before turning to an examination of these provisions, it might be appropriate to ask whether the rights, which Articles 5 (3) and (4) guarantee to a person deprived of his liberty, do not impose a corresponding duty on the state authorities to inform him that he has these rights? Without being prepared at this time to examine this question, I am inclined to think that elementary notions of fairness require an affirmative reply.

(*a*) *Article 5 (2)*

Article 5 (2) entitles an individual to be 'informed promptly, in a language which he understands, of the reasons for his arrest and of any charge against him'. In seeking to understand the meaning of this provision, it should be noted that it parallels to a certain extent the right accorded to a criminal accused in Article 6 (3) (*a*), who must be 'informed promptly, in a language which he understands and *in detail*, of the nature and cause of the accusation against him'. From a juxtaposition of these two provisions, the Commission has concluded that the information that must be given a person arrested but not yet charged with a criminal offence need not be detailed or specific. It will suffice, if he is informed in general terms of the reasons for his arrest and the charges against him.[2] This requirement will be complied with if the requisite information is conveyed orally, either by a simple explanation on the part of the arresting authorities[3] or if the warrant of arrest is read to the detained.[4] Surprising as it may seem, the Commission has even concluded that Article 5 (2) was not violated in a case where the Applicant was interrogated in detail for a considerable time and confronted with a witness because, as a result thereof, he 'must have been fully aware of the reasons for

---

[1] This question suggests itself in App. No. 858/60, *Yearbook*, IV, 224, where it did not have to be resolved.

[2] App. No. 343/57, *Nielsen* v. *Denmark* (Admissibility), *Yearbook*, II, 412, 462.

[3] App. No. 1211/61, *Yearbook*, V, 224, 228 (1962).

[4] App. No. 1216/61, 11 *Collection* 1, 5 (1963).

his arrest and the nature of the charges against him'.[1] Surely Article 5 (2) requires more than that. Since under Article 5 (4) the arrested individual has the right to take legal proceedings to determine its legality, it is obvious that the extent to which he is informed of the particular reasons for his arrest and the charges against him, could determine whether he will and effectively can avail himself of this right. That Article 5 (2) contemplates more than the Commission has to date required, is further apparent from the wording of this provision. It requires that the information be given *promptly*. That condition is not satisfied if the reasons for the arrest and the charges are revealed to the detained person piecemeal during prolonged periods of interrogation. Besides, the stipulation in Article 5 (2) that the information must be conveyed to the arrested person 'in a language which he understands', refers in part at least to the nature of the information and not merely to its linguistic aspect. If it were not so, this phrase would be superfluous. Assuming the ordinary meaning of the words 'shall be informed', it is clear that a person who understands only Italian would not be 'informed', if the reasons for his arrest are explained to him in Dutch. Thus, it seems to me that the phrase 'in a language which he understands', indicates that the information conveyed must give the arrested person promptly a clear and readily understandable indication why and on what grounds he is being held.

(b) Article 5 (3)

By far the largest number of applications decided by the Convention Institutions under Article 5 have charged violations of paragraph (3). It provides that a person deprived of his liberty in cases involving the application of Article 5 (1) (c), must be brought promptly before a judge and is entitled to be tried within a reasonable time or to release pending trial, which 'may be conditioned by guarantees to appear for trial'. Article 5 (1) (c), it will be recalled, applies to deprivations of liberty effected on suspicion that the arrested person has committed an offence, to prevent him from committing it or fleeing the country after having done so. We have already noted that in the *Lawless case* the Human Rights Court held that the rights guaranteed in Article 5 (3) apply with equal force to all three categories of cases subsumed under Article 5 (1) (c).[2] It follows from this that the arrest and detention of a person to prevent the commission of an offence will be unlawful, unless he is brought promptly

---

[1] App. No. 1936/63, *Neumeister* v. *Austria* (Admissibility), 14 *Collection* 38, 50 (1965).

[2] *Lawless* v. *Ireland* (Merits), Judgment of 1 July 1961, *Yearbook*, IV, 438, 464–6.

M

before a judicial officer and tried within a reasonable time, which in turn presupposes that planning a crime is a punishable offence.

Interestingly enough, the Commission has so far only had to consider cases charging delays in bringing the Applicant to trial and none involving complaints that they were not promptly arraigned. The Commission has made it quite clear in deciding the former, that it is empowered under Article 5 (3) 'to judge whether a period in custody is of reasonable duration'.[1] And it has emphasised that 'the question whether a period of detention pending trial is reasonable or not, is not a question to be decided *in abstracto* but to be considered in the light of the particular circumstances of each case'.[2] In making this assessment, the Commission has in the past usually found that the complexity of a case justifies long periods of detention pending trial. Thus, it has characterised as reasonable lengthy delays, if the pre-trial investigation was slowed down because, due to the special facts of the case, the authorities encountered difficulties in gathering the requisite evidence,[3] or if it was deemed advisable to subject the individual to thorough psychiatric examinations before trying him.[4] As part of this same enquiry, the Commission has in some cases also considered as relevant the fact that the ultimate sentence was reduced by the time served pending trial.[5] It has furthermore upheld as reasonable lengthy delays on the ground that they were attributable to legal actions instituted by the Applicant, wherein he challenged the legality of his detention, because they resulted in the unavailability of his case file and thus prevented the prosecution from proceeding on the merits.[6]

One might seriously doubt whether these considerations should be regarded as factors bearing on the reasonableness of a lengthy detention pending trial. The fact that the period of detention resulted in the reduction of the final sentence surely cannot affect the legality of the detention. At most, it goes to the measure of damages to which the person so detained would be entitled to under Article 5 (5). As far as the unavailability of the case file is concerned, it seems rather absurd to contend that the exercise of the right, expressly given by

[1] App. no. 530/59, *Yearbook*, III, 184, 192.

[2] See e.g. App. No. 920/60, 8 *Collection* 46, 48 (1962); App. No. 2077/63, 14 *Collection* 56, 61 (1965).

[3] App. No. 222/56, *Yearbook*, II, 344, 347; App. No. 2077/63, 14 *Collection* 56, 61 (1965); App. No. 920/60, 8 *Collection* 46, 48–9 (1962).

[4] App. No. 1546/62, *Yearbook*, V, 248, 254.

[5] App. No. 222/56, *Yearbook*, II, 344, 347. But see App. No. 1546/62, *Yearbook*, V, 248, 254, where the period of detention pending trial exceeded the final sentence but the Commission nevertheless found no violation of the Convention.

[6] App. No. 530/59, *Yearbook*, III, 184, 192; App. No. 297/57, *Yearbook*, II, 204, 210–12; App. No. 2137/64, 14 *Collection* 54, 61 (1965).

the Convention, to challenge the legality of one's deprivation of liberty,[1] can be used to justify a prolonged detention pending trial. While the Commission has in the past accepted as reasonable what seemed to be unusually lengthy periods of detention, some recent cases indicate that it will no longer uncritically accept governmental assertions that the complexity of the case justifies imprisonment of up to two or three years pending trial. Since the Commission has now at least ruled admissible three cases involving such charges,[2] it may be more willing in the future to give some meaning to this important provision of the Convention. In doing so, the Commission might want to reconsider the validity of its earlier assumption that the complexity of the case makes a lengthy detention reasonable under Article 5 (3). By stipulating that a person who has been deprived of his liberty is entitled 'to trial within a reasonable time or to release pending trial, release may be conditioned by guarantees to appear for trial', Article 5 (3) makes any prolonged detention pending trial a necessary exception, it is arguable, only to assure that the defendant will appear for trial. Accordingly, it seems to me that the term 'reasonable' has reference to the period of detention pending trial that is reasonable for *any* person in a democratic society, irrespective of the complexity of the crime that he is alleged to have committed. If that were not so, the size and facilities of the State's law enforcement agencies would *ipso facto* determine the reasonableness of any period of detention. Of course, this problem cannot be considered solely in terms of statutory construction. It must also be discussed in light of the needs of the law enforcement agencies. This I shall do when dealing with the domestic application of Article 5 (3). Let me submit, however, that in interpreting Article 5 (3), the Commission has so far completely disregarded the rights of the individual. It has to date not recognised that lengthy police detention not only affects the continued willingness and ability of a person to establish his innocence, but that it can also seriously affect his financial capacity to do so, for it might deprive him and his family of the needed resources to put up a really effective defence. The proper administration of justice in a democratic society does not compel such a sacrifice of individual rights.

---

[1] Convention, Article 5(4).

[2] App. No. 2122/64, *Wemhoff* v. *Federal Republic of Germany* (Admissibility), 14 *Collection* 29 (1965) (31 months' detention pending trial); App. No. 1936/63, *Neumeister* v. *Austria* (Admissibility), 14 *Collection* 38 (1965) (two years' detention pending trial); App. No. 1602/62, *Stögmüller* v. *Austria* (Admissibility), 14 *Collection* 62 (1965) (detention pending trial in excess of two years).

(c) *Article 5 (4)*

We have in the course of our discussion already referred to Article 5 (4). It accords an individual deprived of his liberty the right to institute judicial proceedings, in which the legality of his detention 'shall be decided speedily by a court and his release ordered if the detention is not lawful'. This provision has not as yet given rise to much litigation before the Convention Institutions. That this could well change in the foreseeable future may be indicated by a number of recent decisions rendered by the Commission. They raise a question basic to the interpretation of Article 5 (4), that is, whether the judicial proceeding it envisages must conform to the 'fair trial' requirements expressed in Article 6 (1) of the Convention. In two decisions rendered in 1963, the Commission answered this question, by implication at least, in the affirmative.[1] It has now done so expressly in ruling admissible two cases, in which the Applicants charged that they were denied a fair hearing during proceedings conducted to determine the lawfulness of their detention due to the fact that they were excluded from the hearing whereas the Public Prosecutor was allowed to be present.[2] In these cases the Austrian Government took the position that Article 6 (1) did not apply to proceedings under Article 5. Surely, a judicial hearing designed to determine the legality of a person's detention is as much concerned with a 'determination of his civil rights and obligations' as any other proceeding to which Article 6 (1) could possibly apply.

Regarding the nature of the proceedings envisaged by Article 5 (4), the Commission has so far only indicated that it requires a speedy decision by a court of law on the legality of a person's detention.[3] It has emphasised in this connection, however, that 'the judicial inquiry provided for in Article 5, paragraph (4), of the Convention is concerned . . . with the lawfulness of the measures complained of, but not necessarily with the grounds on which they were taken'.[4] As a result, the Commission concluded that so long as the court in question could pass on the legality of a person's detention under a deportation order, the requirements of Article 5 (4)

---

[1] App. No. 1802/63, 10 *Collection* 26, 37–8 (1963); App. No. 1599/62, 10 *Collection* 5, 8 (1963).

[2] App. No. 1936/63, *Neumeister* v. *Austria* (Admissibility), 14 *Collection* 38, 51–3 (1965); App. No. 2178/64, *Matznetter* v. *Austria* (Admissibility), 15 *Collection* 40, 48–9 (1965).

[3] App. No. 858/60, *Yearbook*, IV, 224, 236. But see App. No. 2077/63, 14 *Collection* 56, 60 (1965), where the Commission found that the Applicant was not prejudiced by a one month delay in the adjudication of his plea challenging the lawfulness of an outstanding detention order, because he was during that time imprisoned on other grounds.

[4] App. No. 858/60, *Yearbook*, IV, 224, 238.

were satisfied, even though that tribunal lacked the power to pass on the validity of the grounds for the deportation.

(d) Article 5 (5)

Article 5 (5) of the Convention gives 'the victim of arrest or detention in contravention of the provisions of this Article . . . an enforceable right to compensation'. The Convention Institutions have not yet had an opportunity to interpret this provision. As I have shown elsewhere, a decision by the Convention Institutions based on this provision could present difficult constitutional problems as far as concerns its domestic implementation.[1] I need accordingly not deal with it here.[2] However, a few remarks regarding its meaning are in order. First, this provision does not specify against whom a victim of an illegal deprivation of liberty may proceed. It would nevertheless seem to be clear that the unavailability of this remedy against the State itself would not constitute a violation of Article 5 (5), if under its laws such an action can be instituted against a guilty individual. Second, it is important that defence attorneys in the Member States understand the full import of this provision. Since it speaks of victims of both illegal arrests and detention, it is quite possible that a person, whose detention was lawful, might have a cause of action under this provision because his arrest was unlawful. Here I have in mind particularly cases of police brutality or abuses in effecting an arrest. Such conduct might be illegal under Article 5 without being of a type outlawed in Article 3.[3] Finally, a detention lawful in all other respects, may give rise to a cause of action because of the manner in which it is carried out. It is not inconceivable, for example, that the internment of a minor or person awaiting deportation in a cell with convicts might under certain circumstances violate Article 5.

---

[1] Buergenthal, 'The Effect of the European Convention on Human Rights on the Internal Law of Member States', *Int'l & Comp. L. Q.* Supp. Publ. No. 11, p. 79 (1965).

[2] Parenthetically, it might be noted, however, that the 'enforceable right to compensation' guaranteed in Art. 5 (5) need not necessarily be one enforceable in a court of law if the claim is based on a ruling rendered by a Convention Institution. This would enable Member States to establish administrative procedures or claims courts to compensate persons ruled by the Convention Institutions to have been victims of measures contravening Article 5. In certain countries, where it might be impossible to give domestic legal effect to such decisions by the Convention Institutions, such methods might have to be devised. See Buergenthal, op. cit. at pp. 95 *et seq.*

[3] Article 3 of the Convention provides: 'No one shall be subjected to torture or to inhuman or degrading treatment or punishment'.

In National Courts

1. General application of Article 5

In examining national jurisprudence relating to Article 5, it should initially be noted that two domestic courts have ruled that this provision lacked the status of directly applicable law.[1] The Austrian Constitutional Court ruled in 1961 that Article 5 was not self-executing in nature.[2] And in the famous *Lawless case*, the Irish Supreme Court held that the Convention as a whole had not acquired the status of Irish law, so that Article 5 could not be invoked as a legal norm binding national authorities.[3] The ruling of the Austrian Constitutional Court has in the meantime, however, been reversed by the Austrian legislature, which in 1964 designated the Convention as a constitutional law.[4]

2. Rights of persons arrested or detained

(a) Article 5 (3)

(i) Detention pending trial

Of the rights guaranteed in Article 5 of the Convention, the provision that has received the most extensive interpretation by national courts is paragraph (3). This is not surprising, because in certain Member States it is not uncommon for persons suspected of having committed some types of criminal offences to be held in custody pending trial for a considerable length of time. Since Article 5 (3) entitles an individual so detained to be tried within a reasonable time or to be released pending trial, national tribunals, just like the Convention Institutions, are confronted with the problem of determining what is 'reasonable'. The standards these courts will apply may very well depend upon the particular legal systems under which they operate.

In those legal systems where the suspect, once arraigned, can

---

[1] On the application of the Convention by national courts, see Buergenthal 'The Domestic Status of the European Convention on Human Rights', 13 *Buffalo L. Rev.*, p. 354 (1964).

[2] Austria, VfGH, Judgment of 14 October 1961, 84 *J.B.* 145 (1962). For an eloquent criticism of this decision, see Ermacora 'Die Menschenrechte und der Formalismus', 84 *J.B.* 118 (1962).

[3] Ireland, *In re Lawless*, Judgment of 3 December 1957, [1960] *Irish Reports*, 93 (1957).

[4] See Constitutional Law of 4 March 1964, Article II, para. 7, promulgated on 6 April 1964, [1964] *Bundesgesetzblatt für die Republik Österreich*, No. 59, p. 623. See in this connection Austria, OGH, Judgment of 30 April 1964, 19 *Ö.J.-Z.* 578 (1964), where the Austrian Supreme Court ruled that the lower court, by conditioning the appellant's release pending trial on his promise not to enter a house owned by him, violated Article 5 of the Convention.

refuse to make statements to the police, the judge or the prosecution, and where that right is respected by the authorities, detention pending trial only serves the purpose of preventing escape. Accordingly, except in capital cases, he will find no great difficulty in obtaining his release by posting bond or giving some other guarantees. In other words, the authorities here derive no benefit from his detention. In these countries, therefore, the question what is a reasonable detention poses no real problem. The courts operate on the presumption that the detained is to be set free promptly and all they have to ascertain is whether the guarantees for this ultimate appearance at the trial are adequate from the prosecution's point of view and not unrealistically burdensome as far as the individual is concerned.

In those legal systems, however, where the arraigned individual can be extensively interrogated during his detention, either by the police, the prosecution or the investigating judge, detention pending trial plays a very important role in the eyes of the authorities. Here, the more complicated a case the longer the detention tends to be, because the case against the accused is made while he is in custody. This is not to say or even to imply that innocent people are convicted under such a procedure any more than under any other system of criminal justice. As a matter of fact, it often leads to the speedy exculpation of those wrongly suspected. All I am trying to show is that, in such a system, the judiciary tends to look upon detention pending trial in a different light. It views it as an important part of the entire law enforcement process, with the result that in determining what is a reasonable detention pending trial, it has to resolve a conflict. The conflict is between the interest of the authorities in discharging the investigatory functions assigned to them and that of the individual in his freedom. Once the lines are thus drawn, the question of what is a reasonable detention tends to be examined less in terms of what is reasonable *per se*, that is, from the point of view of the human being not yet tried. Instead, the enquiry proceeds in terms of the complexity of the case, the time that has elapsed since the commission of the crime, the lack of witnesses, the diligence of the prosecution, the unavailability of the case file resulting from the suspect's legal actions instituted to obtain his release, etc. As a consequence, what is 'reasonable', takes on a very relative meaning, in which the right of the suspect to his freedom is, to be sure, one of the elements to be considered, but only one of many. It follows that his chances of obtaining his release are often rather slim, except where his detention has lasted for a number of years or where it has already exceeded the sentence that will most likely be imposed.

This latter approach is, with some exceptions, the general pattern one encounters in examining the relevant national decisions. It is, as we have seen, consistent for the most part with the jurisprudence of the Commission. But this is not to say that it is a correct interpretation of Article 5 (3) or that some national courts have not departed from it in favour of a more individual-oriented approach.

The rule enunciated by the Belgian Supreme Court in a recent case is rather typical of the manner in which many national courts have interpreted Article 5 (3). This tribunal ruled that a detention pending trial lasting a number of months did not violate Articles 5 (1) (c) and 5 (3), because the preliminary investigations (*actes d'instruction*) were still in progress and were carried on without any unjustified delay.[1] Some German courts have reached similar conclusions. In upholding lengthy periods of detention pending trial, they stress the complexity of the case, the danger that the suspect might abscond or that he will seek to hinder the investigation by influencing witnesses.[2] Two decisions depart from this general pattern. In a 1960 case, the Court of Appeals of Saarbrücken concluded that a detention of 21 months pending trial was unreasonable and thus required the suspect's release, despite the probability that he might use his freedom to flee the country.[3] The Court here found that the authorities were not diligent enough in bringing the appellant to trial and that the delay was not attributable to the complexity of the investigation. This being the case, it was irrelevant, in the Court's view, that the detention was shorter than the anticipated sentence might be. It would only be relevant if the delay was due to actual difficulties encountered at the investigatory stage.[4] Recently, however, a lower German court even questioned the validity of this dictum in a decision that shows a genuine appreciation for the rights of the individual.[5] The appellants, who were suspected of having participated in killings of Nazi concentration camp inmates, had by 1964 already spent six years in detention awaiting trial. It appeared, furthermore, that due to the difficulties encountered in preparing the case for trial, it was unlikely that it would take place before 1967. Despite the fact that the Court was persuaded that this delay was not due to any lack of

[1] Belgium, Cour de Cassation, Judgment of 16 March 1964, [1964] *Pasicrisie Belge*, I, pp. 762, 763.
[2] See German Fed. Rep., OLG/Bremen, Judgment of 17 February 1960, 13 *N.J.W.* 1265 (1960); OLG/Saarbrücken, Judgment of 15 February 1960, 13 *N.J.W.* 1731 (1960); BVerfG, Judgment of 14 January 1960, 13 *N.J.W.* 1243, 1244 (1960).
[3] German Fed. Rep., OLG/Saarbrücken, Judgment of 9 November 1960, 14 *N.J.W.* 377 (1961).
[4] Ibid., 378.
[5] German Fed. Rep., Landgericht/Köln, Judgment of 9 June 1964, 17 *N.J.W.* 1816 (1964).

diligence on the part of the authorities investigating the case, it ruled that it exceeded the bounds of reasonableness. In reaching this conclusion, the tribunal reasoned that, even though it be admitted that the anticipated sentence would be longer than the detention pending trial and even though the delay resulted from the complex nature of the case, these considerations did not necessarily justify such a lengthy detention. In the Court's view, an individual has to be released from custody if it is of such duration that it cannot but destroy his morale and impair his continued desire to prove his innocence. A detention of six years pending trial was, in the Court's opinion, calculated to reduce the individual to a totally dispirited cog in the wheels of justice. Such a destruction of the personality of one theoretically presumed innocent could not be tolerated.[1]

Needless to say, judgments of this type are to be welcomed and one can only hope that the detained person does not have to wait six years to hear it pronounced. The notion that a person suspected of having committed a crime can be detained for substantial periods of time pending trial so that the authorities are not inconvenienced in establishing the truth, provided only that the period in custody does not exceed the anticipated sentence, not only shows a basic disregard of the rights of the individual to his personal liberty. It is also inconsistent with the principle that a person is to be presumed innocent until proved guilty. Surely this principle cannot be reconciled with the assumption made by the Commission and some national courts that a detention is not unreasonably long, so long as the anticipated sentence can be expected to be longer. It strikes me as blatant sophistry to argue the theoretical difference between imprisonment following conviction and detention pending trial, for to the individual involved it is a meaningless distinction. It is one thing to make the punishment fit the crime, it is quite another to punish before the crime has been proved. Detention pending trial is just as much a punishment as is a prison sentence. If a legal system is truly interested in guaranteeing the rights of the individual, its law enforcement machinery would not be unduly hampered if, instead of detaining a person for lengthy questioning, it would leave him at liberty and require him to appear before the investigating magistrate at designated intervals.[2]

[1] Ibid., 1817.
[2] Considering past practices in some Member States, the recently enacted amendment to Article 121 of the German Code of Criminal Procedure constitutes a step, but only a step, in the right direction. It limits detention pending trial to a maximum of six months, except 'in cases where the special difficulty or extent of the investigations or some other important reason renders the passing of judgment temporarily impossible and justifies such prolongation'. See translation prepared by the Secretariat of the European Commission of Human Rights, Doc.

(ii) *Preventive detention*

Before concluding our discussion of the manner in which national courts have interpreted Article 5, attention must be called to certain Greek adjudications relating to preventive detention. On two occasions, in 1954[1] and again in 1961[2] the Greek Council of State ruled that the internment apparently without a trial of persons suspected of illegal Communist activities did not violate Article 5 of the Convention. The Court reasoned in both cases that these preventive detention measures were permissible under Article 15 (1) of the Convention, since they were designed to cope with a public danger threatening the nation. Besides, as is apparent from a later decision of the same tribunal,[3] the determination whether such an emergency exists, is a political decision not reviewable by the courts.

It is rather surprising to learn that the existence or non-existence of the conditions precedent to the application of Article 15 is not subject to judicial review, especially in a country where the Convention has supposedly acquired the status of domestic law.[4] It is even more surprising to find that Greece neither reserved the right to apply these laws in accordance with Article 64 of the Convention, nor exercised its right of derogation to do so under Article 15 by notification addressed to the Secretary-General of the Council of Europe.[5]

(b) Article 5 (4)

Domestic litigation involving the rights guaranteed in Article 5 (4) has so far only concerned itself with the question, whether the proceeding to determine the lawfulness of a person's arrest or detention envisaged by this provision must conform to the 'fair trial' standards set forth in Article 6 (1). To me it therefore seems analytically more desirable to examine this jurisprudence later in the context of my discussion of the domestic application of Article 6 (1).

D.5.322. That it does not, however, meet the basic objections to detention pending trial which I have expressed, would appear from a reading of the exceptions stipulated in the new Article 121.

[1] Greece, Council of State, Judgment No. 724/1954, 7 *Rev. Hellénique de Droit Int'l*, 278 (1954).

[2] Greece, Council of State, Judgment 35/1961 (unreported).

[3] Greece, Council of State, Judgment 182/1961 (unreported).

[4] Greece, Arios Pagos (Supreme Court), Judgment No. 386/1955, 9 *Rev. Hellénique de Droit Int'l*, 206 (1956), *Yearbook*, II, 606.

[5] See Convention, Art. 15(3), *Lawless* v. *Ireland* (Merits), Judgment of 1 July 1961, *Yearbook*, IV, 438, 484–6. See also Vasak, *La Convention européenne . . .*, op. cit., 248.

III. ARTICLE 6

Before the Convention Institutions

1. Fairness in the administration of justice

Unless the legislator has formulated detailed rules relating to fairness in the administration of justice, courts have to wrestle with this problem on a case-by-case basis. If they take their duty seriously, especially in criminal cases, they will strive to balance the rights of the individual against the needs for maintaining an effective law enforcement system. This is not an easy task for, of necessity, the standard has to be flexible and has to change with the spirit of the times. The result usually satisfies neither the defendant nor the law enforcement agencies, not to mention the legal profession as it looks for judicial certainty. But when justice is better served by a certain amount of uncertainty, it is a price worth paying.

The European Convention on Human Rights does not contain comprehensive rules relating to the standard of fairness in civil and criminal proceedings. It lays down only broad guidelines. The Convention Institutions charged with the duty of applying them thus face an even more difficult task than do national courts. While it is not easy to evolve some workable norms of fairness for one country, the task becomes profoundly more difficult when it is to be uniform for sixteen countries, whose rules of criminal procedure have not grown identically and whose legal systems vary. The judicial balancing process thus often has to take into consideration different factors present in one legal system but not in another. Accordingly, in interpreting the 'fair trial' provision of Article 6, efforts to formulate hard and fast rules are doomed to failure. If we approach our task realistically, we will have to assume that the result in one or the other case will turn on the sense of fairness, changeable and unpredictable as it may often be, of those who render the final judgment. All we can do is to seek to ascertain what legal factors seem to influence their decisions.

(a) In criminal cases

Article 6 (1) provides in part that 'in the determination of his civil rights and obligations or of any criminal charge against him, everyone is entitled to a fair and public hearing within a reasonable time by an independent and impartial tribunal established by law'. It then goes on to stipulate that, while judgment must be pronounced publicly, the public may under certain specified conditions be excluded from the trial. Under Article 6 (2) a person charged with a criminal offence is entitled to the presumption of innocence, while Article 6 (3) accords him certain 'minimum rights' of a procedural nature. Accordingly, in seeking to understand Article 6 (1), the basic question to be resolved is whether the notion of a 'fair trial' that it enunciates for criminal cases, is limited and defined exclusively by the rights guaranteed in Articles 6 (2) and 6 (3). The Commission has unequivocally answered this question in the negative.

Article 6 of the Convention does not define the notion of 'fair trial' in a criminal case. Paragraph 3 of the Article enumerates certain specific rights which constitute essential elements of that general notion, and paragraph 2 may be considered to add another element. The words 'minimum rights', however, clearly indicate that the six rights specifically enumerated in paragraph 3 are not exhaustive, and that a trial may not conform to the general standard of a 'fair trial', even if the minimum rights guaranteed by paragraph 3—and also the right set forth in paragraph 2—have been respected.[1]

According to the Commission, the determination whether a criminal defendant has been denied a fair trial must be approached in the following manner:

In a case where no violation of paragraph 3 is found to have taken place, the question whether the trial conforms to the standard laid down by paragraph 1 must be decided on the basis of a consideration of the trial as a whole, and not on the basis of an isolated consideration of one particular aspect of the trial or one particular incident. Admittedly, one particular incident or one particular aspect, even if not falling within the provisions of paragraphs 2 or 3, may have been so prominent or may have been of such importance as to be decisive for the general evaluation of the trial as a whole. Nevertheless, even in this contingency, it is on the basis of an evaluation of the trial in its entirety that the answer must be given to the question whether or not there has been a fair trial.[2]

The Commission has repeatedly reaffirmed this principle, which simply asserts that the fairness of a trial cannot be judged on the basis of abstract concepts.[3]

Its emerging jurisprudence provides us, however, with some insights as to what the Commission regards to be inherent elements of a fair trial. In *Pataki and Dunshirn* v. *Austria*, the Commission ruled that 'equality of arms' is an inherent element of a fair hearing, the denial of which violated the Convention.[4] Here the Attorney General,

[1] App. No. 343/57. *Nielsen* v. *Denmark* (Merits), *Yearbook*, IV, 494, 548.
[2] Ibid. 548–50.
[3] See e.g. App. No. 788/60, *Austria* v. *Italy*, Report of the Plenary Commission of 31 March 1963, Council of Europe, Doc. A. 84.548, pp. 224–5 (1963).
[4] App. Nos. 596/59 and 789/60, *Pataki & Dunshirn* v. *Austria*, Report of the Commission of 16 September 1963, Council of Europe, Doc. A. 78.768, pp. 49–50 (1963). The Commission reached the same conclusion in App. Nos. 834/60 et seq., *Glaser et al.* v. *Austria* (Admissibility), Report of the Commission of 17 December 1963, Council of Europe, Doc. 12.417 p. 65 (1964).

who appealed the conviction to obtain a heavier sentence, appeared before the Austrian appellate tribunal at the hearing of the case while the defendants and their counsel were excluded therefrom. To the Commission this was a violation of the procedural equality basic to a fair hearing, notwithstanding the fact that the defendants were given an opportunity to submit written pleadings. The mere possibility that the presence of the Attorney General enabled him to exert an influence on the Court, constituted a violation of the Convention, because it was denied to the defendants to their possible detriment.[1] In passing on the fairness of criminal proceedings the Commission has, furthermore, indicated that it would in this context look into charges of prejudicial press coverage, coerced confessions, prosecution behaviour calculated to arouse the jury, and bias attributable to the composition of the jury, especially in a territory torn by ethnic strife.[2] Consistent with its view, however, that isolated instances of unfairness need not necessarily vitiate the legality of the entire proceedings, the Commission has in such cases also been careful to ascertain whether these objectionable practices could and were in fact cured at the appellate[3] or even the trial level.[4]

(b) In civil cases

Concern for fairness in the administration of criminal justice seems as a rule to relegate the proper adjudication of civil claims to a minor position. This is unfortunate. The effect on the individual may often be equally harmful in either type of case. Article 6 (1) accordingly and properly so guarantees to an individual 'in the determination of his civil rights and obligations . . . a fair and public hearing within a reasonable time by an independent and impartial tribunal established by law'. But, unlike in criminal cases, Article 6 does not even articulate any minimum standards that must be complied with in adjudicating civil claims. The scope of this

---

[1] *Pataki & Dunshirn* v. *Austria*, see note above. It is, of course, arguable that the principle of equality of arms has its source in the provisions of Articles 6 (3) (*b*) and 6 (3) (*c*). The articulation of this concept would thus not compel giving the fair trial provision of Article 6 (1) a meaning broader than that implicit in Articles 6 (2) and 6 (3). However, the Commission has expressly, and I think wisely, refused to adopt this approach. Leaving open the question whether such an interpretation would be permissible, it has concluded that it did not have to pass on this point 'since it is beyond doubt that in any case the wider and general provision for a fair trial, contained in paragraph (1) of Article 6, embodies the notion of "equality of arms".' App. Nos. 542/59 and 617/59, *Ofner & Hopfinger* v. *Austria* (Merits), Report of the Commission of 23 November 1962, Council of Europe, Doc. A. 78.827, p. 78 (1963), *Pataki & Dunshirn* v. *Austria*, loc. cit.

[2] See *Austria* v. *Italy*, loc. cit. App. No. 1476/62, 11 *Collection* 31, 42–3 (1963).

[3] *Austria* v. *Italy*, above, loc. cit. at 209, App. No. 323/57, *Yearbook*, I, 241.

[4] *Nielsen* v. *Denmark*, loc. cit. at 556.

provision must accordingly be supplied by those charged with its interpretation.

In a case[1] that is of particular interest to international lawyers, the Commission rendered an extensive interpretation of the rights accorded to a civil litigant under Article 6 (1). The Applicant, a Polish national residing in Germany, sought in Swedish courts to obtain visitation rights to his infant child living with his divorced wife in Sweden. His application for entry into Sweden to participate in the proceedings was denied. In passing on the admissibility of this Application, the Commission first noted that the Convention did not necessarily guarantee a litigant the right to participate in person in every civil proceeding. However, there are certain types of case where the personality and moral character of the litigants are of vital importance in determining the rights of the parties. Here, in the Commission's view, since the absence of one party could be detrimental to his interest, the notion of a fair trial as expressed in Article 6 (1) may imply the right for both litigants to be present, especially when, as in the instant action, it was accorded to one of them.[2] Under these circumstances, and notwithstanding the fact that general international law leaves states free to control the admission of aliens and that a foreigner's right to enter the territory of a member State is not as such guaranteed by the Convention, a High Contracting Party must be understood to have agreed 'to restrict the free exercise of its rights under general international law, including its right to control the entry and exit of foreigners, to the extent and within the limits of the obligations which it has accepted under the Convention'.[3] Since Sweden subsequently granted the Applicant an entry visa, the Commission did not have to decide whether its initial denial violated his rights under Article 6 (1).[4] That it might well have reached this conclusion is, however, apparent from its opinion.

In applying Article 6 (1) the Commission has also ruled that the adjudication of civil claims by arbitration under a procedure departing from that which is consistent with proper judicial practice, was not *ipso facto* a violation of the Convention.[5] A waiver of judicial adjudication in favour of arbitration might, however, in the Commission's view, be incompatible with the rights guaranteed in the Convention if not given voluntarily.[6] This would also be true, if the conduct of the arbitrator was incompatible with the spirit of Article 6 (1). Such would presumably be the case, if the arbitrator, for example, acted in a way which raised serious doubt about his impartiality. In this connection, one might ask parenthetically whether a

---

[1] App. No. 434/58, *Yearbook*, II, 354.   [2] Ibid., 370.   [3] Ibid., 372.
[4] See App. No. 911/60, *Yearbook*, IV, 198, 206.
[5] App. No. 1197/61, *Yearbook*, V, 88.   [6] Ibid., 96.

member State, by delegating judicial powers to an international institution, would violate the Convention, if in the determination of his civil rights an individual is not accorded by that body the rights assured him under Article 6 (1). It is not inconceivable that the Convention Institutions will have to face this question. Accordingly, it should be noted that the Commission has on at least one occasion indicated that a State, in concluding an international agreement, is 'bound not to disable itself from giving effect to the rights and freedoms which it had guaranteed by entering into the European Convention'.[1]

To round out our discussion of Article 6 (1), a number of points remain. There is first the obvious observation that the minimum rights guaranteed in Article 6 (3) apply as such only to criminal cases.[2] A denial of similar rights in a civil case may, however, violate Article 6 (1). Thus, to refuse a civil party the opportunity of introducing certain relevant evidence might amount to a denial of a fair trial.[3] This might equally be true, if a person is not allowed to be represented by counsel in certain civil proceedings[4] and, conceivably, if counsel is not assigned to him in some special civil cases.[5]

Finally, it should be pointed out that the Convention Institutions, in interpreting Article 6, are not bound by the legal classification ascribed to a case by national legislation. In other words, whether a given dispute involves a person's civil or other rights, is a determination that is ultimately governed by the law of the Convention. This at least has been the holding of the Commission in a case arising out of a defamation action, which under the applicable Austrian law was criminal in nature.[6] The Commission here concluded that, since the action was instituted by the defamed person to protect his reputation, it involved his civil rights, even though Austrian law characterised it as criminal.[7] This interpretation, which makes a great deal of sense, would seem to compel a different result from that reached by the Commission in another case.[8] The facts giving rise to this Application turned on a decision suspending the Applicant's visitation rights to her children by a former marriage. The court which had granted the underlying divorce had left to administrative authorities the task of working out the appropriate custody arrangements. They awarded custody of the children to the Applicant's

---

[1] App. No. 655/59, *Yearbook*, III, 280, 286.
[2] See e.g. App. No. 265/57, *Yearbook*, I, 192.
[3] See App. No. 852/60, *Yearbook*, IV, 346, 354; App. No. 1092/61, *Yearbook*, V, 210, 212.
[4] See App. No. 1013/61, *Yearbook*, V, 158, 164–6.
[5] See App. No. 727/60, *Yearbook*, III, 302, 308–10.
[6] App. No. 808/60, *Yearbook*, V, 108.   [7] Ibid., 122.
[8] App. No. 1329/62, *Yearbook*, V, 200.

former husband and accorded the Applicant visitation rights. These were subsequently sustained by the courts in a proceeding instituted by the father. Thereafter they were, however, suspended by the Ministry of Justice without granting the Applicant a hearing. She challenged this decision before the Commission relying, *inter alia*, on Article 6 of the Convention. In ruling the Application inadmissible, the Commission held that Article 6 applies only 'to proceedings before courts of law'.[1] Since the decision to suspend the Applicant's visitation rights was 'an administrative decision, solely within the competence of that Ministry', the Commission concluded that Article 6 was inapplicable, because 'the right to have a purely administrative decision based upon proceedings comparable to those prescribed by Article 6 for proceedings in Court is not as such included among the rights and freedoms guaranteed by the Convention'.[2] While one may seriously doubt whether Article 6 governs only judicial proceedings,[3] it certainly begs the question to say that Article 6 applies only to proceedings in a court of law. The pertinent question is whether the Applicant's 'civil rights and obligations' were determined in these proceedings. If the answer is yes, as it must be in this case, the Applicant was entitled 'to a fair and public hearing within a reasonable time by an independent and impartial tribunal established by law'. A different conclusion would permit a state to delegate the adjudication of an individual's civil rights to administrative bodies, thereby effectively circumventing the safeguards established in Article 6. One may accordingly hope that the Commission will reconsider the reasoning underlying this decision, because it is patently incompatible with the purpose of Article 6. Its applicability in any given case must be determined by asking whether a person's civil rights and obligations are at stake, and not by reference to a formalistic dichotomization that distinguishes between administrative and civil proceedings.[4]

2. *Specific rights of the criminal defendant*

The beneficiaries of the rights guaranteed in Article 6 (2) and 6 (3) are those 'charged with a criminal offence'. It must accordingly be determined who qualifies as such a person. Here it should again be

[1] App. No. 1329/62 *Yearbook*, v, 208.   [2] Ibid.

[3] See Schwelb 'On the Operation of the European Convention on Human Rights', 18 *International Organisation* 558, 575 (1964) who subjects this decision to a searching analysis and concludes that its soundness 'is open to very serious doubts'.

[4] See, in this connection, the very valuable analysis by Velu, 'Le Problème de l'Application aux Juridictions Administratives, des Règles de la Convention Européenne des Droits de l'Homme Relatives à la Publicité des Audiences et des Jugements', 38 *Revue de Droit International et de Droit Comparé* 129 (1961).

emphasised that this determination cannot be made exclusively by reference to the meaning ascribed to this phrase by the domestic law of any one state. This the Commission recognised in a 1963 decision. Taking note of the fact that the German Code of Criminal Procedure distinguishes between a so-called accused (*Angeklagter*), who has already been 'committed for trial', and an individual who has merely been indicted (*Angeschuldigter*), the Commission ruled that the latter 'although not yet an "Angeklagter" under the Code of Criminal Procedure, becomes at that stage "charged with a criminal offence" within the meaning of Article 6. . . .'[1] The Commission has also repeatedly held that a convicted person cannot invoke the rights guaranteed in Articles 6 (2) and 6 (3) since he is no longer merely 'charged with a criminal offence'. This issue presents itself in cases involving convicts who, in seeking to obtain retrials or the re-opening of the original proceedings, claim that the determination of their motion is subject to the provisions of Article 6.[2] The Commission has, however, rightly noted that Article 6 would apply notwithstanding a final conviction, if it is subsequently re-opened and new charges are lodged against the defendant.[3] Logically, the same result should obtain even if no new charges are filed, once the case is re-examined on the merits.

(a) The presumption of innocence

Article 6 (2) provides that 'everyone charged with a criminal offence shall be presumed innocent until proved guilty according to law'. The Commission has had the opportunity of considering the scope of this provision in considerable detail in the case of *Austria* v. *Italy*.[4] This litigation had its genesis in criminal proceedings that took place in Italian courts and which resulted in the conviction of a number of youths belonging to the German-speaking minority in the Bolzano area, who were charged with the killing of an Italian customs official. One of the many charges advanced against Italy related to an alleged breach of the presumption of innocence. In support of its claim, Austria contended that confessions were extracted from the accused by threats and by actual maltreatment, that the prosecution was permitted by the Court to indulge in vitriolic attacks calculated to prejudice the jury against the defence, and that certain legal conclusions were not substantiated by the evidence. The Commission

---

[1] App. No. 1216/61, 11 *Collection* 1, 6 (1963).
[2] See e.g. App. No. 914/60, *Yearbook*, IV, 372, holding that persons seeking a re-opening of the proceedings (Wiederaufnahme des Verfahrens) are not entitled to protection under Article 6 (2). Ibid., 376.
[3] See App. No. 2136/64, 13 *Collection* 116, 120 (1964).
[4] *Austria* v. *Italy*, loc. cit.

rejected these allegations on the merits,[1] but in doing so provided us with considerable insight as to how it will interpret Article 6 (2). Basic to this provision, in the Commission's view, is the notion that courts must not approach a criminal case with the assumption that the accused committed the crime in question. To use the Commission's words, 'the onus to prove guilt falls upon the Prosecution and any doubt is to the benefit of the accused'.[2] The defendant must accordingly be permitted to refute the evidence. To be lawful, furthermore, the conviction must be based on direct or indirect evidence 'sufficiently strong in the eyes of the law to establish his guilt'.[3] To the Commission, 'Article 6 (2) is thus primarily concerned with the spirit in which the judges must carry out their task . . .'.[4]

In assessing it, the Commission will, for example, examine charges of misbehaviour by the prosecution. The assumption here is that, if the Court does not check it, this may indicate that the tribunal has itself prejudged the case. By the same token, if the Court accepts confessions procured by illegal means, the Commission will hold that the defendant was denied the right guaranteed him under the Convention to be proved guilty according to law.[5]

A question that is by no means easy to answer, and that seems to have been left unresolved in *Austria* v. *Italy*, concerns the power of the Convention Institutions to examine allegations that the prosecution did not sustain the requisite burden of proof. The Convention does not, of course, tell us what the extent of that burden must be. As we have seen, the Commission has indicated that the evidence must be 'sufficiently strong in the eyes of the law to establish . . . guilt'. The question remains: in the eyes of what law, the law of the convicting state or the law of the Convention? Presumably, there is a limit beyond which the law of the convicting state may not go; it may not expressly or implicitly, for example, shift the burden of proof on the defendant. But apart from this, there is a wide range of cases that cannot be so easily decided. Here the demarcation line between errors of law or fact, which the Convention Institutions may not pass upon, and violations of the Convention, is blurred. Accordingly, it is interesting to note that in rejecting the Austrian contention that the Italian courts based their findings of homicidal intent on insufficient evidence, the Commission stated that it was 'not competent to substitute its own assessment of the evidence for that of the national courts, but can only pronounce as to whether the domestic courts have committed any abuse or procedural irregularity'.[6] This formula does not, of course, help resolve our question. It may nevertheless indicate that the Commission will leave to national courts

---

[1] *Austria* v. *Italy*, loc. cit., 207–12. [2] Ibid., 208. [3] Ibid.
[4] Ibid. [5] Ibid. [6] Ibid., 211.

wide discretion in appreciating the evidence, provided only that in doing so they proceed on the assumption that all reasonable doubts must be resolved in favour of the accused. In other words, since it will not substitute its own evaluation of the facts for that of the national courts, it would seem that the Commission's enquiry will be concerned primarily with the attitude which domestic tribunals bring to the case, rather than with their ultimate assessment of the evidence.

(b) *The enumerated minimum rights*

(i) *Article 6 (3) (a)*

The Convention, in Article 6 (3), accords a person charged with a criminal offence five so-called 'minimum rights'. The first of these, set out in Article 6 (3) (*a*), entitled him 'to be informed promptly, in a language which he understands and in detail, of the nature and cause of the accusation against him'. In interpreting this provision, the Commission has ruled that under it the defendant 'has the right to be informed not only of the grounds for the accusation, that is, not only the acts with which he is charged and on which his indictment is based, but also of the *nature* of the accusation, namely, the legal classification of the acts in question'. (Italics in original).[1] To the Commission, this right is closely linked to Article 6 (3) (*b*), which entitles the accused to adequate time and facilities for the preparation of his defence.[2] It follows from this that an allegation charging a violation of Article 6 (3) (*a*) will be examined in the light of the adverse effect it may have had on the effective preparation of the defendant's case.[3]

It is no doubt true that all of the rights guaranteed in Article 6 are closely interrelated. But it should be noted that the Commission, by examining a charge under Article 6 (3) (*a*) from the point of view of the rights guaranteed in Article 6 (3) (*b*), may well have watered down the meaning of Article 6 (3) (*a*). This results from the fact that by interpreting this provision in terms of the effect its non-compliance may have had on the preparation of the defence, the Commission has ascribed a relative meaning to a right formulated in absolute language. That such was not the intention of those who drafted the Convention, would seem to be apparent from the fact that they expressed Article 6 (3) (*a*) as a right separate and distinct from that accorded in Article 6 (3) (*b*). By giving Article 6 (3) (*a*) an identity of its own, they must be understood to have determined that the defence is, as a matter of law, prejudiced whenever the defendant is not informed 'promptly' and 'in detail' of the charges against him.

---

[1] *Ofner & Hopfinger* v. *Austria*, loc. cit. at 31.
[2] Ibid.   [3] Ibid., 74–7.

If this assumption is correct, it is the Commission's task under Article 6 (3) (*a*) to ascertain whether the requisite information was conveyed promptly and in sufficient detail. It may accordingly not speculate whether, in any given case, non-compliance with this requirement adversely affected the preparation of the defence because the Convention proceeds on that assumption.

In the light of the foregoing, I have some doubts as to the soundness of the Commission's adjudication of one of the allegations advanced in the *Nielsen case*.[1] The Applicant here contended that he was not informed of the charges against him in sufficient detail. The indictment charged him with having planned and instigated an attempted robbery that caused a homicide, but it did not describe the manner in which the crime was perpetrated. Specifically, it contained no indication that the prosecution intended to prove that the defendant committed these offences by virtue of the hypnotic influence he exercised over the actual perpetrator. Besides, the Danish courts denied counsel's motion to compel the prosecution to indicate whether the term 'instigate', referred to in the indictment, encompassed the notion of hypnotic suggestion. The Commission, nevertheless, ruled that Article 6 (3) (*a*) had not been violated.[2] It reasoned that the term 'instigate' was sufficiently broad to cover hypnotic influence. According to the Commission, furthermore, counsel must have been aware of the nature of the prosecution's case, because he was furnished with a lengthy report relating to psychiatric and hypnotic tests performed on the actual perpetrator of the offences allegedly masterminded by the defendant.[3]

These findings are actually irrelevant. In the first place, the issue under Article 6 (3) (*a*) is not whether the language of the indictment was broad enough to cover hypnotic suggestion but whether, being so broad, it conveyed to the defendant in detail the requisite information about the nature of the charges against him. Besides, the fact that the defence could surmise how the prosecution planned to prove its case, is not enough to satisfy the requirements of Article 6 (3) (*a*). If it were not so, the right guaranteed in Article 6 (3) (*a*) would be illusory, for sooner or later every defendant can figure out what it is that he is being charged with. In my opinion, the whole purpose of Article 6 (3) (*a*) is to obviate this type of speculation on the part of the defence.

(ii) *Article 6 (3) (b)*

As indicated earlier, Article 6 (3) (*b*) entitles a person charged with a criminal offence 'to have adequate time and facilities for the preparation of his defence'. Here it should initially be noted that of the five

---

[1] *Nielsen* v. *Denmark*, loc. cit.   [2] Ibid., 538.   [3] Ibid., 536.

minimum rights guaranteed in Article 6 (3), this one is the least susceptible to concise definition. Whether or not it has been violated, is of necessity a question that will depend upon the specific facts of the case, the issue always being whether the defendant's right to put up an effective defence was protected. A number of general observations can, however, be made. It may be assumed for example, that this provision would be violated if the prosecution interfered unreasonably with necessary consultations between defence counsel and his client. The same would be true if counsel were denied access to relevant documents, although here it should be noted that its denial to the accused will not constitute a breach of the Convention, provided it was accorded to his attorney in due time to permit him to consult with the defendant.[1] It is equally clear that, as a rule, short time limits within which to file appeals will not give rise to a cause of action under this provision, especially if the pleadings can be supplemented at the subsequent hearing.[2] But, where the documentary evidence is voluminous, the failure to grant a reasonable extension of time to enable counsel to examine it, may amount to a violation of Article 6 (3) (b).[3]

(iii) *Article 6 (3) (c)*

Article 6 (3) (c) guarantees the right to counsel. Under it the accused on a criminal charge is entitled 'to defend himself in person or through legal assistance of his own choosing or, if he has not sufficient means to pay for legal assistance, to be given it free when the interests of justice so require'. Thus Article 6 (3) (c) clearly indicates that the indigent defendant's right to counsel is not absolute. It is limited by the requirements of justice.[4] The Commission has, furthermore, held that, even if in a given case counsel must be assigned, the indigent accused does not have the right to compel the designation of the attorney of his choice.[5] Besides, in the Commission's view, a comparison of the English and French text of Article 6 (3) (c) indicates that the right expressed therein does not even require the appointment of an attorney as such, but merely a person qualified to provide legal assistance.[6] As a result, the Commission found that Article 6 (3) (c) had not been violated where the attorney assigned to

---

[1] See *Ofner & Hopfinger* v. *Austria*, loc. cit. at pp. 34–6.
[2] App. No. 441/58, *Yearbook*, ii, 391, 395.
[3] See App. No. 2122/64, *Wemhoff* v. *Germany* (New complaints), 15 *Collection* 1, 5 (1965).
[4] App. No. 127/55, *Yearbook*, i, 230, 231.
[5] App. No. 646/59, *Yearbook*, iii, 272, 276–8.
[6] App. No. 509/59, *Yearbook*, iii, 174, 182. The Commission reached this conclusion even though the French text of Article 6 (3) (c) refers to an 'avocat', because its English counterpart only speaks of 'legal assistance'.

182 HUMAN RIGHTS IN NATIONAL AND INTERNATIONAL LAW

the defendant did not handle the case himself, but was represented in the proceedings by his law clerk (*Referendar*).[1] Without necessarily disagreeing with the Commission's theoretical construction of Article 6 (3) (*c*), it should be emphasised that this provision authorises the Commission to ascertain not only whether legal assistance was provided but also whether in a particular case the interests of justice were fully served by the appointment of, or the legal services rendered by, a law clerk rather than an attorney.[2]

While the language of Article 6 (3) (*c*) appears to guarantee an accused, who has the requisite means to hire his own attorney, the unrestricted right to do so, at least one case indicates that the Commission does not so construe it.[3] From the rather skimpy facts given, it seems that in this case the accused was not allowed to employ a certain attorney to defend him in a criminal prosecution arising out of the defendant's political activities on behalf of an outlawed political organisation. In all likelihood, the attorney in question was thought to be associated with this group. While the Commission noted that it could reject the Application for failure to exhaust domestic remedies, it chose instead to decide the case on the merits by holding that

... the right to defend oneself through legal assistance of one's own choosing, as guaranteed by Article 6, paragraph (3), subparagraph (*c*), of the Convention ... is not an absolute right, but limited by the right of the State concerned to make regulations concerning the appearance of lawyers before the courts; ... therefore, the State has full discretion to exclude lawyers from appearing before the courts; ....[4]

The Commission, would, of course, be right if the selected attorney was disbarred or not qualified to appear before certain courts. To that extent the right to be represented by counsel of one's own choosing is not absolute. This and not more follows from the power of each state to control and regulate admissions to its Bar. But where the attorney has not been thus disbarred or disqualified, the right of an accused to choose any willing Member of the Bar would seem to be absolute. A different interpretation of Article 6 (3) (*c*) deprives it of any real meaning.

(iv) *Article 6 (3) (d)*

Of the minimum rights set forth in Article 6 (3), probably the most

[1] App. No. 509/59, *Yearbook*, III, 180–2. A *Referendar* is a person who has obtained his law degree but who has not yet completed the statutory training in the courts and law offices required for admission to the Bar.
[2] This would seem to be but another aspect of the equality-of-arms problem. See *Glaser et al. v. Austria*, loc. cit. at p. 31.
App. No. 722/60, *Yearbook*, V, 104.　　　　[4] Ibid., 106.

difficult to apply is that accorded to an accused in subparagraph (*d*). It entitles him 'to examine or have examined witnesses against him and to obtain the attendance and examination of witnesses on his behalf under the same conditions as witnesses against him'.

It must be remembered, in the first place, that under the rules of procedure in force in some member States, the decision whether to call a witness is made by the judge who, in doing so, has to determine whether the testimony the witness could give would be relevant. This differs from the Common Law system, where counsel is free to call any witness he desires and where the Court will be required to rule on the admissibility of the testimony only after having heard either all of it, part of it, or counsel's questions designed to elicit it. Thus, at least with regard to one requirement of Article 6 (3) (*d*), that the defendant is entitled to obtain the attendance of witnesses on his behalf 'under the same conditions as witnesses against him', the task of the Common Law judge is an easy one, because the parties rather than he decide who shall be called. Besides, if a witness refuses to attend voluntarily, counsel can have him subpoenaed as a matter of course. Since the Continental judge must initially decide whom to call as a witness, he will not find the standard contained in Article 6 (3) (*d*) as easy to apply. This is due to the fact that he will be confronted not only with the problem also faced by the Common Law judge under Article 6 (3) (*d*), that is, ensuring that the defendant's right to examine witnesses on his behalf under the same conditions as witnesses against him is protected, but he will also have to apply this standard in ensuring the defendant's right to obtain their attendance. Since this decision is of necessity made in terms of the probative evidence the witness might provide, it requires a further value judgment, which the Common Law judge does not have to make and which offers additional opportunity for error or a violation of the Convention, because as a practical matter no two witnesses will be able to provide the same probative evidence. Thus, as far as the attendance of witnesses is concerned, Article 6 (3) (*d*) furnishes the Common Law judge with a simple mechanical rule, i.e. all witnesses must be allowed to take the stand. Its application by the Continental judge is by no means as simple.

The second difficulty which Article 6 (3) (*d*) presents is closely related to the first. It has to do with the function which the Convention Institutions perform in applying this provision. Since they are not appellate tribunals, they lack the power to review errors of law or fact committed by domestic courts. Accordingly, the following question presents itself: if a Continental judge has not called a witness whose anticipated testimony he ruled to be irrelevant, or if a Common Law judge has excluded certain testimony as being inadmissible, how do we determine whether they merely erred or whether they violated the Convention?

The jurisprudence of the Commission throws some light on this question. Initially it should be noted that the Commission has repeatedly stated that Article 6 (3) (*d*) does not entitle 'the accused to call everyone, in particular persons who are not in a position to assist by their statements in elucidating the truth; . . . in other words, paragraph (3) (*d*) does not prohibit the Court from refusing to summon persons who cannot be "witnesses on his behalf" within the meaning of that . . . paragraph'.[1] In its view, this provision is designed to place the defendant 'on an equal footing with the prosecution as regards the hearing of witnesses'.[2] The application of these formulae presented a real challenge in the case of *Austria* v. *Italy*.[3] The defence here sought to rebut the prosecution's contention that the deceased customs official was either thrown into the river bed alive or that he was already dead when pushed in. It contended that he had fallen in accidentally while trying to escape his pursuers. Thus, the state and position of the body was a crucial element in the case. The question which the Commission accordingly had to resolve was whether the Italian courts, by hearing two witnesses for the prosecution, who had seen the body before it was moved, violated Article 6 (3) (*d*) because they refused defence counsel's request to call the medical examiner who had certified the decedent's death. Since this physician had examined the deceased after the body had already been moved, his testimony on that point would have been immaterial. It was argued before the Commission, however, that his testimony regarding certain traces of rock fragments he had noticed on the body tended to substantiate the defence theory regarding the cause of death and that this same physician was present at the autopsy performed twelve hours later by a medical expert, who was heard by the Court.

In deciding whether the Italian courts had deprived the defendants of the rights guaranteed them in Article 6 (3) (*d*), the Commission initially noted that its enquiry would not be limited to ascertaining whether under Italian law the right to call witnesses is assured to the defence and prosecution alike on conditions of equality. It had to be determined also 'whether the . . . Court created any inequality of treatment in its application of the law'.[4] This question the Commis-

---

[1] See e.g. App. No. 617/59, *Hopfinger* v. *Austria* (Admissibility), *Yearbook*, III, 370, 390–2. Parenthetically, it should be noted that this test would not be applicable, for the reasons previously explained, to cases coming from Common Law jurisdictions.

[2] App. No. 1134/61 *Yearbook*, IV, 378, 382.

[3] *Austria* v. *Italy*, loc. cit.   [4] Ibid., 113.

sion seems to have examined from two aspects. It looked first to the information available to the judge when he made his decision not to call the witness in question. Here the Commission concluded that he had not been apprised of the fact that the witness had been present at the autopsy. All he knew was that the prospective witness had seen the body only after it had been moved. The latter factor the Commission considered especially important, because the defence's motion to hear this witness at the scene of the crime was made after the prosecution had been granted permission to question its two witnesses regarding the position of the body.[1] In other words, due to the fact that the defence motion was made in that context, the judge could reasonably assume that this witness was offered to give evidence concerning the location of the corpse with regard to which he was, in the Court's opinion, not competent to testify. The Commission's next step in passing on this case consisted merely of a verification of the Italian court's conclusion that the witness offered by the defence could in fact not have testified to the position of the body.[2] Significantly, the Commission never examined the question whether the failure to call this witness at any stage of the proceedings violated Article 6 (3) (d), although it is at least arguable that the information he could have offered regarding the physical condition of the body might have been relevant.[3]

What light does this case throw on the application of Article 6 (3) (d) by the Convention Institutions? In answering this question we must first emphasise that it is not entirely clear what the Commission would have decided, had it found that the witness in question, notwithstanding the contrary conclusion reached by the Italian court, could in fact have testified to the position of the body. As a result one can do no more than speculate on the wider implication of this case; that is, how the Commission for one will draw the demarcation line between errors of fact and law on the one hand, and violations of Article 6 (3) (d) on the other. It seems, however, that the Commission will limit its review functions under the second half-sentence of Article 6 (3) (d) to a single enquiry. It will simply ask whether, at the time the decision was made to call or not to call a certain witness, the judge acted arbitrarily by denying one side an equal hearing on the specific point in issue, considering all the information reasonably available to him. But, the mere fact that the Court erred or that reasonable men might disagree with this decision will not result in a violation of Article 6 (3) (d).[4] What seems to be needed to make

---

[1] Ibid., 114–15.   [2] Ibid.
[3] See, in this connection, the forceful dissenting opinion by Professor Ermacora. Ibid., 116–19.
[4] See App. No. 1476/62, 11 *Collection* 31, 43–4 (1963).

out a violation of Article 6 (3) (*d*) is a showing that, on the facts known to the judge or which he should have known, his decision was clearly calculated to favour one side to the detriment of the other.

Article 6 (3) (*d*), as will be recalled, also guarantees to the accused on a criminal charge the very important right 'to examine or have examined witnesses against him'. One aspect of the case of *Austria* v. *Italy*[1] presented an interesting and by no means easy question relating to the interpretation of this right. In the course of the proceedings, the Italian court ordered the hearing moved to the scene of the crime to clarify the evidence relating to the position of the deceased's body. That inspection was attended by the Court, the two witnesses who had found the body, one of the defendants, the prosecution and counsel for the other defendants. It appears that the defence attorneys had previously informally asked the Court to permit the remaining defendants to be present and that this was denied. No formal motion, was, however, made. It also appears that once at the scene, the investigation was broadened beyond its original purpose, with the result that the only defendant who was there, and whose testimony incidentally had incriminated the other accused, was also questioned. The Austrian Government accordingly contended before the Commission that the absence of the remaining defendants violated their rights under Article 6 (3) (*d*). The Commission rejected this argument. It noted that the defendants, according to their own testimony, had no knowledge regarding the location of the body. And while it admitted that it 'would have been better' if the one defendant had not been questioned in the absence of the remaining accused, it found that the failure of the defence attorneys to ask for an adjournment to permit their attendance constituted a waiver and could be regarded as such by the Italian court.[2]

This decision raises two interesting points. The first has to do with the fact that Article 6 (3) (*d*) does not expressly state that the defendant has the right to be present when witnesses against him are examined, although this may be implied from the words 'to examine or have examined'. Nevertheless, it is quite clear that to deny him this right would be inconsistent with the notion of a fair hearing. The Commission, at any rate, seems to have proceeded on the assumption that a defendant is entitled to be present when witnesses against him are examined.

The second point was expressly considered by Father Beaufort in his dissenting opinion. He argued that even if one were to assume that the defence had through error or omission waived defendant's rights, this was not dispositive of the case. In his view 'judges are

[1] *Austria* v. *Italy*, loc. cit.   [2] Ibid., 142.

obliged to protect and safeguard the rights of an accused person as enumerated in the Convention. There is no need for the accused to make formal application to exercise these rights. Judges should guarantee them automatically'.[1] In his dissenting opinion, Professor Ermacora makes the same point.[2] While, considering all the circumstances of the case, one might seriously disagree with the Commission's conclusion that the defence had in fact waived its rights,[3] the argument of the dissenting Members of the Commission regarding the duty of domestic judges under the Convention presents certain problems. Under an adversary system of criminal procedure of the Common Law type, the function of a judge is primarily that of a referee between two contending parties. Except in certain exceptional cases, for example, if the accused is not represented by an attorney, he cannot on his own motion enforce rights which counsel for the defence does not invoke. Given this legal setting, the argument made by the dissenters, if accepted, could interfere with counsel's conduct of the defence and would require a complete reshaping of the governing rules of criminal procedure and, for that matter, a large body of substantive civil and criminal law doctrine having its source in the peculiarities of the adversary system. On the other hand, in a system of criminal justice where the judge performs a much more active role in the conduct of a trial, the argument made by the dissenters, that the Court has a duty to assure to the defendant the rights guaranteed in the Convention whether or not he invokes them, may well have greater validity. At any rate, it is clear that this question cannot be decided abstractly. It requires a comprehensive evaluation by the Convention Institutions of the functions a judge performs in one or the other member States.

(v) *Article 6 (3) (e)*

The final provision of Article 6 (3) stipulates in subparagraph (e) that a person charged with a criminal offence is entitled 'to have the free assistance of an interpreter if he cannot understand or speak the language used in court'. The Convention Institutions have not as yet been called upon to interpret this provision. While it is self-explanatory, one might note that a person who has sufficient understanding and command of the language in which the judicial proceedings are conducted to defend himself effectively, would not be entitled to invoke this provision merely to gratify his ethnic or nationalistic convictions.[4]

---

[1] Ibid., 146.   [2] Ibid., 149.
[3] On this point I find Professor Ermacora's contrary argument more persuasive. Ibid., 150–1.
[4] See, in this connection, App. No. 808/60, *Yearbook*, v, 108.

In National Courts

As we have seen, domestic court litigation involving Article 5 has been limited largely to an interpretation of the provisions contained in Article 5 (3). The provisions of Article 6, on the other hand, have been invoked more extensively before national tribunals. These cases have dealt with questions involving the type of legal proceedings to which Article 6 (1) applies, the presumption of innocence, the right to counsel, to examine witnesses, to gratuitous services of an interpreter, etc. In other words, the jurisprudence of the domestic courts has in the meantime considered most of the legal questions presented by Article 6.

1. *Fairness in the administration of justice*

In approaching the rights guaranteed in Article 6 (1), some national courts were initially called upon to ascertain whether this provision applies only to civil and criminal cases or whether administrative proceedings are also governed by it. Here it should be noted that, in making this determination, the domestic tribunals have generally approached the question by defining legal proceedings as civil, criminal or administrative not in terms of their substantive character, but along the public-private law dichotomy adopted in their legal system. Illustrative of this approach is a judgment rendered by a German appellate court, which held that decisions of administrative tribunals did not have to be pronounced publicly, because Article 6 applied only to civil and criminal courts.[1] This conclusion was based in part at least on the German text of Article 6 (1) under which such an interpretation is not unreasonable, but only because the translation is erroneous. The German translation of Article 6 (1) speaks in part of 'an independent and impartial tribunal established by law, authorised to adjudicate his civil rights and obligations or any criminal charges brought against him'. While this language comes closer to the more ambiguous French wording of Article 6 (1), it is totally at variance with the English text, which provides that 'in the determination of his civil rights and obligations or of any criminal charge against him, everyone is entitled to a fair and public hearing . . . by an independent and impartial tribunal established by law'. In other words, a reading of the German text might justify the assump-

---

[1] Germ. Fed. Rep., OVG/Münster, Judgment of 25 November 1955, 9 *N.J.W.* 1374, 1375 (1956). See also to the same effect OVG/Münster, Judgment of 24 June 1955, 9 *N.J.W.* 157 (1956); BVerwG, Judgment of 16 September 1957, 11 *M.D.R.* 697 (1957); OLG/Celle, Judgment of 17 November 1959, 13 *N.J.W.* 880 (1960). But see BGH, Judgment of 21 April 1959, 12 *N.J.W.* 1230 (1959), recognising the danger inherent in this approach.

tion that Article 6 (1) refers only to courts having jurisdiction to decide civil and criminal cases. The authentic English version, however, permits no such conclusion, notwithstanding the fact that the Commission seems to have adopted a position similar to that taken by German courts.

But that is not to say that Article 6 (1) necessarily applies to all types of administrative proceedings. It governs only those which affect a person's civil rights or obligations or which are criminal in nature. This characterisation must be made not in terms of the particular classification adopted for it under one or the other legal system, but by reference to the substance of the claims involved. This is particularly true in situations where a person challenges the legality of his detention. A case in point is a 1960 decision rendered by a Bavarian Appeals Court. The appellant here contended that the proceedings leading to his detention in an asylum for the mentally ill did not conform to Article 6 (1) of the Convention. His appeal was rejected on the ground that the proceedings in question were administrative in nature and thus not governed by Article 6.[1] The Court based its decision in part on the erroneous German translation of Article 6 (1) as well as on Article 13 of the Convention. In relying on the latter provision, the tribunal emphasised that it merely entitled the victim of a violation of the Convention to 'an effective remedy before a national authority notwithstanding that the violation has been committed by persons acting in an official capacity'. It therefore concluded that, since the order detaining an individual in an asylum for the mentally ill was under its law a sovereign or official act and since Article 13 refers only to 'an effective remedy before a national authority' without prescribing that the national authority be a court, it followed that Article 6 (1) did not apply to administrative proceedings challenging the sovereign acts here in question. What the Court overlooked is that even persons of unsound mind detained under Article 5 (1) (e) are, under Article 5 (4), entitled to have the lawfulness of their detention decided by a 'court'. Thus, notwithstanding the meaning one might ascribe to Article 13, a person detained or to be detained in an asylum has the right to a judicial proceeding and, since his civil rights are obviously at stake, to have the hearing conducted in accordance with the standards prescribed in Article 6 (1). This conclusion, furthermore, finds support in recent Commission jurisprudence[2] and is not inconsistent with its

---

[1] Germ. Fed. Rep., BayObLG, Judgment of 21 September 1960, 14 *N.J.W.* 270 (1961).

[2] See App. No. 1936/63, *Neumeister* v. *Austria* (Admissibility), 16 *Collection* 38 (1965); App. No. 2178/64, *Matznetter* v. *Austria* (Admissibility), 15 *Collection* 40 (1965). Both cases were ruled admissible over the Austrian Government's

decisions that Article 6 (1) does not apply to administrative proceedings. These ostensibly contradictory rulings are reconcilable, for even accepting the Commission's opinion that Article 6 (1) applies only to judicial and not to administrative proceedings, it must not be forgotten that Article 5 (4) expressly accords an individual the right to have the lawfulness of his detention decided by a *court*. Since this court, according to the jurisprudence of the Commission, must be a court of law, it follows that a proceeding under Article 5 (4) is subject to the provisions of Article 6 (1).

Article 6 (1) does not, however, articulate those standards beyond requiring a fair and public hearing by an independent and impartial tribunal. What constitutes a 'fair hearing', for example, in an action designed to determine the legality of a person's detention, is still largely an open question. The Convention Institutions, as has been indicated, have so far only held that in such proceedings the individual may not be placed at a procedural disadvantage *vis-à-vis* the law enforcement authorities, i.e. that he has the right to equality of arms. Whether this means that he is entitled to legal counsel at that stage is not clear, although one might imagine cases where such a right will have to be accorded. The important thing to keep in mind, in my opinion, is that the individual must be in possession of all those rights without which, in his particular case, the hearing to determine the lawfulness of his detention cannot be meaningful. One of the questions that will in this connection have to be determined was recently considered by a national court. The case had to do with the right of a person, against whom a warrant of arrest had been issued, to obtain access to his dossier prior to the hearing. This was denied on one ground, among others, that the appellant was not a person charged with a criminal offence within the meaning of Article 6 (3). Not being an accused, he could accordingly not claim that to deny him the possibility of inspecting his dossier deprived him of adequate facilities to prepare his defence.[1] It is, of course, true that the rights guaranteed in Article 6 (3) can be invoked only by those charged with a criminal offence. There may well be cases, however, where a person might be unable meaningfully to assert the illegality of his detention, unless he can inspect his case file. Given these facts, the fair hearing requirements of Article 6 (1) could conceivably apply to compel the disclosure of information contained therein.

---

contention that Article 6 (1) did not apply to proceedings under Article 5 (4), since under Austrian law they were neither civil nor criminal in nature.

[1] Belgium, Cour de Cassation, Judgment of 25 March 1963, [1963] *Pasicrisie Belge* 808, 809. See also Cour de Cassation, Judgment of 22 July 1960, [1960] *Pasicrisie Belge* 1263.

2. Specific rights of the defendant on a criminal charge

(a) The presumption of innocence

The right to be presumed innocent until proved guilty, guaranteed in Article 6 (2) of the Convention, raises a very interesting question with regard to one German penal law provision. Under Article 245a of the German Penal Code[1] the possession of burglar's tools by a person who has previously been convicted, for example, of grand larceny or larceny recidivism, is a criminal offence, unless it appears from the surrounding circumstances that they 'were not intended for use in the commission of punishable acts'. In 1958 a lower German court refused to enforce this provision on the ground that it violated Article 6 (2) of the Convention.[2] In its view this resulted from the fact that the German law in question required the conviction of an individual, not because it had been proved that he intended to use these tools to commit an offence, but because the law makes this assumption whenever the defendant cannot rebut it. This, the Court ruled, was inconsistent with the principle *in dubio pro reo* and with the Convention, because it compelled the accused's conviction without proof of illegal intent. In 1963, however, an appellate tribunal expressly rejected this interpretation.[3] It reasoned that the applicable provision of the German Penal Code did not establish a presumption of guilt (*Schuldvermutung*) but merely a rebuttable evidentiary presumption (*widerlegbare Beweisvermutung*). Once it was interpreted in this manner, Article 245a could not, in the Court's opinion, be said to violate Article 6 (2) of the Convention. I am not sure that I understand this subtle distinction. But, if in this oblique way the Court is trying to say that Article 6 (2) does not prevent a State from enacting laws making it unlawful for convicts to do certain things, i.e. having possession of some types of tools, one would have to agree with it.

(b) The enumerated minimum rights

In interpreting the minimum rights guaranteed to a criminal accused, domestic courts have so far mainly had to deal with three of these: the right to counsel, the right to examine witnesses, and the right to the services of an interpreter.

---

[1] For an English translation see Mueller & Buergenthal, 'The German Penal Code', 4 *American Series of Foreign Penal Codes* (1961).

[2] Germ. Fed. Rep., Landgericht/Heidelberg, Judgment of 3 October 1958, 12 *N.J.W.* 1932 (1959). For a critical discussion of this case, see Schröder, 'Zur Zulässigkeit gesetzlicher Beweisregeln im Strafrecht', 12 *N.J.W.* 1903 (1959).

[3] Germ. Fed. Rep., OLG/Braunschweig, Judgment of 11 April 1963, 18 M.D.R. 342 (1964).

(i) *The right to counsel*

As we have seen, the Commission has on a number of occasions ruled that Article 6 (3) (c) of the Convention did not require national authorities to assign an indigent defendant a defence attorney of his choice. Under German law, his choice will as a rule be respected. The Federal Constitutional Court in a 1958 decision, however, ruled that neither the Federal Constitution nor the Convention was violated by a denial of the defendant's motion to be assigned a lawyer whose appointment he had requested.[1] In reaching this conclusion, the Court noted that the defendant was accused of engaging in illegal activities on behalf of an outlawed political organisation and that the attorney in question appeared to be subservient to the wishes of that group. It was, therefore, not unreasonable to conclude that he might for political reasons act contrary to the best interests of his client. Since his motion was denied for these reasons the defendant, in the Court's opinion, could not validly contend that Article 6 (3) had been violated, especially since the right to counsel accorded him under German law exceeded the requirements imposed by the Convention.[2]

(ii) *The right to call and examine witnesses*

Consistent with the established jurisprudence of the Commission, the Belgian Supreme Court has held that Article 6 (3) (d) does not deprive a judge of his right to refuse to call a witness if in his view the proffered testimony could not affect the outcome of the case. The Court reasoned that such a decision could not be said to impair the requisite procedural equality between the prosecution and the defence, since the judge had the power to deny similar requests by the prosecution.[3] While the facts given in this case are inadequate to examine this question, it should be noted that the Commission has taken the position that the mere existence of formal equality between prosecution and defence may nevertheless give rise to a violation of Article 6 (3) (d) if a court, by not calling a certain witness, in fact prejudiced the rights of the defence. Thus, domestic courts will here have to do more than merely examine the formal equality of the parties.[4]

---

[1] Germ. Fed. Rep , BVerfG, Judgment of 16 December 1958, 9 *Ent. d. BverfG* 36 (1959).
[2] Ibid., 38–9.
[3] Belgium, Cour de Cassation, Judgment of 20 July 1962, [1962] *Pasicrisie Belge* 1238, 1239.
[4] While it is clear that the failure of a court to call a witness, who cannot by his testimony help in elucidating the truth, does not violate Article 6 (3) (d), it may still be an open question, as far as concerns the jurisprudence of the Convention Institutions, whether the Court has the duty on its own motion to examine witnesses capable of providing probative evidence, even if the defence has

Article 6 (3) (*d*) does not only entitle an accused to obtain the attendance and examination of witnesses on his behalf. It also gives him the right 'to examine or have examined witnesses against him'. One important issue which this provision presents has to do with the admissibility in a criminal trial of evidence obtained from police informers. At least one domestic court has considered this question. It had to decide whether the defendant's rights under Article 6 (3) (*d*) had been violated, because police officers were permitted to give evidence regarding incriminating testimony they obtained from informers, whose names they would not divulge and whom the defendant could accordingly not examine. The Court ruled that this practice did not violate Article 6, since the police officers rather than the informers were the witnesses against the defendant within the meaning of Article 6 (3) (*d*) and he was not denied the right to examine them.[1]

The notion implicit in this judgment is, to say the least, preposterous. If accepted, a State could, for so-called reasons of national security, dispense with witnesses at a trial altogether by substituting police officers instead. That would certainly lead to much more expeditious criminal proceedings. It would, however, be totally inconsistent with the notion of a fair and public hearing guaranteed in Article 6 (1) and with Article 6 (3) (*d*). Article 6 (3) (*d*) assures the defendant the right to examine witnesses against him. It does not say that this function can be performed by the police out of court who can then testify thereto. In such a case the police officer is not a witness. He is a conduit of one-sided information, no matter how fairly he may have conducted the interrogation, because his interests are not the same as those of the defendant. The defendant, if he knows who the informer is, might be in a position to impeach his veracity by evidence not known to the police. This he cannot do by questioning the police officer, who is not at liberty to divulge the name of the informer. To call this an examination of a witness against him would be ludicrous, were it not such a serious denial of basic human rights as to be totally inconsistent with the notion of a fair trial in a democratic society. Needless to say, it also violates Article 6 (3) (*b*), because it deprives the accused of adequate facilities in the preparation of his defence, due to the fact that he can only rarely defend himself against charges made by anonymous persons.

---

inadvertently failed to make such a request. At least one domestic court has answered this question in the negative. See Italy, Corte Suprema di Cassazione, Judgment of 6 February 1962, 87 *Foro Italiano*, II, p. 315 (1962).

[1] Germ. Fed. Rep., BGH, Judgment of 1 August 1962, 15 *N.J.W.* 1876, 1877 (1962).

(iii) *The right to services of an interpreter*

Under German rules of criminal procedure, a convicted person is chargeable with the costs of the proceedings. In an interesting decision rendered by a lower German court, it was held, however, that the costs incurred in providing an interpreter could not be assessed against a foreigner.[1] The tribunal correctly reasoned that, as far as this item was concerned, Article 6 (3) (*e*) superseded the otherwise applicable German law, so that henceforth the services of an interpreter have to be provided free of charge by German courts.[2]

IV. ARTICLE 13

Article 13 of the Convention provides that 'everyone whose rights and freedoms as set forth in this Convention are violated shall have an effective remedy before a national authority notwithstanding that the violation has been committed by persons acting in an official capacity.' In interpreting this provision, the Commission has consistently held that it would only consider an allegation based on Article 13 after the Applicant has established a violation of a right guaranteed in the Convention.[3] The Commission has not explained, however, what useful purpose would thereby be served. It would seem that once the complainant has established himself as a victim of a violation of a substantive right guaranteed in the Convention, the relief to which he is entitled will be the same whether or not he invokes Article 13. Thus interpreted, Article 13 is incapable of performing a useful function in litigation before the Convention Institutions. If one accepts the Commission's view, it would follow that this provision was incorporated in the Convention for the sole purpose of preventing, out of an over-abundance of caution, the interposition of governmental immunity in one form or another as a defence to an action in domestic courts seeking redress for a breach of the Convention.[4]

This is a permissible interpretation of the Convention, albeit one that ascribes to Article 13 a very limited purpose. As a result, a

[1] Germ. Fed. Rep., Amstgericht/Bremerhaven, Judgment of 18 October 1962, 16 *N.J.W.* 827 (1963).

[2] But see Austria, OGH, Judgment of 22 January 1960, 2 *Z.f.R.V.* 170 (1961) (with the interesting comparative note by Liebscher), where the fact that an indictment in the German language was served on a Belgian defendant, although he indicated that he could not read German, was held not to be a reversible error because he failed to file a formal objection thereto and because at the trial he was assigned an interpreter.

[3] App. No. 472/59, *Yearbook*, III, 206, 212; App. No. 655/59, *Yearbook*, III, 280, 286; App. No. 1092/61, *Yearbook*, V, 210, 212.

[4] See Robertson, *Human Rights in Europe* 38 (1963).

number of commentators have argued that this provision was designed to perform a much more important function, namely, that it requires the member States to give the Convention the status of domestic law.[1] One national court, furthermore, seems to have accepted this view.[2] Since enough has been written on this subject, I need not go into it here in any length. It should be said, however, that sound arguments can be made for and against this theory.[3] Basically, its proponents contend that the Convention was intentionally drafted in precise statutory language to permit its direct transformation into domestic law, because its draftsmen assumed that the 'remedy' of which Article 13 speaks can only be 'effective', in the sense that it will assure speedy relief by domestic courts, if its provisions bind these tribunals directly.[4]

This argument presents certain conceptual problems, because a State cannot be said to violate the Convention, unless it has deprived a person of a right guaranteed therein. Thus, if its national law assures an individual the same or even greater rights than the Convention assures, it cannot be charged with its violation. The Commission is, therefore, right in saying that an individual cannot claim to be a victim of a violation of Article 13 until he has shown the breach of a substantive right accorded him by the Convention. It must, however, be remembered that an individual is, *ex hypothesi*, prevented in a State where the Convention lacks the status of domestic law from effectively testing the proposition that its own laws accord him the same rights as does the Convention. Therefore, it is arguable that Article 13 does authorise the Convention Institutions in such cases to require a defendant State, if it seeks the rejection of an Application for non-exhaustion of domestic remedies, to show that these remedies would actually have been effective.[5] Whether the Convention Institutions will accept this argument remains to be seen.

---

[1] See Golsong, *Das Rechtsschutzsystem der Europäischen Menschenrechtskonvention* 8 (1958); Süsterhenn, 'L'Application de la Convention sur le plan du Droit Interne', *La Protection Internationale des Droits de l'Homme dans le Cadre Européen* 303, 318 (1961).

[2] See Germ. Fed. Rep., OLG/Bremen, Judgment of 16 May 1962, 15 *N.J.W.* 1735 (1962).

[3] See especially Golsong, op. cit. at 6–15, who supports it. But see Vasak, *La Convention Européenne . . .*, op. cit., 232–5; Scheuner 'Die Grundrechte der Europäischen Menschenrechts . . .', op. cit., 355, 371–2, who reject these arguments.

[4] See Buergenthal 'European Human Rights: A Review', 13 *Am. Journal Comp. Law* 301, 307–8 (1964).

[5] See Vasak, op. cit., at 28, who seems to suggest that Article 13 permits the Commission in such cases to pass on an allegation of a violation of the Convention without having to determine first whether there exists a *primia facie* cause of action.

The Commission has, in the past, only upheld the admissibility of an Application against the charge that domestic remedies had not been exhausted because the Applicant failed to invoke a specific provision of the Convention in the national courts. The Commission here found that these courts had previously ruled that the provision in question was non-self-executing. Therefore, in the Commission's view, 'it would in no way have been an effective remedy for the Applicant to invoke Article 6 in proceedings before the Austrian courts; . . . under Article 26 of the Convention he was therefore not so obliged before introducing his Application before the Commission of Human Rights'.[1]

In interpreting Article 13, domestic courts have uniformly held that an individual cannot in reliance on this provision assert a right to judicial or constitutional review, where none is provided for under the applicable domestic law.[2] This view conforms to the position taken by the Commission. It has repeatedly held that 'no clause of the Convention obliges a High Contracting Party to allow its citizens access to a Constitutional Court as well as to the normal courts of appeal, and . . . if a High Contracting Party sets up a Supreme Constitutional Court, . . . it is entitled to lay down its own regulations regarding access to that Court'.[3] The Commission has also ruled that every litigant is not necessarily entitled to have his case reviewed by three successive domestic tribunals,[4] because the Convention does not deprive the member States of the right to impose various conditions regulating access to their courts of last resort, 'provided that such regulations do not deviate from their exclusive purpose of assuring justice according to law'.[5]

As we have already seen, some national courts have in reliance on Article 13 contended that the rights guaranteed in Article 6 of the

[1] App. No. 808/60, *Yearbook*, v, 108, 122.

[2] Austria, VerwGH, Judgment of 11 December 1958, 13 Erkenntnisse und Beschlüsse des Verwaltungsgerichtshofes (Adm. Teil) 990, 992 (1960), Ger. Fed. Rep., VerfGH/Rheinland-Pfalz, Judgment of 16 March 1959, 12 D.O.V. 578 (1959); Netherlands, *X* v. *Inspector of Taxes*, Hoge Raad, Judgment of 24 February 1960, 8 *Ned. Tijdschrift* v. *Int'l Recht* 285, 286 (1961); Germ. Fed. Rep., BGH, Judgment of 20 July 1964, 17 *N.J.W.* 2119 (1964).

[3] App. No. 673/59, *Yearbook*, IV, 286, 292–4; App. No. 436/58, *Yearbook*, II, 386, 389; App. No. 441/58, *Yearbook*, II, 391, 395.

[4] App. No. 690/60, 3 *Collection* 1, 4 (1960).

[5] App. No. 727/60, *Yearbook*, III, 302, 308. Here the domestic court rejected the Applicant's request to have counsel assigned to him to appeal his case to the Federal Court of Justice, where all litigants have to be represented by an attorney. Under German law such a request will only be granted if there is a chance that the appeal might be successful. In the Commission's view this system did not violate the Convention because it was enacted for the very purpose of 'assuring justice according to law'.

Convention do not apply to proceedings within the jurisdiction of administrative tribunals.[1] They reason that Article 13 only requires member States to accord an individual 'an effective remedy before a national authority' without even stipulating that it be a court of law. From this they conclude that the Convention left the States free to provide administrative remedies not subject to the 'fair hearing' provisions of Article 6.

While some Commission jurisprudence tends to support this conclusion, this argument cannot in principle be accepted. It is, of course, true that certain rights guaranteed in the Convention can be adequately enforced without any recourse to judicial authorities. From this it does not, however, follow that a governmental organ having exclusive jurisdiction to pass on claims relating to a person's civil rights and obligations can disregard the requirements of Article 6 simply because it is not designated as a court of law. A State is no doubt free to describe its institutions in any way it sees fit. But when such an institution is given the power to render final decisions relating to a person's civil rights and obligations, it must conform its procedure to the standards prescribed in Article 6. If it does not, and the domestic law offers the individual no effective remedy to obtain it, Article 13 has also been violated. In this context no other meaning can be ascribed to Article 13 without thereby effectively nullifying the provisions of Article 6.

In conclusion, it should be noted that Article 13 can perform a very useful function as far as concerns the domestic application of the Convention. National courts are, of course, free to interpret the Convention more liberally—and some have done so—than might the Convention Institutions. But if, in applying the Convention, they interpret it more restrictively than is consistent with the jurisprudence of the Convention Institutions, they subject their Governments to the risk of being adjudged guilty of conduct inconsistent with their obligations under the Convention. In practice, therefore, Article 13 is an 'elastic clause'. As the jurisprudence of the Convention Institutions develops and grows, domestic law will have to adjust its interpretations of the Convention to it. Only in this way will the domestic remedy of which Article 13 speaks retain its requisite effectiveness. Viewed in this light, Article 13 can play a very significant role in bringing about uniformity in the application of the Convention. If this is to be achieved, domestic courts and attorneys appearing before them will have to pay close attention to the jurisprudence of the Convention Institutions.

[1] See Germ. Fed. Rep., OVG/Münster, Judgment of 21 November 1955, 9 *N.J.W.* 1374, 1375 (1956); BayObLG, Judgment of 21 September 1960, 14 *N.J.W.* 270 (1961).

V. CONCLUSION

The case law discussed in this study indicates that the rights guaranteed in Articles 5 and 6 of the Convention are beginning to play an important role in shaping the administration of justice in certain member States. These provisions are flexible enough and have for the most part been interpreted in this manner, to permit the Convention Institutions and the national courts to develop these 'minimum standards' into an ever growing body of law designed to maximise the rights of the individual. This is only proper, for the evolution of human rights shows that what is today regarded as not inconsistent with democratic principles may tomorrow appear almost barbaric.

As we have seen, despite its relatively short existence, the Convention has already made a significant contribution to this development. The notion that a person suspected of having committed a crime may be detained pending trial for months and even years simply because the investigation is complicated, is beginning to crumble. All forms of deprivation of liberty not expressly permitted by the Convention have been outlawed. The proceeding in the nature of a writ of *habeas corpus*, guaranteed in Article 5 (4) of the Convention, is slowly emerging as a full-fledged judicial enquiry subject to the evolving 'fair trial' standards expressed in Article 6. While the full scope of the 'fair trial' principle proclaimed in the Convention is still largely unexplored, it has already produced the 'equality-of-arms' doctrine. By according the individual the right to procedural equality in his judicial confrontation with the State, this doctrine is capable of profoundly influencing domestic law enforcement practices and of serving as the foundation of legal norms designed to balance the interests of the individual in his liberty with those of the State in upholding law and order. This balancing process will, furthermore, characterise the judicial application of all the rights guaranteed in Articles 5 and 6. Since it cannot be charted in terms of simple rules, it will require a great deal of enlightened imagination on the part of those charged with its implementation. It will also call for exhaustive comparative research in criminal and civil procedure to help formulate legal principles that can be applied in all member States without sacrificing valuable aspects found in each of their legal systems. As this jurisprudence grows and uncovers problems that the courts cannot solve by themselves, it might also serve as a guide in drafting uniform European laws relating to some or all areas of civil and criminal procedure.

Our comparison of the interpretation of Articles 5, 6 and 13 by the Convention Institutions with that of domestic courts indicates that these national and international tribunals do not for the most part reach divergent theoretical conclusions. They sometimes arrive at conflicting results, but this is due mainly to differences in the evaluation of the facts, which are unavoidable because reasonable men can honestly differ in their adjudication of concrete cases.

On the whole, therefore, our study justifies considerable optimism regarding the future effectiveness of the Convention. It must, however, be tempered by the recognition that our survey presents a somewhat distorted picture of its actual significance, because it is very limited in scope. This is due to a variety of factors. First of all, we have only considered domestic cases decided by a small number of States, because we were of necessity limited to those countries which accord the Convention the status of domestic law. Secondly, with the possible exception of the German Federal Republic, the Convention has not as yet, even in these States, produced any substantial body of case law. This, in my opinion, is attributable largely to the failure of their legal professions to recognise the full scope of the rights guaranteed by the Convention. Thirdly, the Convention Institutions have been prevented from applying the Convention to certain patently illegal practices condoned by some member States—the Greek adjudications relating to preventive detention is a case in point—because these countries have not recognised the right of individuals subject to their jurisdiction to appeal to the Commission. Fourthly, many cases have been improperly presented by the Applicant to the Convention Institutions, with the result that they were rejected on procedural grounds and thus offer no clues as to how they might have been decided on the merits. Finally, as we have seen, most of the jurisprudence emanating from the Convention Institutions are Commission decisions, even though some cases could and should have been referred to the Court for an authoritative ruling on important legal questions. It is most unfortunate that this has not been done because, due to the fact that the Commission is only a quasi-judicial body and notwithstanding the high and well-deserved professional reputation of its members, Commission decisions necessarily lack the authoritative character enjoyed by judgments of the Human Rights Court. Besides, since this Court is composed of quite a number of the finest and most respected European legal minds, whose judicial contribution to the development of the Convention would certainly enrich it immensely, it is regrettable that it has not had the opportunity to settle certain disputed issues relating to its interpretation. Thus, for example, until the Court has spoken, it is not at all clear whether or not the 'fair trial' guarantees of Article 6 apply to some types of administrative proceedings. As a result, our study does not by any means present a truly comprehensive picture of the impact Articles 5, 6 and

13 have or could have on the administration of justice in all or even a substantial number of the member States. It cannot, however, be denied that what it indicates in this limited setting about the influence and application of the Convention is surely most encouraging.

WRITTEN COMMUNICATION BY
NICOLA PICARDI

The right to liberty and security of person, guaranteed in Article 5 of the European Convention on Human Rights, is one of the fundamental rights which form the pivot of every liberal and democratic legal system.

The Italian system conforms strictly with this principle. Article 2 of the Constitution reads:

The Republic acknowledges and guarantees the inviolable rights of man both as an individual and in the social organisations where his personality is developed and requires the fulfilment of the essential duties of political, economic and social solidarity.[1]

In the first and second paragraphs of Article 13 it is stipulated that 'personal liberty is inviolable' and that 'no form of detention, inspection or personal search or any other restriction of personal liberty is permitted except by a duly authorised act of the judicial authorities and then only in cases and under the procedure prescribed by law'.

This provision, as affirmed by the Constitutional Court,[2] safeguards personal liberty against any forms of physical restraint exercised without the intervention of the judicial authorities; hence it concerns the supreme guarantees, the 'corner-stones of life in a democratic society', embodied in the Anglo-Saxon concept of *habeas corpus*. This protection is ensured in two ways: every measure affecting human rights must be laid down in a general law and every decision restricting the liberty of the individual must emanate from the judicial authorities and be adequately substantiated.

In one of its first decisions[3] the Constitutional Court, examining, in the light of the above-mentioned principles, certain provisions of the Public Safety Act concerning persons considered dangerous to society, decided as follows:

---

[1] The English translation of this and subsequent Articles is taken from Peaslee's *Constitutions of Nations*.
[2] Decision of 15 July 1959, No. 49, *Giurispr. Cost.*, 1959, 778.
[3] Decision of 1 July 1956, No. 11, *Giurispr. Cost.*, 1956, 612.

According to the principle of the recognition of the fundamental rights of the citizen (Article 2 of the Constitution), these rights are the heritage of all free men. Liberty of person is an inalienable personal right in so far as the Constitution prohibits the public authorities from exercising their power of physical restraint; in the Constitution, liberty of person is not an unlimited right granted to the individual to dispose freely of his person, but a guarantee that the power of physical restraint vested in the State shall be exercised within the limits of the strict observance of the law, that is to say, in specific cases and in accordance with a prescribed procedure (limitation of freedom as provided for by law, judicial proceedings, duly substantiated decisions by the judicial authorities). The provisions on admonition in Sections 164 and 176 of the Code of Public Safety are inconsistent with Article 13 of the Constitution since they confer, not on the judicial but on the administrative authorities, the power to limit personal liberty by decisions which are subject to no supervision and without the guarantees of a fair trial. Article 13 of the Constitution is self-executing, at least in so far as it denies the public authorities power of decision in the matters specified therein; it is through this judicial guarantee that the right to liberty of person acquires its legal force.

*   *   *

Hence the rules of judicial procedure are dictated by the principles of *habeas corpus*.

Article 6 of the European Convention states that everyone is entitled to a fair and public hearing by an independent and impartial tribunal established by law, which shall pronounce judgment publicly.

Italian judicial procedure is based on these principles, which have been formally recognised in the Constitutional Charter. In regard to the rights and duties of citizens and to civil relations in particular, Article 25 (1) of the Constitution provides that 'no one may be deprived of the right to be tried by the appropriate, legally constituted courts'. Articles 101 (2) and 111 (1) concerning the magistrature provide that 'judges are subject solely to the law' and that 'all judicial measures must be duly supported by reasons'.

Owing to the importance attached, in our system, to the role of the courts in guaranteeing the fundamental rights of citizens, the methods whereby this role is fulfilled are of the greatest consequence, for any arbitrary action here would obviously render the proclamation of these rights in the Constitutional Charter ineffectual. The Italian legislature has endeavoured, by means of constitutional and other provisions, to place the exercise of the judicial function above suspicion. To this end it has guaranteed the independence of judges in regard to the litigants and to any other influence likely to affect the rectitude of their decisions, e.g. by precluding a judge appointed *a posteriori* from trying a case; it has also ensured the application of two fundamental principles: that all hearings shall be in public and all decisions supported by reasons.

The principle of *precostituzione*, that is to say, of the pre-determination of the competence of the judge and the importance attributed thereto under the present Italian system, is clearly illustrated by the Constitutional Court's decision No. 88 of 7 July 1962,[1] in which the clauses of Sections 30 and 31 of the Code of Criminal Procedure and Section 10 of the *Decreto Legge* (legislative decree) of 20 July 1934, No. 1404, concerning the extension of competence in legal matters, are declared incompatible with Article 25 of the Constitution; these clauses provided that a judicial organ could, by a decision without appeal, in specific cases, order the transfer to the 'pretore' of a case falling within the jurisdiction of an ordinary or juvenile court. In the grounds for its decision, the Court explained that the principle of the pre-determination of competence must be understood to mean that competence shall be determined immediately and exclusively by virtue of the law, in a general, abstract manner, so as to preclude that a choice between different judges should be exercised *a posteriori* in individual cases.

As regards the second of the above-mentioned fundamental principles, it was emphasised during the *travaux préparatoires* of the Constitution that the compulsory motivation of decisions protected the right of the person concerned, and of society in general, to know the grounds for any Court decision by revealing the logical process whereby the judge reached a particular decision. This obligation to motivate a decision is approved by jurists as in keeping with the publicity principle underlying our judicial procedure and evidenced by the presence of the public at hearings and by the disclosure of the arguments on which judgment is founded; publicity in its dynamic form, spurring on the judge to greater precision in his decisions, and in its static form, dispelling all doubt and suspicion regarding the decisions given.

Numerous judgments of the Supreme Court prove that the obligation to motivate decisions is one of the principles on which our legal order is based, and that it is strictly applied in everyday court practice through the appeal system.

Supreme Court rulings consistently reflect the view that the absence of grounds referred to in Section 360, No. 5 of the Code of Civil Procedure exists whenever a judgment does not set out the arguments which led the judge to give a particular decision in a specific case. They also make it clear that, even if the judge is not bound to give a detailed analysis of all the evidence adduced and the arguments advanced by the parties, enabling a general appreciation to be made of

---

[1] *Giurispr. Cost.*, 1962, 959.

all the material submitted to him for examination, he must nevertheless take all the said material into consideration and explain the logical process whereby he arrived at his decision, so that the criteria on which he based his verdict can be examined at all times.[1]

*   *   *

Where criminal justice is concerned, problems arise regarding the treatment to be given to an accused person both prior to and following his conviction. Such treatment must obviously comply with the requirements of *habeas corpus* and, in general, of the protection of the fundamental human rights already referred to.

Articles 3, 5 and 6 of the European Convention lay down fundamental principles in the matter: the prohibition of torture or inhuman or degrading treatment; the right of persons arrested to be informed of the grounds for their detention and to be brought to trial promptly; the right of everyone charged with an offence to prepare an effective defence; everyone charged with a criminal offence shall be presumed innocent until proved guilty according to the law.

Our Constitutional Charter conforms strictly with these principles: Articles 13, 24 and 27 lay down the following fundamental rules: 'penal responsibility is personal'; 'an accused person is not deemed guilty until convicted'; 'physical and psychological violence against persons placed under some form of restriction of personal freedom shall be punished'; 'the right to defence is inviolable in every state and at every stage of the judicial process'; 'sentences may not consist in treatment contrary to humanity and must tend to promote the rehabilitation of the convicted person'; 'the death penalty is not permitted except in cases provided for by military laws of war'.

Detailed illustration of the above principles seems unnecessary, for they are not abstract affirmations but have for long been the essential rules of our civilised legal order; it will suffice to refer the reader to the classic works of Verri and Beccaria. It is expedient, however, to recall, in view of the dramatic happenings with which our contemporary world is familiar, that the Supreme Court of Appeal[2] has had occasion to affirm that 'the interrogation of prisoners awaiting trial while they are under the influence of the truth drug and thus deprived of their physical liberty, constitutes a violation of one of the fundamental principles of our legal system confirmed by Article 13 of the Constitution'.

Considering the ancient legal tradition of our own and of the other countries which have signed the European Convention, and the fact

---

[1] V. Cass., 20 November 1964, No. 2770, Guist. civ. Mass., 1964, 1290; Cass. 20 January 1964, no. 111, 50; Cass., 21 May 1964 No. 1254, 571.
[2] Decision of 10 November 1948, *Giurispr. It.*, 1949, II, 129.

that certain general principles and fundamental guarantees for the protection of persons charged with an offence can be regarded now and henceforth as established, it seems to us more essential to call attention to a practical and very difficult problem—that of the demands of the defence as regards the expeditious conduct of proceedings and gathering of evidence. This problem arises in connection with the preliminary investigation, the indispensable preparatory phase preceding the trial proper.

The Italian Code of Criminal Procedure provides for two forms of preliminary investigation: summary investigation in cases where there is clear proof and in other specific cases, and ordinary 'formal' investigation. In the latter case, the accused is accorded all the rights of the defence, even during the investigation.

In its decision No. 52 of 16 June 1965, the Constitutional Court noted that the provisions designed to safeguard the defence of the accused, applicable to formal investigation, had been regarded by the ordinary magistrature as inapplicable in practice to summary investigation, on account of the special nature of this much more rapid procedure. Consequently, the Court declared Section 392 (1) of the Code of Criminal Procedure unconstitutional in so far as concerns the parenthetical phrase to the effect that the provisions relating to formal investigation must be observed in summary investigation only 'where applicable'. It was, in substance, a question of determining whether the provisions governing the accused's right of defence in formal investigation could be applied, in the more delicate phases of the proceedings, even to summary investigation. In the grounds for the said decision (as well as for that of 4. 2. 1965, No. 11), the Constitutional Court reaffirmed that the right of the defence, as stipulated in Article 24 of the Constitution, was inviolable in every state and at every stage of the judicial process, that consequently exercise of that right was not incompatible with summary investigation. In short, the defence must be able to fulfil its function effectively, even in this form of investigation.

However, if such incompatibility existed, the logical outcome would be not the denial of the rights of the defence, but the abolition of summary investigation proceedings as being inconsistent with the above-mentioned constitutional principle.

SUMMARY OF THE DISCUSSION

W. J. Ganshof van der Meersch: I should like to make certain comments on what has been called the 'relative character' of the right to liberty.

Article 5 of the European Convention on Human Rights, as

Professor Buergenthal's report has emphasised, permits restrictions on individual freedom of movement. It is quite true to say that the notion of individual liberty thus becomes relative; this is justified by the necessity of action by the public authorities.

Two reservations, however, must be made as regards the relative character of the right to liberty in the strict sense:

(1) In the context of the rights of the defence, the right to liberty has an absolute character; this results from the solemn character attached to the 'general principles of law', among which are included the rights of the defence.

(2) The view has been expressed that the criterion for determining the lawfulness of detention on remand should be related to the probable sentence; in other words, that detention on remand which is not longer than the probable length of sentence is legitimate. This criterion is dangerous. On the one hand, it is difficult to know in advance what view will be taken by the judge; on the other hand, it may be feared that at a later stage the judge's decision may be influenced by the desire to equate the prison sentence with the period of detention on remand.

The 'relative character' of the right to liberty in the strict sense evokes the procedure of friendly settlement. It is important to bear in mind that this is not a procedure of conciliation as regards the substance of the right, but a procedure of reparation for the harm suffered.

Far from affecting the substance of the right itself, the attempt at friendly settlement must be based on 'respect for human rights as defined in the Convention'. The objective which is expressly recalled in Article 28 is therefore the *maintenance* of the protection of the right; this is irreconcilable with any compromise on the right itself.

The Belgian *Cour de Cassation* has on many occasions referred to the Convention in order to evaluate the lawfulness of certain procedures; it has defined the right guaranteed by Article 5 (3) in a decision of 16 March 1964. Perhaps the definition is not sufficient in itself, but it enables one to establish two criteria:

(1) Article 5 (3) of the Convention is not violated as long as the procedure of investigation which is necessary to discover the truth is still under way and as long as this procedure is being carried on without unreasonable delay.

(2) The legality of detention on remand does not necessarily come to an end when the procedure of investigation has been completed.

I should be grateful if Professor Buergenthal would explain the situation in the United States. I think that in several States it is a common practice to release the accused person on the posting of bail. The general adoption of such a system of bail does not seem to me consistent with the idea of justice in a democratic country. In Belgium, there is still a provision of this sort in the law about remand in custody, but it is never applied in practice.

Finally, I would like to draw attention to the basic distinction to be made between the *right* which exists as such in the individual, and the *exercise* of this right. This distinction must not be lost sight of when we come to consider to what extent and under what conditions it is possible to renounce the right to avail oneself of the guarantees established by the Convention.

M. J. van Emde Boas: paragraphs 3 and 4 of Article 5 of the Convention may be considered as *leges speciales* of Article 13.

Even in countries in which the Convention is self-executing, such as the Netherlands, there should be a judge who is authorised by national law to receive complaints under there provisions. Unless he is so authorised, the judge should declare himself incompetent to receive petitions, in which case the rights guaranteed in paragraphs 3 and 4 of Article 5 could not be enforced.

This opinion is confirmed by a judgment issued by the High Court of Rotterdam on 19 July 1962.[1] An American detained pending deportation to the United States requested the judge's ruling on the lawfulness of his detention. At that time, the Government alone could order the deportation of an alien and there was no remedy at law in such a case. Nevertheless, the alien concerned instituted proceedings under Article 5, paragraphs 4 and 1 (*f*), of the Convention. The Court of Rotterdam dismissed the action, the judicial authorities not being empowered by Netherlands law, at the time, to examine Government decisions concerning the deportation of aliens. The judge could not claim competence on the strength of the provisions of the Convention alone, which was normal, since a national judge's absolute and relative competence is, as a rule, founded solely on internal law.

The law has been amended in the meanwhile. The new Aliens Act of 13 January 1965 (*Staatsblad*, 40) provides for remedies in conformity with the Convention.

V. Liebscher (Articles 5 and 6 of the Human Rights Convention and national criminal procedure): the Convention refers expressly in its Preamble to the signatory States' common heritage of political traditions, ideals, freedom and the rule of law. But what constitutes this common heritage is, in practice, very often a matter of controversy, especially where the law of criminal procedure is concerned. Anglo-Saxon and Continental jurists hold widely divergent views regarding, for instance, the concept of a 'fair trial' within the meaning of Article 6 of the Convention. Both legal systems have institutions with age-old traditions, which are, nevertheless, totally dissimilar, e.g. the

[1] *Nederlandse Jurisprudentie*, 1964, no, 388.

position of the Prosecution. The systems differ also as regards the principle of equality of arms and the form of appeal procedure. Terminological difficulties are easier to overcome, but difficulties seem insurmountable when they arise out of methods of procedure which are not comparable with one another. Mr Buergenthal illustrated the extraordinary difficulty of the task imposed on the organs of the Convention, and particularly the Commission, by contrasting the position of the judge in the respective systems. Whereas, under the Common Law, the judge is merely an arbiter between the parties, i.e. between prosecutor and defendant, he plays an active role in the Continental legal system. This role lays an obligation on the judge to grant the accused all the rights to which he is entitled. But these difficulties—and I have mentioned only one of many—must not make us pessimistic about the future of the Human Rights Convention. The utmost discretion, reserve and understanding for national legal systems must, however, be exercised in our efforts to achieve the ultimate aim of European legal integration. This applies, above all, to reforms of penal law and penal law procedure, such as those being carried out in Austria at present. Even though the development of the Human Rights Convention in individual member States tends to be rather independent, the primary aim of these reforms is nevertheless to bring the new laws into line with the leading principles of the Convention.

F. Capotorti: Article 6 of the Convention cannot be applied without reference to municipal law, for it can only be enforced by lawfully constituted and independent courts. It follows that Article 6 cannot be applied except under internal law. Procedural measures, such as the examination of witnesses pursuant to Article 6, paragraph 3 (*d*), can only be carried out in accordance with domestic rules of procedure. This also determines the role which the judge must play in the procedure. The acceptance of the possibility of complaint provided for in Article 6 makes it a rule of *ordre public* and thus an integral part of the procedural rules, in such a way that it overrides all previous procedural rules which conflict with the Article. This applies in particular to countries where the Convention has the force of internal law. The rules which do not conflict with Article 6 continue to be applicable and form the framework for the Article.

This has two consequences:

1. Before a court which hears the parties to a case, the defence must expressly invoke the rights guaranteed by Article 6 (this is in conformity with the internal logic of the procedure).

2. Where the competence of a court of last resort is confined to deciding points of law, and where any appeal to it must be supported by reasons, Article 6 can only be taken into account if it is claimed

that it has been violated. Thus the question arises of application *ex officio*; the Court can apply Article 6 *ex officio* only in the same way as other procedural rules. The fact that Article 6 is a rule of *ordre public* makes no difference. The application of Article 6 also depends on the Court's relation to the parties, as defined in the various judicial systems. Only if Article 6 were regarded as a constitutional provision would it have to be applied *ex officio*.

Hans Weiler (significance of the judgments of the organs of the Convention, particularly those concerning Article 6): the Convention has had the effect of implanting fundamental rules in national legal systems, rules whose real content is revealed for the first time by the decisions of the Court, the Commission and the Committee of Ministers. Hence the necessity for an abundant case-law. These distinguished bodies have already issued many judgments. They have assumed their task with that circumspection which is essential in the transition period, if only because each of their decisions profoundly influences national legal systems. We Europeans have, of course, a common set of basic values to which the Convention gives expression. But—as stated again and again—there is also much in the Convention which, on account of the unequal development of the different legal systems, involves dissimilar values. Hence the need for caution, above all. For there is a danger of inconsistency in the decisions of the organs of the Convention as well as a danger of extraneous influences on national law, with its own values and traditions, a danger which, in view of the principle of the Constitutional State—the ultimate aim of the Convention—must be taken seriously. These dangers can be avoided if the Convention is interpreted teleologically, i.e. in the light of its aims. Article 6 is an outstanding example of a provision which raises problems on account of the disparate development of legal systems. The Anglo-Saxon view of a State based on justice here conflicts with the continental philosophy of the State as an administrative entity. Austria, which is characterised by administrative structures, has striven for many decades to shape its administration according to the rule of law (or Constitutional State) principle and hence to the principle of human rights. For example, administrative procedure has been organised to conform with the rule of law and the administration has been subjected to the control of specialised courts. Doctrine and practice have recognised this system as being consistent with the rule of law. It is the wording, not the meaning, of Article 6 that has posed problems for Austria. Hence the special interest taken by Austria in the development of the case-law of the organs of the Convention on Article 6.

Karl Doehring: according to Article 6, para. 1, of the Convention, everyone has the right to a fair and public hearing by a domestic court in the determination of his 'civil rights and obligations' or of a criminal charge against him. This provision has generally been interpreted (above all by national courts) as meaning that such protection does not have to be guaranteed in *public* law disputes. Let us leave aside the question whether a subjective interpretation (reference to *travaux préparatoires*, etc.) demands such a conclusion. An objective interpretation (reference to the text alone) would suggest that everyone is entitled to this protection in public law disputes, assuming that the terms used cover everything which States subject to the rule of law can offer by way of judicial guarantee. However that may be, at least from the point of view of *lex ferenda*, there appears to be an urgent need to recommend the inclusion of judicial protection against the sovereign power. The effect of developments in all States subject to the rule of law, (particularly since the Second World War) has been to shift the emphasis of the problem to another level.

Protection of the individual against the civil power is nowadays the most urgent problem within the general context of judicial protection. The fact that certain States have not instituted any special system of administrative jurisdiction would not bar such protection from being included, for even if it is provided by ordinary Courts (which is generally the case where there is no special administrative jurisdiction) such protection against the civil administration could surely be established without any particular difficulty.

I. Seidl-Hohenveldern (access to the Austrian Administrative Court is sufficient, according to Article 6, for the determination of civil rights by administrative authorities): an important question arises for Austria in connection with Mr Weiler's remarks. In some cases Austrian law provides that civil rights shall be determined by administrative authorities. The relevant proceedings are conducted according to the principles of the rule of law, the hearing of the parties is ensured—hence the provisions of Article 6 appear to be fulfilled.

But a further question arises: is this procedure admissible within the meaning of Article 6 which stipulates that civil rights shall be determined by *judges*?

I associate myself with Professor Buergenthal's criticism of the Commission's decision on Application No. 1329/62.[1] From this decision it would appear possible to remove the judgment of an essentially judicial instance from the control of Article 6, simply by calling that instance an 'administrative authority'.

The important question is: when is a court decision final? Under Article 26, the Commission and the Court may deal with a matter only after all domestic remedies have been exhausted. But such decisions of the administrative authorities are subject to control by the

---

[1] *Yearbook*, v, p. 200.

Administrative and Constitutional Courts, which are undoubtedly Courts within the meaning of Article 6.

Specialists have, however, questioned whether the conditions of Article 6 are satisfied thereby, since the decision of the Administrative Court merely quashes the decision of the administrative *authority* which ultimately is required to take a new decision. Nevertheless, by virtue of this control the requirements of Article 6 are fulfilled, for the subordinate authority required to take a new decision is bound, when so doing, by the opinion of the Administrative Court. It would be absurd, in my view, if, after the Administrative Court had issued a final decision, a person applied to the Commission on the ground that his civil rights claim had not been heard by a court.

Peter Benenson (Article 13—Effective remedy): Magna Carta secured protection for all free men against the denial or deferment of justice. Article 13, which appears to contain a safeguard against denial of justice, seems also to be violated when a court decision is unduly delayed. In the highly developed legal systems of present-day States denial of justice is a rare occurrence, but not so deferment of justice, which is met with extraordinarily frequently.

The introduction of a system patterned on the well-known Swedish Ombudsman has been proposed in Great Britain with a view to remedying this evil. The Ombudsman (Parliamentary Commissioner) can, however, be seized of a matter only through a member of Parliament.

This leads one to consider another means of preventing deferment of justice, namely parliamentary procedure which, over the years, has assumed two forms:

(1) A member of Parliament can draw the attention of the secretary of the Minister to a defect in the administration of justice. The Minister thereupon investigates the complaint, which scarcely ever becomes the subject of a parliamentary discussion.

(2) Ministers are regularly invited to answer questions on television. No Minister can refuse such an invitation. Intervention is made on these occasions, too, on behalf of victims of bureaucratic tardiness and the Minister, after investigation, remedies the evil complained of.

These systems might be adopted on the Continent also. Perhaps a similar procedure could be introduced before the Consultative Assembly of the Council of Europe.

A. Kobzina referred to his written communication (Chapter II above) part of which referred to the application of Article 13 in Austrian law.

SUMMING UP BY
THOMAS BUERGENTHAL

In reply to Professor Ganshof van der Meersch

I fully agree that it is improper and dangerous to assume that Article 5 (3) is not violated so long as the detention pending trial does not exceed the anticipated sentence or the sentence that is ultimately imposed. Such considerations are relevant only in deciding upon the measure of damages (compensation) to which the individual so detained is entitled to under Article 5 (5), since any lengthy detention that can only be justified on these grounds violates Article 5 (3).

Any detention pending trial in excess of a few weeks should be held to be inconsistent with Article 5 (3), unless there is clear showing that such detention is required to assure that the accused will appear at the trial or unless he actively hampers the investigation when set free. I am, therefore, in agreement with Mr Ganshof van der Meersch that it is erroneous to assume that Article 5 (3) permits a lengthy detention merely because the investigation is still in progress and is being carried out without unnecessary delay. Until he has been duly convicted the accused must be presumed to be innocent. To me this means, among other things, that he cannot be deprived of his liberty to suit the convenience of the authorities, who could just as easily summon him for questioning at reasonable intervals without having to detain him.

As to the U.S. practice of releasing prisoners on bail, I must admit that I consider it to be patently undemocratic in practice. It continuously results in the lengthy detention of persons lacking the requisite means to obtain bail. In New York City and elsewhere prisoners are now being released without bail on an experimental basis. This practice has to date proved to be highly successful and may therefore eventually, I hope, find general acceptance in America.

In reply to Mr Van Emde Boas

It is entirely proper under Articles 5 (1) (*f*), 5 (4) and 13 for a national court to hold that it lacks the power to examine the *grounds* justifying the deportation of an alien. Articles 5 (4) and 13 do, however, require the Contracting States to afford an individual the opportunity to test judicially the *legality* of his detention pending such deportation. That means, *inter alia*, that he must be accorded the right to show that his detention violates applicable domestic law or that it was effected for purposes other than to assure his deportation. Accordingly, I think that a national court, sitting in a country where the Convention is domestic law, could and should conclude that Articles 5 (4) and 13 read together are explicit enough to empower it to review the legality of such a detention order even without additional implementing legislation.

In reply to Professors Seidl-Hohenveldern and Kobzina

The requirements of Article 6 would seem to be satisfied in an administrative proceeding, if somewhere along the line the individual has the opportunity to challenge fully the factual and legal basis of the administrative determination before a court where the rights guaranteed in Article 6 are accorded to him. To that extent I share Professor Seidl-Hohenveldern's view. In this connection it should be stressed, however, that *both* the legal and factual findings of the administrative body must be reviewable by such a court. It follows therefrom that where this court is bound by any findings of fact or law made by the administrative authority, the Convention will be violated unless the administrative authority, in making its findings, has complied with the requirements of Article 6.

In reply to Mr Benenson

I am in complete agreement that justice delayed is justice denied. In countries subject to the Convention such delays are closely related to lengthy detentions pending trial. A rigorous application of Article 5 (3) by national courts and the organs of the Convention would largely resolve this problem.

Article 13 comes into play, in my opinion, in countries where the Convention lacks the status of domestic law. Here, if the Convention has in fact been violated, it will take a number of years before the individual's rights might be vindicated by the organs of the Convention. This is contrary to the letter and spirit of Article 13. Accordingly, I think that Article 13 should be read either as requiring the Member States to give the Convention domestic law status or, in countries failing to do so, as authorising an individual to appeal directly to the Commission without having to exhaust the *ipso jure* 'ineffective' domestic remedy.

In reply to MM. Picardi, Capotorti, Liebscher and Weiler

All these gentlemen emphasise that in applying Articles 5 and 6, the organs of the Convention must take into account the divergent legal systems subject to the Convention; their historical and institutional traditions and patterns; and the doctrinal differences between Common Law and Continental systems of criminal and civil procedure. In principle I share these sentiments. One legal system can safeguard human rights just as effectively as another even though their methods differ. The Convention organs must therefore guard against formalistic dispositions of cases which take no account of the legal, institutional and doctrinal divergence within the Council of Europe.

At the same time, however, one must guard against the disproportionate exaggeration of these differences. They are sometimes more apparent than real. This can easily be demonstrated if one looks to substance rather than form. I think, therefore, that one should be cautious in accepting the validity of such contentions, for they may well hide an attempt to perpetuate legal institutions patently in conflict with the principles enunciated in the Convention.

Let me add, in this connection, that the Convention does enunciate a standard to which domestic law must conform. It cannot therefore be admitted that an awareness of and a respect for institutional divergence requires more than the recognition by the Convention organs that fairness in the administration of justice can be achieved in various ways. But if the particular method does not *in practice* measure up to the standard set by the Convention, the fact that it is a cherished and long-established principle or institution of national law is not enough to justify its continued existence.

CHAPTER VI

Comparison of the jurisprudence of national courts with that of the organs of the Convention as regards other rights

REPORT BY

ULRICH SCHEUNER

I. THE ROLE OF THE EUROPEAN CONVENTION ON HUMAN RIGHTS AS GUARANTOR OF A COMMON TRADITION OF FUNDAMENTAL FREEDOMS

1. *Human rights as an element of national constitutions and of international protection*

The notion of human rights did not originate in international law but developed within the constitutional law of individual States. The idea that the individual shall continue to enjoy certain fundamental rights and freedoms *vis-à-vis* the political community has its roots in the conception of natural rights which in England in the seventeenth century was linked with the tradition, to be found throughout Europe, of the guarantee of individual freedoms and rights for the higher classes, for the citizens of towns or indeed for the whole population of a country.[1] According to this conception, the protection of property and personal liberty came first, soon to be supplemented by the idea of religious freedoms and tolerance. They underwent further development through political philosophy (Locke, Rousseau) and formed the starting point for the Declarations of Fundamental Freedoms in the constitutions adopted by individual American States after their secession from England and in the amendments made in 1791 to the Constitution of the United States. The Declaration of the Rights of Man issued by the French National assembly in 1789 was undoubtedly of decisive importance to developments in Europe. It became a model of constitutional legislation which explains why, despite all the diversity of national conceptions, the lists of fundamental freedoms and

---

[1] On the subject of the origin of the idea of fundamental rights, see J. Bohatec, *England und die Geschichte der Menschen und Bürgerrechte*, Graz, 1956; my comments: 'Grundlagen und Sicherung der Menschenrechte', *Salzburger Jahrb. f. Philosophie*, III, 1959, p. 7, et seq. In regard to the medieval tradition of liberties guaranteed by political contract, see J. C. Holt, *Magna Carta*, Cambridge, 1965, p. 43 et seq.

civil rights of the countries of the European Continent nevertheless have many common features and relationships on which the European Convention on Human Rights and Fundamental Freedoms can today build. The development of human rights in the Netherlands (since 1798), in Belgium (1831) and Switzerland (1848), as well as in Germany (since 1818, 1848), Italy (1848) and Austria (the State Basic Law of 1867 is still in force today), was largely based on the tradition of the French Revolution. In the nineteenth century there was, however, a noticeable trend to regard the freedom rights granted under the constitutions not as human rights for all men, but as civil rights for the nationals of a State; in practice, however, this limitation affected by and large only political rights. It was very significant, on the other hand, that in the nineteenth century Parliament assumed a Sovereign position in most countries and that, as a result, applications to the legislative body by individuals invoking freedoms guaranteed under constitutional law generally remained ineffectual. Prior to 1914, there was no jurisprudence in Europe comparable to American jurisprudence in regard to civil rights, apart from some initiatives taken in Switzerland and Austria. The position has changed considerably since the First World War. A few large European countries, such as England and France, which had always attached especial importance to freedom of the individual, maintained the principle of the unrestricted power of the legislator. Many other countries, however, adopted the principles of the supremacy of the Constitution and of the Fundamental Freedoms laid down therein, and also subjected the legislator to judicial control in regard to the observance of the Constitution.

The content of the fundamental freedoms embodied in constitutions, or guaranteed by national legislation or merely recognised in common law has undergone considerable change and development in the course of time. It is possible, without going into details, to distinguish three groups of constitutionally guaranteed rights. First there is the group of fundamental rights in respect of the protection of the life of the individual, his personal freedom, his family circle, his freedom of religion, thought and property. The primary object of these rights is to protect the freedom of the individual against the power of the State. This group also includes certain political freedoms: freedom of association, of assembly and of the press. This group of freedoms as a whole may be described as the group of civil or liberal rights. They form the nucleus of the constitutionally guaranteed freedoms and the main content of the European Convention on Human Rights. Alongside this group, a second series of social and cultural rights has now developed. They arise out of the changed position of modern man who seeks independence of the political power in certain respects but in others remains dependent on State encouragement and support. Alone the individual can no longer procure employment, the necessary educational facilities, insurance against illness and old age. These rights entitle him to protection and advancement which can be ensured only by appropriate State action. They include the right to education (Protocol No. 1, Art. 2), the right to work and to social insurance or to an adequate standard of living(Universal Declaration of Human Rights of the United Nations, Arts. 22, 23 and 25). If these rights are to become effective, the legislator must intervene and take the necessary measures to implement the cultural and social programme laid down.[1] These fundamental social rights are in many respects wholly different from the liberal rights pertaining to personal freedoms[2] and they obviously lend themselves less to international protection, since they call for influence to be brought to bear upon the legislator. They do not play a role in the European Convention. The third group of constitutional provisions are to be found primarily in the constitutions of the countries of central Europe. They do not relate to individual rights but to material law guarantees, pertaining to the protection of certain public institutions or certain basic features of the legal order, such as marriage, the family, the position of the church *vis-à-vis* the State, certain principles governing education in schools or the independence of municipalities (Basic Law of the Federal Republic of Germany, Arts. 6, 7, 28, 140).[3] These constitutional guarantees known as 'institutional guarantees' are not to be found in Western constitutions and are also absent from the European Convention. Their importance resides in the fact that they have greatly contributed to the interpretation of fundamental freedoms. Today German jurisprudence recognises that basically many individual freedoms also embody a guarantee of material rights, such as the protection of marriage and the family(European Convention, Arts. 8, 12), property (Protocol No. 1, Art. 1) or the press (Art. 10).[4] This conception can

---

[1] In regard to the change in conception of man's independence in the era of the *homme situé*, see G. Burdeau, *Les libertés publiques*, Paris, 1961, p. 20 et seq.; M. Duverger, *Institutions politiques et droit constitutionnel*, 6th ed., Paris, 1962, p. 213 et seq.; my comments in *Veröffentlichungen der Vereinigung Deutscher Staatsrechtslehrer*, vol. 22 (1965), p. 43 et seq.

[2] With their call for social welfare, they may even induce a country to restrict individual freedoms. In regard to a possible conflict between individual freedom and social rights, cf. Hans Huber, 'Speziale Verfassungsrechte', *Die Freiheit des Bürgers im Schweizerischen Recht. Zur Hundertjahrfeier der Bundesverfassung*, 1948, p. 149 et seq.

[3] In regard to institutional guarantees afforded by the constitution, cf. v. Mangoldt-Klein, *Das Bonner Grundgesetz*, 2nd ed., 1955, p. 83 et seq.

[4] In regard to the simultaneous protection of an individual right and material institution, cf. Hans Huber, *Festgabe des Schweizer Juristenvereins*, 1955, p. 128 et seq.; P. Häberle, *Die Wesensgehaltsgarantie des Art. 19, Abs. 2., Grundgesetz*,

lead to an extended application of freedoms if general principles are derived from them, i.e. if they are regarded as laying down standards which are in a general way binding on the legislature.[1] In some cases German courts apply objective principles derived from fundamental freedoms, in their jurisprudence in respect of the Human Rights Convention. The Federal Administrative Court derives from Article 8 the general principle of the protection of the family and in the case of expulsion (*Aufenthalts-verbot*) of a foreigner, which could lead to separation of members of a family, opposes it to the interest of national security.[2] From Article 7 the Federal Court derives the principle of the administration of criminal justice in strict accordance with the law (*strenge Gesetzmässigkeit der Strafrechtspflege*) and therefore considers extended application of the provisions of the penal code on the confiscation of illegal publications as inadmissible.[3] It would seem that this interpretation of fundamental rights is to be found primarily in German jurisprudence.[4] In comparing the application of the Convention by international bodies with national jurisprudence, it is necessary to take these differences in interpretation into account. In Germany the extension of jurisprudence to questions of fundamental rights has led to the development of new viewpoints which broaden the field of application of constitutionally guaranteed rights.

Compared with the development of constitutional protection of fundamental freedoms, international law has up to now lagged behind in this field. In the seventeenth and eighteenth centuries attempts were made to protect individual rights on the basis of natural law and of a *jus gentium* recognised as a law common to all

Karlsruhe, 1962, p. 80 et seq.; Bachof in: *Bettermann-Nipperdey, Die Grundrechte, Bd. III*, p. 155 et seq.; P. Dagtoglou, *Wesen und Grenzen der Pressefreiheit* 1963, p. 12, et seq.; my comments in *Veröffentlichungen d. Staatsrechtslehrer*, Heft 22, p. 55 et seq.

[1] This idea is to be found in the jurisprudence of the German Constitutional Court: Equality of man and woman B. *Verf. GE*, 10, p. 8 et seq.; protection of marriage and the family 6, p. 76; 12, p. 163; 13, p. 298, 317; 17, p. 317; property 14, p. 277; freedom to work 16, p. 217. In regard to theoretical motivation, see Zippelius, *Wertungsprobleme im System der Grundrechte*, 1962, p. 2 et seq.; my comments, *Veröff. d. Staatsrechtlehrer, Heft* 22, p. 51 et seq.

[2] B.VerwG in *Deutsche Verwaltungsblätter*, 1957, p. 57.

[3] *NJW*, 1962, S. 499.

[4] The same applies to other principles of interpretation, e.g. the attempt to embody fundamental freedoms in a system and to develop an order of precedence among them and, in certain cases, extend their scope to relations between private individuals (so-called third party effect). These conceptions are also to be found in Austrian and Swiss doctrine. Cf. F. Ermacora, *Handbuch der Grundrechte und Menschenrechte*, Wien, 1963, p. 29 et seq.; Hans Huber, *Ztschr. f. Schweiz. Recht*, 1963, A.; J. P. Müller, *Die Grundrechte der Verfassung und der Persönlichkeitsschutz des Privatrechts*, Bern, 1964, p. 74 et seq., p. 160 et seq.

States.[1] According to nineteenth century doctrine, on the other hand, international law was applicable only to relations between States and it was left entirely to the individual countries to determine the legal status of their citizens. The international community or the big powers acting on its behalf concerned themselves only occasionally with the promotion and protection of human rights from the point of view of humanity, the protection of religious minorities or the promotion of individual rights in certain, narrowly limited spheres (prevention of slavery and white slave traffic).[2] These interventions were only of an incidental nature and were not without political repercussions. Certain individual rights were protected permanently and effectively solely because the big powers granted their nationals diplomatic protection and thereby achieved the international protection of certain minimum basic rights of foreigners.[3] This protection was, however, only afforded to foreigners and today this method of safeguarding general principles of the law of aliens, which can lead to differences in the legal status of nationals and foreigners, is politically more difficult to exercise and has therefore declined in importance. It constitutes an example of an older trend which is in line with present day efforts to draw up a list of certain human rights. After the first war, the agreements on the protection of religious, ethnic and linguistic minorities and the acceptance by the League of Nations of petitions from the mandated territories constituted forms of geographically and substantively limited protection of human rights through international bodies. Apart from the establishment of a Mixed Commission and Arbitral Tribunal under the Convention between Germany and Poland of 15 May 1922, and from individual cases concerned with questions of this kind referred to the Permanent

[1] Under natural law, the individual was still regarded as the direct holder of certain rights also *vis-à-vis* his own State and in some cases held certain rights in the international sphere (law of aliens, martial law, etc.). Cf. my comments, *Festschrift Hermann Jahrreis*, Cologne, 1964, p. 361 et seq.; Mosler, *ZaöRuVR*, 22, 1962, p. 30 et seq.; P. P. Remec, *The Position of the Individual in International Law according to Grotius and Vattel*, The Hague, 1960, p. 125 et seq. At that time the protection of human rights was already provided for in a number of peace treaties, particularly in the form of guarantee of religious tolerance and maintenance of existing civil rights. Cf. R. Chakravarti, *Human Rights and the UN.*, Calcutta, 1958, p. 6 et seq.

[2] On the subject of these occasional measures to protect individual rights, see M. Ganji, *International Protection of Human Rights*, Geneva, 1962, p. 9 et seq.; p. 88 et seq.

[3] On the subject of a minimum degree of protection for foreigners in the form of diplomatic protection, see Dietrich Schindler, *Gleichberechtigung von Individuen als Problem des Völkerrechts*, Zürich, 1957, p. 28 et seq.; K. Doehring, *Die allgemeinen Regeln des völkerrechtlichen Fremdenrechts und das deutsche Verfassungsrecht*, Cologne, 1963, p. 85 et seq.

Court of International Justice by States,[1] action of the international community was limited to political interventions.[2]

Today the legal position has changed considerably. The view that the application of international law should be strictly limited to States as subjects is giving way more and more to the conviction that under international law individuals can personally have a legal status as holders of rights and duties, not only in respect of a *locus standi* in international proceedings but also in substantive law.[3] Going beyond the initiatives of 1919, promotion of respect for human rights is today a fundamental task of the United Nations. This aim has found expression not only in special fields but in general through the adoption of the Universal Declaration of Human Rights by all Members of the United Nations. The Declaration is, it is true, only of limited legal importance. It is not a binding convention imposing obligations on States. Its legal force has been compared to that of a recommendation of the General Assembly,[4] embodying directives for the action of member countries and of international bodies, and providing a legal basis for it in the Charter. This provision of the Charter is therefore not without legal importance. By virtue of the principle of sovereign equality [Art. 2 (1) UN Charter] it is in principle left entirely to the State to determine the legal status of its inhabitants. This independence is, however, limited where international obligations, whether arising from a treaty or from a general rule, are concerned. Article 2 (7) of the UN Charter cannot, therefore, be invoked against the activities of UN bodies concerned with the protection of a minimum number of human rights in a country, even where the nationals of that country are concerned.[5] The United Nations

[1] *P.C.I.J. Reports*, Ser. A, No. 15 (Upper Silesia) and Ser. A/B, No. 64 (Minorities in Albania). Cf. also Ganji, op. cit., p. 52 et seq.; 64 et seq.

[2] See Ganji, op. cit., p. 45 et seq.; G. Ezejiofor, *Protection of Human Rights under the Law*, London, 1964, p. 38 et seq. The hearing of petitions from the inhabitants of mandated territories by the League of Nations and of trusteeship territories by the United Nations constitutes a protection of individual rights through international bodies, although the petitioners do not have any procedural rights.

Cf. C. A. Nørgaard, *The Position of the Individual in International Law*, Oslo, 1962, p. 109 et seq. See also the reference to the International Court of Justice of questions of this nature in connection with the disputes over South-West Africa, *I.C.J. Rep.*, 1962, p. 319.

[3] In regard to present-day determination of the legal status of the individual under international law, see Mosler, *ZaöRuVR*, 22, 1962, p. 20 et seq.; Nørgaard, loc. cit., p. 82 et seq.; G. Dahm, *Die Stellung der Menschen im Völkerrecht unserer Zeit*, Tübingen, 1961.

[4] Cf. Robinson, *The Universal Declaration of Human Rights*, New York, 1958, p. 52; Ezejiofor, loc. cit., p. 77 et seq.

[5] This interpretation of the duty to protect human rights as against Article 2 (7) of the UN Charter is supported by both Ganji, loc. cit., p. 50 et seq., and R.

can, however, give protection only through discussion, recommendation and peaceful action. In the limited sphere of the human rights protected by the Conventions of the International Labour Organisations, the Organisation proposes several kinds of procedure for dealing with complaints against States; such complaints can, however, be lodged only by corporate bodies or international organisations and not by individuals.[1] In all these cases of promotion and protection of individual rights through the United Nations or specialised agencies, apart from special cases referred to the International Court of Justice,[2] protection is provided only by political action through discussion, publication or recommendation.

2. *Common principles of law as a basis for European Conventions*

The European Convention for the Protection of Human Rights and Fundamental Freedoms takes its place as a regional institution among endeavours to strengthen the protection of human rights which under present-day international law exist primarily in the United Nations context. By virtue of its content, the extent of its binding effect in both international and municipal law and its means of enforcement, the place it occupies is, however, a special one. As far as the *content* is concerned, the Universal Declaration of Human Rights of the United Nations—and the same applies to the draft Covenants on Civil and Political Rights and Economic, Social and Cultural Rights —embodies a very broad field of guarantees encompassing not only liberal freedoms but also a large number of social rights and institutional guarantees. This is in conformity with the aim of the Declaration to constitute a model for the development and protection of human rights throughout the world; but it would be difficult to apply

---

Higgins, *The Development of International Law through the Political Organs of the UN*, London, 1963, p. 118 et seq. Another opinion limits the United Nations' right to intervene to cases when the violation of human rights entails a threat to or breach of the peace or of security; otherwise protection is left to the State and only the promotion of individual rights to the United Nations: Kelsen, *The Law of the UN*, 1950, p. 29 et seq.; G. Schwarzenberger, *The Inductive Approach to International Law*, 1965, p. 167 et seq. This interpretation is too narrow and takes too little account of the obligation arising from Article 2 (5,6) for the Members of the United Nations. As for the limits to the action of the UN, which has only peaceful means of enforcing its attitude, see I. Brownlie, *International Law and the Use of Force by States*, Oxford, 1963, p. 341 et seq.

[1] In this connection, cf. C. W. Jenks, *Human Rights and International Labour Standards*, 1960; *Law, Freedom and Welfare*, London, 1963, p. 101 et seq.; Nørgaard, loc. cit., p. 139 et seq.

[2] The attempt to implement the provisions on the protection of human rights embodied in the peace treaties of 1947 was unsuccessful. Cf. *I.C.J Rep.*, 1950, p. 121 et seq.; and p. 221 et seq.

the Declaration as directly enforceable law.[1] The European Convention, on the other hand, confines itself to guaranteeing a limited but clearly defined standard of individual freedom enforceable through the courts and refrains from formulating programmes and promises of a social character. The United Nations Declaration is not in the form of a binding undertaking. It is true that in a few cases domestic courts have invoked the Declaration, not as applicable law but as an expression of the political principles of the international community.[2] The European Convention, on the contrary, is directly binding law, at international level as well as under the municipal law of many countries. The principles of the Universal Declaration can only be applied by means of political action by the United Nations institutions. Its implementation therefore depends on States taking up a violation by a member of the United Nations and referring it to the General Assembly or Security Council.[3] Under the European Convention, on the other hand, individuals and groups of persons have direct access to the European Commission of Human Rights and, its provisions being applicable at national level, also to the municipal courts of many signatory States. The question dealt with in this study, namely the uniform application of an international convention on the protection of the rights of individuals by municipal courts and international bodies and courts, can therefore arise only in connection with the European Convention. International texts which are non-binding declarations and do not afford individual legal protection can only in exceptional cases be applied and interpreted by a national or international body.

The special position of the European Convention is also apparent in the fact that its legal provisions are firmly rooted in the common legal concepts of member countries. The Universal Declaration of Human Rights, too, is designed to promote such a nucleus of human rights in all countries and foster a common attitude. In view of the great political and social differences between the countries of the

[1] The Declaration on the elimination of racial discrimination, which is in course of preparation, is similar in character. Cf. *Int. Organisation*, 1964, p. 374 et seq., *UN Monthly*, 1965, pp. 11, 62. There are other rights which form the subject of special conventions. See Ganji, loc. cit., p. 225.

[2] In *Fuji* v. *the State of California* (1952, IIR 312), the American Supreme Court describes the UN Declaration as 'entitled to respectful consideration by courts' and as a 'moral commitment' which does not, however, affect municipal law. For other references to the Universal Declaration, see Chakravarti, loc. cit., p. 77 et seq.; Robinson, loc. cit., p. 95 et seq.; and C. W. Jenks, *The Prospects of International Adjudication*, London, 1964, p. 443. See also Schwarzenberger, *The Changing Structure of International Law*, London, 1964, p. 240 et seq.

[3] Implementation of the Conventions of the International Labour Organisation, too, is entrusted mainly to international bodies and States. Cf. Ganji, loc. cit., p. 22 et seq.

world, there are only few legal principles which are common to all and can be taken as a starting point in this broader context. Despite the noticeable influence of the Universal Declaration on many modern constitutions,[1] there is no common tradition of constitutional law. In the world context, a 'Common Law of Mankind' providing a common basis for human rights can be adopted only progressively.[2] With its narrower regional context and its clearly worded Articles, the European Convention can, on the contrary—as mentioned above—base itself on a common tradition of constitutional law and a large measure of legal tradition common to member countries. Its aim is not only to present this common heritage as a model but to make it an effective source of legal interpretation.[3] Its provisions thus become common law (*droit communautaire*)[4] for all signatory States, a *patrimoine commun*[5] which is based on a common foundation of legal conceptions.[6] The international bodies set up under the Convention and municipal courts can naturally also interpret the Convention according to the general principles of international law, the 'general principles of law recognised by civilised nations' referred to in Article 38 of the Statute of the International Court of Justice, i.e. according to a kind of joint law of all nations, a *jus gentium*;[7] the law applied by them is, however, the law of European tradition and represents a system of regional standards and principles.[8] It does not, however, suffice merely to lay down such legal principles; it is also necessary to ensure their uniform recognition in all countries and their uniform application and interpretation despite differing national legal systems and traditions.

[1] In regard to the influence of the UN Declaration on recent constitutions, see Chakravarti, loc. cit., p. 75 et seq.; Robinson, loc. cit., p. 93 et seq.

[2] See also Schwarzenberger, *The Changing Structure of Int. Law*, p. 241 et seq. A more hopeful assessment of the degree of development is made by C. W. Jenks, *The Common Law of Mankind*, 1950, p. 46 et seq., although he does not underestimate the difficulties of uniform interpretation (p. 164 et seq.).

[3] The Commission describes the aim as 'to proclaim and define certain human rights and fundamental freedoms and to furnish guarantees for their enjoyment', *E.C.H.R.*, Series B, 1962, p. 125 (*De Becker Case*).

[4] Dupuy, *Annuaire Français de droit international*, II, 1957 p. 461.

[5] Janssen, *Chronique de Politique étrangère*, xv, 1962, p. 204.

[6] In the Preamble to the Convention reference is made to such a 'common heritage'. Cf. also the reference to this basis in the decision of the Commission 788/60 *Yearbook*, IV, p. 138, which speaks of 'common public order of the free democracies of Europe'.

[7] Such a series of fundamental human rights applicable under international law is proposed by Bernhardt, *ZaöRuVR*, 24, 1964, p. 446. Cf. also Eustathiades, *Friedens-Warte*, 52, 1955, pp. 345–6. For a reference to general principles of international law, see decision of the Commission 323/57 *Yearbook*, I, p. 247.

[8] In regard to the possibility of adoption of such a common legal view, see Sir Humphrey Waldock *Br. Yearbook Int. Law*, 24, 1958, p. 363.

The acceptance of such a common legal view is implied when, in deciding whether or not a claim for political asylum is admissible (Art. 16 of the Basic Law), the German Federal Court takes the view that it is admissible if the person had to apprehend a violation of his human rights within the meaning of the European Convention.[1] In the definition of the term 'asylum' under municipal law, the common human rights provisions are here used as a yardstick in assessing the political danger in the home country. An even more direct application of the provisions was made by the Federal Administrative Court when, in ruling on claims by refugees from the eastern part of Germany, it defined the conception of violation of 'the principles of humanity or constitutionality' in invoking the contents of European human rights.[2]

3. The need for a uniform interpretation of the Convention

The principle can be agreed that a uniform interpretation of the Human Rights Convention is required of both international bodies and national courts and constrains them to bear in mind the need for harmonisation.[3] This applies all the more to the European Convention in that its law does not include any machinery for ensuring uniform interpretation, as does the law of the European Communities—Article 41 of the ECSC Treaty, Article 177 of the EEC Treaty, Article 150 of the Euratom Treaty. Here national courts are to a certain extent obliged to refer questions of interpretation of the Treaty which arise in national disputes to the Court of Justice of the Communities.[4] The task of ensuring uniform interpretation of provisions in the context of the European Communities is very similar to that in respect of the European Convention on Human Rights. It is not a question of the rights of individuals but of

---

[1] *BGHSt.*, 8, p. 59; the extradition of a man sought by Greece for committing several murders during the civil war does not constitute an infringement of human rights; hence there can be no claim to political asylum.

[2] Federal Administrative Court, reproduced by Morvay, 'Rechtsprechung nationaler Gerichte zur MRK', *ZaöRuVR*, 21, 1961, p. 96.

[3] The need for uniform interpretation of European Community law is urged by R. Pépy in *Revue critique de droit international privé*, 1963, p. 491; also by H. J. Glaesner in *Zehn Jahre Rechtsprechung des Gerichtshofs der Eur. Gemeinschaften*, Cologne, 1965, pp. 159–60.

[4] Article 177 of the EEC Treaty is the most important of these provisions. It governs only the interpretation of the provisions of the Treaty and not the discussion of its bearing upon municipal law. Cf. Case 28–30 *RsprGH*, 9, p. 81. On Article 177 of the EEC Treaty in general, see H. van Heuvel, *Prejudiciele vragen en bevoegdheidsproblemen in het europees recht*, Deventer, 1962; Steindorff, *Rechtsschutz und Verfahren im Recht der Eur. Gemeinschaften*, 1964, p. 66 et seq.; Chr. Tomashek, *Die gerichtliche Vorabentscheidung nach den Verträgen über die Europäischen Gemeinschaften*, Cologne, 1965.

economic law. Here there are common legal conceptions and notions, such as evaluation, discrimination, subsidy, competition, command of the market, etc., which must be interpreted uniformly. Many of these conceptions—and this also applies to the Human Rights Convention—have their origin in municipal law. Where they are applied under an international treaty, they will have to be interpreted by means of comparative law.[1] Where there is concordance between systems of municipal law, the application can be based on this common foundation.[2] Municipal law provisions for which there is no equivalent in the law of the other member countries can, however, have no bearing.[3]

Through the medium of comparative law, the interpretation of the European Convention will be able to evolve from the legal systems of member States common principles of law which will be of great value for the understanding of certain concepts such as 'private and family life' (Art. 8), 'freedom of expression' (Art. 10), 'possessions' (First Protocol, Art. 1), 'national security' and 'public safety' (Arts. 8, 9, 11). Hitherto the organs of the Convention have had little recourse to the comparative method for the establishment of uniform interpretations, wherein they differ from the Court of Justice of the European Communities which frequently does so.[4]

---

[1] On the subject of the comparative law method in public law, cf. Bernhardt, *ZaöRuVR*, 24, 1964, p. 431 et seq.

[2] From the practice of the Court of Justice of the European Communities, see Case 2-10/63, *Rspr.*, 9, p. 727 (Invoking by a party of equivalent provisions of mercantile law on the preservation of bills of exchange in the EEC countries). From the practice of the Commission of Human Rights, see the invoking by a party in the *De Becker case* of provisions of penal codes of other countries (*E.C.H.R.*, Series B, 1962, p. 99).

[3] *VerfGH* Koblenz, *Neue Juristische Wochenschrift* (*NJW*), 1959, p. 1628: Article 13 of the Convention does not make it compulsory to lodge a constitutional application, as is the case in the Federal Republic by virtue of the law governing the Federal Constitutional Court of 12 March 1951, Articles 90 et seq. Apart from Austria, no other member country has similar machinery. An interesting decision was rendered by the Court of Justice of the European Communities in a case in which it refused to recognise the validity of a reservation of owner's rights peculiar to German law, and accordingly to exempt a firm from payment of a tax on scrap metal. Case 17 u. 20/61, *Rspr.*, 8, p. 691. Cf. also Case 6/60 *Rspr.* 6, p. 1, 195. For a criticism of decision 17 u. 20/61, see Wille, *Zehn Jahre Rechtsprechung* (Ann. 33), p. 149 et seq.

[4] Cf. Cases Nos. 8–13/57, *RsprGH*, vol. 4, pp. 257, 408, 445, 483, 523; the 'generally recognised principle of law in the legal systems of member States', namely that of equality in economic legislation, does not preclude the introduction of different prices for different categories of consumers; cases Nos. 22 and 23/60, *RsprGH*, vol. 7, p. 421, Attorney-General Roemer: 'The generally recognised principle of administrative law' that an official has no absolute right to promotion; Case No. 25/62, *RsprGH*, vol. 9, p. 260: Attorney-General Roemer: Admissibility of rectification of a claim during procedure in an administrative

Following this practice, the Court of the European Communities takes care, however, not to give universal application to national concepts and interpretations which derive from peculiarities of national law and legal traditions.[1] It would seem legitimate, however, to invoke such legal principles as within the circle of member States are generally recognised in municipal law for the interpretation of the guarantees given in the Convention, even when they are principles which enjoy regional rather than world-wide acceptance.[2] Indeed this method was adopted by the European Court of Human Rights to justify the communication of the Commission's report to the parties in the Lawless case. The Court pointed out that the proceedings before it were of a judicial character and that, according to the generally accepted principles of civil and criminal law, judicial proceedings had to be conducted in the presence of the parties and in public.[3]

There is of course an important difference in one respect between the European Convention on Human Rights and the Community Treaties when it comes to their interpretation. The purpose of the latter is to unify the law of member States in their sphere of application.[4] This tendency of the treaties to foster the evolution of uniform

---

court in French and German administrative law; Cases Nos. 53 and 54/63, *RsprGH*, vol. 9, pp. 513, 555, Attorney-General Roemer: Liability for costs of a party to proceedings by whom they have been incurred without due cause, as a general principle of procedural law. Case No. 6/60, *Jurisprudence*, vol. 6, p. 1195; Decision on the measure of freedom from taxation enjoyed by European civil servants on the basis of a comparison of fiscal law in member States. For questions relating to this form of comparative work see Bernhardt, *ZaöRuVR*, 24, 1964, p. 448 and idem, *Die Auslegung völkerrechtlicher Verträge*, Cologne, 1963, p. 156 et seq.

[1] Case No. 33/59, *RsprGH*, vol. 8, p. 820, Attorney-General Lagrange: The difference between subjective right and interest in Italian law (in connection with a decision on the admissibility of a claim for damages) does not concord with the system of the European Treaties; cases Nos. 17 and 20/61, *RsprGH*, vol. 8, p. 691: No consideration of peculiarities of German law in regard to the reservation of owner's rights which is incompatible with the basic principles of property law in all the member States and could result in legal possibilities which do not exist in other legal systems being open to German firms. Cf. also Donner, *Zehn Jahre Rechtsprechung*, p. 6 et seq., Karl Wolf, op. cit., p. 198, and Wille's criticism, p. 149 et seq.

[2] Thus rightly Bernhardt, *Auslegung*, p. 157; Mathijsen, *Le droit de la Communauté Européenne du Charbon et de l'Acier*, The Hague, 1958, p. 137 et seq.; G. Cassoni, *Diritto Internazionale*, 13, 1959, p. 448 et seq.

[3] *Lawless Case*, Decision of 14 November 1960, p. 13. See also Bernhardt, *Auslegung*, p. 158.

[4] Cf. Rome Treaty, Art. 3h, 27, 54, 56 (2), 57 (2), 99, 100–102. For this trend towards the harmonisation of legal systems see Beitzke, 'Probleme der Privatrechtsangleichung in der Europäischen Wirtschaftsgemeinschaft', *Ztschr. für Rechtsvergleichung*, 1964, p. 50 et seq.

Q

law makes it easier for the Court of Justice to compare national laws and rely on the establishment and recognition of common legal principles. But such is not the purpose of the Convention on Human Rights, which does not seek to introduce any superior law or to bring about the amendment or unification of municipal law, but asks simply that in their own law the contracting States should stand by the undertakings they have given.[1] Whether the Convention, after some time, may lead to a certain harmonisation of legal principles and of substantive law in relation to fundamental freedoms is another matter.

II. JURISPRUDENCE AND THE GENERAL PROBLEM OF THE CONVENTION'S APPLICATION IN NATIONAL AND INTERNATIONAL LAW

1. *The Convention as international law*

The fact that the European Convention is binding on the contracting States for the framing and application of their law makes it necessary to compare national law—constitutional and other—and its application by the administration and the courts, with the terms of the Convention. Furthermore, the Convention is not invoked in international courts alone, but also in national courts in many countries. This requires a further comparison—indeed the main one that interests us here—of the effects of the application of the Convention. Here the questions which arise may be divided into three groups:

(*a*) Is the Convention interpreted in the same way by international judicial authorities as by national courts? Has international practice binding force at national level?

(*b*) When international authorities are enquiring into the conformity of national law and its application to the terms of the Convention, they have at the same time to interpret national law. To what extent ought they to go into the details of national law and its interpretation? Are they bound by the prevailing national opinion? Or ought they at least to accept it without further enquiry?

(*c*) When national courts apply the Convention directly as part of municipal law they too have to compare its terms with national legal provisions in order to establish the relationship between them. Are there any general principles governing procedure for the interpretation of the Convention and are they the same in all countries? Or are

---

[1] The Commission accordingly rejects the theory that Article 1 of the First Protocol was designed to prohibit the imposition of fines. That would have been *une véritable révolution juridique* (333/57 *Yearbook*, I, p. 247). Cf. also the decision of the Police Court of Aubel, *Yearbook*, v, p. 374.

differences in the legal systems and traditions of individual States to be observed in this connection.[1]

These questions can receive only a general answer here. It is clear that the European Convention is an international treaty and therefore the international organs it sets up need have regard to their own opinions only and not to any considerations of national law. The violation of the rights and freedoms guaranteed by the Convention alone confers competence on the international organs.[2] It is not their duty to decide, in the manner of a supreme court, whether national law—even when it conforms to the Convention—is properly applied. Neither the invocation of general clauses of the Convention nor the prohibition of punishment except in accordance with the law (Art. 7) can cause the international organs to enquire into details of national law and procedure which do not directly affect the substance of the international guarantees.[3] The European Commission, as it has itself pointed out, 'cannot deal with any errors of fact or law imputed rightly or wrongly to the courts of the Contracting States'.[4]

This attitude rests on a dualist view of the relationship between international and municipal law. It is also that taken by international judicial authorities in deciding whether the Convention has immediate force of law in member countries, since they agree that individual constitutions are decisive on this point.[5] Even if we adopt the more recent doctrine that no longer requires the transformation of an international treaty into municipal law for its application in the contracting State but accepts that the treaty as such acquires force of municipal law through an internal order of execution which does not affect its international character,[6] it is still for national constitutional

---

[1] For the problems of uniform interpretation of international treaties and the establishment of common principles among the contracting States, see F. Capotorti, 'Sulla interpretazione uniforme dei trattati Europei', *Rivista di diritto internazionale*, 43, 1960, p. 1 et seq.; Mann, 'The Interpretation of Uniform Statutes', *The Law Quarterly Review*, 1946, p. 278 et seq.; G. Cassoni, 'I principali generali comuni agli ordinamenti degli Stati membri quale fonte sussidaria del diritto applicato dalla Corte di Guistizia delle Communità Europee', *Diritto Internazionale*, 13, 1959, p. 428 et seq., 457 et seq.

[2] Cf. 1802/62, *Yearbook*, VI, p. 479.

[3] 154/57, 172/57, 258/57, *Yearbook*, I, p. 152, 216, 254, 462/59, *Yearbook*, II, p. 388, 1169/61, *Yearbook*, VI, p. 528.   [4] 1103/61, *Yearbook*, V, p. 190.

[5] In its decision as to whether Belgian applicants had a legal remedy in municipal law against a law passed subsequently to the Convention, the Commission at the same time goes into the question of the force and status of the Convention in Belgian law (1661/62, *Yearbook*, VI, p. 367 et seq.).

[6] For this 'execution doctrine' see H. Mosler, *Das Völkerrecht in der Praxis der deutschen Gerichte*, Karlsruhe, 1957, p. 15 et seq.; idem, *Recueil des Cours*, 91, 1957, p. 640 et seq.; K. Partsch, 'Die Anwendung des Völkerrechts im innerstaatlichen Recht', *Berichte der Deutschen Gesellschaft für Völkerrecht*, 6, 1964, p. 44 et seq., 156 et seq.

law to decide whether the Convention is directly applicable in municipal law and what its status is in relation to that law.

2. Application of the Convention in municipal law

The question of the application of the European Convention on Human Rights in municipal law and the status of its provisions in relation to the Constitution and other legislation is one that has often been investigated and we shall do no more here than give a brief account of the findings.[1] Of the 18 member States of the Council of Europe, 2 have not yet signed the Convention (Switzerland[2] and Malta) and one (France)[3] has not yet ratified it. Although it has adopted several clauses in the Convention into its Constitution, nothing definite can be said in regard to Cyprus.[4]

In six countries the direct application of the Convention in municipal law is impossible owing to the terms of the Constitution and the prevailing conceptions on the relation between international and national law. This has been established for Iceland,[5] Ireland[6] and in effect also for Norway[7] by court decisions and must be recognised in the case of Denmark, Sweden and Great Britain likewise.[8]

In three countries, on the contrary, the Convention takes precedence over ordinary laws and accordingly even over subsequent laws.

[1] For an outline see Golsong, *Das Rechtsschutzsystem der Eur. Menschenrechts-konvention*, 1958, p. 9 et seq., and *Br. Yearbook Int. Law*, 38, 1962, p. 448 et seq.; Morvay, *ZaöRuVR*, 21, 1961, p. 91 et seq.; K. Vasak, *La Convention européenne des Droits de l'Homme*, 1964, p. 227 et seq.; Bürgenthal, *The European Convention on Human Rights*, (British Institute of International and Comparative Law, Intern. Law Series No. 5) 1965, p. 84 et seq. See in addition for similar research in connection with the Treaties of the European Communities: Schlochauer, *Archiv d. Völkerrechts* 11, 1962, p. 1 et seq.; van den Heuvel (Note 50), p. 20 et seq.; *Bericht über den Vorrang des Gemeinschaftsrechts vor dem Recht der Mitgliedstaaten, Europ. Parlament Sitzungsdokumente*, Doc. 43, 1965–6.

[2] For the accession of Switzerland to the European Convention on Human Rights see the report of the Federal Council of 26 October 1962, *BBl*, 1962, p. 1096.

[3] The predominance of an international treaty over municipal law (Art. 55 of the Constitution of 4 October 1958) should in fact be of little practical significance in relation to subsequent legislation. Cf. J. Schilling, *Völkerrecht und staatliches Recht in Frankreich*, 1964, p. 158 et seq., 167 et seq. See however Pépy, *Dall. Chron.*, 1964, p. 9 et seq., and idem, *Revue Critique de droit international privé*, 1963, p. 695 et seq. On the other hand, cf. *Cour d'Appel de Douai, Dall*, 1964, p. 299 and *Conseil d'État*, Lebon, Rec., 1964, p. 344.

[4] Cf. Vasak, p. 244; Bürgenthal, p. 94.

[5] Court of Reykjavik, *Yearbook*, III, 643, 646.

[6] Supreme Court, *Yearbook*, II, 609, 623/24. Cf. Bürgenthal, p. 84.

[7] The evasive formula adopted by the Norwegian courts (see Supreme Court of 16 December 1961, *Journal Clunet*, 90, 1963, p. 789) changes nothing as regards the result. Cf. Hambro, *Journal Clunet*, 90, p. 790.

[8] For these countries see Bürgenthal, p. 84.

In Austria the theory was at first that since the Convention was approved by the Austrian Parliament by the majority required for amendments to the Federal Constitution, this, according to Articles 50, 44, gave it the same status as the Constitution.[1] The Austrian Constitutional Court rejected this claim on the grounds that under Article 44 (1) of the Constitution a Bill acquired that status only if it were specifically described as a 'constitutional law', (*Verfassungsgesetz*). In this instance that was not the case.[2] Subsequently, the amendment to the Constitution of 4 March 1964 (*BGBI* No. 59) Article II, laid down that certain treaties, among them the Convention on Human Rights, were to be regarded as 'constitutional laws', so that it is now clear that since this amendment came into force (7 April 1964) the Convention has constitutional status in Austria.[3] In the Netherlands, according to Articles 65–7 of the Grondwet, the Treaty has precedence over municipal law and even subsequent law.[4] The same is true in Luxembourg on the basis of jurisprudence.[5]

In the remaining countries the Convention has the status of an ordinary law, so that subsequent legislation can validly set it aside. In Germany, legal authors have championed its precedence over ordinary law.[6] And yet it is right to consider the opinion established in jurisprudence, that the Convention has the status of an ordinary law,[7] as the prevailing one. The same is true of Belgium[8] and

---

[1] Cf. Ermacora, *JurBlätter*, 1959, p. 396 et seq.; Pfeifer, Festschrift Hugelmann, Aalen, 1959, p. 420.

[2] Decision 2/61 Slg. 1961 No. 4049 (*Yearbook*, IV, p. 604). See also Slg. 1962, No. 4260 and Ermacora, *JurBlätter*, 1962, p. 117 et seq.

[3] Cf. Kunst, *OJurZeitung*, 1964, p. 198; Bürgenthal, pp. 90–1.

[4] Erades and Gould, *The Relation between International Law and Municipal Law in the Netherlands and the United States*, 1961, p. 346 et seq. *Hoge Rad Ned. Jurisprudentie*, 1960, p. 993, *Yearbook*, III, p. 649; *Yearbook*, IV, p. 641.

[5] Judgment of the Supreme Court of 5 June 1950, 15 *Pas. Lux.* 41, Report of the Europ. Parliament. Nos. 50, 90/91. Cf. however, the Luxembourg Court of Summary Justice, *Yearbook*, IV, p. 622.

[6] Cf. a review of legal literature by Münch, *Juristenzeitung* 1961, p. 153; Morvay, p. 91 et seq.

[7] It is enough to quote the Constitutional Court (*BVerfGE* 6, 440, *Yearbook*, II, 595). See also the Higher Administrative Court of Münster, *Yearbook*, II, 573; the Federal Administrative Court, *Yearbook*, II, 585; the Berlin High Court, *NJW*, 1962, 2209. The opinion that certain clauses of the Convention belong to general international law which, according to Article 25 of the Basic Law takes precedence over municipal law (cf. Meyer-Lindenberg, *Berichte der Deutschen Gesellschaft für Völkerrecht*, 4, 1961, p. 103 et seq.; Klein, *Jahrb. f. Internat. Recht*, 11, 1962, p. 149 et seq.) has never yet been put into practice.

[8] Thus the Commission of Human Rights, 1661/62, *Yearbook*, VI, 366. See also the Cour de Cassation, *Pasicrisie*, 1961, p. 207; 1963, p. 808; 1964, 1, 762. See also Janssen, *Chronique de Politique étrangère*, XV, 1962, p. 287; *Les conséquences d'ordre interne de la participation de la Belgique aux organisations internationales*, Institut Royal des Relations Internationales, 1964, p. 172 et seq., 181 et seq.

Italy[1] while in Greece and Turkey opinion is similar except that by emphasising the exceptions in the Convention jurisprudence gives its provisions a narrower interpretation.[2]

In connection with the application of the Convention in municipal law a further question arises which deserves attention. An individual can invoke in national courts only those provisions of the Convention which are recognised as directly applicable (self-executing). In some cases national courts have shown an inclination to regard clauses of the Convention simply as guides which legislation is bound to follow but which are not capable of direct application. Apart from Article 13, which in the main is certainly not regarded as self-executing,[3] such an attitude is likely to conflict with that of international judicial authorities.[4] Articles 1 to 12 of the Convention are, without exception, immediately applicable.[5]

A question related to the recognition of the provisions of the Convention as self-executing is that as to whether an applicant in whose country a provision of the Convention is not recognised as directly applicable is nevertheless obliged to appeal first to the national courts. According to international jurisprudence,[6] it will always be possible to require that domestic remedies be exhausted if this would really promise to put an end to a breach of international law.[7] But the plea does not need to rely on the Convention on Human Rights. It can invoke provisions of municipal law whose substance corresponds to the terms of the Convention.[8] This is a case in which the international judicial authorities, when investigating the ful-

---

[1] Corte Suprema di Cassazione, *Foro Italiano*, 1962, II, 315.

[2] For Greece see Arios Pagos, *Yearbook*, II, 607 and also Kyriakopoulos, *Festschrift Spiropoulos*, Bonn, 1957, p. 285 et seq.; for Turkey, Constitutional Court, *Yearbook*, VI, 820. Both judgments stress the exceptions authorised to the provisions of the Convention. Cf. Bürgenthal, p. 87 et seq.

[3] Cf. Morvay, p. 95, 105; Boas, *European Yearbook*, X, 1963, p. 231 et seq.

[4] This is true of the decision of the Austrian Constitutional Court that Article 6 was to be regarded as a directive only (*Programmsatz*). Slg. 1960, No. 3767, *Yearbook*, III, 617; 1961, No. 4122; *Oest. Juristenzeitung* 1963, 327. Cf. also 808/60, *Yearbook*, V, 120–2.

[5] See Supreme Court of Bremen, *Yearbook*, V, 359; *Hoge Rad Ned. Jurisprudentie* 1961, No. 273; 1964, No. 239.

[6] *P.C.I.J.*, Series A/B No. 76, *Panevezys-Saldutiskis Railway Case* quoted in 1661/62, *Yearbook*, VI, 368.

[7] 343/57, *Yearbook*, II, 436; 788/60, *Yearbook*, IV, 168; 1727/62, *Yearbook*, VI, 398: 'effective and adequate means of redressing the grievances set forth, on the international plane, against the respondent State'. Cf. also Janssen, op. cit., p. 198 et seq.

[8] Thus the Commission, in 722/60 (Collection 8, 38, 41) compares Article 103 (2) of the German Basic Law with Article 7 of the Convention.

filment of the terms of Article 26, have to compare the guarantees given in national law with those of the Convention. Individuals cannot be required to have recourse to useless remedies and in that respect a national concept of the self-executing character of the provisions of the Convention may sometimes play a part. The Commission requires basically, in the Federal Republic, the lodging of an appeal under the Constitution (*Verfassungsbeschwerde*) (Section 90 of the Constitutional Court Act of 12 March 1951)[1] although the Constitutional Court does not authorise this when the appellant invokes the European Convention on Human Rights,[2] since proceedings instituted on constitutional grounds can be concerned with breaches of the German Constitution only, whereas in the Federal Republic the Convention has only the status of ordinary law. Here too, therefore, when investigating the question of the exhaustion of domestic remedies, the Commission has constantly to compare the substance of German law and the terms of the Convention. If the Applicant could invoke a basic right guaranteed by the German Constitution which corresponded in substance to a provision of the Convention, he ought to institute proceedings in the Constitutional Court.[3] Indeed Article 26 of the Convention does not require that the domestic remedy should relate directly to the terms of the Convention; a parallel provision in municipal law may equally well be invoked.[4] The problem takes this special form only in German law, because the Federal Constitutional Court is competent only to hear cases of alleged infringement of municipal law. In Austria, where Article 144 of the Constitution likewise allows individuals to appeal to the Constitutional Court against alleged breaches of their constitutional rights, it was not possible until 1964 to plead in the Constitutional Court on the grounds of a clause of the Convention, because until then the Convention did not have constitutional status. The amendment to the Constitution has now changed this state of affairs if it be accepted that thereby the provisions of the Convention have become 'constitutionally protected rights' in

---

[1] 1661/62 *Yearbook*, VI, 368; Collection 8, 41.

[2] Federal Constitutional Court, 4, 111; 6, 440; 9, 39; 10; 274. Also the Constitutional Court of Bavaria, Decision 8, II, 74, Cf. Morvay, p. 105.

[3] 1086/61 *Yearbook*, V, 156: 'Whereas she now alleges violations of Article 6 of the Convention and Article 1 of the Protocol; whereas these provisions correspond, to a certain degree, to Article 14 and Article 103 paragraph (1) of the Basic Law ...; whereas however, the Applicant failed to lodge a constitutional appeal based on these articles; whereas it follows that she has not exhausted the remedies available to her under German law.' This obligation ceases only when the national courts do not regard the provisions of the Convention as directly applicable law. 808/60 *Yearbook*, V, 122.

[4] 712/60 (Retimag), *Yearbook*, IV, 404; *Collection of Decisions*, 14, 25.

Austria.[1] That pre-supposes that the provisions of the Convention are regarded not as directives but as immediately applicable law.[2]

In regard to the status and force of the provisions of the European Convention in municipal law no comparison can be made with the situation in the European Communities. According to one concept, which is coming to the fore both in doctrine and in jurisprudence, the European law created by the Treaties, inasmuch as its provisions are directly applicable, prevails over national law, even in the case of *leges posteriores*. This view can be supported only on the basis of certain specific clauses of the Community treaties (Arts. 11, 189 (2) of the Treaty setting up the European Economic Community).[3] It is irrelevant to our present subject.

3. *Influence of the international organs of the Convention on national law and jurisprudence*

The way the Convention itself and its relation to municipal law are interpreted by the international organs, is of importance for municipal law in three respects:

(a) The opinion of the international organs serves to clarify the extent and nature of the obligations of contracting States, which are led, thereby, to bring their law into line with the provisions of the Convention.

(b) Although the decisions of the Court and the Commission are not binding on member States, they are liable to influence national courts in their interpretation of the Convention and even of municipal law.

(c) The international organs judge national law by the yardstick of the Convention. There are other questions too (exhaustion of domestic remedies) in which they have to compare municipal law provisions with those of the Convention. What relation between national and international decisions results from this?

The Convention makes it incumbent upon the contracting States to

---

[1] To this effect see Ermacora, *JurBlätter* 1959, 403, Pfeifer, *OeZöR* 12 (1962) 5, 57, and Kunst *OeJuristenzeitung*, 1962, p. 199.

[2] In support of this see also Kunst, op. cit., pp. 198–9. When national jurisprudence regards the provisions of the Convention as directives only, the situation is different. Cf. Golsong, *JurBlätter*, 1961, p. 531, and Klecatsky, *JurBlätter* 1964, pp. 354 et seq.

[3] This point cannot be dealt with in any more detail here. For further information see the Report of the European Parliament referred to above; Ipsen in *Aktuelle Fragen des Europäischen Gemeinschaftsrechts*, 1964, p. 1 et seq. In support of the predominance of European law, cf. also the decision of the Court of Justice of the Communities in case No. 6/64. *RsprGH*, 10, p. 126 et seq. A different opinion is given by the Italian Constitutional Court in its judgment of 7 March 1964 (*Foro Italiano*, 1964, I, 416).

bring their municipal law and its application into line with the provisions of the Convention, irrespective of whether the Convention
has force of municipal law or not.[1] That includes the obligation to
amend national legislation in so far as States have not secured their
position by means of reservations. Thus Norway, in spite of a reservation, amended Article 2 of its Constitution which forbade
Jesuits to settle in the country.[2] In other cases proceedings pending
have caused States to amend their legislation. In connection with
Article 6, Austria made two amendments to its Code of Criminal
Procedure.[3] In connection with Article 10 Belgium attenuated the
provisions of an article of its Criminal Code which imposed professional restrictions without a time-limit on persons convicted of
political crimes committed in time of war.[4] The Federal Republic, in
the face of two cases pending before the Commission,[5] introduced an
amendment into its Code of Criminal Procedure to ensure more
effective control of the duration of remand in custody.[6]

Since the decision of the Committee of Ministers or of the Court is
binding on the signatory States which are parties to a case (Arts.
32 (4) and 53) it accordingly obliges them to repeal any provisions of
municipal law or administrative measures which conflict with the
terms of the Convention.[7] Difficulties arise in the case of decisions of
national courts which the international organ cannot set aside as it is
not a court of appeal. There are some international treaties which
confer on international courts the power to set aside national
judgments[8] but the Convention is not among them.[9] The States

---

[1] Cf. Waldock, *Br. Yearbook Int. Law*, 34, 1959, p. 358. The Commission in
the *De Becker case*, *E.C.H.R.*, Series B, 1962, p. 128: 'The Convention entered
into force with respect to Belgium on 14 June 1955. Thereafter the Belgian
Government, which had made no reservations with respect to Article 10 when
ratifying the Convention, was under an obligation to make any modifications in
its laws which might be necessary to bring them into harmony with the provisions
of the Convention.'

[2] Modinos, *Internat. and Comp. Law Quarterly*, 11, 1962, p. 1102.

[3] Acts of 18 July 1962, *BGBl*, No. 229, and of 27 March 1963, *BGBl*, No. 66,
Yearbook, v, 340; vi, 804.

[4] Act of 30 June 1961. See texts in *E.C.H.R.*, Series B, 1962, pp. 139, 183 et seq.
and the declaration of the representative of the Belgian Government to the
European Court, p. 189. Cf. also the Commission's statement, p. 125 et seq.

[5] Wemhoff, 2122/64 *Collection of Decisions* no. 14, p. 29 and Gericke, 2294/64,
Collection no. 15 p. 50.

[6] Act of 19 December 1964, *BGBl*, i, 1067.

[7] The decision cannot of itself repeal internal measures. Cf. Hallier, *Völker-
rechtliche Schiedsinstanzen für Einzelpersonen und ihr Verhältnis zur innerstaatlichen Gerichtsbarkeit*, 1962, p. 100 et seq.

[8] Hallier, p. 100, n. 430; for an outline of such treaties see D. Heise, *Internationale Rechtspflege und nationale Staatsgewalt*, Göttingen, 1964, pp. 66, 85, 128.

[9] Bürgenthal, p. 95 et seq.

concerned cannot, under the rule of law, set aside judicial decisions that have acquired force of law. In German and Austrian law it is possible to reopen proceedings. However, this is not authorised by a decision of an international judicial authority which does not either constitute a new fact or new evidence but is simply another legal decision.[1] In these circumstances the only obligation imposed on the State is that of compensation; such cases are provided for in Article 50 of the Convention.

The binding effect of a decision by the Committee of Ministers or the Court is confined to the individual case. There is no *erga omnes* effect.[2] The doctrine of *stare decisis* is unknown in the law of most member States and so cannot be regarded as applying to the Convention.[3] However, for the Commission, decisions of the Committee of Ministers or the Court are authoritative.[4] In countries where the Convention has no force in municipal law, the national courts are unlikely to have to define their attitude to decisions of the international organs, but in countries which apply the Convention as law decisions of the Committee of Ministers, the Court and even the Commission will in practice be recognised in the same way as decisions in the national courts of higher instance.[5] There has so far been no reference in national jurisprudence to decisions of the European judicial organs.

4. *Application of national law by international judicial authorities*

The points of contact between applied international law and national jurisprudence in similar spheres are very much more numerous in the case of the Convention than is normal with other international instruments. The reason for this is quite simple. Not only do international and national judicial authorities apply provisions of the Convention—which is also possible in the case of other treaties applied as municipal law—but the Convention is directly concerned with relations between the individual and the State, which are the province of municipal law. The Convention requires national legislation to be brought into line with its provisions and this closely affects the application of municipal law in many spheres. Normally, for international courts, municipal law is a phenomenon to be considered only in relation to its effect on the fulfilment of the State's inter-

---

[1] For this reason Austria, by the Act of 27 March 1963, *BGBl*, No. 66, instituted a special procedure for the rehearing of cases which the Commission had declared admissible.

[2] Bürgenthal, p. 95.　　　　　　　　　[3] Bürgenthal, p. 100 et seq.

[4] On the other hand, I hold, with Bürgenthal, that the Committee of Ministers is not bound by the judgment of the Court.

[5] Bürgenthal, p. 101.

national obligations, that is, to some extent as a simple fact which needs no further analysis.[1] And even when in connection with specific points—the exhaustion of domestic remedies, the effect of national legislation on the fulfilment of international obligations, etc.—the international authority is obliged to interpret a provision of municipal law, it adopts the prevailing national interpretation rather than forming any opinion of its own.[2] In relation to the validity and interpretation of a provision of national law, international courts may even leave it to the party who invokes such a provision or pleads wrongful application to supply the necessary arguments.[3] In dealing with the European Convention, whose provisions impose rules not for relations between States but for the position of the individual in municipal law, it is essential to enquire much further into the conformity of national legislation with the terms of the Convention. In many cases this necessitates a very careful analysis of national law[4] particularly when, as in Article 7 (1) and Article 12, the Convention itself refers to national law.[5] And yet the

---

[1] Cf. the pronouncements of the International Court in the *Chorzow Factory Case*, *P.C.I.J.* Series A, No. 7, pp. 18–19; Judge Badawi, *diss. op.* in *Norwegian Loans Case*, *I.C.J. Reports* 1957, p. 32; Judge Read, *diss. op.* in the *Nottebohm Case*, *I.C.J. Reports* 1955, pp. 35–6. Recognition that national legislation merely constitutes a 'fact' does not, however, eliminate the need to interpret it in certain circumstances. Cf. Judge Badawi, loc. cit., p. 78. For a relevant treatment of the question see C. W. Jenks, *The Prospects of International Adjudication*, London, 1964, p. 547 et seq., p. 557 et seq.

[2] Cf. the Court in the *Brazilian Loans Case*, *P.C.I.J.* Series A/B, Nos. 20/21, p. 124: 'Once the Court has arrived at the conclusion that it is necessary to apply the municipal law of a particular country there seems no doubt that it must seek to apply it as it would be applied in that country.'

[3] *Ad hoc* Judge Guggenheim, *diss. op.* in *Nottebohm Case*, *I.C.J.* Reports 1955, p. 51/52; Cf. also Jenks, p. 587 et seq.

[4] Examples of this may be found in: 712/60 (*Retimag*), *Yearbook*, IV, 384. In this case a provision of German criminal law (Art. 86, par. 2, *StGB*) was examined closely in relation to Article 7 of the Convention and Article 1 of the Protocol. Also 1169/61 *Yearbook*, VI, p. 20: this was concerned with an offence against rent regulations and necessitated a careful investigation of the continuing force of penal provisions in order to decide whether the Applicant had been punished under law that was in force at the time (Art. 7). The Commission outlined its task as follows: 'Whereas the Commission, being charged to watch over the observance of the Convention by the Contracting States (Art. 19) is empowered to satisfy itself, if need be *proprio motu*, that domestic courts are not continuing to apply criminal laws which are no longer in force; whereas although it is not normally for the Commission to check on the proper administration of municipal law by such courts (. . . *quotation*), the case is otherwise in matters where the Convention refers to municipal law, as it does in Article 7; whereas in these matters, any violation of municipal law involves conflict with the Convention so that the Commission can and must take cognisance thereof, without thereby assuming the status of a supreme court.'

[5] Cf. 1169/61 *Yearbook*, VI, 588/89.

established rules of international jurisprudence are not without importance here. The organs of the European Convention accept the principle that the international application of national provisions normally follows the prevailing interpretation in the country concerned.[1] The Commission even stressed that it had to exercise caution in interpreting national law and that a margin of appreciation had to be left to national authorities in the promulgation and interpretation of national law with regard to its compatibility with the terms of the Convention.[2] In short it can be said that in regard to the comparison of its terms with those of national law, particularly in connection with the references to national law in Articles 7 and 12 and the application of the general concepts in respect of which restrictions are authorised in Articles 8, 9, 10 and 11, the Convention confers considerable responsibility on the international organs in interpreting national law but in so doing it may rely on the generally accepted interpretation in the law of the country concerned.

5. *Principles of interpretation*

The foregoing section shows that the European Convention makes use of the rules that have been established in international jurisprudence, a fact, moreover, that can be observed from other indications.[3] The question is now whether, in the application of the Convention by international and national judicial authorities, criteria of interpretation have been established which concern specific fundamental freedoms or correspond to ideas which have developed in the law of certain contracting States for the application of fundamental rights. In this respect the development is as yet only rudimentary. Theories which regard fundamental freedoms as an aspect of natural law have had no influence so far in practice.[4] Similarly the

---

[1] Cf. 458/59 *Yearbook*, III, 232: 'Whereas, even if all domestic remedies had been exhausted it should be stressed that it is not for the Commission to give a ruling on the application and the interpretation of domestic law by national courts unless the law itself constitutes a violation of the Convention or the domestic courts have committed such violation in the application or interpretation of this law.' See also 1068/61 *Yearbook*, IV, 285/86.

[2] The Commission's report in the *Lawless Case*, Series B, 1960–1, pp. 82, 114, 130, 135, 154 (existence of the 'emergency' referred to in Article 15); 753/60 *Yearbook*, III, 318 (limits of freedom of expression according to Article 10); 1068/61 *Yearbook*, V, 248 (limitations in a democratic society as defined in Article 9): here the Commission speaks of the 'considerable measures of discretion left to national Parliaments in appreciating the vital interests of the community'; 1449/62 *Collection*, 10, 3 (Art. 8; 1169/61 *Yearbook*, VI, 590 (Art. 7 (1)).

[3] Reference to principles of international law in 712/1960 *Yearbook*, IV, 401; 1662/62 *Yearbook*, VI, 368.

[4] Natural law is referred to by the Higher Administrative Court of Koblenz, *NJW*, 1959, 1628 to the effect that it does not prescribe the lodging of an appeal

idea that fundamental freedoms may be concerned not only with the relationship of the individual to the State but also, in certain circumstances, with relations between individuals (the so-called *Drittwirkung*) has never been recognised in any practical way and indeed has been rejected.[1] The theory, too, that some of the individual fundamental freedoms might be specially important and take precedence over others is foreign to the application of the Convention. On the other hand, traces of an objective interpretation of the provisions of the Convention are to be glimpsed in the doctrine of the institutional elements of fundamental rights and freedoms. The Commission stresses that the obligations of the contracting States are 'essentially of an objective character, being designed rather to protect the fundamental rights of individual human beings from infringement by any of the High Contracting Parties than to create subjective and reciprocal rights for the High Contracting Parties themselves'.[2]

A point of specific importance for fundamental rights and freedoms is the distinction to be made between provisions directly establishing individual rights and those which simply constitute directives for the legislator. Apart from Article 13 and the obligation placed on contracting States under Article 3 of the First Protocol to hold free elections, which establishes no individual right to partake in such elections,[3] the international organs have expressed themselves in favour of the direct force of the provisions of the Convention.[4]

---

on constitutional grounds (*Verfassungsbeschwerde*) within the meaning of German law.

[1] The question is touched on by Woesner, *NJW*, 1961, 1384 who claims that Article 2 of the Convention—apart from the exceptions in paragraph 2—prohibits all deprivation of life and hence the killing in defence authorised in German criminal law (*StGB*, Art. 53) when the attack is not against a person but against an object. Article 2 is thereby applied to the behaviour of individuals. This reasoning is contested in German law. Against it and the recognition of an effect for individuals see Welzel, *Das deutsche Strafrecht*, 9. *Aufl.* 1965, p. 80. In 172/56 *Yearbook*, I, 215, 218, the Commission rejects the application of Articles 8 and 9 to matters concerning divorced parents and their children's education. Cf. p. 18: 'Whereas, without underestimating the moral obligation under Canon law, Article 9 of the Convention and Article 2 of the Protocol cannot validly be invoked by an Applicant because his complaint, in this respect, concerns the action of a private individual and in no way involves the responsibility of the Swedish Government.' See also 852/60 *Yearbook*, IV, 352 and Guradze, *Festschrift Nipperdey*, 1965, 2, p. 759 et seq.

[2] 788/60 *Yearbook*, IV, 140. The legal consequence is that Austria could claim that Italy had committed a breach of the Convention before Austria had acceded to it. Cf. Mosler, *Festschrift Jahrreis*, 1964, p. 301.

[3] Cf. 530/59 *Yearbook*, III, 190; 1065/61 *Yearbook*, IV, 268.

[4] Cf. national case-law in the Netherlands, *Hoge Rad in Ned. Jurisprudentie*, 1961, No. 273; 1964, No. 402.

Lastly we may mention as one of the principles of interpretation the Commission's readiness, for the proper understanding of a text, to look back to the *travaux préparatoires*.[1]

III. THE INDIVIDUAL HUMAN RIGHTS EMBODIED
IN THE CONVENTION

If we look at the Convention's application in the international and the national spheres, we see immediately that it is possible to speak of a national application only in those States which regard the provisions of the Convention as part of municipal law. Among these countries, there is a greater body of jurisprudence in the Netherlands, Belgium, Austria and the Federal Republic. How does the national concept compare with the international? Here the following general points are to be observed.

(*a*) A large number of the cases referred to the Commission are concerned with the principles laid down in the Convention in regard to judicial procedure, particularly criminal procedure, (Arts. 5, 6, 13) with which we are not concerned here. In addition, the Articles of the Convention invoked have frequently a connection with criminal procedure. This is, of course, true in particular of Articles 3 and 7 which by their nature are concerned with criminal procedure.

(*b*) The cases in which the international organs have disagreed with a national decision have been concerned chiefly with questions of procedure. In regard to the other Articles of the Convention far-reaching agreement between national and international authorities is to be observed.

(*c*) Where national law contains the same guarantees as the Convention or gives even more protection, the Convention is as a rule never invoked. The realm in which national and international decisions may conflict is that in which the European Convention gives more extensive guarantees than municipal law and where its clauses are consequently invoked by individuals even in national courts.

In this connection, too, it is significant to note the tendency of jurisprudence in some countries, especially in the Federal Republic, to interpret extensively the rights embodied in the Convention.

(*d*) Of the Articles of the Convention not concerned with judicial procedure, Article 1 of the First Protocol is couched in such general terms that it is very seldom mentioned in judicial disputes. The same is true of Article 2 of the Protocol, although it is more frequently invoked. Article 11 of the Convention seems to be covered by municipal law in all the contracting States and is accordingly rarely

---

[1] Cf. 788/60 *Yearbook*, IV, 140; 1028/61 *Yearbook*, III, 336. Commission's report in the *Lawless Case*, Series B, 1960–1, p. 327.

cited. On the whole, concern with the Convention seems to concentrate on three main spheres and the Articles invoked are frequently bracketed; in the first place, the protection of the person and freedom from retrospective punishment or degrading treatment (Arts. 3, 4, 7); secondly, the guarantees of freedom of religion and expression (Arts. 9 and 10); and, thirdly, the guarantee of the right to marriage and to private and family life (Arts. 8 and 12).

(e) When Applications are lodged with the Commission against decisions, they often complain, not of the Court's failure to recognise the provisions of the Convention, but of the law's failure to recognise them. They are thus disguised appeals for control over legislation.[1] Otherwise, it is the Court's application of municipal law or of the Convention itself by a national court which is complained of. In that case, the Application is directed against a court judgment. When administrative measures are complained of, on the other hand, it is usually in the form of an appeal against a court judgment, since the principle of the exhaustion of domestic remedies leads first to judicial proceedings in municipal law.

1. Security of life and personal freedom (Articles 2, 3, 4, 7)

(a) Article 2

The question of the protection of life has cropped up in connection with only one decision of a national court. The Turkish Constitutional Court decided in the light of the Turkish Constitution that Article 14 of the Constitution, recognising every individual's right to life, did not preclude the death penalty as prescribed in the Turkish Penal Code. The Court referred to Article 2 (1) of the Convention, which authorises capital punishment, in order to justify this interpretation of the Turkish Constitution.[2] The meaning of Article 2 is presumably correctly understood in this context.

In a trial in Germany, it was sought to make out of Article 2 a general guarantee of the full development of the personality as defined in Article 2 (1) of the Constitution of the Federal Republic. The Federal Constitutional Court rightly rejected this view whereby it was sought to prohibit the punishment of homosexuality in German criminal law. Article 2 is concerned with the protection of life and not with freedom to live as one wishes.[3]

---

[1] Cf. as basic to this question E. Schumann, *Verfassungs-und Menschenrechts-beschwerde gegen richterliche Entscheidungen*, Berlin, 1963, p. 246 et seq. Cases of disguised attacks against legislation in 1468/62 *Yearbook*, vi, 278 (Norwegian law on the period of public service for dentists, Art. 4 of the Convention), 1068/61 *Yearbook*, v, 279 (Netherlands legislation on old age insurance, Art. 9); 1474/62 *Yearbook*, vi, 332 (Belgian language Act of 1935).
[2] *Yearbook*, vi, p. 820.   [3] *BVerfGE*, 6, 441.

(b) Article 3

The prohibition, in Article 3, of degrading punishments or treatment has given rise to a whole series of questions. However, attempts to attack specific provisions of the law on such grounds have necessarily failed. Austrian criminal law provides for an additional penalty to imprisonment, namely 'hartes Lager', on certain days, in the case in question once every three months. The Commission did not regard this as an infringement of Article 3.[1] This opinion seems justified. The judgment of the High Court of Bavaria which denied that the higher sentences prescribed for robbery with aggravating circumstances (Art. 243 StBG) and for recidivism (Art. 244) constituted a breach of Article 3 of the Convention.[2] A gradation of punishment according to the seriousness of the crime was not considered degrading.

The possibility of executing in the Federal Republic sentences imposed by courts in the German People's Republic for non-political crimes, in respect of persons who had emigrated to that part of Germany, has raised difficult problems. The fact that the German Legal and Administrative Assistance Act of 2 May 1953 requires a preliminary investigation to establish the absence of political circumstances precludes, however, any breach of Article 3.[3]

The really important cases are connected with expulsion and extradition. With regard to the expulsion of a foreigner,[4] it is to be considered as an administrative act which infringes no individual right. Article 3 of the Convention does not protect foreigners' rights to remain in a country. Expulsion is not degrading treatment.[5] Article 3 can only be concerned when the person is deported to a country in which he is exposed to political persecution or where no guarantee of fundamental freedoms can be expected.[6] Also, when the

---

[1] 462/59 Yearbook, II, 385. Similarly in connection with the disciplinary punishment of a prisoner. Bremen Administrative Court, DöV, 1956, 705.

[2] NJW, 1964, 2025.

[3] 1322/62 Yearbook, VI, 521. The question of an excessively long period of remand in custody has no relation to Article 3, although it may arouse doubts in connection with Articles 5 and 6. Cf. 1546/62, Coll. 9, 63; 2294/64, Coll. 15, 50.

[4] The expulsion by a State of one of its own nationals is forbidden in Article 3 of the Fourth Protocol which, however, is not yet in force (cf. Report of the Committee of Ministers to the Consultative Assembly of 10 March 1965, Doc. 1897, para. 289).

[5] One can agree with this attitude on the part of the German courts. Cf. Federal Administrative Court, Decision 3, 236; Münster Higher Administrative Court, NJW, 1954, 1821; Stuttgart Administrative Court, Verwaltungsrechtsprechung, 8, pp. 357 and 861. Cf. also the Commission in 1211/61 Coll. 9, 46 and 1465/62 Yearbook, V, 260.

[6] The Commission refers to this reasoning, which is also valid for extradition, in 1802/62 Yearbook, VI, 480; 2143/64 Coll. 14, 24.

person concerned would be severely affected in his human relations, e.g. his family life.[1] Asylum for political refugees is not a right protected by the Convention, even if the law of certain contracting States recognises such a right (Art. 16 (2) second sentence of the Basic Law of the Federal Republic).[2] Hence it always requires what the Commission refers to as 'exceptional circumstances'[3] for expulsion or extradition to constitute degrading treatment. In German case-law such circumstances are held to exist if the expulsion could lead to the separation of the family.[4] This view can be accepted only if there is no grave cause for the expulsion and the spouse cannot be deemed to have a moral obligation to follow the person expelled.

These principles apply similarly to extradition. We can agree with the decision of the German Federal Constitutional Court that extradition to a State party to the Convention (Turkey) did not constitute a breach of Article 3, since that State might be expected to respect human rights and because the political circumstances pleaded by the person concerned were not adequately proved.[5] The extradition of a person exposed to a political threat would indeed constitute an infringement of Article 3. The decision in regard to the expulsion from Germany to his home country of an Egyptian who pleaded his opposition to President Nasser, would no doubt have needed to be different if the declaration of the German authorities had not left expulsion out of account from the start.[6] The Berlin Higher Administrative Court did not regard the extradition of a foreigner to Czechoslovakia as a breach of Article 3, although in all likelihood the person concerned had to expect punishment for desertion and espionage.[7] The case awakens doubts. True, in such cases it is very

[1] For this context see 434/58 *Yearbook*, II, 374: refusal of entry into a country to fight a legal action with a former wife over the care of a child of the marriage is not a breach of Article 8 of the Convention.

[2] 1465/62 *Yearbook*, V, 260; 1802/62 *Yearbook*, VI, 477, 479.

[3] 2143/64 Coll. 14, 24.

[4] For this reason the Bavarian Administrative Court considered that expulsion was inadmissible if the (German) wife of the expelled person was not prepared to follow him. On the other hand the Federal Administrative Court (Decision 3, 61) held that the wife could be expected to follow her husband to his country of origin (Italy) where her rights would be fully protected. Schorn, in *Die Europäische Konvention zum Schutz der Menschenrechte und Grundfreiheiten*, Frankfurt, 1965, p. 112, agrees with the Bavarian Court.

[5] *BVerfG*, 15, 252/53.

[6] 1465/62 *Yearbook*, V, 257. See also Mosler, *Festschrift Jahrreis*, 1964, p. 307. On the other hand, the fact that capital punishment exists in the country to which the person concerned is to be extradited and not in the country which is handing him over is irrelevant in this context. Failing any political circumstances, capital punishment does not constitute a breach of human rights. Cf. the German Federal Constitutional Court, *BverfGE*, 18, 112 et seq.

[7] *Yearbook*, III, 641. Quoted in support in 2143/64 Coll. 14, 24.

R

difficult to draw the dividing line between acts with a political background and purely criminal acts. It is also true that it should not be automatically considered inadmissible to hand over an individual to a State with a Communist régime when the existence of political circumstances has not been adequately proved.

Examples of a last group of cases are to be found in German jurisprudence only. For perjury German criminal law imposes the accessory penalty of permanent incapacity to serve as a witness or expert on oath (*StGB*, Art. 161). Certain courts judged this penalty as inhuman, because it was unlimited in time and would place the person concerned in a difficult position in court proceedings. The punishment was regarded as out of proportion to the offence.[1] On the other hand, a more recent decision stressed that there was no disproportion as between the crime and the measure. The sentence was intended for the protection of justice and could only weigh heavily on the person concerned if he had to appear in court as a witness. In any case, he would have to expect, in such circumstances, to be questioned by the judge about earlier convictions for perjury, so that he could not always avoid exposure in court.[2] I feel that this latter view is to be preferred. Severe or painful measures are not necessarily inhuman.

A difficult question is raised by the attitude of the German Federal Court in a case in which an illegitimate child was called as a witness against its natural father. Since German family law recognises no relationship in this case, there is no cause to reject such a witness (Art. 52 of the Code of Criminal Procedure). This rule of German law may be regarded as unsatisfactory, but it is not inhuman, particularly if the child does not live with the father.[3]

(c) *Article 4*

Forced or compulsory labour in the sense of Article 4 means work that a person is made to do against his will in unjust or oppressive conditions or accompanied by unnecessarily harsh treatment.[4] It is thus a question of work imposed unilaterally by the State, which

---

[1] Lower Court (*Amtsgericht*) of Wiesbaden, *NJW*, 1963, 965 and Regional Court (*Oberlandesgericht*) of Cologne, *NJW*, 1963, 1748. The Cologne court lays emphasis chiefly on the absence of a time-limit. A similar opinion was expressed by a Senate of the Federal Court (*NJW*, 1964, 176) and the same question was submitted to the *Grosser Senat* of the Court. It was withdrawn, however. The fact that a draft of a new Criminal Code no longer contains this measure has some influence. Cf. *Entwurf eines Strafgesetzbuches*, Bonn, 1962, 431, 443, and *Begründung*, p. 625 et seq.

[2] OLG, Oldenburg, *NJW*, 1965, 509.

[3] Federal Court, *NJW*, 1956, p. 1286. For critical analysis see Schom, op. cit., p. 129.

[4] *Iversen Case*, 1468/62 *Yearbook*, VI, 328.

takes up a considerable time and interferes seriously with the career and above all with the professional freedom of the person concerned. The exceptions to Article 4 are extensive.[1] In any case the Article does not apply to services to the State which are restricted in time, such as the practice in German fiscal law for the employee's taxes to be deducted by the employer, particularly as the service is not performed by the employer in person but through his pay-office.[2] Nor is indirect compulsion to work to be regarded as compulsory labour, if the pressure exerted is purely financial, there is no threat of punishment and the circumstances are not such as to make the pressure irresistible. If relief is withheld from an unemployed person because he refuses to do certain specific work for the community, the services demanded of him are not forced, although the financial loss through failing to perform them may be considerable.[3] For the same reason the implementation in the Netherlands of the Royal Decree of 5 October 1945 on labour relations does not constitute a breach of Article 4. According to the decree, neither an employer nor an employee can terminate their mutual relations without the authorisation of the labour authorities. The question of the termination of such relations can of course be taken to court, but a money payment is the only consequence of refusal to continue as before. Netherlands jurisprudence[4] does not hold that this is a case of forced labour. This view has been criticised[5] and it has rightly been pointed out that today the emergency clause, which applied in 1945, can no longer be invoked in this context. I believe that such measures against the unilateral termination of labour relations, if the consequences are purely financial, are not relevant to Article 4 unless they cause prejudice to the worker concerned for a considerable period of time.

Another case, however, is highly controversial. A Norwegian Act of 21 June 1956 made it compulsory for dentists who had qualified after 1955 to place themselves at the disposal of the Minister for Social Affairs for two years (since 1962 for 18 months) for posting to a post in the public health service which, although advertised, could not be filled. In this way dental services were to be ensured in the thinly populated North. The Commission rejected the application

---

[1] Friesenhahn, in *Der internationale Schutz der Menschenrechte*, Hannover 1960, p. 40, draws attention to the far-reaching restrictions placed on Article 4 by the exceptions in its paragraph 3.

[2] Federal Finance Court, *NJW*, 1963, 2191. The Court finds that this is a civic obligation as referred to in Article 4 (3) (*d*). I do not think that there can be any question here of obligation or forced labour.

[3] Federal Administrative Court, *NJW*, 1961, 1082.

[4] Rechtsbank Rotterdam, *Ned. Jurisprudentie* 1961, No. 470; Amsterdam Court *Ned. Jur.*, 1962, No. 441.

[5] J. van Emde Boas, *European Yearbook*, XI, 1963, p. 237 et seq.

concerned by a majority of 6 to 4. Of the majority, four were of the opinion that the service required did not fall within the definition of forced labour, since it was for a short period, well-paid and corresponded to the qualifications of those affected. Two members thought that in any case the service was justified by the state of emergency in the rural areas to which Article 4 (3) (c) applied. The minority held, however, that the favourable outward circumstances did not preclude the application of Article 4, since, in addition, failure to perform the service was punishable. The minority also thought that the existence of a state of emergency needed further investigation.[1] Jurists[2] have suggested that the phrase 'forced or compulsory labour' is not to be understood as a single concept but as two concepts.[3] 'Compulsory labour' would thus have a wider meaning than 'forced labour' and would mean more than just labour characterised by unjust or arbitrary treatment. In that case, Article 4 (2) would not only afford protection against inhuman and criminal oppression but would also prohibit compulsion to perform services required for the rational and normal needs of the community. It is certain that the Norwegian Act arose from a humane and social concern for the welfare of the people of the northern districts. The same result might perhaps have been achieved by other means which would not have been likely to conflict with Article 4. Admission to practice as a dentist could possibly have been made subject to a period spent in the public health services or the dental course might have been arranged accordingly.[4] Nevertheless we must come round to the view that Article 4 is not concerned solely with the restricted field of inhuman and arbitrary compulsion to work, but applies also to services which constitute normal social duties of various kinds but are not voluntary and which oblige the persons concerned to devote to the community a considerable part of their professional life or abilities. And so Article 4 also gives protection against State intervention of a kind which fulfils a useful social purpose. A not too narrow interpretation of the 'emergency' and the 'normal civic obligations' in Article 4 should do justice to cases in which the imposition of certain services is vital for the maintenance of proper living conditions or the safety of the community and they cannot be secured in any other way, even at great expense. The State must be prevented from finding compulsion more convenient than making the effort to get the necessary work

---

[1] *Iversen Case*, 1468/62 *Yearbook*, VI, 278.

[2] H. G. Schermers, *Nederlands Tijdschrift voor Internationaal Recht*, 11, 1964 p. 366 et seq.; Mosler, *Festschrift Jahrreis*, 1964, p. 310 et seq.

[3] As was the opinion of the Norwegian Government, *Yearbook*, VI, 302. See on the other hand the Applicant, p. 213 et seq.

[4] This was mentioned by the Norwegian Government (loc. cit., p. 306).

done in another way or at greater cost. On the other hand, Article 4 contains no real guarantee of freedom of occupation as exists in the law of some countries. Care must also be taken not to involve Article 4 in the problems relating to economic practice and principles in connection with the guarantee of general economic freedom or freedom of occupation.

(d) Article 7

For the application of Article 7 it must be borne in mind that the principle *nulla poena sine lege* grew up in the eighteenth century during the Age of Enlightenment and was universally recognised on the Continent[1] but its legal consequences are still much in dispute. In particular, there is no generally accepted legal view as to whether an act is punishable retrospectively when, at the time it was committed, it offended against general principles of law recognised by all nations (Art. 7 (2)). The German reservation in respect of this clause shows that the possibility of waiving the general prohibition of retrospective punishment is not recognised everywhere. And however clearly the prohibition in Article 7 may exclude an analogy as regards what are the elements of a crime, it is not altogether possible to avoid certain differences of interpretation due to custom, in connection with general concepts (e.g. premeditation, omission) and in the interpretation of less well-defined terms (e.g. public security, common danger).[2]

The absence of complete agreement over Article 7 (2) has been brought out in the views expressed regarding the punishment of certain serious war crimes which constituted infringements of human rights.[3] German opinion is strongly against retrospective punishment in general, and the only point contested by German jurists is whether the establishment of the legality of the penalty at the time the act was committed involves also the determination of statutory limitation or whether statutory limitation is a purely procedural question. This latter view, that statutory limitation is not a factor in ascertaining the legality of the penalty, is supported by the Act of 13 April 1965 on

---

[1] Since English criminal law rests partly on Common Law, the requirement of legal provisions governing the act and its punishment cannot be taken here in the strict sense. However, precedent in this case plays much the same part as the principle accepted on the Continent.

[2] For the role of interpretation in connection with vague formulae in criminal law and the application of general legal concepts, see Welzel, *Das deutsche Strafrecht* 9. Aufl., 1965, p. 20 et seq. Here again punishability must not be extended. See also Grünwald, *Zeitschrift f.d. gesamte Rechtswissenschaft* 76, 1964, p. 1 et seq.

[3] For questions of principle see the Pierson report to the Consultative Assembly of the Council of Europe of 27 January 1965, Doc. 1868.

the calculation of periods of statutory limitation in criminal law, which has prolonged the time-limit for the prosecution of all offences by fixing the beginning of the period of statutory limitation at 31 December 1949.[1]

Article 7 has not played an important part in the application of the Convention. Apart from applications which invoke Article 7 against criminal judgments without any clear reason,[2] only a few cases of slight importance can be cited. The question of the legality of a penalty arose in all its complexity in a case where punishment for exceeding fixed rents depended on whether such price-fixing regulations—which are not a part of criminal law—existed for the rent case in question. The Commission decided that they did and, following its principle of adopting the national interpretation of municipal law, after careful investigation upheld the national court judgments.[3] In another case, the Commission also endorsed the national decision. It did not consider the entering of a sentence pronounced by a court in the German Democratic Republic in the Federal Republic's register of criminal convictions as a further punishment, but simply as the recording of a sentence pronounced by a court which had jurisdiction at the place of the offence.[4] In regard to Article 7 the Commission also holds that it precludes any extension of punishability *in malam partem* and therefore prescribes a restrictive interpretation of criminal law.[5]

In accord with this attitude is the German decision rejecting the applicability of the additional penalty of confiscation of gains in the case of the offence of illegal association (Section 128 StGB) by analogy with Section 86 of the Penal Code, which prescribes this penalty in the case of treason, considering that both Article 103 (2) of the Basic Law and Article 7 of the Convention require an explicit basis in legislation.[6]

The exception permitted by paragraph 2 of Article 7 to the prohibition on the retrospective effect of criminal law is a very extensive one, according to the intention to be discerned in the *travaux préparatoires* on which the Commission relied. It covers penalties

---

[1] The majority of German authors hold that the establishment of the legality of the punishment has nothing to do with determining the statutory time-limit, which is only of procedural importance for the prosecution of the offence. This view is contested. See the latest review of the question by Grünwald, *Monatsschrift für Deutsches Recht*, 1965, p. 521 et seq.

[2] 217/56 *Yearbook*, I, 239; 1103/61 *Yearbook*, v, 190; 1592/62 Coll. 10, 11. There was in addition an application relating to the severity of a sentence, which, however, is unrelated to the substance of Article 7: 458/59 *Yearbook*, III, 234.

[3] 1169/61 *Yearbook*, VI, 588.   [4] 448/59 *Yearbook*, III, 270.

[5] 217/56, *Yearbook*, I, 239; 1169/61, *Yearbook*, VI, 587-8.

[6] Federal Court, *NJW*, 1963, 499.

introduced after the Second World War to punish retrospectively persons guilty of treason and collaboration with the enemy. This interpretation shows that in the law of many of the contracting States the principle of no retrospective effect has no precedence over other considerations of criminal law.[1]

2. Protection of family life, marriage and education (Articles 8, 12 and Article 2 of the First Protocol)

(a) Article 8

The reason why such a body of jurisprudence has grown up around Article 8 must be sought in the fact that this provision protects an aspect of human life which is in part unconnected with the traditional sphere of liberal freedoms and whose general description ('private and family life') allows a wide field of application. Article 8 is to some extent complementary to national law which does not give any exactly corresponding guarantee. However, Article 8 (2) authorises very far-reaching restrictions.

The protection of the home and of correspondence has given rise to no serious problems. It is obvious that Article 8 does not entitle individuals to attack the State in regard to the allocation of appropriate housing but only forbids interference with established homes.[2] The restrictions authorised in Article 8 (2) clearly allow the prison authorities to watch prisoners' correspondence in the interests of public safety and the prevention of crime.[3] However, the access to the European Commission must not be impeded or unduly delayed.[4] In this connection, the action of a judge towards a person remanded in custody in returning to him a letter with instructions to reconsider the factual inaccuracies in his complaint against the court is on the borderline of what is permissible.[5]

Article 8 does not prevent the State from punishing homosexuality among men. Nor does the fact that it is not a punishable offence for the other sex constitute a breach of Article 14, since concrete reasons for the difference can be put forward.[6]

The protection of family life is illustrated in two ways in the jurisprudence of the Convention: in the first place, in cases where a parent, after divorce or separation, claims a right to educate a child of

---

[1] Cf. *De Becker Case, Yearbook,* IV, 226; *E.C.H.R.*, Series B, 1962, p. 60. Also case 1038/61 *Yearbook,* IV, 336.

[2] 159/56 *Yearbook,* I, 202.

[3] 530/59 *Yearbook,* III, 190; 646/59 *Yearbook,* III, 278.

[4] 793/60 *Yearbook,* III, 448.   [5] 2122/64 Coll. 15, 6.

[6] The international view (104/55, 167/56, 261/57 *Yearbook,* I, 228, 235, 255) coincides here with the national one (German Federal Constitutional Court, 6, 441).

the marriage; in the second place, in connection with police measures in respect of an alien (refusal of entry or expulsion) when this may lead to the separation of a husband and wife. The first group of cases concerns individual disputes which are not the concern of the Convention. It is, accordingly, not for the Commission to determine whether the child's welfare, moral considerations, etc., justify forbidding one of the parents access to the child; it can only verify whether the provisions of the Convention are infringed thereby.[1] Thus, in consideration of the child's welfare, a father convicted of misconduct with his own daughter could properly be forbidden access to her,[2] and it was no breach of Article 8 when Sweden refused entry into Sweden to plead his case to a non-Swedish father living abroad whose wife had obtained a separation and the custody of the only child of the marriage in the Swedish courts.[3]

The invocation of Article 8 raises more serious problems, however, in the case of the expulsion of foreigners, when a family is thereby separated or kept apart. We have already touched on the question in connection with Article 3. German courts have already repeatedly expressed the opinion that this is a case where the public interest must be weighed against the preservation of family life.[4] This view corresponds to a broad interpretation of the Convention which, however, is not necessarily a generally accepted legal doctrine.[5] The guarantee of private life has been invoked in German case-law only as an accessory plea to Article 1 of the Basic Law, to claim that the sound-recording of a person's utterances against his will, whether in private or in court, is inadmissible.[6] In my view, to cite Article 8 as a basis for the protection of the personal sphere of life is to go beyond its recognisable limits. In regard to the protection of the intimate aspects of human life from outside interference, no firm legal opinion

---

[1] Cf. 172/56 *Yearbook*, I, 216; 911/60 *Yearbook*, IV, 218. Similarly a law which gives the custody of an illegitimate child not to the mother but to the youth authorities, as in Austria, does not constitute an infringement of Article 8 (514/59 *Yearbook*, III, 204).

[2] 1449/62 *Yearbook*, VI, 266.

[3] 172/56 *Yearbook*, I, 216; 434/58 *Yearbook*, II, 360; 911/60 *Yearbook*, IV, 216 .

[4] Federal Administrative Court, *Deutsches Verwaltungsblatt* 1957, 57; idem, *Decisions*, 5, 61; Bavarian Constitutional Court, *Bayerische Verwaltungsblätter*, 1959, 256 (Lifting of expulsion for minor offences against public safety in the interests of the family).

[5] The decision of the Belgian Court of Cassation (*Pasicrisie* 1960, I, 98) seems to follow a stricter line; it simply sets the legal authorisation to expel against the considerations of family unity. The published text of this decision does not make it clear, unfortunately, what danger to public safety existed. Cf. Janssen, loc. cit., p. 218; Morvay, p. 328.

[6] German Federal Court, Decisions 27, 286; idem, *NJW*, 1960, 1580. In both judgments Article 8 is only mentioned briefly in conjunction with the Basic Law.

has yet been established in the contracting States and consequently no support could be found in common legal tradition for such a broad interpretation of the concept of 'private life'.

The application of Article 8 to the protection of the home in the case of aliens is based less on a right accruing to the individual than on an objective principle of the unity of the family, which enjoins the State authorities to take this into account.[1]

The same is true in one last context in which Article 8 is invoked, namely the language disputes in Belgium. As they are still *sub judice* I shall refrain from expressing an opinion on them and confine myself to showing their connection with Article 8. The Belgian Act of 28 June 1932 on language in schools allows communities whose inhabitants belong to one of the two language groups only one school using the language of the locality. Parents speaking the other language—in the cases in question Walloon parents in Flemish-speaking districts—must either send their children to the local Flemish-speaking school or, in places bordering on French-speaking areas, send them long distances to school or, failing this, be separated from them. The applications of these parents[2] are based on Articles 8, 9 and 10 of the Convention and Article 2 of the First Protocol. They claim that Article 2 protects the right of parents to educate their children according to their wishes. Article 8 they allege to be violated because the children have had to leave home. Lastly, they claim that freedom of language forms part of freedom of expression and of thought. The Commission has rejected the claims based on Articles 9 and 10, since freedom of language is not among the freedoms protected by the Convention and the freedom of thought of the parents themselves is not affected. On the other hand, the applications have been declared admissible on the grounds of Articles 8 and 14 of the Convention and Article 2 of the First Protocol.

(b) *Article 2 of the First Protocol*

Apart from the invocation of Article 2 of the Protocol in the language cases just referred to, it has only been applied in one case in the Netherlands. A dancing teacher gave lessons at a café without possessing the necessary licence to dispense alcoholic beverages. He appealed against his sentence on the grounds of the unrestricted right to education which he claimed was guaranteed by Article 2 of the Protocol. The Netherlands court, which is not competent to

---

[1] Vasak in *La Convention Européenne*, 1964, p. 51, speaks rightly here of '*la protection de la famille dans son unité*' as forming the substance of Article 8.

[2] See Vasak's review of the four existing groups of applications, *Journal Clunet*, 1964, p. 370. The declaration of the admissibility of Application 1474/62 has been published, *Yearbook*, VI, 333.

determine whether a law is compatible with the Constitution,[1] could not consider the law on the sale of alcoholic beverages in conjunction with the Constitution (Art. 208), which declares that education is free but allows the State the right to supervise it. However, it pointed out that freedom of education did not preclude certain restrictions and declared that the law did not infringe the terms of the Convention. This decision has been criticised[2] because Article 2 provides for no restrictions. However, in my view, it has been overlooked here that all freedoms must submit to the rules of public safety and order when they do not affect the real substance of the freedom concerned but only its outward aspects. And this seems to me to be the case. The dancing lessons would not have suffered if the teacher had complied with the general regulations relating to the sale of alcoholic beverages.

It would certainly not be right to see in Article 2 the guarantee of absolute freedom of instruction. In this respect the legal opinions and the regulations of the various States are too different. It should be noted that Article 2 refers only to 'education' and not to 'instruction'.[3] Article 2 merely protects the individual's access to education in the sense of access to the existing educational facilities[4] and obliges the State to respect the religious convictions of parents. It is not concerned, however, with the question of State education as opposed to private schools or with the thorny problem of religious education. Education may also be provided by a State school system.[5]

(c) Article 12

The right to marry is not one of the older fundamental rights and the reason for that may readily be understood. In European legal tradition there has long been no general impediment to marriage except those of civil law. Here the law varies very widely from country to country as regards the number and nature of the impediments, the minimum age for marriage and the nature of the marriage tie (possibility of divorce, duties of the spouses). The reference in Article 12 to municipal law does not mean, in practice, that municipal law is adopted into the Convention,[6] but simply that great latitude is allowed

---

[1] Cf. Boas, *European Yearbook* x, 1963, p. 250 et seq. For the decision see *Nederlandse Jurisprudentie*, 1959, No. 361.

[2] Boas, loc. cit., p. 252.

[3] Weil, *The European Convention on Human Rights*, Leyden, 1963, p. 184.

[4] See Vasak, loc. cit., p. 58.

[5] For the question of the organisation of a State school system see Schorn, loc. cit., p. 434 et seq. Several States have availed themselves of their right to make a reservation in respect of this Article (cf. *Yearbook*, I, 54/55).

[6] Vasak, loc. cit., p. 50 treats the question from this angle and draws the conclusion that the international organs are called upon to examine the law in the same way as a national court. This view does not appear to me consistent with

for restrictions. These must not go so far, however—and here again the interpretation touches the question of the absolute protection to be afforded to the essential substance of a freedom—that they threaten the principle of the right to marry, and it is by this criterion that the international organs must judge national law.[1]

The number of problems arising here is considerable, although some of them have only yet emerged in case-law. German and Netherlands practice follows the view that the State is not required to allow a prisoner to marry. The Commission concurs in this, provided the prisoner is serving such a long term of imprisonment that no normal married life is to be expected.[2] It may be argued against this that imprisonment certainly stands in the way of the establishment of family life—that is also consistent with Article 8—but the object of the punishment does not necessarily require that the prisoner should be forbidden to marry.[3] True, it must be considered that Article 12—bearing in mind Article 8 and the expression 'to found a family'—is not concerned simply with the legal act of contracting marriage but with the married life of the couple.

Even greater problems are raised by cases in which marriage is not forbidden but entails legal or financial prejudice, which poses the question of the indirect violation of the principle of Article 12. This occurs for example with legal provisions forbidding members of the armed forces or of the police to marry for a certain period without permission, with the result that to marry without authorisation means dismissal (the so-called 'celibacy clause'). In German case-law it has been recognised that to give such an undertaking voluntarily, when entering the service, constitutes a personal decision and there is no infringement of the terms of Article 12. Here the right to give personal undertakings must be weighed against the protection of the right to marry. However, in cases where marriage was urgent (a child expected) jurisprudence has held the State to be legally bound to give the required permission and dismissal has been regarded as unjustified.[4] The differentiation seems to me to meet the situation

---

the reserve practised in international jurisprudence in regard to the interpretation of national law.

[1] This limitation does not mean, however, that Article 12 is a mere directive (see, on the other hand Münch, *JZ*, 1961, 152; Schorn, p. 268). Article 12 is 'self-executing' but allows national legislation wide discretion.

[2] The Netherlands judgment (*Hof s'Gravenhage, Ned. Jur.*, 1964, no. 54) specifies that the State is not bound to remove the material obstacles to marriage that result from the execution of a sentence. This is not entirely convincing. See the German case in 892/60 *Yearbook*, IV, 256.

[3] Cf. Vasak, loc. cit., p. 50 et seq.

[4] Higher Administrative Court of Coblence, *Zeitschrift für Beamtenrecht*, 1955, p. 314; Federal Administrative Court, Decision 14, 25–9. The Coblence Court

fairly. Undertakings given freely for a fixed period—in the cases in question for three years—which do not prevent marriage, but only attach certain consequences to it, are not incompatible with Article 12.

A similar question was raised by the case of a woman teacher in a Catholic *Land* who was employed in Catholic schools and married a divorced Catholic. German law recognises divorce but Canon Law does not. The Bavarian education authorities accordingly decided to transfer the teacher to another locality to a non-denominational school (*Gemeinschaftsschule*). Here again it was not a case of preventing marriage, but merely of the administrative prejudice suffered by it. The Bavarian Administrative Court—with a brief reference to Article 12—upheld the transfer on the grounds that teachers in religious schools are bound to live by the tenets of that religion.[1] The Federal Administrative Court—without referring to the Convention —decided otherwise on the basis of Article 6 of the Basic Law. Against the teacher's duty to practice the religion of the school, not only at school but also in private life, it set the protection of marriage and so arrived at a restriction of the obligation to follow religious principles in private life.[2] The decisions can be properly understood only in the light of the provisions regarding State religious schools contained in German legislation and of the Concordat of 1924 between Bavaria and the Holy See.[3] But even so it seems right to give the protection of marriage precedence over the duties of teachers in religious schools. It should also be considered that the main duty, namely that of teaching according to the religion of the school, is not affected thereby.

On the other hand, Article 12 cannot be applied in connection with the indirect prejudice suffered as a result of marriage when the impediments derive from civil law, or when private international law recognises foreign impediments to marriage. Article 13 of the Introductory Act (*Einführungsgesetz*) to the German Civil Code prescribes that, when contracting marriage, each partner shall be judged according to his or her own law when one of the partners is of German nationality. The purpose of the provision is to prevent the German party from entering into a marriage that would be considered

---

regarded the marriage as a breach of discipline with extenuating circumstances. The Federal Court stressed the obligation to seek permission. It did not think that Article 12 was relevant, a too narrow interpretation which overlooks the fact that even indirect consequences can prevent marriage. In both cases, which concerned different people, Article 6 of the Basic Law was the deciding factor in the decision.

[1] *Bayerische Verwaltungsblätter*, 1959, 58. See also Morvay, p. 343 et seq.

[2] *BVerwGE*, 17, 267 (here too the decisions concerned different persons).

[3] These lay down that teachers at religious schools shall belong to the Church in question and teach according to its tenets.

null and void in the partner's country of origin and thereby suffering legal prejudice on settling in that country. An alien who marries in Germany has as a rule to produce a certificate from his country of origin stating that no impediment to the marriage exists under the law of that country (Section 10 of the Marriage Act of 30 February 1946). Exemption may be granted, but the German judicial authorities refuse it if under the law of the foreign country the marriage contracted in Germany would be considered null and void. This occurred in the case of a Spaniard who married a German woman who was a Protestant and divorced. Spanish law requires for the Spanish partner marriage in accordance with Canon Law and imposes the same requirement on the foreign partner to the marriage. This means that the Protestant woman's first marriage is a valid marriage according to Canon Law 1099 CIC and is indissoluble, so that it presents an overriding impediment to any other marriage. It may be possible to criticise from the point of view of private international law or of German constitutional law (freedom of religion) the taking into consideration a foreign legal provision that subjects marriage so completely to Canon Law, but it constitutes no threat to *ordre public* nor is there any breach of Article 12. It is simply a question of recognising an impediment that exists in civil law and not of adding any further impediment.[1] The existing impediment is not inconsistent, even in its religious aspect, with the traditional principles of European law and the German courts were accordingly right in denying the applicability of Article 12.[2]

Generally speaking, it can be seen that in national jurisprudence Article 12 is increasingly applied, while the Commission, on the other hand, remains reserved as regards its application.

3. *Protection of freedom of thought (Articles 9, 10, 11, 16)*
(a) *Article 9*

The significance of Articles 9–11 of the Convention is weakened by the fact that national Constitutions often contain far-reaching guarantees to the same effect. This is why the jurisprudence of the

---

[1] Federal Court, *BGHZ*, 41, 137; see also the critical comments of E. Fischer, *NJW*, 1964, p. 1323 and in support Matz, *NJW*, 1964, p. 2015. See also Regional Court of Munich, *NJW*, 1963, 2233.

[2] One may criticise the recognition in similar circumstances of an impediment to marriage in Iranian law which makes the marriage of Iranian civil servants and students abroad subject to the authorisation of the Iranian authorities (Berlin Court of Appeal, *NJW*, 1961, 2209). It is doubtful whether the recognition of such an administrative impediment is compatible with Article 12. Article 12 refers to national law in the sense of recognising the generally accepted rules of civil law relating to marriage, and to its effects and impediments, but not additional restrictions placed on marriage on political grounds.

Federal Republic, which is so considerable in the case of other articles, has been less concerned with these clauses. Articles 4, 5, 8 and 9 of the Basic Law have a wide sphere of application far beyond that of the Convention. The same is true of other countries. The questions referred to the Commission in this connection are not representative and do not bring out the full significance of the fundamental freedoms concerned. There have nevertheless been some interesting and important cases of this kind; this shows that the additional guarantee of the Convention can have its importance even side by side with a long tradition of national constitutional and other law.

All three articles contain far-reaching restrictions in the interests of what is necessary in a democratic society for the protection of public safety and order, health or morals or the rights of others. In their details, these restrictions differ slightly from article to article so that in many cases the crux of the matter lies in their interpretation.

The fact that Articles 9 and 10 do not relate to freedom in the use of language has already been decided by the Commission, as already mentioned in connection with the Belgian linguistic cases.

The correct application of the principle of religious freedom in the sense of true tolerance is illustrated by the decision of the Appeals Division of the Belgian National Labour Office in Brussels, which restored to an unemployed Jewish craftsman the relief that had been withheld from him because, it was alleged, on account of the Sabbath day of rest, he had not shown that he had been unemployed for six successive days and had not submitted to official control. It was rightly decided that the Sabbath day of rest belonged to the practice of his religion (Article 9) and the law had accordingly to be interpreted so that he could fulfil his religious obligations.[1] On the other hand, Netherlands jurisprudence has considered the invocation of the principle of religious freedom unjustified in a number of cases in which pleas were entered against financial or social regulations applying to all citizens in general, or to certain sections of the population, on the grounds of religious freedom or conscientious objections. This was the case with the invocation of Article 10 against the general rules concerning shop-closing, since it was a question of selling religious tracts in the street. Here it is sufficient to point to the permissibility of restrictions based on considerations of *ordre public*.[2] But the decisive factor is the realisation that funda-

[1] *Yearbook*, v, 365; American jurisprudence on the other hand concluded in another case that Sunday was also the day of rest for Jewish businesses since this was a general rule that had to be strictly obeyed. *McGowan* v. *Maryland* 366 US 420; *Braunfeld* v. *Brown* 366 US 599 (1961).

[2] *Hoge Rad Ned. Jurisprudentie* 1961 No. 273. See also Röling, *Ned. Tijdschrift voor Internationaal Recht*, 9, 1962, p. 316.

mental rights and freedoms, when their essentials are not threatened, must adapt themselves to the State legal system. The practice of a religion in the street can be kept away from places where traffic is congested and the law that all publications must bear the name of the publisher and the place of publication is no offence against freedom of opinion.[1] The situation becomes quite different as soon as there is any question of interference with or supervision of the contents.[2]

From this point of view it seems unjustified to plead freedom of conscience against the regulations requiring information to be supplied to the '*Landbouwschap*' as the organisation representing agricultural employers and workers. Not only can Article 9 (2) be invoked, but it seems fundamentally impossible in modern society to plead conscientious scruples against general social and financial regulations which have a negligible effect on individual freedom.[3] This point of view applies to yet another case. A farmer refused to join the State Association of cattle-owners for the suppression of tuberculosis in cattle, pleading conscientious objections as the member of a church which was against the imposition of legal obligations on farmers. This claim could be immediately rejected on the grounds of the protection of health referred to in Article 9 (2).[4] However, it is clear that legal systems, to whatever extent they have to give way in important questions relating to the life of the individual, cannot allow measures affecting public safety and health to depend on the individual conscience which rejects even unimportant services to the community.[5]

Another case takes us into the realm of doubt. A minister of the Dutch Reformed Church refused to pay his contribution to old age insurance because, according to the doctrine of his church and Article 13 of the Church Constitution of Dordrecht, his parishioners

---

[1] This is not the theory of *interêt distinct* which Boas opposes, loc. cit., p. 254 et seq. The question here, on the contrary, is as follows: in cases when a fundamental freedom is not affected in its essential substance by a general law which does not specifically concern the subject matter of that freedom, the full exercise of that right must not be weighed against all the other interests that have not yet been taken into consideration.

[2] The situation is different when the regulations make the access to publishing difficult, e.g. by requiring professional training or financial guarantees, as in the case of a Netherlands regulation. It was regarded by the *Hoge Rad* as incompatible with Article 10. *Ned Jurisprudentie*, 1960, No. 274; see also Boas, p. 247.

[3] Hof Leuwarden, *Ned. Jurisprudentie*, 1964, no. 401, 402.

[4] The Commission upheld the opinion of the Netherlands courts: 1068/61 *Yearbook*, v, 283 et seq.

[5] For this reason—though without reference to the Convention—German jurisprudence allows no exemption from vaccination against smallpox on conscientious grounds, since otherwise the protective effect of the measure would be lost: Federal Administrative Court 9, 78.

were bound to take care of him in his old age. The *Hoge Rad* regarded Article 9 as self-executing, but held that while the Convention and the earlier legislation regarding the protection of religious freedom in the Netherlands guaranteed everyone freedom 'to manifest his religion', nobody was entitled to appeal on religious grounds against obligations imposed on all citizens alike. The payment of the contribution required of everybody to old age insurance could not affect religious freedom.[1] The Court draws a line here between freedom to practise a religion and the opposition of religious convictions to provisions of municipal law. It does not extend the concept of the practice of a religion to compliance with religious principles in everyday life, but restricts protection to specifically religious activities. This view seems too narrow. It is a question here, as Röling[2] has rightly pointed out, of the demarcation line between the sphere proper to the Church, which includes care for its ministers, and the sphere of law which applies equally to all. The sphere guaranteed to the Church and its members by the principle of religious freedom is not confined to participation in religious services but, as is shown by the respect for the Sabbath as a day of rest, reaches out into various spheres of everyday life[3] and here conflicts arise with municipal law. The only possibility once more, is to weigh the considerations of *ordre public* against the independence of the Church,[4] in the manner described above. Röling is right when he says[5]: 'Het blijft immers steeds een afweging van de intensiteit van het wettelijk voorschrift en van de kerkelijke regel'. This weighing of the one against the other must take place even when it is possible with justice to invoke the protection of public order referred to in Article 9 (2) to uphold State insurance legislation as against freedom of religion. For one of the

---

[1] *Hoge Rad, Ned. Jurisprudentie*, 1960, No. 436, *Yearbook*, v, 293.

[2] Note in *Ned. Jurisprudentie*, 1960, p. 999 et seq.

[3] This extension of religious freedom must be stressed but at the same time it is accompanied by an obligation to exercise it as a 'responsible freedom' and to recognise the individual's duties to the community. Cf. A.B. Carillo de Albornoz, *The Basis of Religious Liberty*, World Council of Churches, New York, 1963, p. 108 et seq. For what is meant by the practice of a religion see also P. Lanarès, *La liberté religieuse*, Annemasse, 1964, p. 55, et seq., which refers to the abolition of the caste system (of religious origin) in India by Article 17 of the Constitution.

[4] The jurisprudence of the German Federal Constitutional Court contains many examples of such weighing up of opposing considerations. Cf. *BVerfGE*, 7, 208; 15, 78; 16, 202. See also the American Supreme Court in *Communist Party of the U.S.* v. *Subversive Activities Control Board*, 367 US 97 (1961) (Judge Frankfurter) and *Scales* v. *United States* (Judge Douglas) 367 US 270/71: 'balancing the right of speech and association against other values in society'. Cf. my remarks in *Pressefreiheit, Veröffentlichungen der Vereinigung Deutscher Staatsrechtslehrer* 22, 55 et seq.

[5] *Ned. Jurisprudentie*, 1960, p. 999 et seq.

basic principles of the interpretation of fundamental rights in Germany[1] is that even when judging restrictions on such rights their essential substance must always be taken into account and its limits defined. In this light the interpretation of the expression 'manifest his religion' seems too narrow. In the result, however, the attitude of Netherlands jurisprudence is justified. The Commission upheld it and further pointed out that Netherlands law expressly authorises conscientious objectors to pay amounts due as insurance contributions in the form of taxes.[2]

In one last case, however, we can support the critics who disagree with the denial by Netherlands jurisprudence of the application of Article 9. A Catholic priest was punished for having organised a procession without official authorisation in a locality called Gertruidenberg.[3] Article 184 (2) of the Netherlands Basic Law (*Grondwet*) allows religious services to be conducted in public (in the open air) if they are in accordance with the laws and regulations. More detailed provisions are to be found in the Act of 1853 on the State supervision of churches. There is no doubt that a procession comes under the heading of conducting religious services. The problem is only whether authorisation can be required on the grounds of the 'protection of public order' in accordance with Article 9 (2). The *Hoge Rad* considered that it could, because from the history of Article 184 of the *Grondwet* it was clear that the purpose of the article was to prevent the tension and unrest that might be caused between the different religious sects by public manifestations. The Court did not go into the question whether Article 184 was still valid today, considering that in Netherlands law its competence did not extend to this. The criticism must be made that the restriction in question does not derive from considerations of public order (such as traffic conditions) but from the threat represented by the relations between the religious sects. Thus the measure is directed against the very substance of religious freedom, which it restricts in the interests of another religion. It must be remembered that the concept of religious tolerance has changed vastly in European countries. In former times religious demonstrations on the part of a minority might have appeared offensive to the majority,[4] but the modern concept of

---

[1] This has been developed in Federal Constitutional Law in connection with Article 5 of the Basic Law (freedom of the Press); *BVerfGE*, 7, 207; 12, 124.

[2] 1497/62 *Yearbook*, v, 299. It must be borne in mind that for many religious sects compulsion to belong to a State organisation already places a burden on the conscience.

[3] The relevant judgments are: *Rechtbank Breda, Ned. Jurisprudentie* 1959, No. 254; *Hoge Rad* 1959, No. 560 (referred back); *Hof Arnhem* 1961, No. 424; *Hoge Rad* 1962, No. 107.

[4] As an example it may be recalled that in 1908 King Edward VII of England

tolerance calls for a much greater measure of give and take and the opinion of the Court that the restriction imposed is 'in itself justified' cannot at first sight be seen to rest on a generally accepted view.[1]

The decision of the Greek Areopagus that the authorisation of the competent religious authority and of the Ministry of Education for the erection or fitting up of premises for religious use can be required by Greek law without any breach of Article 9 adds yet further to the possible restrictions. Without a closer knowledge of the application of this decision no judgment can be passed on it here.[2]

Generally speaking, the decisions relating to Article 9 show that the modern trend towards increased State intervention in the life of the individual is enlarging the possibilities of conflict between considerations of *ordre public* and the principle of freedom of religion as regards the effects of religious beliefs on everyday life. For this reason, the interpretation of the expression 'to manifest his religion' in practice will acquire special importance. In no circumstances must its meaning be restricted to participation in religious services.

(b) Articles 10, 16

If we omit the cases in which Article 9 and Article 10 are invoked together (Belgian language question, shop-closing), the litigation relating to Article 10 is even more closely confined to the question of the admissibility of the restrictions enumerated in its paragraph 2. Among the measures necessary for the prevention of disorder and crime and for the protection of morals are without doubt the provisions of criminal law making the circulation of literature likely to be harmful to the young a punishable offence and also those prohibiting national-socialist activities.[3] And so it is no breach of Article 10 if an alien is expelled on the grounds that he is engaging in an undesirable political activity that is liable to prejudice peaceful relations with a neighbouring country.[4] National constitutional law seems rather inclined, of recent years, to allow aliens some measure of political

---

intervened with the Prime Minister Mr Asquith to oppose a procession that was planned in London on the occasion of a Eucharistic Congress. In the event its cancellation was secured. Cf. Roy Jenkins, *Asquith*, 1964, p. 189 et seq.

[1] Against the decision see also Boas, loc. cit., p. 240 et seq. Vasak, loc. cit. p. 55.

[2] *Yearbook*, II, 606.

[3] 1747/62 *Yearbook*, VI, 444. The Commission rightly referred in addition to Article 17 of the Convention.

[4] Austrian Constitutional Court, Decisions 1962 No. 4233; activities in an organisation of Croatian exiles caused the alien's police authorities to intervene, Austrian municipal law recognises the protection of the public interest against expressions of opinion. According to Article 16, Articles 10 and 11 of the Convention do not protect the political activity of aliens.

activity and association.[1] Owing to the growing mobility of population in Europe, the question whether freedom of opinion and association should not be guaranteed under the same conditions to everybody, including aliens, is sure to arise in countries where the law affords these guarantees only to nationals.[2]

The decision relating to Article 10 which has aroused the most comment, namely the *De Becker case*, is on closer inspection the least suited to illustrate general principles. Its details are closely bound up with the exceptional circumstances following on the Second World War and the emphasis again is chiefly on the admissibility or otherwise of certain restrictions. It can be regarded as admissible for a State sometimes to impose professional restrictions as an accessory penalty in the case of certain offences which constitute serious breaches of professional duty.[3] In regard to professions connected with the forming of public opinion and its diffusion such measures require particularly careful investigation,[4] for there can be no doubt that they interfere with freedom of opinion. In its Report, the Commission held such restrictions on the exercise of a profession to be permissible and recognised that, to a limited extent, even permanent restrictions might be allowable, in the presence of exceptional circumstances and if confined to political utterances.[5] However, this view cannot be separated from the special circumstances which surround the case, and it would be unwise to draw conclusions from it for the purpose of judging restrictions imposed in normal circumstances.

Two further decisions raising general questions may be quoted. In a case in the Netherlands the question arose whether the restrictions authorised in Article 10—in this case regulations governing open air assemblies—had to be imposed by Act of Parliament or whether a ministerial order was sufficient.[6] The Court held that it was, since the legal systems of all European countries recognise the possibility of amplifying legislation by issuing regulations. This is also my view.

[1] The German Aliens Act of 28 April 1965 (*BGB1*, I, 353) seeks to reduce the restrictions on the political activity of aliens (Section 6) by defining more closely the forbidden activities. The expression used (*erhebliche Interessen der Bundesrepublik*) are certainly vague. For the question of the political rights of aliens see Hans Huber, *Festschrift Jahrreis*, 1964, p. 101 et seq.

[2] It is enough to refer to Articles 48–66 of the Treaty setting up the European Economic Community.

[3] The German Criminal Code (Section 42, 1) prescribes this accessory penalty for all professions (up to 5 years). However, its application to the Press is contested.

[4] The Commission accepted such a restriction in the interests of public safety but required that it be considered 'with the utmost care'.

[5] Loc. cit., pp. 127/28, 214, 227, Cf. also 924/60 *Yearbook*, VI, 151.

[6] *Hoge Rad, Ned. Jurisprudentie*, 1964, No. 239.

The expression 'by law' (*par la loi*) is to be understood generally and not in the sense of by Act of Parliament alone. A clearer expression would have been preferable. A German decision regarded as justified in the interests of *ordre public* |a restriction of the freedom of the Press whereby the Employment Act made publications advertising posts for Germans abroad subject to authorisation by the Federal Employment Institute.[1] This measure, introduced in the interests of the control of employment, did not restrict the freedom of the Press, inasmuch as it was directed against offers of employment and not against expressions of opinion. One must agree with that decision.

(c) *Articles 11, 16*

If one passes over the few cases in which Article 11 has been invoked in conjunction with Article 10—these have already been discussed—the Commission's decision to reject the application of the German Communist Party against its prohibition under Article 21 of the Basic Law raises no important questions.[2] The application of Article 17 in this context was appropriate. The more far-reaching questions of the State democratic order, raised not so much by this decision as by Article 21 of the Basic Law, cannot be discussed here.

4. *Protection of material situation* (*Article 1 of the First Protocol*)

The protection afforded to possessions in Article 1 of the Protocol is expressed in general terms and allows far-reaching restrictions to be imposed by national legislation. The State retains the right to impose restrictions in the general interest and to secure the payment of taxes and other contributions. This limited protection of property is understandable when one bears in mind what a good example it affords of how the evolution of legal opinion can lead to the weakening and restricting of fundamental freedoms. Out of the *droit inviolable et sacré* of Article 17 of the French Declaration of the Rights of Man of 1789 modern Constitutions have developed, under the influence of social or socialist ideas, a legal principle whose substance seems limited by civic obligations and whose application can be considerably restricted in the common interest.

Article 1 leaves the decision as to what constitute rights of property largely to national legislation. The situation is similar to that created by Article 12. Here too national law is not left completely free. The international organs are entitled to judge national laws by the criteria of the principles established by the Convention. As

---

[1] Federal Social Court, *NJW*, 1964, 1691.
[2] 250/57 *Yearbook*, I, 222; Vasak rightly points (loc. cit., p. 72) to the agreement in substance between Article 21 of the Basic Law and Article 17 of the Convention.

regards the differences in national opinion as to what is meant by rights of property, the principles derive in the first place from international law, as is stated in Article 1 (1), and from the rules for the protection of aliens' property. Even these rules do not go uncontested today, but they constitute an adequate basis.

All the applications to the Commission have been concerned with the imposition of taxes or contributions. States were allowed from the outset great latitude in this respect. Article 1 authorises even heavy taxation. The Commission rightly considered contributions to the German *Lastenausgleich* as a tax. They were originally intended as a means of redistribution of income, but in the long run they amounted to differential taxation. The Commission rightly appreciated the social intention of these contributions whose purpose was to share out fairly the burden of the war.[1] Paragraph 2 of Article 1 has only properly been invoked in the case of the Netherlands old age insurance contributions referred to in connection with Article 10 of the Convention.[2]

The decision concerning the Icelandic Act, No. 44, of 3 June 1957 raises serious difficulties. Here it is a question of a contribution which might seriously have been held to amount to a confiscation of property. A tax of 25 per cent was imposed on all property over a certain value and followed a similar contribution exacted in 1950. It applied to a small section of the population only. The Icelandic courts were in no doubt that this contribution was to be regarded as a tax and the Commission agreed with them, pointing out that its payment could be spread over ten years. It was exacted in the public interest and derived from the sovereign power of States to levy taxes. The Commission also expressed the opinion that the principles of international law could not affect the application of Article 1 in relations between a State and its citizens.[3] If we adopt this point of view, the content of Article 1 is greatly restricted. It does not seem to me to follow that internal relations cannot be judged by minimum standards of international law. This view is supported by the wording of the Article. In the event, however, it is possible to agree with the decision, considering that the contribution was spread over a number of years.

Inasmuch as national Constitutions protect property, their provisions go so far beyond those of Article 1 that no important application of this clause is to be expected.

5. *Prohibition of discrimination (Article 14)*

Article 14 of the Convention is among the articles most frequently quoted. In reality it is of slight importance, since it can only be

[1] 551/59 *Yearbook*, III, 250; 673/59 *Yearbook*, IV, 291.
[2] 1497/62 *Yearbook*, V, 298.   [3] 511/59 *Yearbook*, III, 421 et seq.

applied in conjunction with other fundamental rights guaranteed by the Convention. Only when there is any question of discriminatory treatment is Article 14 involved.[1] It does not constitute an independent ground for complaint and can in no way be compared with the provisions of national Constitutions establishing the equality of all men. In addition, the Commission has drawn attention to the fact that material differences do not constitute discrimination[2] and that legislation frequently distributes the burden of contributions quite unequally.[3] The only cases in which Article 14 has found an application have been those relating to the Belgian language question and there no decision has yet been reached.[4]

6. *Restrictions on fundamental rights and freedoms (Articles 15, 17, 18)*

The question of restrictions on fundamental rights raises one of the most serious problems in municipal law when these restrictions are not clearly defined, but are couched in general terms, or when their application has to be weighed systematically against other considerations. In the face of this the Convention has sought to define precisely the restrictions that may be imposed on the rights it guarantees, but it must be admitted that the question of the limits of fundamental rights and freedoms has not been entirely solved, as may be seen from the decisions relating to Article 9. The problem, however, is a strictly limited one. Articles 15 and 17 already afford to some extent the possibility of restrictions deriving from generally accepted opinions. The really important limitations lie, however, in the restrictions authorised in the individual articles.

Article 15 has found too wide an application in certain judgments of national courts which invoked it to justify political emergency measures which, however, had not been notified in accordance with paragraph 3.[5] The most significant application of Article 15 was in the *Lawless Case*. Here the national[6] and international[7] authorities agreed that the excesses of the nationalists against Northern Ireland

---

[1] In this sense cf. 86/55 *Yearbook*, I, p. 199; 95/55 *Yearbook*, I, 202; 238/56 *Yearbook*, I, 206; 551/59 *Yearbook*, III, 252; 436/58 *Yearbook*, II, 390.

[2] Thus in connection with the repression of homosexuality among men only: 167/56 *Yearbook*, I, 235; 261/57 *Yearbook*, I, 257.

[3] 511/59 *Yearbook*, III, 424.

[4] 1474/62 *Yearbook* VI, 343; 1769/62 *Yearbook*, VI, 457. Another case in which Article 14 was applied was in that of *Austria* v. *Italy*. The Committee of Ministers examined the claim that the sentences were excessive in the light of Article 14 and found it unjustified, *Yearbook*, VI, 795.

[5] Cf. the decisions of the Greek State Council quoted by Bürgenthal, loc. cit., p. 87 et seq.

[6] *International Law Reports*, 24, 420.

[7] Report of the Commission, *E.C.H.R.*, Series B, 1960–1, p. 9 et seq. Judgment of the Court, of 1 July 1961, Series A.

had created for Ireland an emergency threatening the life of the nation. The court had carefully investigated the matter, which involved various political issues, and had concluded that it was competent to judge the facts. It did not refer expressly to the margin of appreciation left to the national authorities, but it appreciated the subjective considerations that had influenced the Irish Government and thereby indirectly recognised the freedom of decision that existed in this sphere.[1] Whether the unrest on the border really constituted a situation threatening the life of the nation has been questioned by many critics. However, it cannot be overlooked that, when it comes to judging emergency measures taken by the Government, national courts too have always set limits to their competence. In any case Article 15 has rather gained in its possibilities of application than otherwise through the decision in the Lawless case.

Article 17, on the contrary, raises no special problems. The fact that it is directed against groups or individuals engaging in activities which constitute a threat to freedom authorises action against political movements which reject and oppose democracy. The duty of the international organs is rather to ensure that Article 17 is not taken as the basis for restrictions on fundamental freedoms aimed at left-wing movements.

The really essential questions of the limits of fundamental freedoms where the Convention is concerned lie, however, in the interpretation of such concepts as 'public order', 'morality', 'emergency', etc. which are to be found in individual articles. Whether, in addition, a doctrine will grow up, as in national law, in regard to the limits of fundamental rights and the necessity of weighing the values guaranteed against one another and against other basic values of society is doubtful, but no judgment can be passed on that question as yet.

7. *Conclusion*

The above review has shown the vast range of national and international decisions. The number relating to the various articles varies, but in general the existing opinions make it possible to sum up the position as regards the Convention in a small number of points.

1. The importance of the Convention for the individual contracting States does not depend on the acceptance of the right of individual petition (Art. 25) or the acceptance of the jurisdiction of the Court (Art. 46), but to a large extent on the rules of national constitutional law which determine whether the clauses of the Convention are

---

[1] Cf. also to this effect the detailed appreciation of the judgment by Hans Huber, *ZaöRuVR*, 21, 1961, p. 664 et seq.

directly applicable as municipal law and decide their status in relation to the other laws of the land. Only in those countries where the Convention has direct force of law can any national jurisprudence grow up in respect of it.

2. The importance of the question whether in municipal law the Convention takes precedence over ordinary law should not be overestimated. Even in countries where this is not the case the Convention is constantly being invoked.

3. The extent of the actual application of the Convention in the contracting States depends in a large measure on the rights and freedoms guaranteed in the Constitution of the country concerned. Where the Constitution guarantees fundamental freedoms which coincide with or go beyond those guaranteed by the Convention, national jurisprudence will concentrate chiefly, if not entirely, on municipal law and the Convention will be invoked only in isolated cases. Since the aim of the Convention is not to be a substitute for national guarantees of rights and freedoms but to afford an additional guarantee, and in some cases make good the deficiencies of national law, the present state of affairs fulfils that aim. The situation described arises frequently in connection with Articles 10 and 11. A very large body of national jurisprudence has grown up around the freedoms guaranteed in these two clauses, but it is concerned primarily with the provisions of the Constitutions of the countries concerned. However, it is not possible, even in countries which have accepted the right of individual petition, to measure the effects of the Convention by the number of applications that reach the Commission. The Convention has, so to speak, a considerable 'disguised' effect.

It follows that the Convention has the strongest international and national influence in those spheres where it guarantees fundamental rights and freedoms which go beyond those that are traditionally recognised, or where its provisions are more specific than the often very general formulae of national law. The former applies to Articles 4, 8 and 12, the latter is illustrated chiefly by Articles 5 and 6.

4. A comparison shows that, on the whole, the construction placed on the provisions of the Convention by international and national authorities agree. That is so in spite of the fact that national jurisprudence has taken little notice so far of the decisions of the international organs, and conversely the international organs—in accordance with their principle of reticence in the interpretation of municipal law—rarely go deeply into national jurisprudence relating to the Convention or to the corresponding clauses of the Constitution.

The differences from country to country in the application of the

Convention depend in the first place on the manner in which various countries interpret their own Constitution and its guarantees. The methods adopted in interpreting the Constitution is carried over in general by national Courts to the application of the Convention. That may lead in a few cases to a tendency to place a very wide interpretation on the provisions of the Convention, and sometimes it may have the opposite effect.

To review and compare with one another, and with the attitude of the international organs, the results of the interpretation of the Convention, in the different contracting States can accordingly represent an essential contribution on the part of legal science to the uniform application of the Convention and to the harmonisation of legal concepts.

5. An examination of jurisprudence shows that the Convention rightly derives its origin from the conviction that a common tradition of protection for fundamental rights and freedoms exists in the contracting States and member countries of the Council of Europe. There is often a wide measure of agreement between jurisprudence in the various countries. That agreement would emerge more clearly if it were judged not only by the decisions which expressly refer to the Convention, but also by those which are concerned with questions touching the substance of the Convention but which refer not to it but to provisions of municipal law. An international comparison on this scale of the application of fundamental rights and freedoms is however only in its early stages. It should be pointed out, however, that cases can be quoted in which national courts, interpreting clauses of the national Constitutions, have expressly referred to the opinions of courts in other countries regarding corresponding provisions.

From this point of view of the comparison and harmonisation of legal opinion it is particularly gratifying that the decisions of the Commission, the Committee of Ministers and the Court of Human Rights are the product of representatives of all the member countries of the Council of Europe.

6. The influence of the decisions of the international organs of the Convention is to be observed chiefly in connection with the framing of national legislation. Their pronouncements are carefully studied by the framers of national law. However, this influence should not be judged by the number of cases in which the international opinion differs from the national one. In many cases in which the Commission, practising its usual reserve, does not reject the national decision but adds its own comments and references, the influence of the international organs is still felt.

7. The experience of the Convention confirms the view that rules

of a fundamental nature can only achieve their full effect if they are applied, and their application is watched over, with the assistance of a permanent body of jurisprudence. Here the duty of the international organs resembles that of the constitutional courts that exist in many countries today.

SUMMARY OF THE DISCUSSION

J. Unger (Interpretation and Effect of Article 8): I do not agree with the view expressed in the Report that Article 8 cannot be invoked 'as a basis for the protection of the personal sphere of life' as this would exceed the 'recognisable limits' of this Article. Although Article 8 does not define the limits or explain the meaning of the right to respect for private life, it does not follow that these words have no meaning at all. The German Bundesgerichtshof has found meaning in Article 8 when deciding that unauthorised tape-recordings are violations of the right to respect for private life. It is true that these decisions relied in the first place on Article 1 of the German Basic Law, but, as is explained in the third and the final conclusions of the Report, it is inevitable that municipal courts should refer primarily, or even exclusively, to their Constitution whenever fundamental rights are guaranteed there in terms no less comprehensive than those of the Convention.

Professor Scheuner considers that Article 8 must be interpreted narrowly since there has not yet developed a common legal tradition in the contracting States to protect the individual against invasion of his privacy. But it is surely arguable that this assessment of the position reached in most European laws is unduly negative, although it is quite accurate as far as English law is concerned. This is precisely why Article 8 is of crucial significance from the point of view of English law. The List of Decisions of National Courts relating to the Convention which has been distributed[1] does not contain a single decision of an English court. We may claim that this shows that in England Human Rights are well established in law and properly respected in practice, but we cannot possibly maintain this attitude if the Convention has also established a right to privacy.

The problem raised by Article 8 is not limited to the issue of privacy. It raises a question of fundamental importance. Is the Convention to be interpreted as being no more than a restatement of those rights and freedoms which have been proclaimed in the past in such documents as Magna Carta and the Declaration of the Rights of Man? Magna Carta and the Declaration of the Rights of Man

---

[1] A document compiled by the Directorate of Human Rights of the Council of Europe under reference H(65)7 of 12 June 1965.

have served the needs of the past. It cannot be expected that they provide adequate protection against wire-tapping and similar threats to individual freedom and human dignity which have become possible only in this technological age. I hope that rather than interpreting the Convention restrictively it will be possible to use it so that it can serve the changing needs of a dynamic European society.
Felix Ermacora (1. The function of the Convention; 2. Article 3 of the Convention and Article 1 of the Protocol): Professor Scheuner referred to the view expressed by Professor Winkler that the Convention is not meant to interfere with national legal systems. This, however, does not accord with the Preamble; the integrating function of the Convention is fulfilled more by its own dynamism than by any deliberate action on the part of the organs of the Convention.

National law is not applied by these organs, but is simply regarded as an existing fact. The Commission does not constitute the 'fourth instance' of a national legal system. There results a complex process which may culminate in the amendment of national law, as in Austria. A State actuated by good will yields to the tendencies reflected in wise judicial decisions—a fact which the courts must take into account.

The indirect effect of the Convention is illustrated by the following examples: according to Article 3, a person seeking asylum should not be turned away if he is in danger of being subjected to inhuman treatment. In my opinion (even if it conflicts with that of the Commission) Article 1 of the Protocol provides for the protection of nationals as well as of aliens. This opinion derives from Austrian case-law, according to which the payment of compensation constitutes a clear distinction from the notion of expropriation.

It should be noted, in connection with Articles 5 and 6, that the administrative authorities are alleged to be guilty of violations less frequently than the courts; the supervision of administrative acts by the courts is, after all, a century-old tradition in Austria.

I agree with Professor Scheuner that national and international decisions, like the applications themselves, merit further study.
H. Pfeifer (Comments on certain individual Articles of the Human Rights Convention): Article 3 contains provisions which do not, as a rule, appear in older lists of basic rights, the Austrian Basic Rights Schedule of 1867 included. It constitutes a valuable supplement to this Schedule, in that it establishes respect for human dignity in constitutional law. It is self-executing, despite the wide concepts 'inhuman' and 'degrading'. These concepts, which can never be exhaustively defined by law, will have to be worked out in detail in judicial practice. A disproportionately heavy penalty, for example, can also be inhuman.

Article 7 (1) contains the principle already embodied in the French Declaration of the Rights of Man and of the Citizen of 1789: *Nullum crimen et nulla poena sine lege praevia*; international law is put on an equal footing with national law. This fundamental legal principle prevents penal laws and international prescripts from having any retroactive effect. But such laws and prescripts have unfortunately been promulgated or framed since 1945, although ordinary criminal law would have been sufficient for the repression of such criminal offences.

In order to cover up such breaches of the said fundamental principle 'with the trappings of the law', paragraph 2 was added, under which mere 'principles of law', which according to Verdross are based on 'general legal notions', are accepted as a basis for punishment in place of clear penal law provisions. Mindful of Germany's bitter experience, during the period of National Socialist domination, as a result of departures from the principle of *nulla poena sine lege*, the German Federal Government, with the approval of the Bundestag and the Federal Council, referring to the clear provisions of Article 103 (2) of the Basic Law (*Grundgesetz*), made a reservation as regards Article 7 (2). However, as rightly pointed out by certain well-known professors of criminal law,[1] this reservation was not really necessary since, under Article 60 of the Human Rights Convention, the more favourable human right guaranteed to the individual in Article 103 (2) may not be limited by the Convention. The same applies to Austria, for both Article IV Kdm. Pat. (*Kundmachungspatent*—promulgation order) to the Penal Code and Section 1 of the Administrative Penal Code (*Verwaltungstrafgesetz*) contain the principles *nulla poena sine lege praevia* and 'no severer punishment than that prescribed at the time of the offence'. According to Article 60 of the Human Rights Convention, which in Austria has the status of constitutional law, no human right which is 'ensured under the laws of any High Contracting Party' may be limited by the Convention. Hence Article 7 (2), which limits the said human rights ensured under Austrian law and is thus to a certain extent inconsistent with them, may not be applied in Austria.

Article 12 seems to me to mean that any man or woman who fulfils the general requirements of national law on marriage shall have the right to marry and found a family. On the other hand, in the light of Article 14 (prohibition of differential treatment according to status), no special provisions may be issued or applied which prohibit marriage to specific groups of public employees or make it dependent on official authorisation. Provisions of this kind existing in Austria are, in my opinion—an opinion shared by numerous

[1] H. von Weber and Jescheck.

authors—tacitly repealed by Articles 12 and 14. The 1960 Conscription Law (Amendment) Act conceded this view to some extent by repealing the provision prohibiting conscripts from marrying.

To interpret Article 12 as giving Contracting States full powers arbitrarily to prohibit or impede, by legislation, the marriage of persons who fulfil the general requirements of marriage law would be absurd, for any provision in this sense would inevitably lead to concubinage and illegitimate children.

Karl Doehring: Article 1 of the first Protocol to the Convention confers on everyone the right to peaceful enjoyment of his possessions. This provision has been interpreted by the Commission and, to a large extent, in legal literature, as meaning that protection of those rights extends only to aliens. To support this view, reference is made to conditions ' . . . provided for by the law and by the general principles of international law'.

This interpretation must be firmly rejected as being contrary to the Convention, even though the *travaux préparatoires* may, on a subjective reading, allegedly support such reasoning, The Convention guarantees material rights to 'everyone' and draws no distinction except for the traditional distinction relating to the political rights of aliens. Leaving aside the subjective interpretation, it would still remain to prove that the reference to international law has precedence over the reference to the standard of compensation ('conditions provided for by law') and that it is admissible to exclude the concept of a national's rights *vis-à-vis* his own State; the Convention expressly avoids such exclusion. Reference is made to the general principles of international law elsewhere in the Convention, for example, in Article 26 in relation to the exhaustion of domestic remedies. No one, apparently, has ever concluded that this provision applied only to foreigners; on the contrary, it is precisely applications from citizens wishing to establish rights *vis-à-vis* their own State under Article 26 of the Convention which are envisaged.

It is therefore proposed that a change should be made in *lex ferenda* or perhaps that an interpretation more in conformity with the spirit of the Convention should be adopted.

Dr H. Golsong: as I said earlier,[1] in my view the national judge ought to interpret the law of the Convention in the light of the legal tradition of his own country. The rule is similar for the organs of the Convention. The Convention is not designed to put something new in the place of established principles of law; its real purpose is to set strict limits to the abusive application of national law in the sphere of fundamental rights. Reference needs to be made as far as possible to the State's own legal tradition, supplemented, where

---

[1] Chapter II above.

necessary, by comparative legal research. This was what the Commission did, for example, in interpreting Article 8 of the Convention in relation to homosexuality. This does not prevent—but rather facilitates—the gradual approximation of national legal tradition in regard to the Convention.

Here I should like—contrary to Professor Ermacora—to defend the view that for the Commission and the Court, national law, in the context of the Convention, is 'law' and not simply 'fact'.

Lastly, it seems to me important to stress that neither the Commission's decisions as to admissibility nor its opinions in pursuance of Article 31 of the Convention are legal 'precedents' in the English sense. They do not even bind the Commission itself—indeed, in practice, the Commission does not feel itself at all bound by them. At most, they can be of assistance to national judges in interpreting the Convention.

Judgments of the Court are quite another matter. At least in States where the Convention is recognised as directly applying in internal law, judgments of the Court may not be disregarded by national judges, even though, according to Article 53 of the Convention, the judgment is binding on the parties only and has no effect *erga omnes*.

T. Mayer-Maly (Private life and permanent contractual obligations, human rights and third-parties): for specialists in private law Article 8 raises the question: does this provision mean that contractual or legal obligations constitute a barrier to certain forms of private life? In relationships between members of a company or between employers and employees, it may be strongly in the interests of one party to a contract that the other's private life should be such as not to cause prejudice to the company or enterprise. Hence it is natural, for example, to forbid a partner in a trust company or an employee in a savings bank to frequent gaming houses, not so much on account of the temptation to misappropriate the firm's money, as for the risk of damaging its reputation.

Apart from this aspect of Article 8, the question arises whether the fundamental rights guaranteed by the Convention do not tend to have more effect on third-parties than those fundamental rights of the Bonn Basic Law, to which some German law professors (notably Nipperdey) attribute absolute effect. In the interpretation of the Human Rights Convention, the assumption of an effect on third-parties should, in my view, be limited to such acts of private law as general conditions of sale, which, by reason of their social implications, are almost equivalent to substantive law.

K. Vasak (Political Rights): the work begun in 1950 with the signature of the European Convention on Human Rights has been actively continued since that time, since two Protocols concluded in 1952 and 1963 have completed the list of rights which are protected by the collective guarantee. As in 1950, these two Protocols are inspired by the Universal Declaration of Human Rights and, in general, by the work of the United Nations. This illustrates the intention not to consider the achievement of 1950 as final, an achievement which—it must never be forgotten—was due to the active co-operation of the parliamentary organ of the Council of Europe, the Consultative Assembly, with the diplomatic organ, the Committee of Ministers. Does this not prove the desire of European statesmen to give legal expression to a certain political ideology which should become that of the whole of Europe? In other words, is the European Convention on Human Rights based on a specific ideology?

Certainly, the Preamble to the Convention speaks of 'a common heritage of political traditions and ideals'. However, is this common heritage anything more than a liberal approach to all the problems in which it is necessary to reveal the presence of man and to resolve them in function of his humanity? In order to give a definite answer to this question, it would be necessary to analyse the ideological and political content of each of the rights protected by the Convention. I will limit myself to considering a single right—the right of property —which constitutes for all political systems and at all periods of man's legal development a barometer—or even a catalyst—of the political colour of the system and of the country where it exists. It is not hard to see that the right of property—or, more precisely, the right to respect for one's property—as defined in the first Article of the Protocol, is equally consistent with the democratic socialism of the Scandinavian countries and with the traditionally liberal economy of the Federal Republic of Germany, while it is not inconsistent with the so-called 'concerted' or democratically-planned economy of modern France.

Does this mean that the authors of the Convention had no political objective? The fame of these authors, some of whom may be included among the greatest statesmen in Europe since the end of the Second World War, forbids a negative reply. We must nevertheless recognise that these men were inspired by their enthusiasm for the building of a new Europe and really had only one political objective: that the Convention on Human Rights should open the way for European unity and become the final guarantee for democracy in Europe. This was the reason why they selected in the first place from the Universal Declaration the civil and political rights, leaving aside for the moment—but, as they hoped, provisionally—the economic and social rights. Thus the European Convention may be seen as a transposition on to the international plane of the work begun in

1789 by the French Revolution. Indeed, with the Declaration of the Rights of Man and of the Citizen, the revolutionaries of 1789 opened the way for the unity of France, which Napoleon was to achieve by using methods on which the Declaration would have frowned. The authors of the Convention aimed at nothing more nor less than the unity of Europe; they did not wish, however, that a Napoleon on the European scale should appear and complete the work of unity.

What happened to the political objective which underlies each provision of the Convention? When one considers the statistics on the rights which are invoked before the European Commission of Human Rights, one observes that those who claim to be victims are principally concerned with the protection of their individual freedom. Indeed, it is the judicial rights contained in Articles 5 and 6 which are invoked the most frequently, that is to say, the least political of all; by contrast, the real political rights such as the right to freedom of opinion, freedom of the press, freedom of association, and so on, are on the whole neglected by applicants—and these are the rights which may be individual as regards their beneficiaries, but are collective as regards their social effect. Should we conclude that the European of 1966 is only concerned with protecting what is personal to him and ignores the interests of the community? In other words, has the European of today ceased to be a worthy descendant of Athens and of Rome and become a simple *homo economicus*, a Latin formula which barely covers up the customer and the consumer?

Two different replies, which are apparently contradictory, may be given to this painful question. First of all, it is quite clear that this neglect of the political rights protected by the Convention is but a minor aspect—though a very significant one—of the growing political indifference of the European peoples. This indifference has been often noted and is too well known to require demonstration. Nevertheless, this pessimistic conclusion about the future of the European *homo politicus* is only partly correct; if the applicants to the European Commission of Human Rights are led to invoke judicial rights more often than political rights, is this not because the European States are particularly careful to protect the latter? If this conclusion corresponds to the facts, then democracy in the Member States of the Council of Europe has still a promising future.

However, it still remains true that this political indifference in Europe and the consequential character of the applications lodged with the Commission have had the result that the Convention on Human Rights has been transformed into an instrument of legal unification, whereas it should have been, in the first place, an instrument of political unification. However regrettable it may be, this conclusion seems inescapable. Does this mean that we should go into reverse? Probably not; because the Convention, by becoming less political and by constituting a means of legal unification in Europe, is more likely to open up in the direction of that other Europe of which we are more conscious in Vienna than elsewhere. It thus appears that in making the Convention less political, we come back to politics, but to the policy of understanding, of friendship and of peace which the whole of Europe should enjoy.

SUMMING UP BY

ULRICH SCHEUNER

While endorsing Mr Golsong's views, I would like to comment as follows on Professor Unger's statement: I do not agree that the European Convention on Human Rights should be geared to dynamic technological developments, and the like. No uniform solution has as yet been found as regards the right to privacy. It is the task of the Convention to confirm and, if need be, supplement municipal law, but on no account to replace it.

Professor Ermacora recognises that the European Courts promote integration, although the Court of the European Communities and the Court of Human Rights are not of equal importance in this respect. While the Court of the European Communities is virtually a federal institution, the role of the Human Rights Court is to guarantee such human rights as have been acknowledged to date. In this respect, I take an intermediate attitude between MM. Winkler and Ermacora.

I agree with Professor Ermacora's interpretation of Article 1 of the Protocol. Article 3 has assumed importance because of its reflex action.

Professor Pfeifer's account of Articles 7 (2) and 60 does not seem convincing. Where municipal law conflicts with Article 7, the latter is not applicable. There is therefore no contradiction.

Provisions which prohibit marriage are quite defensible. One need only think of a long-term prisoner who wishes to marry.

I agree with Mr Golsong's view that judicial decisions as such are significant for integration. That is why all Council of Europe Member States, even those which have not acceded to the Convention, are represented on the Court (Arts. 20 and 38). As a result, the Convention exerts an influence even in countries which have not signed it.

There is no doubt, as Mr Mayer-Maly said, that the interpretation of fundamental rights has undergone further development; but it is questionable whether objective principles applicable to relations

T

between individuals can be derived from provisions defining fundamental rights.

I agree with Mr Vasak that the centre or centres of gravity of the Convention have shifted.

CHAPTER VII

Consequences of the application of the Convention in municipal and international law

REPORT BY

ROGER PINTO

The application of the Convention to persons subject to the jurisdiction of a Contracting State depends on governmental, administrative and judicial authorities.

The responsibility of Governments—both the executive and legislative branches—is fundamental. It is for them to ensure that the rules laid down in the Convention are applied in the domestic legal system. For this purpose, it is not enough for the Convention to have been duly ratified and published. It must have become law for the administrative and judicial authorities. Nor is it enough for the rules laid down by the Convention to have become law; in addition, their immediate application must be possible. Where this is not the case, the national law-making authorities must adopt internal measures for their application that will give concrete expression to the general principles laid down in the Convention. Lastly, Governments must ensure that no municipal rule which is incompatible with those established by the Convention can take precedence over them. The effect of this obligation is twofold: first, the precedence of the rules established by the Convention over national rules, previously or subsequently adopted, must be guaranteed; then, the interpretation of the rules established by the Convention given by the competent organs of the Convention must be binding on the national authorities, whoever they may be.

Any inadequacy on the part of the Government may prevent the effective application of the Convention by governmental authorities and judges. However, by failing to avail themselves of the full resources of municipal and international law to ensure effective application, such authorities and judges may engage the international responsibility of their State. Their role must not be overlooked. The obligations of Contracting States result from the good faith owing to treaties under general international law; but the Convention itself refers to them in several Articles, which should be recalled forthwith.

275

In Article 1, the Contracting States undertake to secure to everyone within their jurisdiction the rights and freedoms defined in Section 1 of the Convention. These rights and freedoms, therefore, must of necessity be incorporated, without exception, into municipal law. Article 60 stipulates that the provisions of the Convention shall not be construed as limiting or derogating from any of the human rights and fundamental freedoms which may be ensured under municipal laws. This implies that municipal laws may not be construed as limiting or derogating from any of the rights and freedoms ensured by the Convention.

What is more, according to Article 13, everyone whose rights and freedoms as set forth in the Convention are violated shall have an effective remedy before a national authority. Article 24 authorises any Contracting Party to refer to the Commission of Human Rights any alleged breach of the provisions of the Convention by another Contracting Party.

Article 32 provides for a binding decision by the Committee of Ministers, after report by the Commission, to determine whether there has been a violation of the Convention. Articles 45 and 48 establish recourse to the Court of Human Rights, provided its jurisdiction has been accepted as compulsory by the Respondent State. In this case the States which are parties in the action undertake to abide by the decision of the Court (Art. 53). The Secretary-General of the Council of Europe is empowered to ask any State bound by the Convention to furnish an explanation 'of the manner in which its internal law ensures the effective application of any of the provisions of this Convention' (Art. 57).

The problems arising in connection with the application of the Convention should be considered with the foregoing provisions in mind.

1. Introduction of the rules established by the Convention into municipal law.

2. Measures for the application of the rules established by the Convention.

3. The interpretation of the rules established by the Convention by municipal courts and by the organs of the Convention.

In conclusion, we shall consider what remedies are best suited to correct the shortcomings and inadequacies observed.

1. *Introduction of the rules established by the Convention into municipal law*

For all States bound by the Convention, its rules are in a sense part of their internal legal system. It would be a contradiction in terms to maintain the contrary (*pacta sunt servanda*). But it may happen that not all the organs and authorities of the State are capable of applying the rules laid down by the Convention within the limits of the powers conferred upon them by internal law. The powers of Parliaments and Governments are not ordinarily so limited; the rules of the Convention may be said to apply immediately and directly to them.

Administrative agents and departments are placed under the authority of the Government from which they receive their instructions, and so the Government's obligation to respect the rules laid down by a Convention which has entered into force is necessarily extended to them as well.

But, in addition, these bodies, agents and departments of the State must have official knowledge of regularly ratified or approved international agreements. An international agreement, approved or ratified by a head of State, may remain secret, or be known to the Prime Minister alone, or to one or the other of them. In such a case, neither the Parliament nor the governmental or administrative authorities will be able to apply an unpublished agreement. Hence, the French Constitution does not attribute legal effect to treaties until after their publication. This formality has been interpreted strictly by the *Conseil d'État*. Its decisions do not recognise the right of an individual to invoke an international treaty against the authorities if the latter do not know the existence of the treaty.

The publication required for municipal laws and regulations must actually have taken place.[1] In Swiss practice the publication of treaties has only a declaratory value, according to P. Guggenheim.[2] Lastly, it is principally the Courts whose jurisdiction is often restricted to the application of internal laws. Consequently, they cannot apply international conventions which have not been made a part of municipal law.

The force of municipal law must, then, be given to international conventions, but it may also be taken away from them. The Courts will again be powerless to apply the rules laid down by convention.

Two systems have been adopted by positive constitutional law. Under one, the international agreement is incorporated into the State legal system directly, following the same procedure as for the entry into force of internal laws, particularly with regard to publication. Under the other, the international agreement must be incorporated in a municipal law.

[1] Conseil d'État, 30 October 1964, *Société Prosagor et autres*, *Clunet*, 1965, p. 121. Mr Paul de Visscher states that in Belgium publication in the *Moniteur Belge* is also necessary, in pursuance of Article 8 of the Act of 31 May 1961.

[2] On Swiss practice, see P. Guggenheim, 'Le conflit entre le droit des gens et le droit national dans l'ordre juridique suisse', *Mélanges Perassi*, 1957, and *Traité*, vol. I, p. 36 et seq.

A. *Direct incorporation*

Only five States which are Contracting Parties to the Convention on Human Rights use the system of direct incorporation: Netherlands, Austria, Luxembourg, Turkey and Cyprus. Switzerland and France will also belong to this category once they have ratified the Convention.

In this connection, the Constitution of the Netherlands (Arts. 63 to 65) is a model.[1] In Cyprus, Article 169, para. 3, of the Constitution confers binding force upon international treaties, on their publication in the Official Gazette of the Republic. The situation is the same in Luxembourg and Turkey, by virtue of their constitutional practice and the decisions of their Courts.

It follows that in these States the rules laid down by convention should have a legal effect at least equal to that of constitutional rules.

However, the practical implementation of this pre-eminence of rules laid down by convention is contingent upon the existence of an effective control by the Courts of the constitutionality of laws. The Netherlands Constitution stipulates that the laws of the Kingdom are not to be applied when doing so would be incompatible with the provisions of international agreements (Art. 66). During the last ten years, however, there has been no instance of a decision refusing to apply a law because it was incompatible with a previous treaty.[2] In Austria, since the Act of 4 March 1964, granting the force of constitutional law to the Convention, the Constitutional Court has full powers to refuse to apply an ordinary law if it is contrary to the rules established by the Convention. It decided not to avail itself of this right of control in a decision of 14 October 1961 (*Yearbook*, IV, p. 604). In Luxembourg, certain decisions of the *Cour de Cassation* and *Conseil d'État* would seem to imply that such control is in the hands of the Courts, but the Luxembourg Court of Summary Jurisdiction did not consider that it could use it.[3] There is no such test of constitutionality in Turkey. The Convention has, moreover, been 'ratified' by the Legislative Assembly. In that country, therefore, the Convention at the level of domestic law will only have the force of an ordinary law. Its provisions can, therefore, be thwarted by a subsequent enactment. This would also be the case in States in which an Act must be passed to incorporate the Convention into the legal system.

---

[1] Van Panhuys 'The Netherlands Constitution and International Law; a decade of experience', *AJIL*, January 1964, p. 88.

[2] Van Panhuys, op. cit.

[3] Decision of 24 October 1960, *Yearbook*, IV, p. 622.

B. *Incorporation of the rules established by the Convention by means of legislation*

Under this system the Convention is incorporated into the internal legal system by the adoption of a law. By this procedure, its provisions have no greater legal force than those of an ordinary law. Any subsequent law incompatible with it must be followed by the judge. Sometimes the Act authorising ratification provides that the Convention will be fully operative, or will have the force of law, or will be enforced like a State enactment. This is the case in Italy, Belgium, Greece and the Federal Republic of Germany.[1] Sometimes the Convention is ratified without being given the status of municipal law by the legislature. A separate Act is then required for this purpose. Such is the case in the United Kingdom, Ireland, Iceland, Denmark and Sweden. In Norway the Constitution requires action by Parliament before a treaty can become a source of obligations (Art. 26, para. 2); this condition may have been met.[2] In the other States using this system no law has been enacted bringing the provisions of the Convention into effect in the municipal system. Hence, the Courts are officially unaware of the Convention. The consequences of this are not serious in States which allow the right of individual application, such as Iceland, Ireland and the Scandinavian States. But in the United Kingdom, counsel for the defence in Soblen's case were unable to invoke the European Convention on Human Rights in his favour.[3]

It must be stressed that in itself the system which requires enactment of internal legislation to ensure the application of an international convention offers certain advantages—*on condition, of course, that such legislation is in fact enacted.*

The experience of the International Labour Organisation in the application of international conventions may be recalled here. The Committee of Experts to study the technical aspects of the application of conventions suggested in its reports in 1962, and again in

---

[1] M. Valticos, 'Les rapports des traités et de la loi en Grèce', *Revue Hellènique de Droit International*, 1958; P. de Visscher, ' Droit et Jurisprudence belge en matière d'inexécution des conventions internationales', *Revue Belge de Droit International*, 1963, p. 125.

[2] Supreme Court, 16 December 1961, *Yearbook*, VI, p. 286.

[3] Soblen was convicted of espionage in the United States and had to be hospitalised in the United Kingdom while being transferred from Israel to the United States by air. The British Government refused him political asylum, and decided to deport him, not to the country of his choice but to the United States, although Soblen could not, because of the nature of his offence, have been extradited had extradition been requested (24 August 1962, Decision of the Queen's Bench Division; 31 August 1962, decision of the Court of Appeal; cf. letters to *The Times* by R. Pinto, 10 September 1962, and Dr Kaufman, Soblen's solicitor, of 11 September).

1963, that national legislation should be officially made to conform to ratified conventions, even where such legislation is considered to be tacitly modified or superseded by the act of ratification.[1]

The International Labour Conference endorsed these conclusions and emphasised that, even where previous legislation has been implicitly superseded or amended through the automatic incorporation of a ratified convention into municipal law, it is essential that the legislation be adjusted to conform to the Convention, so that all concerned may be aware of the changes and any uncertainty as to the legal position be avoided.[2] The European Convention on Human Rights is, to be sure, generally known to the persons concerned. The number of applications received by the Commission would seem to bear this out.

Adapting national law to conform to the provisions of conventions, however, would simplify the solution of the second problem which we must consider: the necessity for special measures of application.

2. *Special measures for the application of the rules established by the Convention*

Even after they have been incorporated into municipal law, the rules laid down by conventions are not necessarily applied to the persons concerned. National courts may decide that certain provisions of the Convention only relate to States and are valid for them, but also require the adoption by them of measures of application.[3] They may also consider that the provisions of the Convention do not constitute sufficiently specific rules to allow of their direct application and consequently necessitate the adoption of special measures of application.

The Netherlands Court of Cassation, for example, has decided that Article 13 of the Convention cannot, by its nature, be applied directly.[4] Also, the Austrian Constitutional Court held that Article 6 of the Convention, by virtue of the 'lack of precision of the few notions embodied in it', establishes only 'principles constituting a

---

[1] Quoted by M. Valticos, 'les Conventions Internationales du Travail devant le juge français', *Revue critique de Droit International privé*, 1964, 41, 69–72.

[2] Quoted by M. Valticos, loc. cit. However, there is a danger that the implementation of the international convention by municipal law may give rise to differences of interpretations. The International Institute for the Unification of Private Law has observed that some provisions of conventions have been taken over by national law-makers in modified form (cf. Report by Prof. E. Wahl on the uniform interpretation of European treaties, Council of Europe document 1650 of 13 September 1963, para. 11 (2)).

[3] Cf. Luxembourg Court of Summary Jurisdiction, 24 October 1960, *Yearbook*, IV, p. 622.

[4] Decision of 24 February 1960, quoted by K. Vasak, *La Convention européenne des Droits de l'Homme*, Nos. 444 and 447.

programme . . . but which do not in themselves constitute an immediately applicable body of law'.[1]

The Court gave a similar decision relating to Article 5 (3). On the basis of these decisions, M. K. Vasak has concluded that for the Constitutional Court, and thus for Austria, the Convention is merely an 'outline law' which the Courts cannot apply in the absence of measures of implementation.[2]

In the light of these precedents, it should be considered whether or not the provisions of the Convention are *self-executing*. The interpretation adopted by national courts is not necessarily the same in every case. Moreover, their interpretations are not necessarily the same as that of the organs of the Convention.

This is the third problem we shall consider.

3. *The interpretation of the Convention by national courts and by the organs of the Convention*

The problem of diverging interpretations of the provisions of a single treaty by the national courts responsible for applying them is a classic one. Where there is no body competent to ensure uniformity of jurisprudence, Contracting States may endeavour, using diplomatic channels, to arrive at an agreed interpretation that will be accepted by their courts. The Convention may also attempt to accomplish this by means of arbitration, or recourse to an international court.

The European Convention on Human Rights has instituted a coherent system designed to ensure the uniform interpretation of its provisions. Any Contracting State may refer to the Commission any alleged breach of the Convention by another Contracting Party (Art. 24). Such a breach may plainly result from a mistaken interpretation of the Convention by the legislative or judicial organs of the Contracting State. This procedure ends with a decision that is binding upon the parties, taken either by the Committee of Ministers or by the Court.

In fact, Contracting States make virtually no use of this procedure, although it is open to them. If they hesitate to avail themselves of it, one cannot easily imagine that they will accept a new procedure to determine the interpretation of the Convention in the form of references of a point of law to the Court by national tribunals. Similarly, the attempt to empower the Court to give opinions to Contracting Parties on questions of interpretation arising out of their draft laws or regulations had little chance of success. It implied a form of supervision which States are reluctant to accept or to operate effectively.

[1] Decision of 17 June 1960, *Yearbook*, III, p. 616.   [2] Op. cit., no. 457.

I believe that the Convention, in its present form, renders possible the attempt which is necessary to ensure a uniform interpretation. The attention of Contracting States should be drawn in good time to national decisions which seem to be in conflict with the interpretation of the provisions adopted by the Commission or Court, or with other national decisions on the same question. It may be recalled that Contracting Parties have at their disposal the procedure of reference to the Commission under Article 24 for a uniform interpretation of the provisions of the Convention.

In this connection, when the requests go out for an explanation of the method of implementation of the Convention in individual contracting States (Art. 57), the Secretary-General of the Council of Europe might stress the problem of uniform interpretation and the procedures available for settling it.

A decisive step would be if all Contracting Parties were to recognise the right of individual application to the Commission and the compulsory jurisdiction of the Court.[1] Uniform interpretation would then be ensured by the regular process of application and recourse, as it is in municipal systems. The only feature lacking would be appeal 'in the interest of the law', which some legislations have adopted. Recourse to the Commission by States would accomplish this to some extent.

While waiting for the golden age of the Convention to arrive, it is not impossible to contribute towards its uniform application by Contracting States through the unremitting conveyance of information, by word-of-mouth and writing, to jurists, judges, lawyers and professors. A body of precedents has already been created by the organs of the Convention, clarifying its contents and scope. The decisions of the Commission and of the Court, even if they do not have the value of *res judicata*, provide precedents for national courts whose authority cannot be disregarded without serious reasons.

WRITTEN COMMUNICATION BY

A. H. ROBERTSON

There are two points made in Professor Pinto's report on which I should like to comment. These are his statement that the Convention is no doubt sufficiently well known to the interested parties, as evidenced by the number of applications received by the Commission; and his emphasis on the need, in the interest of uniform inter-

---

[1] Only ten States have accepted the right of individual application, and nine the compulsory jurisdiction of the Court. There are eighteen Member States of the Council of Europe.

pretation, to make better known to lawyers, judges and professors the jurisprudence[1] of the Commission and the Court, and of national courts interpreting the Convention.

On the first point, I have some doubts. While it is clear that the Convention is becoming better known—particularly, they say, in certain prisons in Germany and Austria—in my experience it appears that many lawyers in our member countries know little or nothing about it. There are of course exceptions, but we should work to secure that ignorance is the exception and knowledge the rule.

On the need for making better known the jurisprudence—both national and international—relating to the Convention, I am in complete agreement. The conclusion I draw from both points, therefore, is that there is an important task to be undertaken in publicising the Convention itself, the work of the Commission, the Court and the Committee of Ministers, and the jurisprudence of these organs and of the national courts.

A good deal on these lines is already being done—perhaps more than is generally realised. My object here is to say a few words about this work and make some suggestions about how it could be further developed.

Probably the most important task falls on the Universities and Institutes of European Studies in the Member States and a number of them have responded handsomely to this challenge. At least five now have separate courses either on the international protection of human rights in general, or specifically on the European Convention. And about eighty other universities, colleges and institutes in thirteen countries include teaching about the Convention either in their general course on international law or in other courses on international organisations or on European Institutions.[2] The results of an enquiry which we have made on this subject (which are probably incomplete) are contained in a document entitled *Teaching about the European Convention on Human Rights in Universities* (doc. H (65) 13), copies of which we have made available to those interested.

A great deal is also done by the non-governmental organisations to make the Convention more widely known by arranging meetings and study courses, and in their publications. They have a particular role to play in relation to the various specialised groups which they represent and we should be grateful for all that they have already done and will, no doubt, continue to do.

[1] I use the word 'jurisprudence' in the continental sense of decided cases, or case law.
[2] It is also noteworthy that several universities in the United States offer separate courses on the international protection of human rights or include this subject in other courses.

But the Council of Europe itself has a particular responsibility in this respect, as the sponsor and guardian of the Convention. What it has been doing may be considered under three separate headings:

(a) *Publications*

The annual *Yearbook of the Convention on Human Rights* is the most important single source of information. It is generally well-known. I should like to see it in all the university libraries in all our Member States, but regret that this is not yet the case. The same may be said for the publications of the Court.

The Secretariat in Strasbourg puts out a whole series of other publications which are less well-known. They include the volumes of *Selected Decisions of the Commission* (published thrice annually), the *Collected Texts* (which assemble together the Convention and its four Protocols, the Rules of Procedure of the Commission and the Court, the ratifications, optional declarations, reservations, etc.), the *Manual of the Convention* and individual booklets containing the Report of the Commission and the decision of the Committee of Ministers in all cases decided by the latter. These are available without charge to those engaged on teaching or research relating to the Convention.

Other publications relate to particular subjects of topical interest from time to time—for example, the comparison between the European Convention and the draft Inter-American Convention of the Organisation of American States. I make just a passing reference to several books and several dozen articles about the Convention published by members of the Secretariat in their individual capacities.

On the particular subject of decisions of national courts relating to the Convention, which is of special interest to this conference, the Directorate of Human Rights publishes periodically a list, with brief summaries, of all national decisions known to us. The latest edition (of March 1965) includes about 130 such decisions which shows that there is plenty of material available to permit studies being made of uniformity of jurisprudence—as suggested by Professor Pinto.

(b) *Study courses*

The Council of Europe organises from time to time study courses on the international protection of human rights, normally lasting a week. They give a prominent place to the European Convention, but are not limited to it. They have the advantage of permitting the students to hear, and hold discussions with, the officials actually engaged on the work of applying the Convention—as well as university professors in a more independent position. Such courses have been organised for one group from North Africa, for another group of students from all five continents brought together by the World Assembly of Youth; thirdly, for a group of European youth leaders financed by the European Cultural Fund, and in September of this year for a group of lawyers and officials from the French-speaking African territories.

These meetings have been very successful. The participants have expressed great interest in what they have learnt, and their astonishment that so much was being done of which so little was known. Unfortunately we have at present no funds permitting us to organise such study courses on our own initiative, and can only do so when some other body or organisation is prepared to finance them.

(c) Lecturing

There is a great demand by universities, institutes of European studies and other organisations for lectures or courses of lectures about the European Convention. While we cannot comply with all the requests received, officials of the Council do what they can to meet this need. Courses of lectures about the Convention have been given at the College of Europe at Bruges and at the International Faculty for the Teaching of Comparative Law. Individual lectures are given on many occasions (so far about 50 this year, including over a dozen in the United States). Students and others seem to find it of particular interest to hear from those who know the problems involved in the application of the Convention at first hand.

The Directorate of Human Rights also receives a constant stream of individual enquiries for information and documentation about the Convention; several hundred such requests are answered each year.

*   *   *   *

All this shows that a good deal is already being done, but in my view much more could and should be done to make the Convention better known in the Member States. Some suggestions as to possible forms of action are the following:

(1) that other universities and institutes should follow the example of those which already offer courses on the international protection of human rights;

(2) that greater use could be made of the facilities offered by the Council of Europe in the field of documentation. I should be glad to send particulars of what is available to anyone who is interested;

(3) if other universities, institutes or organisations could finance visits of students or others to Strasbourg, we should be glad to organise study courses for them on the lines of those which have already taken place;

(4) in the field of jurisprudence and uniform interpretation, we should be glad to lend our assistance to facilitate research and possibly to arrange publication;

(5) I hope that the time will come when our Member Governments will be willing to enable the Directorate of Human Rights to carry out these tasks on a more important scale, particularly as regards the organisation of study courses in Strasbourg and the award of research fellowships.

In any event, one activity of great value, in my opinion, would be the holding of further conferences such as the present one at reasonable intervals in the different Member States in turn.

SUMMARY OF THE DISCUSSION

Seán MacBride (Ratification of the Convention by France): References have been made to the fact that France has not yet ratified the European Convention. This has, of course, caused great concern to all the friends of France. It is hoped that this failure to ratify the Convention was due solely to the temporary difficulties through which France has passed: now that these difficulties have passed, we all look forward to the ratification of the Convention by France. It is hoped that France will find it possible to ratify without reservations; but should the provisions of the French Constitution be regarded as rendering unconditional ratification difficult, France could, as many other countries have done, ratify subject to reservations. Ratification subject to reservations is better than no ratification.

It has been said that one of the reasons which precluded ratification by France was that the Convention was based on Anglo-Saxon legal concepts. This, I think, does not bear examination; the great inspirers and framers of the Convention were eminent French statesmen and lawyers such as President René Cassin, President Robert Schuman and the former *Garde des Sceaux*, Mr P.-H. Teitgen. The European Convention is largely based on the Universal Declaration, one of whose principal architects was President Cassin. France, in effect, may be said to have exerted the dominating influence in regard to the text and concept of both the Universal Declaration and the European Convention: of this France should be justly proud.

Jacqueline Rochette: 'Libre Justice', the French Section of the International Commission of Jurists, has appointed a committee to examine the French point of view regarding ratification of the Human Rights Convention, as explained by the Minister of Justice in his declaration of November 1964. The conclusions of this committee will be widely circulated.

Michel Gaudet: the Conference has learned much from the functioning of the European Communities concerning the applicability of Community law in the various national legal systems, its place in the hierarchy of rules of law and its uniform application in the Member States. In particular, it has been shown that it is advisable for national courts to apply to the Court of Justice of the Communities, in accordance with the machinery set up by the Treaties of Rome and Paris, for a preliminary ruling on the interpretation and, where necessary, on the validity of Community law. This machinery, which is proving its worth in the framework of the European Communities, is providing, if not a model for the application of the European Convention on Human Rights, at least a concrete contribution to that harmonisation of legal systems which is required by the changes now taking place in international society.

Louis B. Sohn: a remarkable trend is becoming apparent in international law: courts are referring more and more frequently to the precedents set by courts in other States, and in presenting their cases to a court lawyers are making increasing use of material from other legal systems.

The Universal Declaration of Human Rights has undergone an important evolution: although its status is only that of a recommendation under international law, it is often quoted and has even been used as a basis for decisions, with the result that it is assuming more and more the character of a rule of law. The Universal Declaration of Human Rights should be taken into account more frequently in decisions in European States, too, especially in those which are not parties to the European Convention.

Similarly, the European Convention can influence the jurisprudence of the United Nations and the courts of States not bound by the Convention. It might be useful, therefore, to prepare a digest of European decisions on human rights, arranged in accordance with the relevant articles of the United Nations Declaration and Covenants, and to submit it to the United Nations for distribution to all Member States.

C. A. Fleischhauer: it is undoubtedly desirable that the national courts of Member States should adopt the interpretation given by the Strasbourg authorities to the individual provisions of the substantive part of the Convention. On the other hand, it must be remembered that these provisions are worded in such a way that several interpretations are possible; moreover, the Convention does not stipulate that the decisions of the Commission and the Court *must* be taken into account. A divergent interpretation by national courts need not necessarily be a disadvantage, however, for the Member States of the Convention belong to different legal systems and have different legal traditions. An interpretation of the substantive provisions of the

Convention, conforming with the relevant national legal tradition, could, even if it departs in certain details from the precedents of the Commission and the Court, make a greater contribution than by simply following the precedents of the Strasbourg authorities, towards establishing the Convention firmly in the traditions of the individual legal systems. This would also make it easier for the Commission and the Court to evaluate the true European standard for the protection of human rights.

A divergent interpretation would be dangerous only if it conflicted with the letter and the spirit of the Convention. We must agree with Section 3 of the Report on this point. For it is evident that the aims of the Convention can be fully attained only if the competence of the Commission and the Court are recognised, since they provide a means of redress in cases where a divergent interpretation leads to a violation of the Convention.

CHAPTER VIII

The protection of human rights on a universal basis: recent experience and proposals

REPORT BY

J. E. S. FAWCETT[1]

I. INTRODUCTION

The United Nations has since its foundation taken as one of its prime tasks the global implementation of human rights. I use the word 'global', which is to me more concrete than 'universal', to express three ideas: that the modes of implementation which we are now to discuss are those which are not designed for any one region of the world, however large or small; that they must be adequate to meet any situation, in which a human right is in issue, in any part of the world; and that they are primarily international rather than national in form.

This paper will review briefly the possible modes of implementation, try to see what can be inferred from the experience of the last twenty years about their merits and weaknesses, and then to suggest what might usefully be discussed in this field at the present conference.

Global implementation of human rights may be effected, broadly, through publicity; judicial process; or international supervision. I deliberately avoid any attempt to set these modes in an absolute order of effectiveness; for it is possible both to underestimate and to overestimate the effectiveness of each, which must vary with time and place and the kind of right in issue. But at particular stages in the global advancement of human rights, it may be wise to give temporary priority of effort to one of them.

II. PUBLICITY

Publicity for human rights is perhaps itself almost a fundamental human right. To know what is being done is the beginning of any implementation of human rights, and to care, when what is done is

---

[1] This paper was prepared in place of a contribution by Professor Andrew Martin, Q.C., which his duties on the new Law Commission prevented him from making. The writer had the use of a valuable note specially prepared by Mr Samuels of the University of Southampton.

against human rights, is the condition of making that implementation effective. Publicity for human rights consists in making known to every person at least those minimum standards of treatment to which he or she is entitled; in making known violations of human rights, wherever they may occur; and in continual public debate, serving to rationalise and broaden those standards. The vital part of the Press in the protection and advancement of human rights needs no elaboration; but I will recall the words of Jeremy Bentham, who was ready to put all the eggs of progress in the basket of publicity. Of his *Plan for a Universal and Perpetual Peace*, written between 1786 and 1789, he says:

The object is . . . an universal and perpetual peace; the globe is the field of dominion to which the author aspires; the Press, the engine, and the only one he employs.[1]

The Universal Declaration of Human Rights of 1948 has pride of place as a public proclamation of 'a common standard of achievement for all peoples and all nations'; and even the optimists in 1948, amid the disappointment that the Declaration fell short of a binding covenant, can hardly have foreseen the political impact that it was to have. Through public debate in the United Nations, and publicity through the world, it has worked as a formation of an international conscience; and it is the mine from which the UN Draft Covenants,[2] regional conventions and national constitutions, protecting human rights, have been and are being quarried. Invoked in the United Nations over the treatment of Indians, and apartheid, in South Africa, over Soviet labour camps, and over the restriction of movement of the Soviet wives of foreigners, the Declaration has established the principle that the denial of human rights is a matter of international concern, and has gone far to remove Article 2 (7) of the UN Charter as an obstacle to United Nations action; though that clause is still a refuge for those wanting to avoid the implementation provisions of the Draft Covenants.

Perhaps the greatest political impact of the Declaration has been through the idea of self-determination which, on the direction of the General Assembly,[3] was embodied in the Draft Covenants,[4] and

[1] Quoted from F. H. Hinsley, *Power and the Pursuit of Peace*, Cambridge University Press, 1963, p. 86, a most illuminating historical study of international relations.
[2] For texts of and full commentaries on the Draft Covenants see *UN General Assembly Official Records*: Doc. A/2929 and A/5411. The text of the UN Covenants has, in the meantime, been approved by the General Assembly in its Resolution 2200 (xxi) of 16 December 1966. (Editor's note.)
[3] Resolution 545, VI.
[4] Article 1 of both Covenants.

made the subject of a UN Declaration in 1960. The substantive clauses of the article in the Draft Covenants read:

1. All peoples and all nations shall have the right of self-determination, namely, the right freely to determine their political, economic, social and cultural status.

and

3. The right of peoples to self-determination shall also include permanent sovereignty over their natural wealth and resources. In no case may a people be deprived of its own means of subsistence on the grounds of any rights that may be claimed by other States.

There has of course been much debate in the United Nations as to whether these are political principles or legal rights and, if the former, whether they have a proper place in a Covenant containing provisions for judicial settlement, and whether again the concepts of, for example, 'peoples', 'freely', and 'status' are not too large and elusive to be adequately dealt with in one short sentence. Here the experience of the 'Committee of Twenty-four',[1] established to follow up the similar Declaration on Self-determination of 1960, shows that even its political implementation is not untroubled by the conflict that there may be between national independence and self-determination. For example, in the case of Rhodesia the Committee took the right, if for it the perhaps unusual, course of urging the metropolitan country to withhold the granting of independence until the existing constitution be changed to give self-determination to the majority. But it demanded without qualification independence for Fiji, where the indigenous people own 80 per cent of the land but rather more than half the population are Indian immigrants. It is not surprising that the Fijian Affairs Board also asked the United Kingdom to delay independence until constitutional provisions could be worked out protecting the rights of both communities. This experience shows how closely the effectiveness of implementation is limited by the nature of the right.

The formation of public opinion and the proclamation of standards has gone forward in other declarations and other agencies. For example, the UNESCO Convention on Discrimination in Education 1960, the UN Declaration on Racial Discrimination 1963, and the draft Convention, prepared by the UN Human Rights Commission, on the elimination of all forms of religious intolerance[2] are all serving to extend and elaborate the Universal Declaration. The subsidiary organs of the United Nations and their work are well known, but

---

[1] Initially a Committee of seventeen Members.
[2] *Economic and Social Council Official Records*: E/4024 (April 1965).

it is interesting to see the breadth of the studies recently organised through seminars or conferences by the United Nations and its agencies: Criminal Procedure (in this city of Vienna in 1960 and in New York, 1961); Habeas Corpus (Mexico City, 1961); Status of Women in Family Law (Tokyo, 1962); Freedom of Information (Delhi, 1962 and 1964); Rights of the Child (Warsaw, 1963); Role of the Police (Canberra, 1963).

To these may be added the UN Yearbooks on Human Rights. Containing contributions from governments, they are variable in form and quality, though those by France and Germany are usually outstanding, and they may, given their sources, suffer from complacency.

Here then we must not forget the influence at many levels of the independent work and publications of non-governmental bodies such as the International Commission of Jurists, the Civil Liberties Union in the United States, the Ligue Belge des Droits de l'Homme, and Amnesty International.

I have tried to stress the aspect of publicity because, though its effect may be slow and unspectacular, often even unremarked, it is the medium through which human rights come to be understood, recognised, and elaborated, and their denial, where it occurs, made known; it is therefore a real and indeed essential mode of implementation.

III. JUDICIAL SETTLEMENT

The Draft Covenant on Civil and Political Rights would assign certain tasks and responsibilities to the International Court of Justice. In the first place, Article 44 would authorise the Human Rights Committee, which I shall return to later, to recommend to the Economic and Social Council that it give an advisory opinion on any legal question connected with a matter of which the Committee is seized; Article 46 would confer compulsory jurisdiction on the Court in case of failure to reach a settlement of a complaint under Article 43; Article 47 reserves the general jurisdiction of the Court. No other form of international judicial settlement is envisaged by the Draft Covenants.

The choice of the International Court is justified not least by the fact that the Court has, like its predecessor, often handled or had raised before it issues that would fall within the Draft Covenant on Civil and Political Rights. We may recall the *Asylum* and *de la Torre Cases*;[1] the *Ambatielos Case*;[2] the *Guardianship of Infants Convention*

---

[1] Cf. Draft Covenant, Article 13.
[2] Ibid., Article 14.

Case;[1] *the Aerial Incident (July 1955) Case*;[2] the *South West Africa Case*;[3] and the *Cameroun Case*;[4] also the advisory opinions on *Reparation for Injuries*; *Interpretation of the Peace Treaties*; the *Status of South West Africa and its supervision*;[5] *Reservations to the Genocide Convention*; the *Awards of the UN and of the ILO Administrative Tribunals*.[6] In all these cases human rights as set out in the Draft Covenant were directly in issue or the problem of their implementation is, in one form or another, raised.

Two comments may be offered on the proposed advisory opinion procedure. First, it could be a useful device for overcoming the obstacle presented by the fact that the Draft Covenant does not recognise the right of individual petition. The International Court in its advisory opinion on a *Judgment of the ILO Administrative Tribunal on Complaints against UNESCO (1956)*, and the European Court of Human Rights in the *Lawless* and *De Becker Cases* have demonstrated that it is possible to establish an effective 'equality of arms' in hearing a complaint by an individual against public authority, even though the individual cannot himself be a party to the proceedings.

On the other hand, the proposed procedure might under the constitutional law of the United Nations have limitations. When consulted on the point by the Human Rights Commission, the UN Secretary-General reported that, in his opinion,[7] the Human Rights Committee would not be an organ of the UN or a specialised agency,[8] that it would be contrary to the intent and policy of Article 96 of the Charter for ECOSOC to be a mere intermediary in requesting an opinion of the Court on behalf of the Committee, but that it would be legally permissible for the Committee to 'make suggestions to a competent organ that that organ submit a request for an advisory opinion on a legal question arising out of the work of the committee'. The similar course followed by the ILO in obtaining opinions from the Permanent Court may be recalled. However, since ECOSOC may request advisory opinions only on questions arising within 'the scope of its activities',[9] it would appear that the Committee could recommend a request for an opinion only upon a question with which ECOSOC could reasonably be concerned in performing its functions under Article 62 of the Charter. But there is no doubt that access to

---

[1] Ibid., Article 22 (4).   [2] Ibid., Article 6.
[3] Cf. several Articles of the Draft Covenant.   [4] Ibid., Article 23.
[5] Cf. several Articles of the Draft Covenant.
[6] Draft Covenant, Article 14.
[7] *Economic and Social Council Official Records*, E/1732.
[8] It is not obvious why the Human Rights Committee, having a wide international competence, should not be brought into relationship with the UN as a specialised agency under Articles 57 and 63 of the Charter.
[9] General Assembly Resolution 89, I.

the opinion of the Court on legal questions would be not only of the greatest assistance to the Committee but an unrivalled means of objective and orderly interpretation of the Covenant.

The prospects are not bright of a wide acceptance of Article 46, conferring a compulsory jurisdiction on the International Court, at the suit of the State complained of or lodging a complaint, if no solution has been reached by the Human Rights Committee under Article 43.

First, a number of countries in the debates on the Draft Covenant have retired behind the wall of domestic jurisdiction, as a bar to the international judicial settlement of human rights disputes, and we have to listen to arguments from them in defence of national sovereignty which would have been very acceptable to the Holy Alliance. But there is a failing in another quarter. The brute fact is that the new States that have joined the UN since 1946 have shown little confidence in the Court and no enthusiasm for judicial settlement in any form. The great majority have not accepted its compulsory jurisdiction, even with the subtle and numerous reservations that have become fashionable among some of the older countries. Of the sixty or more States that have become parties to the Statute of the Court since that year only six have accepted the optional clause: Cambodia, Israel, Pakistan, Somalia, Sudan and Uganda.

There is the further hindrance to the use of the Court that States, for reasons which often have little or nothing to do with the merits of the case but which they find overriding, show themselves unwilling to litigate with each other in the International Court on matters that might disturb their public relations, so that Article 46, even if adopted, would provide less protection for human rights than it seems to offer.

Reservation is no solution, for even given the principle laid down by the Court for reservations to the Genocide Convention, it would surely be unacceptable that States should be free to accept the Draft Covenant, reserving the application of Article 46; for effective implementation is one of the essential objectives of the Covenant. The problem of reservations to the Covenant has in any case not yet been resolved.

IV. INTERNATIONAL SUPERVISION

It remains to consider the international supervision of human rights. Supervision may be on the one hand indirect and general, a form applicable to those human rights which represent standards of progress rather than rights immediately enforceable; on the other hand, it may be active and specific, a form applicable to those embodied in concrete legal rules, with or without limitations. The first form is represented by what may be called *reporting systems*, the second by *complaint procedures*. The two UN Draft Covenants are constructed broadly on the basis of this distinction.

1. *Reporting systems* have had extensive use. We may recall the work of the Permanent Mandates Commission, the Trusteeship Council, the ILO, and UNESCO, and the important opinions of the International Court on the status of South West Africa and the necessary supervision of its administration.

Periodic reports may be general or directed to the implementation of particular Conventions. The ILO and UNESCO[1] call for both kinds of reports from their members; and ECOSOC has called for triennial reports from members of the UN and of its Specialised Agencies on the progress achieved in the field of human rights on the basis of the Universal Declaration.[2]

In considering the efficacy of a reporting system we may look briefly at how reports are dealt with, the action taken on them, the publicity they can receive, and the measure of co-operation between international agencies working in the same field.

ILO refers reports on the implementation of conventions to a Committee of Experts. The same method is adopted in the European Social Charter. Under the Draft Covenant on Economic, Social and Cultural Rights, ECOSOC *may* transmit the reports submitted by contracting parties, under the obligation assumed in Article 17, to 'the Commission of Human Rights for study and general recommendation or as appropriate for information'.

It will be noted that recommendations are to be 'general', a term which appears to exclude, and to be intended to exclude, recommendations by the Commission to a particular State. Their purpose would then be 'to draw attention to obstacles encountered by States in attaining the full realisation of the rights enumerated in the Covenants and to ascertain what the UN could do to help them to overcome those obstacles'.[3] The international action that might be taken includes 'such methods as conventions, recommendations, technical assistance, regional meetings and technical meetings and studies with governments'.[4] This general approach is feebler than that of the ILO; for its Conference Committee on the Application of Conventions and Recommendations may, on the basis of the report of the Committee of Experts, make observations or recommendations of a general character, or draw the special attention of the conference to particular cases of non-compliance with the ILO Constitution or ratified Conventions; this power has been used to some effect in recent years.

---

[1] For example, in the Convention on Discrimination in Education.
[2] Resolution 624B, XXII.   [3] A/2929, p. 120, para. 19.
[4] Draft Covenant, Article 24.

The Draft Covenant on Economic, Social and Cultural Rights is also not satisfactory in the matter of publicity. An article, to follow Article 24, was at one stage proposed in the following form:

Unless otherwise decided by the Commission on Human Rights or by the Economic and Social Council or requested by the State directly concerned, the Secretary-General of the UN shall arrange for the publication of the report of the Commission of Human Rights. . . .[1]

The Article was deleted, and what is striking is that the arguments made[2] in favour of its retention and of its deletion, both invoke the right of a State to prevent publication of particular matters touching human rights.

There is however recognition of the important need of centralising, as far as possible, the work of global agencies in the field of human rights, and ECOSOC may, under Article 19 of the Draft Covenant, 'make arrangements with the Specialised Agencies in respect of their reporting to it on the progress made in achieving the observance of the provisions of this Covenant falling within the scope of their activities'.[3]

The Draft Covenant on Civil and Political Rights, Article 49, contains requirements for reports by Contracting Parties both initially, and later on request by ECOSOC, on the legislative and other measures, including judicial remedies, which they have adopted to implement the Covenant. These reports may also be referred to the Commission on Human Rights 'for information, study and, if necessary, general recommendations'.

2. *Complaint procedures* are also to be found in ILO practice and the UNESCO Convention on Discrimination in Education.

In January 1950 the ILO established a Fact-Finding Conciliation Commission on Freedom of Association and shortly afterwards ECOSOC decided 'to forward to the Governing Body of the International Labour Office, for its consideration as to referral to the Commission, all allegations regarding infringements of trade union rights received from Governments or trade union or employers' organisations against Member States of the ILO'.[4]

This procedure has already been used with effect on more than one occasion. The inquiries and reports of the Ad Hoc Committee on Forced Labour have also had an important influence.

[1] Viz. made on the basis of reports submitted by Contracting Parties under Article 17.
[2] A/2929, p. 123: paragraphs 36, 37.
[3] Similarly, under Article 17 (2) (*b*), Contracting Parties to the Draft Covenant are required to send copies of their reports made under the Covenant to Specialised Agencies of which they are members.
[4] Resolution 277, X.

The dual function of fact-finding and conciliation as means of dealing with complaints of denials of human rights, is essentially that assigned to the European Commission of Human Rights, and to the Human Rights Committee under the Draft Covenant on Civil and Political Rights.[1]

It is of interest to observe in passing that in the United States, twenty-two States and the District of Columbia have established State Commissions with similar functions in the field of human rights: for example, the New York State Commission for Human Rights.[2] Access is possible for individuals and groups as complainants and provision is made in the enabling law for participation by the Courts both for appeals and for enforcement. In 1962 the New York State Commission heard 1,392 complaints, of which 44 were adjusted by conciliation or consent and 829 dismissed for lack of 'probable cause'.[3]

Procedurally, the systems of the Convention and of the Draft Covenant are very close,[4] but there are three critical differences: first, the proposed Human Rights Committee may receive complaints only from States, there being no right of individual petition; secondly, the report of the Committee is presented to the States concerned and to the Secretary-General of the UN for publication, but no further action is provided for,[5] nor is the Committee granted the power to make recommendations; therefore, unlike the European system where binding decisions by the Court or the Committee of Ministers are envisaged, the effectiveness of the complaint procedure under the Draft Covenant would depend solely on publicity. Thirdly, reference of an issue to the International Court would be exclusively for one or more of the States parties, whereas under the European Convention the Commission may refer cases to the European Court of Human Rights.

3. *A UN High Commissioner of Human Rights*

Two proposals have been made for the appointment of a UN High Commissioner or Attorney-General for Human Rights.

The first proposal, elaborated by Uruguay,[6] would have conferred

---

[1] Articles 27–45 and particularly Article 40.
[2] In Massachusetts it is called 'Commission against Discrimination', in Pennsylvania the 'Commission of Human Relations'.
[3] See Jeffery Jowell, 'Administrative Enforcement of Laws against Discrimination', *Public Law*, Summer 1965, pp. 119–86.
[4] Compare Articles 40–3 of the Draft Covenant with Articles 28–32 of the European Convention.
[5] The annual report which the Human Rights Committee would make to the General Assembly under Article 45 is hardly a substitute.
[6] *General Assembly Official Records*, Sixth Session: A/C 3/654; Ninth Session: A/C 3/L.424.

extensive duties upon him of three main kinds: the collection and examination of information on the observance and enforcement of the Draft Covenant on Civil and Political Rights, including the conduct of on-the-spot studies and enquiries; the reception and examination of complaints of Covenant breaches from individuals, national and international non-governmental organisations and intergovernmental organisations under certain conditions; action on such complaints by negotiations with States parties to the Covenant, and failing a solution, reference to the Human Rights Committee; the submission of annual and special reports to the General Assembly.

The second proposal saw the light of day under the auspices of the International Commission of Jurists. It took the form of a draft resolution, to be adopted by the General Assembly, and was approved in Geneva in July 1964 by representatives of a number of non-governmental organisations including Amnesty International, the International Committee of the Red Cross, the International Press Institute and the World Jewish Congress. This proposal is much more limited than the first, and the role of the proposed High Commissioner is modelled in part on that of the High Commissioner for Refugees. He would:

(i) advise and assist the Commission on Human Rights and other organs of the UN on the periodic and other reports, and submissions made by governments relating to human rights;

(ii) report annually to the General Assembly through the Economic and Social Council and his report shall be considered as a separate item on the agenda of both bodies; at the request of the General Assembly, the Secretary-General, or any other organ of the UN he would make special reports, and he could also make special reports in case of urgency;

(iii) render assistance and services to Governments at their request.

His function under (ii) is the one having most bite in it, and follows at a little distance the Statute for the High Commissioner for Refugees, Article 11 of which provides that 'The High Commissioner shall be entitled to present his views before the General Assembly, the Economic and Social Council and their subsidiary bodies'.[1]

These proposals point to three possible conceptions of the role of a UN High Commissioner, conceptions which differ but are not necessarily mutually exclusive:

(i) that he serve as an international Ombudsman receiving and examining petitions by individuals or organisations;

(ii) that he act as an Advocate-General of the Human Rights Committee in sifting complaints, rejecting those which are obviously inadmissible, and advising the Committee upon them; this function

[1] Taken from a note by Mr Seán MacBride.

would be valuable, and probably essential, if the right of individual petition to the Committee were to be granted;

(iii) that, without being involved in any form of complaint procedure, he act as a global 'watchdog' of human rights, through the centralisation in his office of information, and through his right to present reports with his views, to the UN bodies.

V. CONCLUSIONS

My conclusions, which I offer as possible matters for discussion at the Conference, are these:

If we are to be realistic, we must, at the present stage in the advancement of human rights, recognise that only certain means of global implementation are practicable and we must give priority to them.

Publicity is an essential and effective mode of implementation. Much is being done but, for example, could the efforts of the numerous non-governmental organisations in the field not be more coordinated and even centralised?

Judicial settlement of complaints on a global scale has little prospect at present of systematic adoption, and the fact that little progress has been made with the Draft Covenants for ten years suggests that we should look carefully at the proposals for the appointment of a UN High Commissioner as the best solution for the present. If the Uruguayan proposal seems overambitious, if only for the magnitude of the tasks it gives to the High Commissioner, could not the second proposal be strengthened, for example:

1. could not the High Commissioner 'express his views' to the General Assembly, even on individual cases which came to his knowledge?

2. could the office be distributed, so that there would be, say, six or seven Regional Commissioners around the globe, each with the same role and relationship to the UN?

3. should he not have a power to request information from governments and the right, in certain cases, to publish the fact of their refusal to provide it?

WRITTEN COMMUNICATION BY
JÁNOS TÓTH

THE RECOGNITION OF HUMAN RIGHTS IN EASTERN EUROPE

The following remarks are intended to outline a trend and to draw attention to a growing emphasis on the importance of human rights in the theory and practice of Eastern European countries and to signs of willingness to consider the international protection of human rights.

I. HUMAN RIGHTS IN MUNICIPAL LAW

An essential condition for the recognition of human rights on a universal basis in a world divided into more than one hundred sovereign States, is their recognition as fundamental rights and freedoms in the municipal law of the countries and the provision at the same time of adequate safeguards to protect and implement them.

In Eastern Europe, following the example of the 1936 Soviet Constitution, which included a catalogue of rights and duties of citizens, all constitutions have a chapter dealing with human rights. It is well known, however, that for a considerable period the law on paper did not correspond to the law in practice; that human rights were not respected, indeed violated on a mass scale so that they appeared to be virtually non-existent. These violations were criticised by Western scholars and international organisations concurrently with the sad event. After a certain time lag, Soviet authorities proceeded to a similar criticism from 1956 on, and most forcefully at the 22nd Congress of the Communist Party of the Soviet Union in October 1961.[1] After the Congress many legal tenets of Andréi Vyshinsky, the Procurator of the Great Purge and leading legal theoretician of the Stalinist period, were repudiated. With different timing and different emphasis, similar criticism has been voiced against the neglect of human rights and legality in various other countries of Eastern Europe.

1. Legal science in these countries has now discovered the lack of any socialist doctrine on human rights and freedoms, and first attempts have been made to develop the concept of law in such a way as to include basic rights of the citizens.[2]

The Warsaw Colloquium of the International Association of Legal Science in 1958 provided a revealing survey of the views held by leading jurists of Eastern European countries on the subject.[3] Stanislaw

---

[1] Cf. publications of the International Commission of Jurists; *Justice Enslaved*, 1955; 'Socialist Legality in the Soviet Union as appraised by the 22nd Congress of the CPSU', *Bulletin* 13, May 1962; E. Zellweger 'The Principle of Socialist Legality', *Journal*, vol. 5, no. 2, 1964, pp. 163–202. (In the footnotes *Journal* and *Bulletin* refer to the publications of the International Commission of Jurists.

[2] Georg Brunner, *Die Grundrechte im Sowjetsystem*, 1963, pp. 52–63.)

[3] 'Le concept de la légalité dans les pays socialistes', *Zeszyty Problemowe Nauki Polskiej, Cahiers de l'Académie Polonaise des Sciences*, xxi, Warszawa, 1961.

Ehrlich of Poland underlined that the concept of legality is inextricably linked with the protection of human rights, and that this link is generally admitted in socialist countries.[1] Jivko Stalev of Bulgaria noted that a socialist legal system guarantees different rights for its citizens than a bourgeois one: a socialist State based on the socialist ownership of production puts the right to work and other economic and social rights in the forefront.[2] Ehrlich maintained that the difference in political systems does not lead necessarily to a different catalogue of civil rights, and indeed, in both systems the same rights are recognised as fundamental. Then he sought to answer the basic theoretical question of the role of individual human rights in a socialist system. In his view, socialism offers a possibility of increasing the number of human rights, the basic aim of socialism being the full self-assertion of the individual; the self-assertion itself speeds up the construction of socialism by encouraging individual initiatives in the socialist society. He therefore strongly underlined that it is in the interest of the consolidation of Socialist Legality to assure a harmonious development of the economic and social structure of socialism and of individual rights.[3] Radomir Lukié from Yugoslavia held that a socialist State is obliged to safeguard human rights even if this obligation is of a political and not a legal character.[4] Imre Szabó from Hungary emphasised that rules pertaining to the rights and duties of citizens should be published in the Official Gazette, as is done in Hungary.[5] Winding up the discussions of the Colloquium, P. S. Romashin, then Director of the Institute of State and Law of the Soviet Academy of Sciences, found that the need to insert in the definition of Socialist Legality the concept of the rights and freedoms of the citizen was amply proved.[6] It was also said that human rights and freedoms are derived not from Natural Law, but are the result of a long political struggle for the realisation of these freedoms and have become an integral part of human culture.[7]

2. Law reform has become in the last decade one of the major characteristics of social development throughout Eastern Europe. These reforms have considerably improved the legal position of the citizen and shown a significant tendency to eliminate terror. In the

---

[1] Op. cit., p. 70.   [2] Op. cit., p. 28.
[3] Op. cit., pp. 72, 74.   [4] Op. cit., pp. 260, 266.
[5] Op. cit., p. 55; cf. also: Imre Szabó, *Az emberi jogok mai értelme* (*The meaning of human rights today*), Budapest, 1948; idem, *Az állampolgar i jogok de kötelességek szabályozâsânk elvi kérdései* (*Theoretical problems of the regulation of civic rights and duties*), 1962.
[6] Op. cit., p. 371.
[7] For comments on the Colloquium of Norman S. Marsh: 'The Rule of Law: New Delhi-Lagos-Rio de Janeiro; Some Reflections on a Journey with excursions to Chicago and Warsaw'; *Journal* (vol. IV, no. 2, 1963), pp. 252–68.

Soviet Union this positive trend was manifested basically in the new criminal legislation of 1958, which granted a higher degree of protection for civil rights.[1] Similar law reforms are taking place in other countries of Eastern Europe as well. These reforms all have their limits imposed by the economic and political system of the countries. Indeed, competing trends can also be observed, characterised by the re-establishment of centralised bureaucratic controls.[2] In spite of all its limitations, this process has ushered in a new period, the importance of which for the peoples of Eastern Europe can be assessed by comments made by György Lukács, one of the greatest living philosophers of Marxism:

The Communist Party of the Soviet Union has made a clean break with the Stalinist practice of haughty disdain for legality. If this is described as ending the 'cult of personality', the term is far too modest to convey the extent and depth of what has taken place. What this means is that the Socialist State provides the essential firm guarantees whereby human existence is assured, after Stalin's régime had systematically and contemptuously eliminated the smallest modicum of humanity. . . .[3]

3. The constitutional development of Eastern European countries shows signs that human rights are receiving growing emphasis.

In the Soviet Union, Romashkin has proposed that, in the draft Soviet Constitution which is now being elaborated, all the basic rights and duties of the citizens be set out and that the right of petition and the principles of *nulla poena sine crimine* and *nullum crimen sine lege* be included in the catalogue of fundamental rights and freedoms.[4]

In Hungary, István Kovács has given an account of a new approach in the science of socialist constitutional law, which gives the civil and political rights of citizens equal emphasis with their economic and social rights. In his book he asked for a detailed elaboration of individual political rights and for a differentiated system of legal institutional safeguards for the basic rights and freedoms.[5]

The constitutions enacted recently in Yugoslavia (1963), and in Rumania (1965) reflected the emphasis thus put on such requirements.[6]

[1] J. N. Hazard and I. Shapiro, *The Soviet Legal System*, 1962, reviewed by János Tóth in *Journal*, vol. VI, no. 2, 1963.

[2] Comments in *Bulletins* Nos. 12, 13, 15, 19, 21 and K. Grzybowski/J. L. Alder: Eastern Europe: Legislative Trends; in *Problems of Communism*, March–April, 1965.

[3] Cited by E. Zellweger, op. cit., pp. 166–7.

[4] I. Kovács, *A Szocialista alkotmányfejlödés üj elemei (New Elements of the Socialist Constitutional Evolution)* reviewed by J. Tóth, *Journal*, vol. V, no. 2, 1964.

[5] Ibid.

[6] *Bulletin*, No. 17, December 1963, on Yugoslavia; Radoslav Ratkovic: 'Die ideologischen Grundlagen und Charakteristiken der neuen jugoslawischen

II. INTERNATIONAL PROTECTION OF HUMAN RIGHTS

1. *The policy rejecting international implementation*

The Soviet Union and other States of Eastern Europe have adopted a stand concerning international co-operation in the field of human rights according to which national sovereignty excludes any kind of international implementation. This concept boils down in fact to the negation of an effective international protection of human rights. Yugoslavia held the same view until 1953. Since that time it has aligned itself with the system of implementation as adopted in the final draft of the Commission of Human Rights.[1]

The first (and only) Soviet treatise dealing with the international protection of human rights was written by A. V. Movchan and published in 1958.[2] The book gives a historical survey of the problem starting with the preparation of the United Nations Charter, followed by an analysis of its relevant provisions, a history and evaluation of the draft International Covenants on human rights, prepared by the Commission on Human Rights and the Third Committee of the General Assembly. The author casts the Soviet Union in the role of the active and persevering supporter of the rights of man, whose proposals decisively shaped the United Nations Charter, the Universal Declaration and the draft Covenants. According to him, the Soviet delegation, led in the post-war period by Andréi Vyshinsky, played a major role in securing the incorporation of the protection of human rights among the basic tasks of the United Nations. It succeeded in getting social, economic and cultural rights and the right of nations to self-determination included in the Universal Declaration on an equal footing with the classical political and civil rights. The Soviet delegation, the author continues, proposed to give immediate binding effect to all these rights and met with the opposition of many capitalist States. These States tried first to obstruct the proclamation of the right of self-determination, for fear of losing their colonies. When the majority of the General Assembly proclaimed this right, they resisted the detailed elaboration of social, economic and cultural rights. In this field, too, the developing countries led by the Soviet Union pushed the proposals through. These achievements were credited by Tunkin, in his Preface to the

---

Verfassung', *Jahrbuch für Ostrecht*, bd. v, no. 2, December 1964; *Bulletin*, no. 23, August 1965, on Rumania.

[1] For detailed documentation see Manouchehr Ganji, *International Protection of Human Rights*, Geneva, 1962, pp. 145–8, 186–9.

[2] A. P. Movchan, *Mezhunarodnaya zaschita prav cheloveka* (*International Protection of the Rights of Man*), Gosyurizdat, Moscow, 1958, prefaced by Professor G. I. Tunkin.

work in question, to 'the superiority of socialist democracy' embodied in the 1936 Soviet Constitution. At the same time, the stalemate which developed in the United Nations in the debates on the draft Covenants was also attributed to the reluctant attitude of Western countries, which, according to Tunkin, cooled down towards the international protection of human rights and utilised the idea only 'to launch ideological attacks against the Soviet Union and the People's democracies'. The elements in international protection most criticised by the Soviet Union were the measures of implementation proposed for the draft Covenants in general, the right of individual petition and the establishment of an international adjudication body or of a United Nations Attorney-General for dealing with violations of human rights in particular.

Delegates of the Soviet Union and other East European countries stated on many occasions that the proposed measures of implementation would result in 'unlawful interference in the internal affairs of States, and a gross infringement of Article 2, paragraph 7 of the Charter'. In their view the implementation of those measures was entirely within the internal competence of each sovereign State and represented a primary duty for it.

However, a proposal of the Soviet Union to proclaim that the implementation of the provisions of the Covenants on human rights is entirely for the domestic jurisdiction of States was defeated by a large majority in the fifth General Assembly in 1950.

Though the responsibility for the almost complete failure of the United Nations to arrive at an acceptable arrangement for international protection cannot be attributed, contrary to the Soviet view explained above, to any single State or group of States, it is evident that at that time the negative attitude adopted in Soviet theory as outlined above and in the policy based upon it contributed considerably to the impasse.

It should be mentioned that Lauterpacht drew attention in 1950 to the possibility of changes in this policy.[1] Indeed in the 1960's Soviet policy concerning human rights shows signs of becoming less rigid.

2. The policy of peaceful co-existence

In the first part of this paper new trends were examined in the legal science, practice and constitutional development of countries in Eastern Europe. A similar trend can be observed in the foreign policy and the theory of international law of these countries. Communist jurists refer to this new policy line as that of peaceful co-existence.

[1] H. Lauterpacht: *International Law and Human Rights* 1950, p. 301, cited by Ganji.

Much has been written in all continents on this controversial term. For our present purpose may it suffice to recall that this policy has been defined in its contemporary form and meaning in the 1961 Programme of the CPSU as 'the peaceful competition between socialism and capitalism on an international scale' and as 'a specific form of class struggle' intended to triumph eventually over all adversaries or enemies of world communism. It involves the dropping of the doctrine of the inevitability of war between socialist and capitalist countries and has thereby become the stumbling block for the Chinese group of world communism.

The trend in the development of the doctrine of international law as propounded in the Soviet Union and other Eastern European countries offers a convincing illustration to Harold D. Laswell's thesis that:

The doctrines of any political system are open to changes of many kinds particularly in the intensity with which they are held and the specific interpretations to which they give rise.[1]

These changes 'in intensity' and 'in specific interpretations' should be reviewed here in the particular field of the international protection of human rights. Compared with previous policy, a somewhat modified stand can be observed in a series of recent developments of which the two which seem to be the most significant will be outlined here.

At the seventeenth Session of the Sub-Commission on Prevention of Discrimination and Protection of Minorities, held in Geneva in January 1965, Mr Arcot Krishnaswami of India submitted a draft Resolution asking for further measures in the implementation of the Genocide Convention of 1948.[2] Such measures should include an 'international organ for the investigation and assessment of allegations of genocide'. Mr Krishnaswami pointed out that the General Assembly in adopting the Convention had considered the question of international jurisdiction and had referred to the trial of persons charged with genocide by such international penal tribunal as may have jurisdiction over the contracting States that have accepted its jurisdiction. There is an urgent need, he continued, for an international body which would endeavour to prevent the crime of genocide before it actually occurred on a massive scale. Such a body should be able to investigate and to assess allegations of genocide and to

---

[1] Harold D. Laswell, 'Introduction: Universality versus Parochialism', in M. S. McDougall/F. P. Feliciano, *Law and Minimum World Public Order: the Regulation of International Coercion*, Yale Univ. Press, 1961, pp. xxii-xxiii.

[2] Report of the Seventeenth Session of the Sub-Commission on Prevention of Discrimination and Protection of Minorities to the Commission of Human Rights, E/CN.4/882, paras. 387-95.

take the steps necessary to halt at its outset the deliberate destruction of a national, racial, religious or ethnic group.

The suggestion put forward by Mr Krishnaswami was warmly supported by several members of the Sub-Commission and adopted unanimously.

Mr Nassinowsky of the Soviet Union expressed the view that the proposal was an extremely important and necessary one, as it aimed at the effective implementation of the Convention on the Prevention and Punishment of the Crime of Genocide. He pointed out that the climate of public opinion had changed considerably since that Convention had been adopted in 1948, and that in subsequent years effective measures had been adopted for the implementation of less important Conventions.

At the Twenty-First Session of the Commission on Human Rights in March 1965, and at the Thirty-Ninth Session of the Economic and Social Council in July 1965, a draft Resolution of Costa Rica, entitled 'Election of a United Nations High Commissioner for Human Rights', was examined.[1]

The essence of this proposal was explained by Mr Seán MacBride, Secretary-General of the International Commission of Jurists, before the Sub-Commission, at its Session referred to above.[2] The High Commissioner should be absolutely independent and free to report objectively on all systematic violations of human rights to the Economic and Social Council and to the General Assembly. His task would include the examination of the periodic reports of governments on the implementation of human rights.

The Costa Rican proposal gave rise to interesting discussion both at the Commission on Human Rights and at ECOSOC. In the Commission, Representatives of the Soviet Union and other East European countries opposed the discussion of the proposal as 'contrary to the principle of the Charter of the United Nations, which emphasises non-interference in the internal affairs of States', a standard argument against measures of implementation. At the Session of ECOSOC the Soviet Representative opposed 'any hasty decision which might prejudge the very complex question of the application of human rights which should be considered in the framework of the debate of the General Assembly'.[3] As the main substantive argument against the proposal he advanced that such authority as proposed for the High Commissioner for Human Rights, 'could not be conferred on one person'. Thus the basis of opposition was shifted from the principle

[1] Commission on Human Rights, Report on the Twenty-First Session, 22 March to 15 April 1965, E/4024, paras. 13–24.
[2] E/CN.4/Sub. 2/SR.456.
[3] E/AC.V/SR.518.

of non-interference to the composition of the supervising international organ.

Similar shifts in emphasis observed in the theory of international law have led some scholars in the West to believe that the policy of peaceful co-existence expresses on the part of East European countries 'a common interest in survival and welfare despite national and ideological conflicts',[1] or indeed a 'common interest in minimum rules of world order'.[2] It is to be hoped that future events confirm the validity of these forward-looking appraisals, which would certainly facilitate the implementation of human rights on the international level.

WRITTEN COMMUNICATION BY
EGON SCHWELB

INTRODUCTORY

The European Convention on Human Rights and the machinery which it has established represent the greatest advance so far made toward transforming into reality the United Nations Charter's faith in the dignity and worth of the human person. The European States which have subjected themselves to a scrutiny of their standards by international authorities and in particular those among them which have empowered those authorities to act on the initiative of individuals under the jurisdiction of those States, including their own citizens, have indeed been the spearhead of the movement towards 'better standards of life in larger freedom.' It is perhaps not out of place to present to a Colloquium devoted to the European Convention on Human Rights a background document summarising the activities for which the Human Rights provisions of the Charter of the United Nations have been the point of departure. These very comprehensive and far-flung activities have been undertaken within and outside the United Nations, by specialised agencies, by regional inter-governmental organisations, by international conferences, by Governments, by national legislatures, and by courts. By now spread over twenty years, these activities can, by and large, be divided into three main categories: (1) Action taken under the Charter of the United Nations and under the constituent instruments of other

---

[1] Richard N. Gardner, 'The Soviet Union and the United Nations', *The Soviet Impact on International Law*, Duke University School of Law, vol. XXIX, no. 4, 1964, p. 854.

[2] Edward McWhinney, *Peaceful Co-Existence and Soviet-Western International Law*, 1964, and its review by Ivo Lapenna, in the *International and Comparative Law Quarterly*, July 1965, vol. 14, part 3, p. 1047.

inter-governmental organisations based on the powers vested in these organisations by their constitutional instruments, expressly or by implication; (2) Action aimed at the conclusion of new treaties, importing additional obligations in the Human Rights field of States parties, and creating international supervisory and enforcement machinery; (3) In between these two main categories is the 'twilight zone' of less orthodox 'quasi-legislative' activities through declarations and similar pronouncements.

INTERNATIONAL CONVENTIONS

Because the European Convention on Human Rights, the principal subject of the Colloquium, is the most advanced example, I shall begin with a review of the *second* of these three categories. Since 1945, a by no means negligible body of conventional international law on the subject of human rights has come into being, not only in Western Europe, but also under the auspices of the United Nations family of organisations. A general survey of this body of law, in so far as it was created by the United Nations or, on United Nations initiative, by a Specialised Agency, will now be presented.[1]

The first, in point of time, of the instruments to be considered is the Genocide Convention, 1948 (67) the object of which, in the words of the International Court of Justice, 'is to safeguard the very existence of certain human groups . . . and to confirm and endorse the most elementary principles of morality' (*I.C.J. Reports* 1951, at p. 23). The four Geneva Conventions for the Protection of War Victims, 1949 (not concluded under United Nations auspices) and the UNESCO Convention for the Protection of Cultural Property in the Event of Armed Conflict, 1954, belong to the same body of humanitarian international legislation. A humanitarian convention of a different kind is the Convention for the Suppression of the Traffic in Persons and of the Exploitation of the Prostitution of Others, 1949. The Supplementary Convention on the Abolition of Slavery, the Slave Trade, and Institutions and Practices Similar to Slavery, 1956 (62) outlaws certain institutions and practices similar to slavery such as debt bondage, serfdom, purchase of brides, and exploitation of child labour. It also 'encourages' the prescription of suitable minimum ages for marriage, the use of facilities whereby the consent of both parties to a marriage may be freely expressed, and the registration of mar-

---

[1] The figures inserted in brackets after the particular instruments indicate the number of Contracting Parties to it as of 31 August 1965. The texts of the instruments will, where no other source is indicated, be found in the United Nations Treaty Series, in the *United Nations Yearbook on Human Rights* for the relevant year and in the volumes of resolutions of the General Assembly.

riages. These problems were subsequently dealt with, in a somewhat more concrete manner, in the Convention on Consent to Marriage, Minimum Age for Marriage and Registration of Marriages, 1962 (16). (Cf. Art. 12 of the European Convention on Human Rights.) The International Labour Convention concerning the *Abolition of Forced Labour, 1957* (74) purports to suppress any form of forced or compulsory labour, *inter alia*, as a means of political coercion or education or as a punishment for holding or expressing political views or views ideologically opposed to the established system or as a means of racial, social, national or religious discrimination.

One of the early successes of the United Nations in legislating on the status of women has been the Convention on the Political Rights of Women, 1952 (45), the first world-wide instrument in which States Parties have undertaken a legal obligation concerning the exercise of the political rights of their citizens (cf. Art. 3 of Protocol No. 1, 1952, to the European Convention on Human Rights). Other instruments which represent the culmination of the endeavours of generations of fighters for women's rights are the Convention on the Nationality of Married Women, 1957 (31) and the Equal Remuneration Convention adopted by the International Labour Conference in 1951 (51).

The subject-matter of the latter leads us to two basic treaties against discrimination in very important fields: the (ILO) Discrimination (Employment and Occupation) Convention, 1958 (51) and the (UNESCO) Convention against Discrimination in Education, 1960 (31) with a Protocol of 1962 instituting a Conciliation and Good Offices Commission to be responsible for seeking the settlement of any disputes which may arise between States Parties to the Convention (not yet in force; text in *United Nations Juridical Yearbook*, 1962, p. 187). United Nations Conventions against racial or religious discrimination of a more general scope are still law in the making (Draft International Convention on the Elimination of All Forms of Racial Discrimination and Draft International Convention on the Elimination of All Forms of Religious Intolerance, both on the Provisional Agenda of the Twentieth Session of the General Assembly, UN Doc. A/5950, 23 July 1965).

In the field of nationality and statelessness comprehensive drafts prepared by the International Law Commission in 1953-4 were not acceptable to Governments and the far more modest Convention on the Reduction of Statelessness, 1961 (not yet in force), was adopted. However, measures to improve the position of stateless persons and of refugees were taken. They are based on the principles that there should be as little discrimination as possible between nationals on the one hand and refugees or stateless persons on the other and that there should be no discrimination based on race, religion or country of origin among refugees and among stateless persons. (Convention relating to the Status of Refugees, 1951 (48) and Convention on the Status of Stateless Persons, 1954 (18).)

Out of the very ambitious programme to guarantee freedom of information, i.e. the right to seek, receive, and impart information and ideas, an instrument of very limited scope, the Convention on the International Right of Correction, 1952 (7) has entered into force. The rest of the programme, in particular the draft Convention on Freedom of Information has been before various United Nations organs for many years and the General Assembly continues to be seised of it.

The Freedom of Association and Protection of the Right to Organise Convention, 1948 (70) and the Right to Organise and Collective Bargaining Convention, 1949 (81) were the first great post World War II achievements of the joint efforts of the United Nations and of the ILO to legislate on problems which are in the centre of any system of protecting human rights and of a sound regulation of labour relations.

The above mentioned International Labour Conventions partake of the implementation machinery provided for in the Constitution of the International Labour Organisation (annual reports, representations on non-observance, complaints of non-observance, commissions of enquiry, reference to the International Court of Justice.) None of the other Conventions grants to individuals the right of petition. However, with one exception, all the United Nations Conventions listed above contain clauses that any dispute between Contracting States concerning their interpretation or application which cannot be settled by other means shall be submitted to the International Court of Justice at the request of any one of the Parties to the dispute. The one exception is the Marriage Convention of 1962. The UNESCO Convention of 1960 does not have such a clause either, but the Protocol of 1962 is intended to contribute to the settlement of disputes through a Conciliation and Good Offices Commission.

This is not the place to deal with the *lex ferenda*, in particular the draft International Covenants on Human Rights, 'a project for a piece of international legislation, more ambitious and perhaps more important than any other in the history of international law' (Holcombe) except to say that an earlier draft of one of them, of the present Draft Covenant on Civil and Political Rights, was, to a large extent, used in elaborating the text of the European Convention (see Robertson in *UN Yearbook on Human Rights* for 1950, p. 419) and that by the end of 1963[1] the competent Committee of the General

---

[1] The 1964 Session of the General Assembly was paralysed because of the conflict concerning the application of Article 19 of the Charter.

Assembly of the United Nations had completed the drafting of the general and substantive provisions of both Draft Covenants. The task of revising and approving the 'measures of implementation' and the final clauses still lies ahead.

THE POTENTIALITIES OF THE CHARTER
OF THE UNITED NATIONS

When in 1946 the Economic and Social Council established the UN Commission on Human Rights and defined its terms of reference (Resolutions 5 (1) and 9 (11)) it listed a number of tasks, but added a 'general clause' to the effect that the Commission would submit to the Council proposals, recommendations and reports regarding 'any other matter concerning human rights' not covered by the preceding items. In the following year, however, the Council restricted the Commission's jurisdiction considerably by ruling (on recommendation by the Commission itself) that 'the Commission . . . has no power to take any action in regard to any complaints concerning human rights' (Resolution 75 (V)), a ruling which has been maintained in spite of repeated efforts on the part of some Governments to have it reversed (Resolution 728F (XXVIII), 1959).

However, exceptions from this self-denying ordinance were made for complaints relating to specific human rights subjects, the most important being the establishment of the 'allegations procedure', agreed in 1949–50 between the Economic and Social Council and the Governing body of the ILO for the protection of freedom of association. Machinery was created by the ILO in its own name and on behalf of the United Nations under which trade unions and employers organisations were granted the right of petition. These arrangements (the establishment of the Fact Finding and Conciliation Commission and, later also of the Governing body Committee on Freedom of Association) were made not on the basis of specific new international conventions (such as those of 1948 and 1949 referred to above), but by virtue of the inherent powers of the UN and the International Labour Organisation. The Freedom of Association Committee has, over the years, built up a body of case law which it is quite proper to compare to the case law of the European Commission on Human Rights. Following complaints by trade unions of the infringement of trade union rights in Japan, the Fact Finding and Conciliation Commission undertook a thorough review of the situation of freedom of association and other basic rights in that country which led to the acceptance, by the Government, of a series of recommended reforms (Report of the Commission of 31 August 1965).

PROPOSALS FOR NEW MACHINERY OF IMPLEMENTATION

In 1950 the General Assembly established by resolution the Office of the United Nations High Commissioner for Refugees and created thereby a subsidiary organ to provide a wide range of services for a group of persons in particular need of international protection. For many years the idea has been under discussion to establish a similar office, albeit with a far wider competence, under the designation of 'United Nations High Commissioner for Human Rights'. In 1951 the Government of Uruguay proposed, as part of the measures of implementation of the draft Covenant, the establishment of such a High Commissioner (or 'Attorney-General') for Human Rights as a permanent organ. A modification of this plan, viz. the establishment of the office by mere resolution of the General Assembly and not by treaty was presented to the Commission on Human Rights by the delegation of Costa Rica at its 1965 Session. The Commission included in its 1965 agenda an item entitled 'Question concerning implementation of human rights through a United Nations High Commissioner for Human Rights or through some other appropriate international machinery'. The Commission did not reach the item at its 1965 Session and later in the same year (20 August 1965) Costa Rica proposed the inclusion of the item 'Creation of the post of United Nations High Commissioner for Human Rights' in the agenda of the twentieth Session of the General Assembly (Doc. A/5963). At the time of writing it is not known whether the General Assembly will take action on this proposal in 1965. It is possible to say, however, that the project has the support of some Governments, including at least two major Powers, the United Kingdom and the United States, of Canada and several Latin American States. Whether the support is sufficient is a question on which I would not like to make a prediction.

For those who have the cause of the international protection of Human Rights at heart, a public discussion of the merits or demerits of such an idea and of the concrete proposal which is before the General Assembly, is a very delicate and responsible operation. If a writer or speaker stresses the importance and far-reaching effect of a proposal of this kind, he risks increasing the distrust of Governments of the proposal and thereby adding to the obstacles, very considerable in any event, which are in the way of its passage.

If, on the other hand, he describes the proposal as insignificant or even as worthless, he only contributes to the attitude of cynicism vis-à-vis the United Nations, and its human rights programme in particular, a cynicism which is widespread and very often supported by international lawyers not only of totalitarian countries, but also by quite a few legal scholars of the Western world.

In the comments which follow I shall try to navigate as well as I can to stay clear of both the Scylla and the Charybdis of these two extremes.

In 1947 the Commission of Human Rights adopted, and the Economic and Social Council approved, the self-denying ordinance that the Commission has no power to take any action in regard to any complaints concerning human rights. The ruling has been maintained in spite of repeated efforts to have it reversed, whether the suggestions to reverse or to modify it emanated from the Secretary-General or, as in 1952, from Egypt, or, as in 1957, from Egypt's adversary, Israel. In the light of this dismal history it is of some significance that the proposal, by Costa Rica, has been placed on the Agenda of the General Assembly which would after all give to a newly created organ some power 'to take . . . action'. In my view it can therefore be said at the outset, that a proposal on the general lines of that of Costa Rica is a move in the right direction or, to put it more modestly, in the direction which I consider to be right.

In his report, Mr Fawcett describes the tasks which would be entrusted to the High Commissioner for Human Rights. Fortunately, the draft eventually presented by Costa Rica is, from the point of view of the effectiveness of the proposed institution, better than the text reproduced in Mr Fawcett's paper. Under the draft of which the General Assembly is seised the High Commissioner will 'perform a number of functions under the authority of the General Assembly,' the first of which is defined as follows: (a) He shall assist in furthering the realisation of human rights and shall seek to secure the observance of the Universal Declaration of Human Rights'.

This paragraph of the Commissioner's proposed terms of reference should be read in connection with Art. 13 (1) (b) of the Charter: 'The General Assembly shall initiate studies and make recommendations for the purpose of, among other things . . . assisting in the realisation of human rights and fundamental freedoms for all.' The phrase: '*Assisting in the realisation*' should be noted. The High Commissioner shall '*assist in furthering the realisation of human rights.*' This means, if words mean anything, that the General Assembly would entrust to the High Commissioner the task of assisting in what the general Assembly itself has power to do, i.e. assisting in the realisation of human rights.

As to subject-matter, the permissible activities of the High Commissioner would be co-extensive with the jurisdiction of the General Assembly under the Charter. He would be called upon to assist in everything which comes within the field of activity of the General Assembly in the matter of human rights.

The High Commissioner would also be instructed to seek to secure the observance of the Universal Declaration of Human Rights. In addition he would also perform the specific tasks listed in Mr Fawcett's report.

I believe that if a man of great ability, efficiency and integrity were elected to a unique post with these important duties, he could, and would, contribute to a considerable extent towards the discharge, by the United Nations, of its obligations in the matter of human rights. This is not to say that the Draft Statute of the High Commissioner is not open to criticism in certain respects. Quite unnecessarily, for instance, it contains a provision to the effect that the emoluments of the High Commissioner shall not be less favourable than those of a member of the International Court of Justice. While this provision obviously has the purpose to demonstrate the high status which the General Assembly would grant to the High Commissioner, it nevertheless is apt to attract the criticism, and therefore the opposition, of 117 treasuries. For the same reason, I would respectfully dissent from Mr Fawcett's suggestion that six or seven regional Commissioners be appointed, each with the same role and relationship to the United Nations. Such a proposal, which would considerably increase the financial implications of the project, might be appropriate after several years of successful operation of the world-wide office. Nor would it, I believe, be advisable to spell out the High Commissioner's terms of reference in greater detail as suggested by Mr Fawcett.

INVESTIGATIONS OF ALLEGED VIOLATIONS OF HUMAN RIGHTS BY ORGANS OF THE UNITED NATIONS FAMILY OF ORGANISATIONS

In 1951 the UN and the ILO jointly established an Ad Hoc Committee on Forced Labour to study the nature and extent of the problem raised by the existence in the world of systems of forced labour. In 1953 the Committee submitted a comprehensive report on its world-wide survey which was later followed by further investigative and legislative action by the ILO.

The leading example of United Nations action based on the Human Rights provisions of the Charter is the endless stream of investigations and of resolutions criticising, and trying to remedy, the racial situation in South Africa, a problem of which the General Assembly and a great number of subsidiary bodies which it established for the purpose have been seised since 1952. More recently, the question has also occupied the Security Council.

In 1963 another significant case was added to the list: the question of the treatment of the Buddhists in South Vietnam, a non-member State. The General Assembly accepted an invitation of the South

Vietnamese Government to send a mission there to investigate the matter on the spot. This fact-finding mission submitted to the Assembly a very substantial report on what it had found during its weeks of presence in that country.

In some of the major operations in which the United Nations was involved, the Secretary-General took action, where he had a possibility to do so, in support of human rights. Such a necessity to invoke the Charter provisions on human rights, the Universal Declaration of Human Rights and the Geneva Convention relative to the Protection of Civilian Persons in Time of War arose in 1961 in the course of the Congo operations; the important activities of the Secretary-General's Special Representative in the Dominican Republic (1965) on behalf of the human rights of the parts of the population concerned should also be mentioned in this connection.

In 1955-6 the United Nations embarked upon a programme of continuing activities for which the Charter has supplied the constitutional basis. Details of this programme cannot be given here. It has repeatedly been described and analysed within the United Nations and by learned writers. It has included the 'advisory services in human rights', particularly the regular convening of conferences, called 'seminars'; the undertaking of world-wide surveys of problems such as discrimination in education, discrimination in political rights, protection against arbitrary arrest and detention; and the establishment of a system of periodic reporting of Governments on human rights developments in their countries. The reporting system depends on the voluntary co-operation which has been forthcoming, in the last cycle, on the part of sixty-five Governments. The reporting system and the eventual use to be made of it is still in an experimental stage; recommendations for important changes in it were made in 1965.

DECLARATIONS IN THE HUMAN RIGHTS FIELD

The present paper is of necessity restricted to a mere listing of the main instruments and draft instruments coming within this category. It cannot enter into the constitutional problems involved in this type of quasi-legislation, nor can it describe the impact of particular declarations on legal and political developments. The pronouncements coming within this category are:

(i) The *Universal Declaration of Human Rights, 1948*.

(ii) The *Declaration on the Granting of Independence to Colonial Countries and Peoples, 1960*. For this Declaration a comprehensive machinery of implementation has been established. (The Special Committee of Seventeen (now Twenty-Four) with a great number of subsidiary committees, visiting missions, examination of petitions, hearing of witnesses, etc.).

(iii) The *United Nations Declaration on the Elimination of All Forms of Racial Discrimination, 1963.*

(iv) The *Declaration of the Rights of the Child, 1959.*

The following are among the Declarations which are in various stages of preparation:

(i) *Draft Declaration on Freedom of Information.*

(ii) *Draft Declaration on the Right of Asylum.*

(iii) *Draft Declaration on the Elimination of All Forms of Religious Intolerance.*

(iv) *Draft Declaration on the Elimination of Discrimination against Women.*

(v) *Draft Declaration on the Promotion among Youth of the Ideals of Peace, Mutual Respect and Understanding among Peoples.*

CONCLUDING OBSERVATIONS

There is one statement in Mr Fawcett's report with regard to which I have some reservations. Whether or not little progress has been made with the Draft Covenants for ten years is, of course, a matter of opinion. By the end of 1963 the Third Committee had completed the drafting of all the general and substantive provisions of both Draft Covenants, which covers a rather expanded version of what corresponds to Section I (Articles 1 to 18) of the European Convention on Human Rights and to all the substantive provisions of the European Social Charter, certainly an enormous field. In 1963 the Third Committee started its consideration of the measures of implementation. That the 1964 General Assembly was paralysed was due to the constitutional crisis of the Organisation caused by the controversy over the cost of peace keeping operations and was not due to reasons connected with the human rights work of the Organisation. The rhythm of the work may be disappointing; the achievement is hardly insignificant. In judging the situation we must keep in mind that the drafting agency is now an over-burdened assembly of 117 members. It had 113 Members in 1963. This is almost ten times as many as were the original signers of the European Convention. As Professor Sohn has said, the Covenants will be completed within the foreseeable future, within some three to five years or so. Whether the measures of implementation which the General Assembly will approve will be satisfactory is, however, another question.

It has recently been said[1] that we do not 'render a service to the

[1] Ambassador Franklin H. Williams, *Howard Law Journal*, 1965, vol. 11, p. 383.

cause of international human rights by encouraging the notion that the multiplication of reports and studies and resolutions and declarations and conventions is a measure of progress. On the contrary, by creating the illusion of activity, these voluminous reports and impressive-appearing studies may only serve to invite evasion of true responsibility and to afford Governments a convenient substitute for action.' This writer does not deny that there is a large element of truth in this statement. However, while the conclusion of international treaties does not in itself guarantee that they will in practice be respected, they certainly are a step towards this goal. As to 'declarations', they cannot be made binding upon States in the sense that a treaty is binding upon the parties to it, but they may be considered to impart a strong expectation that members will abide by them and in so far as expectation is gradually justified by State practice, a declaration may by custom become recognised as laying down rules binding upon States.[1] If adopted unanimously, or virtually unanimously, they may constitute an agreement between the parties regarding the interpretation of the Charter or of another treaty. As to surveys, 'studies' and reports, in particular the UN periodic reporting system referred to earlier, the UN Commission on Human Rights has said (1965 Report) that they are 'not only a source of information, but also a valuable incentive to Governments' efforts to protect human rights and fundamental freedoms'.

The United Nations developments do not measure up to the European Convention in neatness and solidity. If it were otherwise, the United Nations would not need to pursue the uphill fight to get the world-wide Human Rights Covenants and measures of implementation adopted, signed and ratified.

However, with all its deficiencies and its lack of system and symmetry, the work of the United Nations in the human rights field has, from its beginning, been a dynamic and by no means insignificant operation and in some of its aspects, particularly in regard to racial discrimination and the status of women, more radical and effective than what has been achieved in Western Europe.

SUMMARY OF THE DISCUSSION

Andrew Martin, deputising for the Rapporteur,[2] summarised Mr Fawcett's paper in the form of ten propositions and three conclusions. He then proceeded to make a few comments of his own: I

---

[1] Statement by the UN Office of Legal Affairs, 1962.

[2] In preparing the Report (in advance of the Conference) Mr Fawcett deputised for Professor Martin. In presenting the Report at the Conference, Professor Martin deputised for Mr Fawcett.

agree entirely with what Mr Fawcett says about the importance of publicity; but I dare not go along with him when he suggests that something, and possibly much, could be gained by further co-ordinating and even centralising the efforts of the many non-governmental organisations which operate in the field of human rights. From my own experience in the United Kingdom, I would say that their co-ordination through the Standing Conference on the economic and social work of the United Nations has reached a point beyond which further centralisation might well be counter-productive of ideas and pressures alike. Co-ordination has the great merit of eliminating overlapping efforts; but it can endanger the capacity of individual organisations to make an immediate response to whatever stimuli may at any given moment require a response to new ideas or fresh complaints. *A fortiori* centralisation has its drawbacks. Many of us know from our war-time experiences that five blasts coming from different directions often had a better chance of hitting the target than one big bomb which, not infrequently, missed it.

The idea of a UN High Commissioner for human rights is very close to my heart. I wholeheartedly agree with Mr Fawcett that the present proposal standing in the name of Costa Rica could be strengthened in various ways and I hope that it will be; but the overriding consideration must be that nothing should be done that would be likely to make the passage of what is the real substance of the proposal unduly difficult or altogether problematical.

Mr Fawcett gives three examples indicating possible ways in which teeth could be put into the office of the High Commissioner. To begin with he suggests a measure of de-centralization, i.e. the appointment of six or seven regional commissioners around the globe, each standing in the same relationship to the UN as the others. I feel a little apprehensive about this, for I am not sure that one can readily find six or seven candidates of that exceptional format which is here required. As in the case of the Ombudsman, so in the case of the proposed High Commissioner, the personality of the incumbent and particularly of the first incumbent counts as much, and possibly more, than the office itself; all depends on his personal drive, stature, persuasiveness, and dynamism. There is much to be learned from the history of the UN High Commissioner for Refugees.

As for Mr Fawcett's other proposals, i.e. that the High Commissioner should have power to express his views on individual cases, and again that he should have power to ask Governments for further information and to publish the fact, should it arise, of their refusal to provide it, I am wholeheartedly in favour of these, subject to the overriding consideration I mentioned before of not jeopardizing the safe passage of the basic proposal. Many will say that such additional powers would be tantamount to introducing the right of individual petition through the back door. I personally do not mind that at all. I have always taken the view, and I have been in good company, that an effective right of individual petition was inherent in those provisions of the UN Charter which referred to human rights. Many people think that since 1947, when the Human Rights Commission made its self-denying ordinance about individual complaints, this has been a closed issue. I do not agree, and I think that today's gathering of distinguished scholars and high officials would be entirely within its rights if it demonstrated that the debate is, in fact, still open.

Paul Weis: as this is the first time that I have the privilege of addressing this Conference, may I express to the Secretary-General of the Council of Europe and the University of Vienna the thanks of the Secretary-General of the United Nations and the United Nations High Commissioner for Refugees, whom I have been asked to represent here, for their kind invitation.

The work of the Council of Europe in the field of human rights and its spectacular achievements are watched with great interest by the United Nations. How could it be otherwise in the case of the United Nations? To use the words of the Secretary-General: 'Concern for human rights and fundamental freedoms goes back to the dawn of history', but ' . . . such concern became, for the first time, a universal goal only under the Charter of the United Nations'.

The activities of the United Nations in the field of human rights have been reviewed by Professor Schwelb in his excellent background document on 'The Human Rights Work of the United Nations' and I can certainly do no better than to refer to his paper. Perhaps the work of the United Nations in this field is viewed by many people too much from the aspect of the efforts to arrive at universal Covenants on Human Rights, which up to now have not yet led to final results, that is to say to the adoption of the Covenants. Some, perhaps less spectacular, efforts of the United Nations and particularly of its Specialised Agencies which have succeeded should, I believe, not be lost sight of. Professor Sohn has drawn attention to the inter-relation between such universal instruments and the European Convention, a problem which is by no means theoretical, as some of these instruments are already on the international statute book and the parties to the European Convention are parties thereto.

This brings me to the problem of implementation. It is known that one of the reasons which so far have held up the adoption of the Covenants is the difficulty to reach agreement on a world-wide basis on methods of implementation. Mr Fawcett in his excellent paper has outlined the various methods of implementation within the framework of the United Nations, designed for States with widely differing standards, methods among which at present the compulsory method of enforcement by judicial settlement has been rarely resorted to.

Apart from publicity, other methods have been evolved, including investigation of complaints by committees, missions on the spot, examination of petitions, hearing of witnesses, etc. It is interesting to note that such methods are used by the United Nations, not only for the implementation of binding obligations, but for the implementation of Declarations which as such are not legally binding, as for example the Declaration on the Granting of Independence to Colonial Countries and Peoples, or the Declaration on Racial Discrimination. This, it would seem to me, is a most interesting development from the aspect of international law.

The Declarations so far adopted, first of all the Universal Declaration of Human Rights, are resolutions of the General Assembly and as such do not entail legal commitments. They are resolutions made in a particularly solemn form and it was certainly the intent of their creators that they should be universally applied. Although not legally binding, their indirect legal effect has been far-reaching, as has been shown so well by Professor Schwelb. The Declaration has been incorporated in treaties, national constitutions and laws and has been the basis for judicial decisions of national courts. This tendency to take account of basic principles of human rights even in the absence of legal obligations has been mentioned in the discussion.

Professor Schwelb has in his paper spoken of a 'twilight zone of quasi-legislative pronouncements'. Surely such methods are difficult to reconcile with the traditional concept of international law as law regulating the relations between States, of which individuals are at best its objects. Does the test of *opinio juris sive necessitatis* as evidence of customary international law—a difficult test in any case in the absence of judicial determination—still hold good? We, as lawyers, must refrain from speculation and declaring to be law what we would wish to be law; but the increased emphasis on the individual and his human rights and the increased resort to 'quasi-legislation' as a substitute for international legislation is certainly a novel development which cannot be disregarded. It would be presumptuous of me in such a distinguished gathering of international lawyers to try and answer these questions. The remarks made by Professor Ganshof van der Meersch in this connection have certainly been most interesting. It must suffice to raise these questions here. Traditional concepts have become blurred, but the new ones are not yet clear. We live, it would appear, in a period of transition.

A proposal for the creation of a United Nations High Commissioner for Human Rights, which is before the General Assembly, as a new method for the implementation of human rights on the international level, has frequently been mentioned in the discussion. This matter being before the General Assembly, it would not be for me to express any views on it. As has been said, the proposal for the establishment of such an institution follows the pattern of an existing body, the UNHCR. Since I have the honour to serve on this body, I may be allowed, before concluding, to say a few words about this institution. The UNHCR has been charged by the General Assembly with the international protection of refugees. Among his tasks, as defined in his Statute, are the promotion of the 'conclusion and ratification of international conventions for the protection of refugees and the supervision of their application'. He shall, 'through special agreements with Governments, promote the execution of any measures calculated to improve the situation of refugees'. Thus, the protection and promotion of the human rights of refugees is his task. The Office has been created and its functions defined by Resolutions of the General Assembly. It thus has a moral not a legal authority; but under the Convention relating to the Status of Refugees of 28 July 1951, to which forty-eight States are parties at present, the Contracting States undertake to co-operate with the Office of UNHCR in the exercise of its functions, and in particular to facilitate its duty of supervising the application of the provisions of the Convention. Thus, what was from the start only a moral authority has, in States parties to the 1951 Convention, become a legal authority. A number of Contracting States have by national legislation or administrative measures, or under agreements with UNHCR, associated the Office with national procedures for the protection of refugees, particularly for the recognition of refugee status. It seems a rather startling phenomenon that the status of a group of persons which under general international law is most precarious has been integrated particularly closely into international law. Within the Council of Europe on the regional level, the protection of human rights has reached, through the safeguards embodied in the European Convention, a far higher degree of integration than on the global scale. We in the United Nations follow your work with close interest, and I may say, for myself, with admiration. The methods may differ, the aims are the same: the protection of human rights and of human dignity.
Georges Aronstein: the originality and significance of the European Convention on Human Rights reside in the right of individual petition and in the competence of the Court. But for these two provisions, the Convention would be ineffectual and would remain a dead letter, for the applications lodged by States so far have had

national political aims. We have not yet acquired a sufficient degree of political morality for one Government to bring an action against another Government in an entirely unselfish manner and solely to serve the cause of human rights.

A serious threat is hanging over the Convention: countries as important as France have not even ratified it, and it is unlikely that the conception of sovereignty held by that country's present rulers will permit ratification. Other countries like Great Britain,[1] Italy, Turkey and Greece have not subscribed to Articles 25 and 46. Moreover, Belgium[2] has not yet renewed its declaration—which expired on 29 June 1965—recognising the compulsory jurisdiction of the Court; this is currently recognised by only eight States, the minimum prescribed in Article 56 of the Convention. The Belgian attitude is due to the Belgian linguistic disputes and to the revival of nationalism in Europe. The abstention of certain great powers is often used as an argument by adversaries of the Convention.

Thus the existence of the Court appears to be threatened. The weakening of the Convention itself can be prevented only by the acceptance, if possible by all the Member States, of Article 25 and of the compulsory jurisdiction of the Court. If the right of individual petition ceased to be recognised, the Convention would lose its entire significance.

*   *   *   *

If the effectiveness of the Universal Declaration of Human Rights is to be comparable with that of the Convention, it is essential not only that the Covenants which have been under discussion for many years should be adopted and ratified, but also that they should provide for machinery for their implementation, for investigation and decision, machinery which so far is practically non-existent.

In order to break out of the present deadlock in the protection of human rights at United Nations level, it has been proposed to appoint a United Nations High Commissioner for Human Rights—his status would, *mutatis mutandis*, be comparable to that of the High Commissioner for Refugees—with certain powers of investigation and study, who, in collaboration with the Governments, could gradually secure the practical application of the Universal Declaration and the Covenants. A certain parallelism might thus develop between the implementation of the Convention and that of the Declaration.

I. C. MacGibbon: two views presented to this Conference prompt me

---

[1] By declaration of 14 January 1966, Great Britain subscribed to Articles 25 and 46 for a period of three years. (Editor's note.)

[2] Belgium has meanwhile renewed, for a period of two years, its recognition of the compulsory jurisdiction of the Court. (Editor's note.)

to counsel caution. The first was expressed elsewhere by Sir Humphrey Waldock, after noting echoes of the Universal Declaration in a variety of national and international instruments, in these words: 'This constant and widespread recognition of the principles of the Universal Declaration clothes it . . . in the character of customary law'. World-wide State practice, however, gainsays such a conclusion and underlines the gap between promise and performance. Compliance has been sporadic and inconstant, often lacking any *opinio juris*. Further, it is difficult to reconcile with the protracted efforts to finalize the Draft Covenants and, with other instruments, to achieve their general ratification, which alone would give the principles of the Declaration normative force. In short, the Declaration still best describes its own status as 'a common standard of achievement'.

The second is that Declarations of the General Assembly create international law—so-called 'instant' or 'pressure-cooked' custom. Resolutions may authorize United Nations action, but they do not become law by being labelled Declarations. Their normative quality differs according to the circumstances of their adoption. None comes nearer to being law-making than the 1963 Declaration of Legal Principles Governing the Exploration and Use of Outer Space —adopted unanimously, without dissent, without abstention, widely equated with existing law, and expressly recognized as such by the two 'space powers' in their undertakings to respect its provisions. These features make it the exception rather than the rule.

Felix Ermacora (Comments on Part IV of the Report): I can share the Rapporteur's optimism only from the theoretical point of view; the facts are quite different. There is a vast gulf between the proclaimed objects of the Universal Declaration of Human Rights and the respect accorded them in the work of the United Nations and in the practice of member States. I need quote only one example of what happens in regard to the protection of minorities within the framework of the United Nations. Events in this field are at once revealing and symptomatic.

There are amongst us several specialists on the work of the United Nations—Professors Sørensen, Zemanek, Capotorti, Sir Samuel Hoare, Professors Weis and Schwelb—who may well subscribe to these critical remarks. Mr Fawcett's report does not draw attention to existing difficulties. I am convinced that this group, full of good will as it is, would soon come to agreement on positive proposals; but we should discuss the difficulties first in order to be able better to appreciate such proposals.

The efforts made to establish *universal* protection of human rights are not very promising at the present time. The following arguments are used to justify delaying the protection of human rights in practice:

1. We must wait until the national conscience of the African States and other new States has been awakened. State sovereignty must be protected.

2. Furthermore, the following difficulties arise:

(*a*) Eastern and Western conceptions of the meaning of human rights are fundamentally different. In the Communist States, for example, it is believed that there is no need for fundamental rights to protect the individual against the community, since the community itself already protects the individual.

(*b*) A differentiation is made between 'true human rights' and 'political human rights', which is world-wide.

(*c*) Heads of delegations, who are politically responsible, are not included in negotiations.

But global agreement alone would constitute progress, global agreement which was not confined to the delegations.

No one seems prepared at present to go beyond the report system. However, the United Nations cannot report on anything without the support of States and *non-governmental organisations*. No one is able to check whether the reports presented by States are correct and complete; there is no authority competent for this purpose. The point is, therefore, on what and in what way, do States make their reports, do they ever criticise themselves?

The hostility of Eastern countries towards non-governmental organisations is well-known.

The system of individual petitions within the framework of the United Nations is a farce.

It is certainly necessary in the Afro-Asian field to endeavour to set up a High Commissioner for Human Rights or an Ombudsman operating *at regional level* with gradually increasing powers.

But let us consider first of all what remains to be done here in our own more homogeneous Community:

(*a*) Ratification of the Convention by France, Switzerland and Malta.[1]

(*b*) Recognition of the right of individual petition and of the compulsory jurisdiction of the European Court by all Member States of the Council of Europe.

(*c*) The abolition of political complaints by one State against another and the appointment of an Ombudsman to act as an international authority to receive complaints within the framework of the Council of Europe.

I would like to add a word in conclusion: do not underestimate the

[1] Malta ratified the Convention in January 1967. (Editor's note.)

significance of supranational protection from the point of view of the rule of law within States. Cases which might become political issues after exhaustion of all remedies in municipal law would once again become essentially legal problems if they could be brought before the European Court, and could be solved in a peaceful atmosphere without external pressure. But there is a still better method to which the Preamble best points the way: if only the State itself gave its citizens no cause for complaint, the situation would indeed be peaceful.

J. J. Cremona (Prospects of world-wide protection of human rights—positive and negative aspects): when, in relation to human rights, we speak of 'recognition' on a universal basis, the very pertinent question arises: what are the prospects of a global implementation of human rights today?

The incorporation of human rights provisions in State Constitutions has, especially of late, become a very common fact. The United Kingdom, without even a written Constitution, stands in this respect in remarkable isolation; but what the British did not do for themselves they have certainly been doing in the last few years for the newly emerging independent members of the Commonwealth. Still, it is true to say that on the whole, at this particular moment in time, the Commonwealth presents a rather heterogeneous picture in this respect.

In Britain and some of the older members of the Commonwealth there is no constitutional formulation of human rights. The view is still being taken that the protection of human rights depends more on the good sense of the politicians and the watchfulness of the people than on formal written guarantees. Of the older members of the Commonwealth, Canada has recently formulated, on a statutory basis, a Bill of Rights with what appears to be a rather limited scope. Of the other members of the Commonwealth, some have an elaborate set of guaranteed human rights, others a shorter and less impressive set, while others still are content with non-justiciable affirmations relating to certain human rights in the preamble of the Constitution or in a presidential declaration to be made on assumption of office. And in some cases the guarantees themselves have varying degrees of effectiveness. My country—Malta—has an extensive and enforceable Bill of Rights in the Constitution.

Even in a Commonwealth which purports to be united by certain common bonds, there is thus a wide diversity of approach to the subject of human rights. Obviously, if human rights are to be effectively dealt with in a Constitution, a mere formulation of them is not enough. There must also be provision for judicial enforcement. And even this would not be enough if the principle of the independence of the judiciary is not jealously safeguarded. What is indeed vitally important, if the concept of human rights is to flourish and spread in the future, is that a political climate should be produced in which not only human rights but also their effective enforcement can really thrive. Let us not forget that the United Kingdom still has no written constitutional human rights guarantees, and we in Malta had consistent adherence to basic human rights much before their constitutional formulation, while in some countries with an elaborate constitutional Bill of Rights the upholding of such rights would encounter, to say the least, some serious difficulties.

The truth is that we lawyers are perhaps a little too apt to look upon a Bill of Rights as a purely legal instrument, whereas it has also political and social implications and connections. Suffice it to consider some newly emergent non-European States which have set their heart on a top-speed achievement of economic and social development. With certain common tendencies and ideologies, countries are apt to form groups and their conception of human rights is adapted to, and essentially coloured by, those tendencies and ideologies. These considerations strengthen the view that the best prospects of a general implementation of human rights, at least for the immediate future, lie in the direction of regional groupings; and in this connection it is reasonable to assume that the European Convention will long remain a source of inspiration.

What I would repeat is that if a global implementation is achievable at all, it can only be achieved if a political climate is created in which effective and enforceable respect for human rights can thrive. This can best be brought about by fostering a general public *awareness* of human rights. Indeed, these are the basic rights of the individual and their full import should be made to reach the individual. After all, the recent proposals for a United Nations High Commissioner or Attorney-General for Human Rights may well be viewed as a personification of this general public awareness.

Peter Benenson (High Commissioner for Human Rights—Article 57 of the Convention): the proposal to appoint a High Commissioner for Human Rights within the framework of the United Nations has so far been sponsored by Costa Rica and Canada. Implementation of this proposal is still a long way off, however, for it is very difficult to persuade the government representatives of the need for such a Commissioner. The proposal should be worded as vaguely as possible, so as to make it acceptable to the maximum number of States.

The Secretary-General of the Council of Europe could assist the High Commissioner by carrying out the function referred to in Article 57 of the Convention. The High Commissioner would have to be in a position to see individual applications. The filtering which would be necessary could perhaps be done by non-governmental organisations. But this, as indeed all our activities, depends to a very great extent on the financial resources available.

Another objective is the effective application of the right of individual application. When this has been achieved, considerable progress will have been made.

Father M. B. Crowe (The influence of the Church in promoting human rights): the Churches should also concern themselves with the doctrine of human rights. The Encyclical *Pacem in Terris* of Pope John XXIII represented a big step in this direction; it was a revolution in the ecclesiastical view of human rights. We must not forget that in our technical work in this field, which I am far from underestimating, inspiration is essential. For this, the Encyclical is a particularly appropriate instrument and should be included in the documentation which it is planned to assemble.

G. O. Warburg (1. Role of non-governmental organisations in implementing the Human Rights Convention; 2. United Nations High Commissioner for Human Rights; 3. Influence of the European Convention on Human Rights on universal Conventions): like Professor Martin, I do not favour Mr Fawcett's proposal to centralize the non-governmental organisations. Where their co-ordination is concerned, Mr Fawcett seems to me to be too pessimistic, for co-ordination has already existed for many years at least in certain countries. Formal co-operation between a large number of non-governmental organisations does exist, for instance, in Great Britain and the USA; another co-ordinating body, to which I belong, and in which twenty-two organisations are represented, has its seat in Geneva. It is doing successful pioneer work in this field. If we are to have any success at all, we must, I think, define the functions of a High Commissioner for Human Rights in as general terms as possible. Publication of the results achieved by the Convention and its implementation to date would, I feel, be an important step towards a world-wide Convention.

Gordon L. Weil: the effective protection of human rights, particularly when an international agreement is applied in a domestic context, depends on the individual being well-informed. Information on human rights protection should be made a part of required instruction in schools, and should also be made available through the publicity media. The European Convention is in a virtually unique position, since it is applied in an area where individuals are aware of public events taking place around them. In other areas of the world, such awareness does not exist and the effective protection of human rights, based on the individual's right to make an official complaint, is impossible.

Human rights protection is clearly both a legal and a political matter. A multiplicity of pressure groups, clamouring for the implementation of the Convention, is both appropriate politically and likely to bring results. The Press depends on the activities of such groups and the admittedly political acts of individuals and States in bringing complaints is news. The Press should be exploited in making individuals aware of the possibilities for protecting human rights.

A provision might be added to the European Convention requiring States to publicise the Convention widely.

SUMMING UP BY

ANDREW MARTIN, Q.C.

I fully agree with Mr Aronstein that Articles 25 and 46 of the European Convention deserve the support of all major powers. I am happy to be able to say that the question whether the United Kingdom ought to exercise its option in regard to these two Articles is even now under active consideration.

I welcome the emphasis placed by Dr Weis on the difference between the traditional techniques of international law and the modern techniques of quasi-legislation, and, in particular, on the highlighting of individual rights. The proposal concerning the UN High Commissioner for Human Rights is entirely in line with these new techniques, the viability of which has been amply demonstrated by the success of the UN High Commissioner for Refugees.

In reply to Professor Ermacora, I would say that on my reading of Mr Fawcett's report he did not overlook the difficulties which stand in the way of the global enforcement of human rights. In fact the appointment of a UN High Commissioner would be the beginning of global enforcement and a significant move away from the present system of dealing with individual complaints which Professor Ermacora has bluntly, and rightly, called a farce.

Mr Justice Cremona has done a great service by stressing the crucial importance of 'public awareness'. There is a tremendous educational job yet to be performed. The only point where I would, with great respect, take issue with the learned Judge concerns his prescription of 'global implementation through regional groupings'. Our real difficulty is at the centre, and it is at the centre, i.e. in the forum of the United Nations, where the battle must continue to be fought. Dr Weil's contribution has linked up admirably with that of Mr Justice Cremona. He too has laid strong stress on the educational tasks which lie ahead in our field and his insistence on the need to harness the techniques of publicity to the tasks of education has been most valuable. And yet, I cannot help feeling that the major emphasis must be on educating the young; it is in our early, formative years that we ought to be made aware of the true meaning of our rights as individuals.

In the more technical field of international law, Dr MacGibbon's warning that we must be careful not to equate mere declarations with positive law was just as timely as Dr Weis's had been. To my mind, however, that is yet another powerful argument for keeping the Universal Declaration constantly before the general public. Declarations, although not law in themselves, have a way of stimulating the development of the law on the lines laid down in them; and we must not give up hoping that in due course the law governing human rights will catch up with the Universal Declaration, either in the precise forms aimed at in the draft covenants or in the form of more general principles. In this respect Professor Schwelb's intervention has been of real help; it has been good to hear an authority of his stature assure us that perhaps a far too gloomy view is being taken, in many quarters, of the progress of the Covenants.

I hardly need to say that I subscribe wholeheartedly to what Mr Benenson has had to say about the importance of public opinion. His practical suggestions about enlisting the support of the universities and of non-governmental organisations of all kinds will, I am sure, be taken to heart by all of us who are assembled here; and most of us, I believe, will agree with his advice that the functions of the High Commissioner should be broadly rather than precisely defined.

Mr Vasak has drawn our attention to the importance of the procedural aspects of the methods of enquiry to be applied to complaints concerning human rights. Whether the time is ripe for thinking in terms of a Permanent Committee of Enquiry is of course an open question; but it is one to which all of us will wish to give serious thought.

Dr Warburg has warned us against any attempts further to centralise the work of non-governmental organisations. I know that his experience of these matters is formidable, and I am sure that all of us have listened to his arguments with the greatest possible respect.

CHAPTER IX

The protection of human rights within the framework of existing regional organisations

REPORT BY
JEAN-FLAVIEN LALIVE

Experience has shown that there can be no hope of achieving effective protection of human rights and fundamental freedoms on a world-wide scale in the near future. The Universal Declaration of Human Rights adopted by the United Nations in 1948 was a reaction against the horrors of war, the result of a noble surge of fellow-feeling; but, contrary to general expectations, it was not supplemented by pacts or conventions providing for compulsory machinery preferably judicial in nature. Without such machinery, the Declaration whatever its juridical scope (in any case a matter of controversy) could not achieve its objectives.

In a situation where States were unable to find general solutions to the problems confronting them, in this field and in others, the idea of regionalism, already embodied in the United Nations Charter, made rapid progress. But what gave this movement its full force was the European Convention for the Protection of Human Rights and Fundamental Freedoms signed in Rome on 4 November 1950 and brought into force on 3 September 1953.

Simultaneously with the rapid growth in the membership of the United Nations (it rose from 51 in 1945 to the present figure of 118 and is still increasing), there has been a proliferation of regional organisations. The initial United Nations 'groups' (pressure groups or electoral groups of Latin-American and Afro-Asian States) became, as it were, institutionalised and, in some cases, split up into smaller groups reflecting more specifically regional affinities. Some of them even became operational (Lebanon, 1956; Cuba, 1960; Congo, 1963). At the same time Economic Commissions were set up for Europe, Asia and Africa; these have extended their activities and, in certain cases, reinforced their independence, while remaining agencies of the United Nations. In addition, mention should be made of the Organisation of American States, already of long standing, and the Arab League, both of which were in existence in 1945. Since then, many other regional organisations have been founded, such as the Council of Europe, the North Atlantic Treaty Organisation (NATO), the Central Treaty Organisation (CENTO), the South-East Asia Treaty Organisation (SEATO), the Organisation of Central American States (OCAS) and the Organisation of African Unity(OAU). As for the famous British Commonwealth, the increase in its membership resulting from the process of decolonisation has been accompanied by a progressive loss of cohesion. Is it still possible to talk of a 'club' whose members are united by a dual common denominator, viz. language and a legal system based on the Common Law? This is less certain than it used to be. Nevertheless, it was in the field of human rights that the Commonwealth could have played—and perhaps still can play—a beneficial role, for the 'Rule of Law', one of the foundations of the Common Law, is closely bound up with respect for the human personality and protection of the rights of the individual.

All these regional organisations, some of which are geared to purely military considerations, while others fulfil a variety of functions, have created a climate conducive to the initiation and development of joint ventures in the field of human rights. The effect which the Rome Convention has had as a stimulus and a catalyst is well known. In the course of numerous journeys which the author of the report made for the International Commission of Jurists between 1958 and 1961 in Asia, Africa and Latin America, the questions most often asked after lectures to jurists, politicians and students were concerned with the operation of the Rome Convention in Europe and the organs to which it had given rise.

It was in 1959, nine years after the signing of the Rome Convention, that a draft Inter-American Convention on Human Rights was adopted. In 1961, the idea of a regional convention was intensively discussed at the first African Congress of Jurists, an occasion which provided French and English speaking African lawyers with their first opportunity of meeting and comparing notes. In recent years the idea of regional conventions has made further progress and there is now talk of such conventions for the Arab world, the British Commonwealth, Asia and, lately, even Eastern Europe.

It has been observed—and the International Commission of Jurists, among other organisations, has repeatedly stressed this—that no matter how excellent constitutions may be, no matter how noble and lofty the terms in which declarations or treaties aimed at safeguarding human rights and fundamental freedoms may be couched, they are of very little worth and may even involve dangers unless they are accompanied by an effective system of control, preferably in the form of judicial machinery guaranteeing the effective protection of those rights by an independent judiciary. The constitutional laws of such countries as the USSR and Spain differ from those, for example, of India and Australia much less in the nature of the rights they guarantee to the individual than in the fact that they provide for no genuine means of control and protection.

It has been very rightly pointed out that the elaboration of regional conventions on human rights is facilitated by the social factor of the closer solidarity found among nations, as among individuals, belonging to the same geographical region. It has also been seen that a framework for regional conventions can often be provided by already existing organisations.

An examination of the efforts made in various parts of the world and of the possible solutions should begin with Europe and the machinery set up by the Convention for the Protection of Human Rights and Fundamental Freedoms, which has now been in operation for more than a decade among fifteen of the eighteen Member countries of the Council of Europe. It is true that lawyers in certain new States have tried to break away from the so-called Western or European solutions. For example, they have sought to elaborate a rule of law which is different both from the European and Western 'constitutional State' (*Etat de droit, Rechtsstaat*) system and from the system of socialist legality. But the rule of law, which has been wrongly regarded as a product of the West, is in fact a universal ideal. It is this ideal that provided the basis for the system of human rights and fundamental freedoms, as laid down in the 1948 Universal Declaration of Human Rights, and, later, in the Rome Convention. Despite certain deficiencies and imperfections, the latter can be properly used as a model and inspiration for other regional conventions, not so much because it came first or because the West has any mission or vocation as a civilising force, but because it was the first convention to embody and institutionalise a set of aspirations that are shared by men in every part of the world, once they have progressed beyond the most primitive level of life.

In the absence of a jurisdiction empowered to make obligatory decisions, and to the extent that the somewhat revolutionary aspect of this solution may frighten certain States, it should be possible to set up a system of conciliation commissions, of an independent and permanent nature, on the model of those which have been tested in international public law in inter-state disputes.

On the practical level, the Rome Convention has shown that it is possible to reconcile two requirements which were once fairly generally regarded as incompatible, i.e. that it is possible to protect, through an independent authority (preferably judicial but not exclusively so), the fundamental rights of man on an international or transnational scale, without paralysing the machinery of the State or impairing its function of upholding law and order and national security. It has also been seen that the system is all the more effective in that it has been kept outside the field of politics. It is designed for individual actions, without the intervention of a State. Moreover, it is intended that the individual should play as large a part as possible in the proceedings. This avoids a drawback which was the bane of the whole problem of the protection of minorities in the inter-war period.

EFFORTS TO ELABORATE REGIONAL CONVENTIONS

I. Europe

The Rome Convention is the achievement of the States of Western, i.e. non-Communist, Europe. Its elaboration benefited to some extent from the Cold War atmosphere in the sense that the Cold War strengthened the solidarity of Western States and facilitated the creation of the various institutions and organisations.

For a long time the countries of Eastern Europe showed no interest in the Rome Convention, seeing it as a by-product of a capitalist civilisation based on the—for them—misguided concept of the rule of law, which they criticised as subordinating the rights and interests of the community, as they are said to exist in the ideal Socialist State, to the egotism of individual rights.

But as the States of Eastern Europe have asserted more and more their independence, and as their intellectual contacts with the West have multiplied, so their interest in the European Convention has grown. Two facts can be referred to in support of this. The first is that a doctorate thesis on the Rome Convention is shortly to be defended at the Prague Faculty of Law. The author, who chose his subject with the agreement of the university authorities, proposes the drawing up of a Socialist charter of human rights. Secondly, on his return from a visit to Poland, the Austrian Minister of Justice recently said how much he had been impressed by the interest shown by the Poles he had met in the system created under the Rome Convention for the protection of human rights.

One swallow does not make a summer. Nevertheless, these developments are encouraging and show that the idea of a regional convention for Socialist States is making headway.

II. America

Unlike Africa or Asia, where regional conventions on human rights are still only at the stage of ideas or intentions and have not yet even produced drafts, on the American continent, where—we must not forget—the States have enjoyed political independence for over a century, they have been trying for some considerable time to find some means of protecting human rights, in particular by the technique of international Conventions. This endeavour has been connected with a certain philosophy, a certain state of mind sometimes called *Americanidad*, defined as being characterised 'by a passionate desire to preserve the individual freedom of the individual American and the political independence of the people'.

The Organisation of American States at its ninth Inter-American Conference at Bogota in 1948—even before the Universal Declaration of Human Rights was adopted by the United Nations—adopted an 'American Declaration of the Rights and Duties of Man.'

At that Conference, the Inter-American Juridical Committee was instructed to draft a 'Statute for an Inter-American Court for the protection of Human Rights'. It had been understood that mere declarations of principle, even if inspired by the highest sentiments—and there are many such in Latin America—were by no means enough, and that it was necessary to provide a system of control to ensure respect for the rights thus promulgated.

A few years later, at the fifth Meeting of Consultation of the Ministers of Foreign Affairs of the Organisation of American States (OAS) held at Santiago (Chile) in 1959, the protection of human rights on the American continent took a considerable step forward. Resolution VIII instructed the Inter-American Council of Jurists to prepare a draft Inter-American Convention on Human Rights.

In the same Resolution, it was further decided to set up an Inter-American Commission on Human Rights, composed of seven members elected in a personal capacity by the Council of the OAS.

a) the Santiago Draft (Draft Inter-American Convention on Human Rights)

This text was prepared by the Inter-American Council of Jurists at their fourth session (September 1959) at Santiago (Chile). On the whole it followed the European Convention very closely, while introducing some appreciable improvements. Thus it covers not only civil and political rights, as does the Rome Convention, but also economic, social and cultural rights (right to free choice of work, to health and safety while at work, to fair remuneration, to social security, to form trade unions, to education, to participation in cultural life, to found a family, to the protection of the law and of the State, etc.).

The Santiago Draft provides for similar institutions as the European Convention: an Inter-American Commission on Human Rights and an Inter-American Court for the Protection of Human Rights. Their functions are comparable to those exercised by the corresponding European bodies.

This text was to have been examined at each of the subsequent Inter-American Conferences, but its examination was repeatedly postponed—most recently in July 1965.[1]

The Santiago Draft also proposes a new method of ensuring respect for economic, social and cultural rights. For the last of these, the Commission holds merely a watching brief (carrying out studies and surveys) with the power to make recommendations and observations to States, a system which is not likely to be very effective.

(b) the Inter-American Commission on Human Rights

This Commission began to function in 1960, when its members were elected. It has held ten ordinary and two extraordinary sessions. It is required by its Statute to promote respect for human rights. To this end it has taken cognisance, for information purposes, of individual petitions alleging violation of human rights in certain American States. It has addressed general recommendations to States, but has considered that it was not itself empowered to take decisions on the petitions received. Thus far, it has examined the situation relating to human rights in Cuba, Haiti, the Dominican Republic, Ecuador, Guatemala, Honduras, Nicaragua and Paraguay. During the recent Dominican crisis it even visited that country to collect information. Its general report, however, has not yet been published.

The Commission recently asked the Second Special Inter-American Conference (Rio de Janeiro, November 1965) for extended powers, so that it could take action on individual applications alleging violation of certain human rights (the right to life, to liberty, to security and integrity of person, and to the proper administration of justice). Even the extension of its powers, however, would not enable the Commission to make its decisions mandatory. At most it could ask respondent Governments for information relating to the petitions, make appropriate recommendations to them and if the recommended action was not taken, publish its report if need be. As can be seen, this would not go very far.

(c) Central American Convention on Human Rights

It was a private organisation, 'Freedom through Law', that prepared a draft Central American Convention. This is largely a carbon copy of the European Convention, though it may be doubted whether this was a wise solution, since the problems are not the same.

In October 1964 a 'Central American Jurists' Chapter' was set up in Nicaragua, comprising jurists from member countries of OCAS —the Organisation of Central American States (Costa Rica,

[1] It was, however, examined at the Second Special Inter-American Conference in Rio de Janeiro in November 1965. (Editor's note.)

Nicaragua, Honduras, El Salvador, Guatemala)—and from Panama. This Chapter is to meet very shortly and will reconsider the draft prepared by 'Freedom through Law'.

Conclusions

It may be wondered why the American States, which in their Constitutions and even in their practical institutions have often taken the lead as regards the protection of human rights, have not succeeded in progressing beyond the stage of preparing drafts which, though generous in their inspiration, have remained pious wishes and mere theories. Probably the true reason for this regrettable stagnation is to be sought not so much in the political instability of some States in that region, nor in a certain Latin tendency to let high-sounding declarations and verbal fireworks take the place of even modest practical achievements, as in the mistake of having associated the United States in this effort. For the United States is showing infinite caution in this field. In the same way as they virtually deprived their acceptance of the compulsory jurisdiction of the International Court of Justice of all real substance (by the Connally Amendment), so too, but more frankly, they have indicated that they have no intention of participating in conventions on human rights, and to this end have invoked certain constitutional bars and the federal structure of the Government.

Very probably the Santiago Draft would have a better chance of success if it were restricted to the Latin American States alone, united as they are by a common conception of human rights and particularly of the judicial institutions required to ensure respect for them. (In Latin America, unlike the common law countries, administrative law is highly developed both in practice and as a separate branch of study and this makes things easier).

The Inter-American Commission on Human Rights, moreover, played a helpful part in the recent crisis in the Dominican Republic. Its powers no doubt are still vague, since its authority is essentially moral and is exercised by recommendations with no binding force. However, even though it is more closely related to the traditional type of conciliation commission than to an arbitration tribunal or international court, it may serve as a necessary stage towards greater integration accompanied by real judicial powers. Its work in the Dominican crisis has been compared to that of the International Committee of the Red Cross—which is by no means a criticism. It is to be hoped, however, that its evolution will be rapid. If the Alliance for Progress as conceived by President Kennedy were to find a place in the thinking of the Latin American countries (which it has not yet done), it might be thought that its essential complement should be an

American Convention on Human Rights. It is known that in many developing countries, contrary to what might have been expected, social questions often take priority over economic interests. But social justice, rightly understood, necessarily implies the existence of individual rights and fundamental freedoms, protected by institutions which provide the indispensable guarantees.

The establishment of an organisation of this kind presupposes, of course, a clear idea of the respective degrees of development of the Latin American nations. This development is extremely varied, and it is therefore bound to be particularly awkward to implement a convention modelled too closely on the European Convention.

If the obstacles persist, it might be necessary to prepare a number of conventions, each covering a few States. This is the system of sub-regional conventions, which would facilitate the establishment of a progressive system for the enforcement of human rights. Nevertheless, the disadvantages of an excessive fragmentation in the field are far from negligible.

To sum up, it is essential to be cautious in making forecasts and to eschew solutions that are too close to the European answer. The danger to be avoided is that of building up an institution whose gleaming and harmonious facade would ill conceal its lack of substance.

At all events, the idea of sub-regional conventions applicable to groups of Latin American States: Central America, South America proper, Greater Colombia, etc., is worthy of close investigation.

III. Africa

We have seen that the idea of an African Convention on Human Rights was first propounded by the African Conference at Lagos in January 1961, organised by the International Commission of Jurists. It was enthusiastically received and, in the 'Law of Lagos', the African Congress stated that the Convention should provide for 'the creation of a court of appropriate jurisdiction and that recourse thereto should be made available to all persons under the jurisdiction of the signatory States'.

Nothing concrete has been done since that time; this is easy to understand, in view of the urgent problems facing the leaders of most African States. However, the idea has been given support in important quarters: for example, in August 1961, Mr Azikiwe, President of the Republic of Nigeria, made a speech containing an explicit reference to the European Convention. A number of other statements of similar purport have been made by African statesmen, from both English- and French-speaking countries; one such was made in 1963 by the President of the Ivory Coast National Assembly. In

z

May 1963, the idea was discussed at the Conference of African Heads of State and of Government at Addis Ababa; but nothing came of this, either. Lastly, in one or two other African States there has been more or less general and unofficial advocacy of an African Convention on Human Rights within the framework of the Organisation of African Unity.

The conclusion of such an instrument should be facilitated by the fact that the Organisation of African Unity is a genuine regional organisation, whose Charter repeatedly proclaims the adherence of African States to the cause of human rights.

In addition, the fact that all African peoples have been the victims of slavery and discrimination should induce them, in their own interest, to see the advantages of adopting an African Convention which would strengthen the bonds uniting them and, by ensuring respect for human rights in Africa, open the way towards unity in their continent. This could not but have a positive influence on the struggle to decolonise Africa and overthrow apartheid.

It is hard, at this time, to say to what extent such a convention should be based on the European Convention. The problems are no more the same here than they are in Latin America. The true face and personality of Africa are gradually emerging and we may therefore hope that before long the right solution will be found in this field as in others.

In practical terms, African jurists should be encouraged to draft an African convention on a private and unofficial basis. Once this has been done, the draft should be submitted to the Commission of African Jurists set up in Cairo in July 1964 by the Organisation of African Unity, and then to the appropriate bodies of that Organisation for adoption.

IV. Asia

Major progress towards the drafting of an Asian Convention on Human Rights would appear to date from the action of the Congress of South-East Asian and Pacific Jurists, held in Bangkok in February 1965 under the auspices of the International Commission of Jurists.

Nothing had been done until that time. The idea had presumably been discussed privately, now and then, but it is surprising to note that even an organisation such as SEATO, which is quite active in the legal and cultural fields, had never taken the matter up seriously. And at a time when the problems of Asia, and South-East Asia in particular, are delicate and so complex, there can be no hope of a rapid settlement of the question. Political difficulties are too great to allow optimism.

The Congress of Jurists admittedly expressed itself in favour of an

Asian Convention on Human Rights, which it felt would constitute 'an important contribution to the protection of human rights and to the solution of the problems of national, racial, religious and other minorities'. But this has not yet produced any positive reaction by the Governments concerned. The Ambassador of India to Paris has expressed rather timid support; nothing more. Despite these great difficulties, there can be no harm in a group of Asian jurists drawing up a detailed draft convention on human rights without delay. This will be a long-term project requiring much thought. A committee might be set up, however, composed of a few Asian jurists and, perhaps, one or two foreign experts. It is possible that, just as the Economic Commission for Asia is doing very beneficial work, a Legal Commission for Asia might also be useful even now. Its task would be considerable: first, it would study existing protection under national constitutions of the region, and then it would consider procedures for international control and make proposals for the protection of human rights, with due regard for the situation and possibilities in the Asian States.

A sub-regional convention has also been proposed—restricted, for example, to the states of the Indian subcontinent, where feeling in favour of the rule of law has been strong since independence. Such a convention might also usefully contribute to the protection of minorities in this part of the world.

V. Arab League

To my knowledge, the idea of an Arab Convention on Human Rights was first broached in 1960 at the meeting of Arab lawyers in Damascus. Little progress has been made since then, although many Arab jurists are following the experience of the European Convention with sympathy.

It is to be hoped that an Arab League stronger than the present one might undertake a project such as this, particularly since it gave very serious consideration to the proposal for the creation of an Arab Court of Justice several years ago. The question should be discussed with the foremost Arab jurists.

VI. British Commonwealth

Here again, the idea of a Commonwealth Convention on Human Rights originated with private institutions. It should be feasible, for the ground is well-prepared in several countries. One of the best-qualified judges of the Supreme Court of India said, a few years ago: 'We are happy to be free today, but we must remain eternally grateful to the British for having bequeathed us their language and the English legal system'.

As we have seen, some of the most important rights of individuals are to be found at the heart of the English legal system based, as it is, on the Rule of Law.

A British Commonwealth Convention would offer several advantages: it would slow down the present centrifugal trend and facilitate a degree of integration of Commonwealth countries, based as this grouping is, on the principles of freedom, equality and tolerance.

The idea of a Human Rights Convention for the Commonwealth has been discussed by 'Justice', the most important British private body of jurists, which is also the national section of the International Commission of Jurists. The organisation 'Amnesty International' should also be interested in this problem, which affects its activities very directly. At a time when disruptive tendencies are becoming increasingly manifest within the Commonwealth, any effort to 'institutionalise' the remaining positive elements—common language and legal system—should by all means be encouraged.

CONCLUSIONS

It seems probable today that the swiftest way to the effective protection of human rights and fundamental freedoms on a universal basis is via the *détour* of regional conventions and institutions. No doubt one can hope to achieve universal institutions one day, such as a World Court of Human Rights, but such a project would at present be premature, while the establishment of a network of regional bodies—courts, commissions of enquiry, conciliation commissions, etc.—would have an indisputable interest and value.

At the level of principles, universality is less difficult. This is in large measure the achievement of the Universal Declaration of Human Rights, even though jurists do not agree on its true scope: has it established or confirmed a common customary law, or is it merely a declaration of intention or, perhaps, of a body of rules of conduct and of moral principles establishing a common standard, without having yet acquired the full effect of compulsory usage? Reference can be made, on this question, to the still too little known Fourth Red Cross Convention, adopted at Geneva in 1949, on the protection of civilians in time of civil war or internal disorder, which gradually but very rapidly has acquired the force of true customary law.

There does not, then, yet exist, on the world level, independent and effective machinery assuring the realisation and protection of human rights, and it is in this field that the idea of regional institutions seems to be particularly fruitful. This has been demonstrated by the European example. It should be remembered that the importance of an

international administrative or judicial institution is not to be meas-
ured by the number of matters which it is called upon to handle.
The very existence of a jurisdiction plays a substantial preventive
role, as is proved by the example of the International Court of
Justice. How many disputes between States have been settled in the
privacy of chancelleries thanks to the simple threat of having recourse to the Court, that is to say of setting in motion a procedure
assured of the greatest possible publicity! For this 'preventive'
reason too, the speedy establishment of other commissions and
courts of human rights is to be desired.

On the other hand, a regional institution, limited to a defined
geographical area, permits full effect to be given to the feelings of
solidarity of the group and to its common juridico-political concepts.

It would be difficult to lay down with precision what the precise
substance and contents, *de lege forenda*, of a regional convention
should be. Too many factors vary from one region to another for it
to be possible to formulate provisions having a general value. It is in
Latin America—subject to the reservations made above—that the
situation seems to be most ripe. A properly concerted effort ought to
result in a rapid result. The precedent of the European Convention
on Human Rights will be of capital importance—not in the least as a
model from which no deviation is to be made, nor yet as an expression of legal perfection—which is not the case—but as an example of
what, in a given social context, a compromise can produce in the
way of strength and efficacity.

In Africa, it would be necessary to arouse a more active interest in
the Organisation of African Unity and leading circles generally,
awakening in them a full awareness of their role and a reassessment
of their position. It is easy to foresee the political and social obstacles
which will lie in the way of the rapid conclusion of a convention of
this nature. The question is equally delicate in Asia, where passions
are exacerbated and where present circumstances, political and
military, can scarcely be said, when viewed as a whole, to facilitate a
favourable evolution. In these regions the best hope of making
progress is by means of work in depth, on the educational and social
fronts. It must also be noted that in the hierarchy of the multiple
problems to be solved, the protection of human rights by no means
appears to present the same degree of urgency everywhere. Individual
rights presuppose a minimum standard of existence, and the objection has sometimes been made that all these rights scarcely count for
starving peoples, just as the freedom of the Press and of expression
only have a limited importance in a region whose population is
illiterate. It would also be necessary to achieve the institution of an
international centre for human rights which would act as a clearing

house and information centre permitting the encouragement of regional efforts without having recourse to over-ambitious methods.

In conclusion, regionalism does indeed appear to be the key to the problem of the effective protection of human rights on a world level. But the obstacles are many. Both discouragement and optimism must be avoided. The example of the fine achievement of the European Convention should inspire those who concern themselves with this massive undertaking in the other regions of the world.

WRITTEN COMMUNICATION BY
GORDON WEIL

HOW SIGNIFICANT AND EFFECTIVE IS THE EUROPEAN CONVENTION ON HUMAN RIGHTS?

The European Convention on Human Rights is something new in the world: an international agreement for the protection of human rights equipped with sanctions. Moreover, the Convention has proved its viability in over ten years of operation.

The significance of the Convention in international and domestic law is evidenced by the scope of publication and discussion of the Convention by legal experts from almost all Western countries during recent years.

Evaluated in terms of the protection it affords to individuals and groups, the Convention marks a major step forward. Compared with the low state of respect for human rights in Europe during the World War II period and the failure of the United Nations to go beyond the Universal Declaration, the Convention must be recognised as a significant, practical measure.

Yet the Second World War is now twenty years behind us and we have had a reasonable period of experience with the Convention. Thus the significance and effectiveness of the Convention must be evaluated by the standards of 1965 not those of 1955 or 1945.

It would in all probability be impossible to create the Convention today if it did not already exist. It will be recalled that the Convention was signed in November 1950. The Council of Europe's Consultative Assembly had held the Member States to their commitment, growing out of the 1948 Hague Congress and the Council Statute, to establish an international human rights agreement. The protracted tug-of-war between the Assembly and the Ministers illustrates the Member States' reluctance to concede more than they could be morally compelled to accept in the Convention.

True, protocols have been added to the Convention in later years. But the lack of enthusiasm of the Member States either to accept the optional undertakings of the Convention or to accept the more liberal proposals for the additional protocols, or to ratify them quickly, can cause doubt about the depth of these States' commitments to the Convention. Thus it is doubtful that the Consultative Assembly could today convince a reluctant Committee of Ministers even to accept the inclusion of the optional clauses of the existing Convention.

The significance of the Convention, if not its potential, is damaged by the relatively small number of valid applications. This is not meant as a criticism of the Commission, which has done an outstanding job in carefully examining each application to determine if it qualifies legally or if it is merely an irresponsible barb aimed at one of the Member States. It is the number admitted by the Commission, not the total number of applications, which must lead us to conclude that the Convention is not overly effective.

The small number of applications is probably due to two factors: the limited number of national acceptances of the right of individual application and lack of awareness of the Convention by potential applicants.

There has been no significant increase in the number of acceptances of the right of individual application or of the Court's jurisdiction since the Convention first came into effect. The one country which did not ratify the Convention at the outset has still not done so. The limiting effect is obvious if one notes that there have only been three inter-state applications. Such applications are the only avenues open in relation to those States which have not accepted the right of individual application. Originally, it was feared that inter-state applications would multiply when one State was seeking to embarrass another politically. This certainly may have been the reason for the three applications that have been made. Yet it is clear that States do not attach much importance to the nuisance value of the Convention, since the number of politically-inspired applications is so small. Of course, the hope that States would not consider the submission of an inter-state application as a hostile act has not been fulfilled. Thus, even this part of the Convention, which binds all States ratifying the Convention, has hardly been used.

Only ten States have accepted the right of individual application.[1] For all intents and purposes these are the only States effectively bound by the Convention. Why were even these States willing to accept the right of individual application? Special historical reasons no doubt dictated the German willingness to accept both of the optional clauses of the Convention. The other States who have accepted individual application are among the smaller States of

[1] The United Kingdom was the eleventh in 1966. (Editor's note.)

Europe; these smaller States have traditionally been the supporters of international arrangements for legal, social and economic matters. Almost all other decisions under the Convention have been made in cases involving these States, most having been related to Germany. None of these States has been caused acute international or domestic embarrassment by the number or nature of the applications.

The other Member States of the Council of Europe could not in good conscience argue that they were free from the reasonable doubt that they harboured some cases of human rights violations. This is, in effect, what they say, of course, since they have agreed in the Convention that human rights in Europe should be protected by means beyond national boundaries, but failed to implement their declaration. In this way they are really no more bound than are the Member States of the United Nations who pay lip service to the Universal Declaration.

Failure to accept the Court's jurisdiction and, to a lesser extent, refusal to include the right of individual application to the Commission are also serious weaknesses in the Convention. The Commission has gone far to minimise the harmful effects this could have on the development of the Convention by converting itself into a judicial body of the highest calibre. The Commission is not merely a sieve to filter out frivolous applications; in deciding on the admissibility of an application, it must and does consider the merits of the case. Its success in fairly rejecting both the frivolous applications and those which must bear the closest legal scrutiny before a decision is made, while accepting the few well-founded applications, has been the key to the durability of the Convention system.

Yet the slow procedure before the Commission must act as a deterrent to potential applicants. Almost all must have undertaken a lengthy Odyssey through the national courts before reaching the stage of Commission investigation, hearing and decision. This built-in delay is manifestly discouraging to an individual who has spent years in court at substantial cost to himself. Obviously, too, this delay discourages inter-state applications, since the plaintiff seeking political advantage through the application must have a reasonable expectation of success in a short enough time for the decision to be useful as a tool of policy. In this regard, it can be argued that submission of an inter-state application alone is useful, because of the publicity value the plaintiff can draw from it. As mentioned earlier, it seems that the Member States have attached less importance to this limited resource at their disposal.

Individuals who might be expected to make applications under the Convention probably do not do so because they are either unaware of the Convention or misunderstand it. This situation results from a lack of publicity and instruction about the Convention. Most people learn the rudiments of their national court systems and the national means available to them for the protection of their rights in the course of their required education. It is true that in some countries the Convention is part of the national legal system, and it is to be hoped that regular instruction contains reference to the Convention and that lawyers can learn about it during their studies. Yet even in these countries and in others where the Convention is not part of national law, ignorance of the Convention's very existence is widespread. It might be argued: 'Why bother telling people in country X about the Convention, since country X has not accepted the right of individual application (or perhaps country X has not ratified the Convention at all)?' This is, of course, the vicious circle, and the obvious place to break out of it is in educating the potential subjects of the Convention.

There are undoubtedly other weaknesses that could be found in the Convention. If it has a great impact on the municipal law, it has, perhaps inevitably, opened some difficult legal problems on both the international and municipal levels. If it represents an innovation on the international level worthy of emulation, the halting and often restrictive efforts in establishing and expanding it have been followed by even more halting and restrictive efforts in other parts of the world.

An effort must be made to overcome the Convention's weaknesses and to render it as effective as it potentially is.

The Council of Europe itself could begin a programme designed to make lawyers and laymen aware of the Convention. A series of seminars for lawyers, preferably with members of the Commission, should be held to acquaint them with the philosophy and the case-law applied by the Commission and with the contribution of the Convention to municipal law. Private groups long associated with the movement for the international protection of human rights could be enlisted in this effort. The Council could also undertake a broad public information drive to teach Europeans about the Convention through posters, travelling exhibits, staging simulated Court sessions for students. The Council could urge upon national educational authorities the inclusion of instruction about the Convention in the school curriculum. In view of the great interest throughout the world in the Convention, a broad programme of information and even of assistance should be started outside Europe.

The greatest fault that must be overcome is the failure of Member States to place the Convention in a political context. Unfortunately, the Convention is regarded as merely a legal document. It is that, but it is much more. The Member States must recognise that the

Convention was created for political purposes, not the least of which was the promotion of European unity. (The preamble of the Convention states: 'The aim of the Council of Europe is the achievement of greater unity between its Members and . . . one of the methods by which that aim is to be pursued is the maintenance and further realisation of Human Rights and Fundamental Freedoms'.) If the problems of making the Convention work well are one of a number of thorny matters which are easier put aside than decided on in the process of unifying Europe, Europe can only be unified by seeking the lowest common denominator among States. This would hardly be real unification. Though no State can expect a material gain from the application of a fully effective Convention, certainly not all of the objectives sought by any country in the unification process are tangible.

Thus the Member States must regard the Convention as a political undertaking (even if that means more politically motivated inter-state applications). They must agree to making the necessary credits available for the public information programme outlined above and for making the Commission a permanent full-time body with adequate staff. They must make the Convention an element of further progress in the field of European unification by inserting the question of ratification or acceptance of its optional clauses or expansion of its provisions into the framework of current negotiations. The alternative to such actions is a 'little Convention' condemned to play a minor role both in the protection of human rights and in the promotion of European unity.

These efforts may seem idealistic or utopian. So, perhaps, would have the Convention in 1945. It is the responsibility of those who are the guardians of the Convention, members of the Court and Commission, the Secretariat of the Council of Europe and the lawyers and others who follow the development of the Convention closely, to take the political risks necessary to reawaken a political appreciation of the Convention.

WRITTEN COMMUNICATION BY
PAUL WEIS

THE RIGHT OF ASYLUM IN THE CONTEXT OF
THE PROTECTION OF HUMAN RIGHTS
IN REGIONAL AND MUNICIPAL LAW

1. *The objective of universal protection of the human rights of all men*

Just as the Universal Declaration of Human Rights proclaims the fundamental importance of the rights of all men, so the European

Convention on Human Rights seeks to secure to everyone within the jurisdiction of the High Contracting Parties the rights and freedoms it contains. This objective of securing the general application of the protection of the Convention is followed in the Protocols to the Convention, which add further rights to those already incorporated in it.

In view of this interest of the International Community, both universally and regionally, in the general protection of human rights, which is reflected in other regional instruments concerning human rights, a serious problem arises with regard to those persons who are in danger of coming within the protection of no such instrument. One particular group in respect of which this danger arises is that of persons seeking asylum. The need of such persons for the protection of their human rights is particularly acute, and yet their protection depends on the goodwill of States which may or may not accept any obligations with regard to them. From earliest times, people have sought asylum from the violation of their human rights or in fear of their being disregarded. Until the protection of human rights is universally assured, they are likely to continue to seek in other countries asylum from persecution, which has been proclaimed as a human right in Article 14 of the Universal Declaration.

As the right to life is the prerequisite for the enjoyment of every other human right, so the right of asylum is the prerequisite for the enjoyment of his basic rights by a refugee. The European Convention recognises the right to life as the first which it seeks to protect and, in the same way, a refugee first needs protection by the grant of asylum.

2. *The development of the law on the right of asylum in international instruments*

Traditional doctrine bases the right of asylum on the right of a State in its sovereignty to decide whom it shall admit to its territory. International law prohibits other States from interfering within its sovereign jurisdiction and, as a result, other States have been barred from challenging successfully the right of a State to harbour within its borders those persons to whom it wishes to give protection.

This traditional doctrine resulted in Article 14 of the Universal Declaration embodying only the right of everyone 'to seek and to enjoy in other countries asylum from persecution'. The UN Commission on Human Rights in their draft for this Article had included the right to be granted asylum, but in the Third Committee of the General Assembly it was amended in order to remove any suggestion that the Article implied an obligation on any State to admit a person seeking asylum.

The chief international instrument relating to the protection of refugees, the Convention of 28 July 1951 relating to the Status of Refugees, to which all the Member States of the Council of Europe are party, contains a strong provision giving effect to the principle of *non-refoulement*, i.e. that no State shall expel or return (*refouler*) a refugee in any manner whatsoever to the frontiers of territories where his life or freedom would be threatened on account of his race, religion, nationality, membership of a particular social group or political opinion. The UN Commission on Human Rights' draft of a Declaration on the Right of Asylum at present before the Third Committee of the General Assembly develops this principle of *non-refoulement* by making it explicitly referable to rejection at the frontier, if this would result in compelling a person seeking asylum to return to or remain in a territory if there is well-founded fear of persecution endangering his life, physical integrity or liberty in that territory.

While it appears to be generally recognised that asylum is granted on humanitarian grounds[1] and that States, in granting asylum, act in fulfilment of their humanitarian duties,[2] a new trend in the doctrine on the law of asylum is appearing which seeks to base the right of asylum on the necessity for the protection of the human rights of the individual and further seeks to equate the right of asylum with a right of the individual to the protection of his human rights.

This trend was the basis of the draft of the UN Commission on Human Rights for Article 14 of the Universal Declaration, before it was amended by the General Assembly. It was also the basis of an amendment proposed by France in the Third Committee to the Commission's draft, which was itself largely the result of French initiatives. France by this amendment sought to add to the Declaration that everyone has the right to seek and be granted asylum, a provision that the United Nations in concert with States should be required to secure such asylum for those who seek it.

3. *The right of asylum in municipal law*

The strongest manner in which a right can be incorporated in the municipal law of a country is for it to be embodied in its Constitution. An ever-increasing number of Constitutions are declaring the respect for human rights and embodying in their provisions some assurances for the general protection of these rights. The number of Constitutions which mention specifically the right of asylum and, of these, the number in which the right of asylum is defined as a right of the individual, is less great but is also increasing.

---

[1] Cf. *I.C.J. Reports*, 1950, p. 282.
[2] *Institute of International Law*, Bath, 1950, vol. 2, p. 389.

The second most secure manner for incorporating a right in municipal law is by means of an Act of the Legislature or some other formal statutory provision. The majority of Acts which refer to the right of asylum are those which regulate a country's extradition procedures. It is general for such Acts to restrict the surrender of any person whose extradition is sought for a political offence. Aliens' laws and regulations frequently limit in a similar way the expulsion of persons who would fear persecution in a territory to which their expulsion was intended. Aliens' laws containing such provisions have only recently been enacted in several States, among them the German Federal Republic and the Netherlands.

A further possibility is the establishment of rights in municipal law by the incorporation of provisions contained in treaties. In those countries where the 1951 Refugee Convention has been incorporated into municipal law, the protection of the right of asylum is assured, although only to those already admitted to its enjoyment.

Extradition has also been the object of many treaties which have been incorporated in municipal law in this way and which have thereby given further protection to political offenders. The European Convention on Extradition of 13 December 1957 is one of the most important in this field. As well as promoting the uniformity of extradition practice between Member States, it increases the protection of persons enjoying asylum by extending to the victims of political events the restriction on the extradition of political offenders and thereby excluding from the operation of the Convention any person whose extradition is sought 'if the requested Party has substantial grounds for believing that a request for extradition for an ordinary criminal offence has been made for the purpose of prosecuting or punishing a person on account of his race, religion, nationality or political opinion, or that that person's position may be prejudiced for any of these reasons' (Art. 3 (2)).

4. *The right of asylum in the Constitutions of Member States*

The French Constitution has the longest history of the formal Constitutions of the Member States of the Council of Europe containing a specific provision on the right of asylum. The Preamble to the Constitution of 4 October 1958 solemnly proclaims the attachment of the French people to the human rights and principles of national sovereignty as they were already defined in the Declaration on the Rights of Man of 1789 and completed by the Preamble to the Constitution of 27 October 1946, which states that anyone persecuted because of his activities in the cause of liberty shall be entitled to the right of asylum within the territories of the Republic. France has constantly been an initiator and a driving force for the protection of human rights and of those of persons fleeing from persecution in particular.

In its brevity and succinctness the German constitutional provision on the right of asylum is perhaps the most general and far-reaching in effect. In Article 16 (2) of the Basic Law of 8 May 1949, the second sentence in only four words states that the politically persecuted enjoy the right of asylum. Already a considerable body of judicial decisions has grown up interpreting this provision.

The new trend equating the right of asylum and the right of an individual to the protection of his human rights is best characterised by the Italian Constitution of 27 December 1947. In its Article 10, paragraph 3, it states that the foreigner who is denied in his own country the effective exercise of the democratic freedoms guaranteed by the Italian Constitution has a right to asylum in the territory of the Republic in accordance with the provisions of the law. This provision adopts for its yardstick to determine who shall receive asylum, the same protection that it grants to all persons within its jurisdiction, demonstrating the faith which it has in the necessity to grant all persons universally the same standard and the same protection without discrimination.

No other Member State has a direct reference to asylum in its Constitution, though references in various other Constitutions are made to extradition and aliens' laws.

5. *European State practice in the grant of asylum*

Whether or not explicit provisions on asylum have been made in the constitutions, statute or treaty law of Member States, their practice, which is itself a source of international law, has on the whole been fairly uniform, generous and virtually all-embracing in granting asylum both within the continent of Europe and from outside. Even when asylum is granted by the Executive as a matter of policy rather than under legal obligations, Governments have frequently made firm statements that they would not deviate from this policy if this would leave the person seeking asylum to the mercy of his persecutors.

Typical of such statements is that made by the Home Secretary of the United Kingdom in the House of Commons on 21 March 1963: 'The tradition of this country is that a person is granted political asylum if, in his own country, he appears to us to be in danger of life or liberty on political grounds, or on grounds of religion or race'.

In the same sense the Swiss Federal Council in its report of 1 February 1957 on the principles to be observed in the practice of asylum in the case of increased international tension or of war, stated the basis of its policy as follows: 'Le droit d'asile n'est pas une simple tradition de la Suisse. Il est un principe politique et une manifestation de la conception suisse de la liberté et de l'indépendance'.

Even in the case of the mass influx of some 200,000 Hungarians in 1956 and 1957, asylum was not denied by neighbouring countries. Austria and Yugoslavia, the international community as a whole and the Member States in particular collaborated to relieve the countries of first asylum most immediately affected. This collaboration of other States with those who shouldered the greatest burden resulted in the spontaneous acceptance by many States of large numbers of refugees without any condition or special requirement for their entry.

Whether Member States grant asylum as a matter of policy or as a matter of law, where their municipal law recognises an obligation to grant asylum, there is little difference in their practice, all recognising the humanitarian duty which they fulfil in so doing.

6. *The prerequisites for the protection of all asylum seekers*

If the objective of States in accordance with the basic humanitarian character of asylum is to ensure the protection of the human rights of all individuals and particularly of persons seeking asylum, means must be found to ensure that they will always be able to find some territory in which they can enjoy asylum. In the first instance, it is the individual States which provide this. In certain circumstances, however, it may become impossible for a particular State to provide the necessary protection in its territory for more than a minimal period of time. In this event it is essential that an alternative solution be sought and the assurance that a territory will be found for all persons seeking asylum can only be given by the international community as a whole, acting in concert.

In this matter national and international action are clearly interdependent. Uniform State practice, whether as a matter of law or of policy, facilitates the reaching of international agreement. Equally, international agreement is bound to influence the favourable development of municipal law on the right of asylum. The readiness of individual States to grant asylum and strengthen the protection of those seeking asylum will be enhanced by the knowledge that other States will act in the same way. It therefore follows that States should consider the strengthening of the right of asylum both in their municipal law and on a regional basis.

The Council of Europe has for some time been engaged in such action on a regional level. In September 1963 and again in April 1964 the Committee of Ministers considered the report of the Committee of Experts on *Recommendation 293*, in which the Assembly proposed the inclusion of an article on the right of asylum in a protocol to the Convention on Human Rights. The Committee of

Experts was of the opinion that an article as proposed by the Assembly, or on the principle of *non-refoulement*, should not be included in a protocol to the Convention, but suggested the possibility of a separate Convention on asylum outside the framework of the Convention on Human Rights or of a recommendation to Member States by way of a resolution of the Committee of Ministers. The Committee of Experts were instructed to prepare a draft declaration on the right of asylum, upon which a resolution or convention might be based in due course, while awaiting the results of discussions on the matter in the UN General Assembly.

In Latin America and the Western hemisphere as a whole, the right of asylum has been the subject of many bilateral, multilateral and regional instruments. The Asian-African Legal Consultative Committee has studied the Law of Extradition and is at present examining the right of asylum within the larger question of the rights of refugees. The Organisation of African Unity is at present considering a Draft Convention relating to the status of refugees in Africa, which it is hoped will include a provision on the right of asylum.

Conclusion

Without individual States and regional organisations taking the necessary initiatives, progress in the protection of asylum seekers is not likely to be achieved. Every opportunity should therefore be sought to enshrine the right of asylum in municipal law as securely as possible. As an example, one may mention the recent initiative of the Austrian Federal Chancellor for the revision of the 'State Basic Law on the general rights of citizens' of 1867, which provides such an opportunity to consider the inclusion of the right of asylum in a new basic law.

The States members of the Council of Europe are perhaps in the best position to reach agreement, on a regional level, on an instrument which could pave the way to the protection of human rights, where necessary, by the grant of asylum being assured by the community of States. The Member States are agreed on a uniformly generous policy; they have the necessary unity of purpose to seek agreement; the wide experience of the last decades has given them an incomparable knowledge of the problems involved.

Whenever States acting individually or within the framework of regional organisations create particular legal provisions and instruments for the protection of persons seeking asylum, they not only assure these rights within their own territory but, beyond this, reaffirm their faith in fundamental human rights and in the dignity and worth of the human person proclaimed in the Preamble to the Charter of the United Nations.

WRITTEN COMMUNICATION BY
LOUIS B. SOHN

PROBLEMS INVOLVED IN OPENING
THE EUROPEAN CONVENTION ON HUMAN RIGHTS
TO ACCESSION BY THE UNITED STATES AND CANADA

In connection with a White House Conference on International Co-operation held in Washington, 29 November–1 December 1965, as part of United States observance of the International Co-operation Year, a Committee on Human Rights of the National Citizens' Commission on International Co-operation has expressed its belief that:

as the United States and Canada share with the European countries a common heritage in the field of human rights, it should be possible for them to join the European countries in their enterprising and successful effort to give international protection to human rights.

After reviewing the European accomplishments, the Committee pointed out that:

Despite close political, military and economic links to Europe, and a common tradition in the field of human rights, the United States has made no attempt to participate in this highly advanced system of protection of fundamental freedoms or to extend it to the whole Atlantic Community. In particular, no action has been taken by the parties to the North Atlantic Treaty to comply with Article 2 of the Treaty obliging them to strengthen 'their free institutions by bringing about a better understanding of the principles upon which these institutions are founded'. The best way to reach that understanding would have been to establish common institutions and procedures to safeguard the rights of their citizens.

This suggestion raises two kinds of problems, those resulting from the federal structure of the United States and Canada and those relating to the opening of the European Convention to accession by non-European States.

It may be assumed for the purposes of this paper that the constitutional problems in Canada and the United States can be solved in view of the recent federal legislation in both countries with respect to human rights, and the consequent change of attitude toward international instruments dealing with human rights. It may be pointed out, for instance, that the President of the United States sent to the Senate for approval in 1963 three conventions relating, respectively, to slavery, forced labour, and political rights of women. The submission to the Senate of several conventions dealing with

AA

discrimination is at present under consideration. In Canada, a major step towards increasing federal concern in human rights matters was taken as a result of the enactment of the Canadian Bill of Rights in 1960.

As far as Europe is concerned, this suggestion seems to reopen the question whether and under what conditions the European Convention on Human Rights, and the additional protocols on human rights, should be opened for signature and ratification, or accession, to States which are not Members of the Council of Europe. This question was raised in 1962 when the Legal Committee of the Consultative Assembly of the Council of Europe presented a report on the subject, prepared by Mr Mathew (doc. 1418). The Committee pointed out that the European Convention on Human Rights is a 'closed' convention 'open to the signature of the Members of the Council of Europe' (Art. 66); and that accession by non-Members can take place only through an amendment of the Convention. It held that the Convention is already universal, as it applies to 'everyone' within the jurisdiction of the Parties to it, regardless of nationality, and as it has been extended to many overseas territories administered by the Parties. The implementing machinery of the Convention has been working effectively for a number of years, and its sphere of application should be expanded 'whenever this is considered appropriate'. The Committee of Ministers is the competent organ to issue to a third State the invitation to accede to the Convention on Human Rights, but before actually issuing an invitation it should first consult the Assembly or its Standing Committee, in the same way as is done in the case of admission of new Members to the Council of Europe. While there are precedents in some European conventions for invitations by a two-thirds vote of the Committee of Ministers, an invitation to accede to the Human Rights Convention should probably require a unanimous vote. Should a non-Member thus become a party to the Convention, additional amendments to the Convention will be required to enable such a State to participate in the elections to the Commission and the Court, and in the decisions of the Committee of Ministers relating to human rights questions.

When this report was discussed in the Consultative Assembly on 17 May 1962, it was pointed out that the proposal was permissive in nature and there was no danger of throwing the door open to Fascist States, to States not having the necessary qualifications, or to States which the Members of the Council of Europe do not wish to accede to the Convention. While it was mentioned in the discussion that the purpose of the proposal was to extend the Convention to countries in Europe outside the Council of Europe, there is no indication of such a restriction in the report itself, as it mentions expressly the desirability of continuing the application of the Convention to formerly non-self-governing territories, such as Cyprus and Nigeria, after they have become independent.[1]

In Recommendation 316 (1962), the Consultative Assembly recommended that 'the Committee of Ministers should instruct the Committee of Experts which is already examining various questions relating to the European Convention on Human Rights to draft amendments to the Convention providing for the possibility of accession by non-member States which possess the necessary qualifications, on the invitation of the Committee of Ministers, after consultation of the Assembly'. The Committee of Ministers took a negative decision on this Recommendation (doc. 1723, p. 61). This decision can easily be reversed should the Committee of Ministers find it desirable to invite the United States and Canada to accede to the Convention and thus give a new expression to the common understanding of human rights which unites the nations on both sides of the Atlantic.

SUMMARY OF THE DISCUSSION

Egon Schwelb: Mr Lalive has performed an extraordinarily valuable task in assembling the material which is presented in his report. For this the legal profession owes Mr Lalive a great debt because, while we knew that some isolated activities on the lines described in his report have been in progress for some time, I for one did not know of their vast extent.

As to the substance of these activities, I consider them extraordinarily disquieting and disturbing. What the report describes is an alarming attempt at the fragmentation of the international action to promote human rights, an artificial creation of parochialism under the pseudonym of regionalism. The ideal of the *one world* which was *en vogue* 20 years ago was clearly an illusion and we have to live with the bipolarization between East and West and—in economic matters —between North and South. The activities described in the paper aim, however, at the creation of some seven or eight worlds with a host of sub-worlds, as it were, such as Central America, Greater Colombia, South America proper.

Western Europe is *sui generis* and the European Convention, Commission and Court of H.R. are going concerns. I am second to none in paying my tribute to them, as I have done in my writings repeatedly and also in the paper for this Conference. I am prepared to concede, albeit reluctantly and with hesitation, that the OAS may

[1] See K. Vasak, *Convention européenne des Droits de l'Homme*, Paris, 1964, p. 260.

conceivably also be a proper basis for separate action in human rights. For the life of me I cannot see why the Arab League, the Organisation of African Unity, SEATO, CENTO could conceivably succeed where on the learned rapporteurs' *ipse dixit* there is no hope of the United Nations achieving its goal. This is hardly the view of, e.g. the Arab statesmen and lawyers like Malik of Lebanon and the late Azmi of Egypt, who made so brilliant a contribution to the human rights programme of the Organisation or, to name a member of the younger generation, the present distinguished chairman of the Sixth Committee, Mr El Erian of the U.A.R. Nor is it the view of the many postgraduate students and postgraduate fellows from Asia, Africa and Latin America with whom I am in constant touch and who look up to the United Nations as the agency for promoting respect for human rights in their regions.

Mr Lalive applies a double standard. When speaking of the United Nations he says that without compulsory judicial machinery it cannot achieve its objectives; when speaking of the Inter-American Convention on Human Rights he gives it credit, and, in part, rightly so, for activities which are not only not performed with the sanction of compulsory judicial machinery, but are not based on any special convention so much as on the inherent powers of the OAS, in the same way as the corresponding United Nations activities are based on the Charter.

I do not propose to reply to Mr Lalive's paper section by section and paragraph by paragraph. On the one hand, he praises the work of the Inter-American Commission on Human Rights in the Dominican crisis; on the other, he criticises the OAS for not having excluded the United States from its human rights work. Incidentally, it is an open question, to say the least, who supported the rule of law in the Dominican affair, whether the Security Council or the Organisation of American States, whether the Inter-American Commission on Human Rights or the Secretary-General's special representative in that country.

The whole paper is permeated by the idea that the 'Greater Colombian Convention, Commission or Court of Human Rights', to take one of his examples, should be encouraged. My submission is that this nightmare should be unambiguously discouraged.

Louis B. Sohn presented his written communication (see above). He added: the courts of the individual States are not sufficient to guarantee the implementation of the Declaration of Human Rights; what is needed to ensure the protection of human rights is, as some States have suggested, a High Commissioner or a permanent Committee of Experts.

The question of human rights was considered recently in the course of preparation for a White House Conference on International Co-operation held in the United States in connection with the International Co-operation Year. To the extent that enforcement of human rights might continue to be regional rather than global, the United States of America is faced with the alternative of relying on the Inter-American Commission on Human Rights or joining the European Organisation. A clause should be inserted in the European Human Rights Convention concerning the accession of States not belonging to the Council of Europe. At one time an invitation to Switzerland to accede to the European Convention was considered, and Finland may be invited in the future. A general clause about accession of non-members would allow also accession by the United States.

János Tóth: our eminent Rapporteur has sketched a general picture of the areas of the world in which the influence of the European Convention is felt. These areas include that half of our continent which, in political geography, is called Eastern Europe. I should like, if I may, to add a few comments to this remarkable report.

The attitude of the Europe of the Human Rights Convention towards Eastern European countries may be described as one of interested expectancy. It found expression in a decision of the Committee of Ministers in December 1964, when advocating technical co-operation with European countries which are not members of the Council of Europe. Moreover, at the Consultative Assembly's session in May 1965, several members tabled a motion for a recommendation on the co-ordination of research into the legal systems of Eastern European countries. The Legal Committee of the Assembly has since been instructed to give effect to this proposal.

Thus there are signs that the Europe of the Human Rights Convention is taking a definite interest in these other European countries which, while sharing its history and 'common heritage of political traditions'—to quote the Preamble to the Convention—have, over the past twenty years, developed a different, a totalitarian economic and political system.

The venerable Hofburg, where this Conference is taking place, seems to me the most appropriate setting in which to examine this growing interest. His Excellency, the Austrian Chancellor, spoke to us in his address about the special role which Austria was anxious to play in bringing the two Europes closer together.

Is this interest which has been expressed by the Europe of the Convention—and also, I may say, by the International Commission of Jurists—in the development of human rights in Eastern Europe shared by the Eastern European countries?

Mention was made in the report which we have just heard of a doctorial thesis written at Karl's University, Prague, proposing the drawing-up of a Socialist Charter of Human Rights. In my written contribution, I gave other examples of this same interest. These, as Professor Martin and Professor Ermacora said today, are only the first steps on a very long and difficult road.

What can we hope for from this interest which the two Europes are taking in each other? Rather than attempt any dubious prognosis, I prefer to note facts. These include the harmonisation of law in Eastern Europe, prompted no doubt by the example of the Europe where the Convention holds good.

In the COMECON countries, an advanced stage has already been reached in the unification of the law on intellectual property, for example. This process is accompanied by increasing co-operation between the COMECON countries and the countries of the European Convention in the framework of the competent international organisations.

Would a move to unify the protection of human rights in Eastern Europe, inspired by the European Convention and accompanied by an intensification of professional contacts across ideological frontiers, be too much to hope for?

That is the question I want to put before you today; perhaps it will fall to a later Council of Europe Conference to supply the answer.

B. N. Esen: I endorse the Rapporteur's opinion and conclusions; the establishment of regional agencies would do much to promote the protection of human rights. I welcome the appeal launched by Mr Aronstein for a campaign in the various countries to secure acceptance of Articles 25 and 46 of the Convention.

A Chair of Human Rights already exists in Turkey. I, myself, have devoted a full year to lecturing on the subject. My colleagues and I are preparing to launch a campaign in favour of the acceptance by my country of the right of individual petition and the compulsory jurisdiction of the Court.

C. W. van Santen: I want to give a serious warning against any action which might encroach upon the validity or the value of the United Nations Universal Declaration of Human Rights.

Its value, I confess, I did not rate highly at first, either from my academic viewpoint at Leiden University or from my practical experience in the Ministry of Foreign Affairs at The Hague.

I made a great mistake. When I was called upon to be the legal adviser of the Sudan Government for international law, I was in a position to notice what great store was rightly set upon the Declaration by that Government. The same appeared from the greater interest taken in the Declaration by the students of Khartoum University when compared with the students at Leiden.

My experience at Khartoum taught me the importance both of international law and of the Universal Declaration for any law-abiding nation, groping for generally accepted and praiseworthy standards of behaviour to assist it in solving the many complex problems of its new nationhood.

Be careful, therefore, of any plans to further the creation of regional standards for human rights differing from the Universal Declaration, by adaptation to regional circumstances and needs. Any watering down of the principles embodied in the Universal Declaration could do great harm.

The point to be made in any propaganda for the Strasbourg achievement should be its more extensive legal force and its enforcement machinery, not its regional character; the first is a virtue, the latter only a practical proposition, admissible and excusable merely in regard to its merits *above* the Universal Declaration. Any regional declaration especially adapted to regional needs and not having great legal force will do irreparable harm to the realisation of the United Nations Universal Declaration of Human Rights.

Paul Weis presented his written communication (above) and added: under Article I of the European Convention, the Contracting States undertake to secure to everyone within their jurisdiction the rights and freedoms defined in Section I of the Convention. Article 15, paragraph 2, of the Convention contains the so-called 'non-derogation clause', according to which certain rights, i.e. the right to life, freedom from degrading treatment, slavery or servitude, and the non-retroactivity of penal law, may not be abrogated, even in time of war or public emergency threatening the life of the nation. The right to life and human dignity are thus recognised to be absolutely basic, since the exercise of all other rights depends on them.

It is because of the violation or the danger of violation of these very rights that men seek asylum and unless they find it none of their human rights are secure.

Where persons already admitted to the national territory are concerned, asylum consists in protection against persecution, protection against surrender to the persecutor. Where persons seeking asylum are concerned, the problem is one of admission, be it even temporary admission, so as not to compel them to remain in, or return to, a territory where they are in danger of persecution. It has been said that such persons are not within the jurisdiction; but unless a person seeking asylum is in a position where admission may be granted or refused—which is the position at the frontier—the question of jurisdiction does not arise. It follows that he is within the jurisdiction, although he may not yet be in the national territory.

Thus the question of asylum is closely related to the question of securing to everyone those rights and freedoms which the European Convention seeks to protect.

At present asylum is granted by all Member States of the Council of Europe, as a matter of law in States which recognize a right to asylum in their constitutions or municipal legislation, and as a matter of practice or policy in others. Even where it is granted as a matter of policy, this policy would not readily be deviated from by the Executive, as it is normally based on long tradition supported by public opinion. The number of States which have enshrined a right of asylum in their municipal law is increasing, and I am glad to learn that in Austria too the question of the inclusion of an individual right to asylum in the catalogue of basic rights (*Grundrechtskatalog*) is under consideration.

By its very nature, international action seems to be called for in the matter of asylum. Just as there is inter-action between customary and treaty law, there is inter-action between municipal law, which itself is evidence of State practice, and international law.

I am not unaware of the difficulties which the regulation of the right of asylum by an international instrument presents. Asylum is of necessity granted by individual States. In so doing, they act in the exercise of a humanitarian duty—a duty which, as the founding fathers of international law have said, is incumbent on the *civitas maxima*; or, as the United Nations Draft Declaration on the Right of Asylum says: 'The situation of persons forced to leave their countries because of persecution or well-founded fear of persecution is of concern to the international community'. However, these difficulties should not deter us from efforts to reach agreement on an international instrument, and such agreement should be easier to reach between the Member States of the Council of Europe which have common standards and traditions in the matter.

The Council of Europe has broken new ground in the Convention on Extradition by adding to the principle of non-extradition of political offenders in its Article 3 (2) that extradition is to be refused 'if the requested party has substantial grounds for believing that a request for extradition for an ordinary criminal offence has been made for the purpose of prosecuting or punishing a person on account of his race, religion, nationality or political opinion, or that the person's position may be prejudiced for any of these reasons'. This new provision has filled a gap in the existing law on extradition, and it is significant that the same formula has subsequently been incorporated in bilateral treaties. However, nowadays the problem of asylum is not normally a problem of extradition, and the work so propitiously started, remains to be completed. The question of asylum has been on the agenda of the competent bodies of the Council for some time and only recently the Consultative Assembly has adopted a further Recommendation on the subject. By approaching the problem in the spirit of the Convention, the competent bodies will, I am sure, be able to reach agreement on a legal instrument which will be a worthy addition to the agreements so far adopted by the Council in the field of human rights.

Pierre Mertens: with regard to the right of asylum, European legislators can still draw lessons from the Universal Declaration of Human Rights, where that privilege is 'enshrined' in Article 14. But, as has occasionally been pointed out, this provision is really meaningless, for, although it recognises the right to seek and to enjoy asylum, it does not recognise the right to demand it. It still deliberately keeps within the limits of a 'traditional' conception of asylum whereas, in order to establish the right of asylum as a subjective and fundamental right, it is necessary to go beyond these limits, as indeed many recent constitutions and legislative texts have already done.

Referring to the regrettable Soblen affair, Professor Pinto has said that since Great Britain has not recognised the right of individual petition provided for in Article 25 of the Human Rights Convention, Soblen's lawyers were unable to invoke the provisions of the Convention in his favour. Is it not a fact that, even if Great Britain acknowledged the right of individual petition, Soblen's lawyers would still have been unable to invoke this right in favour of their client because the right of asylum, as such, is not recognised in the Convention?

Council of Europe efforts to obtain recognition of this right have been only partially successful: Article 3 of the Fourth Protocol prohibits the expulsion by States of their own nationals, Article 4 of the collective expulsion of aliens.

Recognition of their status is for refugees a necessary preliminary to the recognition of other fundamental rights. Without the former, the latter remains illusory. Mr Paul Weis's written communication on the right of asylum deserves to be widely endorsed by participants at the Conference.

SUMMING UP BY
JEAN-FLAVIEN LALIVE

Mr Lalive paid tribute to the principles supported by Mr Schwelb and to the spirit underlying his remarks; but he could not agree with his views. The Rapporteur did not share Mr Schwelb's fears about the danger of fragmentation of international action for the protection of human rights.

From the practical point of view, it is certain that regionalism is indispensable, at least during a transitional period. This is also in conformity with the historical evolution which can be observed in the development of federalism. As regards the dichotomy of compulsory jurisdiction and conciliation, the two systems can be considered complementary and not mutually exclusive. In international law we are far from a general system of compulsory jurisdiction. Even in the European Convention, which has established the most highly developed form of control known to date, the jurisdiction of the Court is not automatic and is not in all cases obligatory, because there is also the machinery of the European Commission of Human Rights.

As regards the statement of Professor Sohn, who would favour the accession of the United States to the European Convention on Human Rights, such an example would have a very considerable effect. However, one may be sceptical as to whether this is a practical possibility. In the first place, it is very unlikely that the American Government could undertake such an initiative; secondly, one may even wonder if it would be desirable. At the present stage, it would be better that the United States should help to develop Pan-American institutions, which would be tremendously reinforced by such support.

As regards Turkey, it was very interesting to learn from Professor Esen the importance of the efforts made and the progress achieved in the field of human rights in his country. If the picture which he painted was not too optimistic, it would appear that Turkey was further advanced in this respect than the Rapporteur's own country, Switzerland.

To his former colleague, Mr Tóth, Mr Lalive replied that much remained to be done in Eastern Europe and that one could not expect any rapid or spectacular developments as regards human rights. Nevertheless, some notable progress was being made, so that co-operation in this field between Eastern Europe and Western Europe (more particularly the States signatory to the European Convention) seemed less Utopian than in the past. At present, however, it appeared probable that the best method was to organise discussions at the university level and on the basis of personal contacts, rather than through government action.

In conclusion, the Rapporteur noted that, with the exception of Professor Schwelb, all those who had spoken appeared to approve the principle of regionalism in the protection of human rights and fundamental freedoms. This was a realistic view. Different opinions might be held on the ultimate objective and on the importance of aiming at universality. But at present, and for the immediate future, the Rapporteur reaffirmed his conviction that regional formulas would enable rapid progress to be made; this was the essential.

CHAPTER X

Conclusions and future prospects

POLYS MODINOS

As Co-Chairman of the Organising Committee I have the very pleasant duty of thanking the Federal Chancellor, Dr Klaus, the Minister of Justice, Dr Broda, and the other members of the Austrian Government for the support they have given to our Committee.

I should also like to thank all the members of our Committee, Professor Schwind, the Faculty of Law in the person of its young and energetic Dean, Professor Winkler, those who have worked tirelessly for several months preparing this Conference, Mr Loebenstein, Professor Ermacora, Mr Pahr and, amongst my own colleagues, MM. Robertson, Golsong, McNulty and Vasak.

Lastly, I should like to express my gratitude to the eminent lawyers assembled here, to our Rapporteurs and to all those who, by their presence and their speeches, have contributed towards the success of our discussions.

I found it relatively easy, Ladies and Gentlemen, to express what were my own sincere feelings. But now my embarrassment, if not my confusion, is acute, for I have no idea how to approach the difficult task I undertook to perform. I have before me as I speak to you, at least a hundred notes, remarks and commentaries, all of which were inspired by the excellent quality of your work. How should I begin, what points ought I to stress and how can I hope to produce a 'synthesis of theses', when these were so rich in substance? I must admit, however, that if I have the courage to go on, it is because, by comparison with those who have already spoken, I am in a privileged position. When I agreed to present the conclusions of the Colloquy, I was cautious enough, Mr Chairman, to ask for more than the ten minutes which the Committee granted to other Rapporteurs. I then took the additional precaution (and I am glad I did, now that I have seen how many people have spoken after each report) of making sure that my conclusions would not be followed by any further discussions. . . .

*　　*　　*　　*

Two main themes were placed before you at this Conference:

I. the place occupied by the European Convention on Human Rights in the legal systems of the Contracting States;

II. the regionalisation of the international protection of human rights and the precedent set by the European Convention.

But before I speak of these themes and their different aspects, I think it would be useful to trace the broad outlines of the development of the Convention since our first symposium in Strasbourg, five years before the present one, which is its sequel. I should like to feel that when you leave this room you will have in your minds a picture of our Convention, covering the most important events which have taken place over the past five years.

On 16 September 1963 the Fourth Protocol to the Convention was opened for signature, which added the following rights to those already recognised: freedom from imprisonment merely on the ground of inability to fulfil a contractual obligation; the right of everyone lawfully within the territory of a State to liberty of movement and freedom to choose his residence; the right of everyone to leave any country freely, including his own; the right of everyone not to be expelled by means either of an individual or of a collective measure from the territory of the State of which he is a national or be refused permission to enter that State; and, lastly, the prohibition of the collective expulsion of aliens.

On 25 October 1963, the Committee of Ministers, at the suggestion of the European Commission of Human Rights, introduced a system of legal aid. After working for ten years, we realised that a number of applicants did not have the financial means to engage a lawyer or to travel as far as Strasbourg to defend their applications before the Commission. Already the Commission has granted two requests for legal aid. The fact that an international tribunal is able to grant legal aid is of great legal importance and should be stressed.

By another Protocol, opened for signature on 6 May 1963, Article 29 of the Convention will be deleted and replaced by the following provision:

After it has accepted a petition submitted under Article 25, the Commission may nevertheless decide unanimously to reject the petition if, in the course of its examination, it finds that the existence of one of the grounds for non-acceptance provided for in Article 27 has been established.

The same Protocol amends Article 30 by providing for the abolition of Sub-Commissions and their replacement by the Plenary Commission.

The aim of these new provisions is to simplify and shorten the procedure before the Commission. By abolishing Sub-Commissions, one stage will have been eliminated. It will no longer be necessary for the Commission to await a report from a Sub-Commission on the results of its preliminary investigation. These operations will now be performed by the Plenary Commission, which is responsible, under Article 31, for drawing up a Report.

Moreover, when the new Article 29 comes into force, the Commission will have the power, which it has not at present, to reject a petition, in certain circumstances, after having accepted it as admissible and having heard the parties.

Another Protocol, signed on 6 May 1963, will grant the Court the power to give advisory opinions on legal questions concerning the interpretation of the Convention.

Since the Strasbourg Colloquy, the Court has, as you know, in addition to pronouncing judgment on the merits of the *Lawless case*, given a decision on the *De Becker case* which is of considerable interest in that it defined the powers of the Court when faced, as on that occasion, with a request for striking a case off the list. The Court has also been seised of the Belgian linguistic cases, whose importance is self-evident.

In October 1964, Article 57 was applied for the first time, as our Rapporteurs and speakers have reminded us on several occasions. In response to a wish which had been expressed some considerable time earlier, in particular at the Strasbourg Colloquy, the Secretary-General of the Council of Europe asked the Parties to the Convention to supply him with information on the manner in which they give effect to the different provisions of the Convention in their internal law. Several replies have already been received, and they will be published later in a form which has yet to be decided.

I should also like to remind you that the Committee of Ministers, acting under Article 32 of the Convention, has taken no fewer than six decisions during the past five years.

Similarly, I must mention the work accomplished by the Committee of Experts on Human Rights. This Committee is at present seised of three questions:

(*a*) the draft protocol granting privileges and immunities to witnesses and experts and other persons appearing before the Court and the Commission;

(*b*) perjury and failure to appear on the part of witnesses and experts;

(*c*) the right of asylum.

In concluding this rapid survey, I should like to make special mention of the European Social Charter, the result of long and difficult negotiations, which entered into force on 26 February 1965. From the beginning, we, in the Council of Europe, have maintained that civil and political rights must be accompanied by economic and social rights. After an interval of twelve years, the Charter is there to prove the truth of our contention.

Taken together, these facts demonstrate that our Convention is working extremely smoothly. But for all that, its effects are very complex. By choosing, from amongst these effects, the two themes which have been suggested to you, the Organising Committee did not seek to shun difficult questions, a point on which it has reason to be satisfied in view of the admirable and thorough treatment these themes have received.

This greatly eases my task, for I do not feel it necessary to analyse the reports and papers one by one, nor need I go into detail as far as the contributions from the floor are concerned. In any case, the Rapporteurs were careful to reply themselves to the numerous speakers, and it would be useless, if not pretentious on my part, to add a rejoinder to their replies.

To my mind, the principal merit of our Conference lies in the fact that, in the space of three days, it has considerably added to the bibliography and, if you will allow me to use the term, the biography of our Convention. Everything that has been written and said at the Conference will retain its value as an instrument of research, comparison and reference. Indeed, the main thing is not to adopt a particular thesis or to contradict another. You know better than I that controversies stimulate jurists and legal science and, more often than not, scholastic progress has its origin in controversy. Hence it would be neither wise nor exact to speak of *conclusions* to our work, as if it were a question of suggesting *solutions* to our problems. I propose rather to make an inventory of the most important questions which arise out of the operation of our Convention.

I. THE EUROPEAN CONVENTION ON HUMAN RIGHTS IN THE LEGAL SYSTEMS OF THE CONTRACTING STATES

The first subject of our Conference comprises in fact three aspects which, though connected, nevertheless deserve to be treated separately:

(*a*) the relations between the international legal order, represented by the Convention, and the internal legal systems, which were examined by Professors Sørensen, Verdross, Ganshof van der Meersch and Pinto;

(*b*) the inter-action between the Convention and other international agreements, studied by Professor Capotorti;

(*c*) a comparison of the case law of the organs of the Convention and that of national courts, made by Professors Buergenthal and Scheuner.

When looking at the first aspect of our subject, we were no doubt all struck by the very special character of our Convention, to all appearances a classic treaty. In the first place, treaties which, like the Convention, deal with a matter as political as human rights, are comparatively rare. But it is perhaps true to say that never has the 'international concept' penetrated so deeply into the field of national policy; might I simply remind you that, by virtue of Article 17, the international organs of the Convention are, in fact, empowered to make a contribution to the internal security of States.

If we take our analysis further, we shall see that, placed in the hierarchy of legal rules, the Convention has the highest rank, that of the constitutional rules. Historically, the demand for a Constitution was bound up with that for liberty and human rights; it is clear that today the international protection of human rights could not fail to affect the Constitutions of the Contracting States.

But our Convention also forms—and this is perhaps its most important aspect—the basis for a Constitution of a United Europe. As a standard of reference, it protects the political institutions of the Member States of the Council of Europe and thus opens the way to the unification of Europe based on democratic principles. Let us not forget that when the Ad Hoc Assembly was instructed in 1952 and 1953 to prepare a draft Statute for a European Political Community, Article 3 of the draft expressly stated that our Convention and its Protocol were 'an integral part' of the Statute of the Community.

Lawyers are aware that in certain member countries of the Council of Europe, there is a strict—perhaps too strict—division between internal law and international law. Yet our Convention belongs both to European international law, as expressed by the Statute of the Council of Europe, and to European constitutional law, since it defines the foundations of an ever greater unity between the Member States. Has the time come to link our Convention with the treaties setting up the European Communities and to say, in the words of the judgment pronounced on 15 July 1964 by the Court of Justice in Luxembourg, that unlike ordinary international treaties, the Convention has instituted a legal system of its own? Perhaps you will allow me to add that this legal system is complete in the sense that it is backed by organs which not only ensure that it is respected, but are also concerned with its further development.

Yet while the Convention has an indisputable originality, the place it occupies in the internal legal system of the Contracting States has been the subject of discussions whose starting point is far from being original. Monists and dualists oppose each other with arguments most of which could be used in relation to many other international treaties. Does this mean that the Convention has introduced nothing new into the classical field of theoretical discussions between jurists? Without taking sides in the controversy that centres in the 'self-executing' character of the Convention, I cannot help asking if, for the sake of its smooth functioning, we should not adopt an attitude of political compromise.

One observation is called for at the outset: the facts oblige us to recognise that the Convention is not considered to be 'self-executing' in all the Contracting States, and that those which do not recognise it as such are not on that account suspected of violating it. That does not mean that the Convention cannot be self-executing: its authors, be it noted, took care that the niceties of drafting should allow the national tribunals to apply it directly. This division of the States into two groups was of no great practical importance as long as the Convention was only rarely applied. Nevertheless, I wonder whether, as the Convention comes to be more widely used in the Contracting States—either before the national courts, or by individual applications to the Commission, or by both means at the same time—its self-executing character will not become a real practical necessity, even for those States which do not at present recognise it? Indeed, to make the Convention directly applicable in internal law will enable national judges to remedy violations without its being necessary to take the matter in the first instance to the European organs. The European Commission of Human Rights also ensures, by virtue of the rule that all domestic remedies shall first be exhausted, that the applicants should invoke the Convention before national courts in States where this is legally possible. The immediate enforcement of the Convention by national tribunals will thus prevent too many cases being brought before the institutions in Strasbourg. It is therefore quite right to maintain that a State which recognises the right of individual petition has a practical interest in rendering the Convention self-executing.

But, even in the case of States which have not yet recognised the right of individual petition, this interest is no less obvious. Indeed, as the law based on the Convention builds up a growing body of precedents and is daily enriched by the contributions not only of the Commission, the Court and the Committee of Ministers, but also of the national tribunals, the Contracting States will have an ever greater interest in taking part in the elaboration of this law. In other words, though these States took part, during diplomatic negotiations, in the elaboration of the law established by the Convention, nevertheless, if they fail to make it self-executing today, they will deprive themselves of the possibility of enriching it through the precedents set by the case-law of their own tribunals. In so far as the Convention constitutes European law, that is to say, not only the law of European

States but also of Europeans, it is important that this law should live and develop, benefiting from the contributions of all States and all Europeans. Both the monists and the dualists could, in my opinion, find common ground here, where our conduct should be inspired by the interest of the Convention as such.

Instead of attempting to bring divergent theories closer together, let us at least try to harmonise judicial practices to make them produce, if possible, the same effect.

We must also recognise that it is not only the different legal systems of the Contracting Parties which give rise to the difficulties pointed out by the Rapporteurs and by several speakers, but also the very provisions of our Convention which often give rise to controversy. Thus, Article 50 of the Convention concedes that a decision or a measure taken by a national authority may conflict with the obligations flowing from the Convention. The same Article goes on to state that: 'if the internal law of the said Party allows only partial reparation to be made for the consequences of this decision or measure, the decision of the Court shall, if necessary, afford just satisfaction to the injured party'. The possibility of a conflict between internal law and Convention law is thus officially recognised and at the same time strangely penalised. Jurists who wish to know why the authors of the Convention spoke of 'just satisfaction', when Article 5 affords 'a right to compensation', will find in the *travaux préparatoires* a brief commentary saying that this provision is in accordance with the international law in force concerning the violation by a State of an international obligation. The same objection, although less strongly worded, could be made to Article 64, which grants a State the right to 'make a reservation in respect of any particular provision of the Convention to the extent that any law then in force in its territory is not in conformity with the provision'.

Yet it seems to me a perfectly 'legal' concept that the aims and the nature of our Convention should exclude even the hypothesis of a violation of the Convention by virtue of a national provision.

Incidentally, the *Boeckmans case*, which was quoted on several occasions, affords proof that the same problem arises in respect of countries which, like Belgium, introduce the Convention into their internal law.

Thus, like Professor Sørensen, I would say: 'if our field is full of weaknesses, the aim of the Conference is to bring them to light in order to overcome difficulties in a European spirit'.

And you will doubtless agree if I add that, in the matter of human rights, international protection does not replace national protection, but reinforces it.

*   *   *   *

The interaction in domestic law between the Convention and other international agreements was dealt with by Professor Capotorti, who performed the extremely useful service of setting out in detail the often fairly ambiguous rules of general international law which govern this matter.

Firstly, it must be borne in mind that this is no theoretical problem: the Convention itself obliges us to look beyond its own provisions since, by its Article 15, it authorises a Party to derogate from its obligations only if the measures taken do not go beyond what is required by the exigencies of the situation and if they are 'not inconsistent with its other obligations under international law'. In the *Cyprus case*—to quote but one example—when it was a question of examining the application of this provision and interpreting Article 3 of the Convention (from which the Parties cannot derogate) it was natural that the 1949 Geneva Conventions should have been invoked. Similarly, in the *Lawless case*, the Court sought to find what other 'obligations under international law' were applicable in the matter.

It is quite clear that it is for the States themselves, as well as for the organs of the Council of Europe, to ensure that conflicts do not arise between the Convention and other international agreements dealing with similar or related questions. Thus, when we were drafting the European Convention on Establishment, we reserved, under Article 23, the provisions of Article 1 of the Protocol to the Convention on Human Rights, which protects the right to own property. Similarly the Resolution on regulations for prisoners, recently adopted by the Committee of Ministers on the proposal of the European Committee on Crime Problems, created several difficulties; a number of amendments were made to the text of the Resolution to bring it into line with the already very abundant case-law of the Commission in the field of penal law.

It is significant that the question of interaction between the Convention and other international agreements was raised in the Commission's early years: in Application No. 235/56, which was declared inadmissible on 10 June 1958,[1] it was a question of finding out if the Federal Republic of Germany was responsible for the working, on its territory, of the Supreme Restitution Court created by the 1954 Convention on the Settlement of Matters arising out of the War and the Occupation. The Commission found on that occasion that 'it is clear that if a State contracts treaty obligations and subsequently concludes another international agreement which disables it from performing its obligations under the first treaty, it will be answerable for any resulting breach of its obligations under the earlier treaty'. This decision, which has been the subject of much doctrinal comment

[1] *Yearbook*, II, pp. 257 et seq.

from the point of view of the competence of the Commission *ratione personae*, has hardly been discussed up to now from the aspect of the inter-relationships between international treaties and, more especially, between the European Convention on Human Rights and the Convention of 1954.

Professor Capotorti's report raised, explicitly or implicitly, two questions which deserve our attention. In the first place, we must ensure that contradictions do not arise between the United Nations instruments on Human Rights—in particular, the Covenants—and our European Convention. As long as the United Nations Covenants have no machinery of implementation, such contradictions, even if they exist will have no direct consequences. But as soon as machinery has been set up, these possible inconsistencies may w ell cause real confusion between the legal decisions taken by the various international organs, as well as those of the national courts. To avoid such a situation, from which a jurist can scarcely see a way out, unless it be by having recourse to extra-legal means (diplomatic and political), we must seek to prevent in order not to have to cure. The only way to ensure such prevention would be by collating, listing and publicising court decisions both national and international, on human rights questions. I apologise for approaching from this angle an idea which is very attractive to me: the creation of an International Institute of Human Rights. I am more and more convinced that from whatever angle one approaches the problem of the protection of human rights, the idea of an Institute is bound to come to mind.

The second question, mentioned in passing by those participating, is that concerning the interaction between the treaties setting up the European Communities and our Convention. There too, the problem was fairly theoretical as long as the application of these treaties remained largely within the field of relations between Contracting States and as long as the creation of a Political Community, of which the Convention would legally be an integral part, seemed close at hand. But the law of the Communities has now ceased to be chiefly an inter-state matter and has increasingly come to concern individuals.

The replies given to the fundamental question whether our Convention is binding on the Communities and whether it is even a part of Community law, have so far been diametrically opposed. Since we are talking of a further Conference in Brussels—and I should like to thank Professor Ganshof van der Meersch, the very active and scholarly Director of the Institute of European Studies at the Free University of Brussels, for his invitation—the 'provisional' seat of the Communities seems to me particularly well suited for a detailed examination of this problem which, in 1968, will no longer be something that we can avoid. At the same time, a comparison might usefully be made between the move towards unification in national legislation resulting from our Convention, on the one hand, and from the Community Treaties, on the other.

* * * *

The comparison of the case-law of the organs of the Convention with that of national courts has produced results which are of obvious interest. Before drawing attention to some of these, I should like to underline the tremendous progress revealed by the mere fact that such a comparison was possible. Indeed, a few years ago it would have been impossible to compare international case-law with internal case-law. On the other hand, we have to recognise that there is still a certain 'hiatus' between international and municipal law. Nevertheless, the comparison made by our Rapporteurs has done much to eliminate this hiatus. Is it not significant that to make such comparisons our Rapporteurs were handicapped only by the need to choose from the great body of decisions taken by the organs of the Convention and the national tribunals?

In this connection, Professor Scheuner very pertinently drew our attention to the fact that national judges are only interested in the Convention to the extent to which its provisions afford more far-reaching and wider guarantees than those provided by domestic law. And he even suggested that, in order to make it more exhaustive, the confrontation between the two types of case-law should also take into account national decisions which, implicitly or indirectly, constitute an application of the Convention. I think this is an ingenious remark. Nevertheless, it happens all too often—and I could easily quote examples—that although the Convention may be mentioned during a case by the litigants or the *Ministère Public*, the judgment makes no mention of the fact. This is doubtless because in most cases the provisions of the Convention correspond exactly to those of national law. Thus, when the judge can choose between an international text and a national text in order to motivate his decision, his training and a certain professional tradition will lead him to select only the latter. Very often, too, the litigants tend only to use the Convention as a supplementary argument, which is subsidiary, if not superfluous.

If we want the Convention to be invoked more often by the national tribunals, then the legal community, judges and lawyers, must penetrate more deeply into the international field and become fully aware of the value and consequently of the effects produced by our Convention.

Like Professor Buergenthal, we must recognise that we are often more sensitive to form than to content. Victims of our training, we feel that a text which has the form of an international treaty should be left to specialists in international law, which is traditionally considered to be a branch of public law. This is why our Convention is taught as a subject of international law, in so far as it is taught at all. The same is true, and the representatives of the European Economic Community will not contradict me on this point, of Community law.

Is there, however, any law which, though international in form and origin, affects to a greater extent the different branches of internal law? The situation is very much the same in the case of our Convention. I would even say that, as the case-law of the Convention grows, its character as a text of internal law becomes more apparent. One would only have to question the members of the Commission to realise that as soon as problems of admissibility are broached, the application of the substantive provisions raises problems which a specialist in private law is much better able to examine than an international lawyer. This virtual 'dis-internationalisation' of the Convention seems all the more desirable in that its ultimate aim is to create a truly European law, a law which would govern not only States, but also all those who come under their jurisdiction. Yet we can only complete this evolution if the Convention ceases to be a subject reserved for international lawyers and becomes a subject for reflection and teaching for the civil lawyer and the criminal lawyer as well. I even wonder whether, before the large Conference in 1968, we should not organise a series of meetings at which lawyers specialising in all branches of the law should consider our Convention in turn.

The problem is, at bottom, that of 'internationalising' the national legal world and, at the same time, of 'dis-internationalising' the Convention. This is a subject—apparently contradictory—which I offer to you for your reflection.

II. THE REGIONALISATION OF THE INTERNATIONAL PROTECTION OF HUMAN RIGHTS AND THE PRECEDENT SET BY THE EUROPEAN CONVENTION

The second subject in the programme was dealt with at length in Mr J. E. S. Fawcett's report, summed up by Professor Andrew Martin, who added his own comments.

Mr Jean-Flavien Lalive's Report was devoted to the very topical problem of the protection of human rights within the framework of the Regional Organisations.

I shall confine myself to picking out the main trends which render these excellent reports so worthy of our attention.

Doubtless you, like myself, were struck by the frequency with which the word 'publicity' occurred in Mr Fawcett's report and in the discussion which followed. This was probably because, without always being conscious of it, we feel that the subject of human rights required publicity more than any other. I have already written elsewhere that everything which is public, which works in the light of day, under the eyes of the public, serves the interests of peace; and it was for this reason that secret pacts were prohibited by the United Nations' Charter, which requires that all international treaties and agreements should be registered and published. We can even say that the Universal Declaration of Human Rights was conceived and drafted with the precise aim of constituting a true source of light. Publicity being the rule at the United Nations, their work takes place in the open; and this doubtless makes the States pay more attention to it.

Thus, there should be no surprise if the only real sanction known to the European Convention is the publication of the Commission's report, if a State fails to take satisfactory measures within the time-limit fixed by the Committee of Ministers. Nevertheless, I cannot entirely agree with certain criticisms concerning the fact that proceedings before the Commission are held *in camera*. When opening the doors of the Commission to individual applicants, the Governments felt it necessary to protect themselves against possible abuses. Petitions motivated by political considerations could have grave repercussions and, in such cases, the guarantee lies less in publicity than in the hearing of both parties by an international Commission composed of eminent persons who are independent of the Governments. Although the enquiry and the preliminary hearing take place before the Commission *in camera* but in the presence of the applicant and his lawyers, the hearings of the Court are, on the contrary, in public. It must not be forgotten, however, that the Commission is present during the public hearings of the Court, and, in the absence of the applicant, it has an important part to play, which was defined in the *Lawless case*. A debt of gratitude is due to the Commission and the Court, which, by their Rules of Procedure and their case-law, have filled serious gaps in the Convention on this subject.

Having said this, we must admit that publicity poses a problem, the consequences of which have been felt by the States themselves in proceedings before the Committee of Ministers. Indeed, it transpired that in certain cases the Governments were anxious to see the Commission's report published, although the meetings of the Committee of Ministers are also held *in camera*. Press Communiqués were no substitute for the publication of the Commission's report, which is not provided for by the Convention if an application is rejected.

I think, therefore, that it would be useful if, at a later Conference, we examined in detail the working of the Convention and tried to introduce the publicity factor whenever the judicial character of its machinery makes this possible.

The proposal, warmly supported by those present here, that a United Nations High Commissioner for Human Rights be appointed is along the same lines: the aim is to make the subject of human rights public property, shared by all men. I have no intention of pronouncing judgment on the merits of this proposal which, when all is said and done, is really a call for the appointment of an international 'Ombudsman'. But there, too, I cannot help saying that certain of the rules destined to govern the working of this suggested new institution have their precedent—and their justification—in the European Convention. Whilst it is tempting to feel that when acting under Article 57 of the Convention, the Secretary-General of the Council of Europe could behave rather as if he were a 'European' High Commissioner for Human Rights, it is probably more exact to think that the European Commission, when drafting its report on an application submitted to it, becomes something in the nature of a European Attorney-General for Human Rights. Was it not a Uruguayan proposal for an International Attorney-General for Human Rights which inspired the present proposal by Costa Rica for the High Commissioner? It is to be hoped that, if this proposal is adopted, the work of the United Nations High Commissioner's office will be co-ordinated with that done under our Convention. It has often been said that co-ordination is the salt which has to go with the daily bread of international organisations; in this instance, co-ordination seems to me a vital necessity, which can only be secured by regular and frank contacts between the Secretariats of the United Nations and the Council of Europe.

Without returning to Professor Capotorti's report, I must say that conventions and agreements due to the action of international organisations are multiplying at a speed with which Parliaments often cannot keep up when called upon to authorise their ratification. Since the end of the Second World War we have seen a proliferation of international organisations which conclude agreements, each in its own sphere of action. All this has or will have the effect of bringing more and more matters which have hitherto been dealt with in the national framework of the State into the field of treaty law. It can even be said that the greater the number of international conventions setting up control procedures or legislative machinery, the smaller will the field become in which national authorities can operate with complete independence. That is a problem which now appears in a new form. The confidence of States in international legislators will be directly related to the extent that international legislation avoids duplication, meets a real need and functions effectively. Here, too, co-ordination constitutes a field open to the wisdom of the research worker, the imagination of the jurist and the pragmatism of the politician.

The need for such co-ordination as regards human rights becomes imperative if one remembers that in addition to regional conventions like ours, there are also the ILO Conventions, one of UNESCO and several United Nations Agreements, including the Convention on the elimination of all forms of racial discrimination, which deal with questions coming within the same field; nor must we forget the four Geneva Conventions of 1949. Co-ordination will thus lead to a comparison, which will be salutary, between the formulations and definitions of rights, as also between the various systems of guarantee.

Regionalisation—and Mr Lalive has shown us this by means of his rapid but complete survey of our planet—is also illustrated by the value acquired by our Convention as an example. During the discussion, the old but ever topical problem of the advantages and disadvantages of regional arrangements for the international protection of human rights was evoked, often with some passion. For my part, I feel that if human rights, in their conception and their principles, are expressed in an analogous form in all continents, the same is not always true of their effects and their realisation. In trying to universalise, one often ends up by procrastination. The Draft Covenants are there to prove it. The protection of human rights on a regional basis, on the other hand, makes it possible to take into account the manners, customs and needs of each group of States, and this will subsequently facilitate the establishment of a world-wide system. Moreover, it is comforting to realise that today even the most fanatical partisans of universalism in the protection of human rights no longer dispute the merits of the European Convention. The various draft regional conventions which, directly or indirectly, have been inspired by the example of the Council of Europe, confirm this opinion.

I could even generalise by saying that the increase in the number of Member States of the United Nations (at present there are 117) makes it ever more difficult to work out a convention on a world scale. It is natural, therefore, that countries belonging to one particular region should settle their common problems by means of regional agreements. The various bodies created by the United Nations, their Specialised Agencies and their Regional Commissions, prove this fact.

From another point of view, the regional approach to the international protection of human rights is even indispensable inasmuch as it constitutes an element in the political and economic integration of a given part of our planet. This is most certainly the case with our

European Convention which, having opened the way to European unification, has remained the corner-stone of our efforts in favour of a United Europe. To appreciate the merits of the other draft regional conventions, it would perhaps be well to place them within the framework of a general system of co-operation between States in a given region. Another subject for a fascinating comparison thus opens up not only for jurists, but also for sociologists and politicians. Will the International Human Rights Year offer us the opportunity for such a comparison? Let us hope so, for this would be useful both for regional organisations and also for the United Nations.

FUTURE PROSPECTS

I could have concluded my remarks at this juncture, had I not been asked to speak not only of the conclusions reached in our work but also of the future prospects of our Convention. When I leave Vienna, I shall be going to Delphi to be present at the laying of the foundation stone for the European Cultural Centre. What a shame it is that I have to predict the future today, when in a few days' time, after consulting the Oracle, I could have talked to you with more confidence and security.

Having heard Mr Aronstein, let us express the hope that the future will disperse the clouds which are at present casting a shadow over our Convention. I like to think that, as far as the renewal by Belgium of her acceptance of the jurisdiction of the Court is concerned, no more is involved than a mere delay in the accomplishment of an act which will reassure us all.

It is true, on the other hand, that three States have not yet ratified the Convention: France, Switzerland and Malta. There is no need to speak at length about Malta which has only just joined the Council; we should note, however, that when declaring itself in favour of Malta's membership, the Assembly was careful to stress the fact that it should be accompanied by the ratification of the Convention. One other point should be singled out: Professor Pinto expressed the opinion that, taking it all in all, it was more correct for France not to ratify the Convention than to ratify it without accepting the right of individual petition and the compulsory jurisdiction of the Court. This reasoning, which is based on the enormous disproportion between the number of applications by States—three—and that of individual applications—more than 2,500—may, however, be countered by pointing out that if the Convention were ratified by France, its provisions would have to be applied directly by the French Courts independently of the Strasbourg institutions, since under French law a treaty, once it is ratified, becomes part of the internal legal system.

Furthermore, I should like to add, as a purely legal argument, that even for a country which does not recognise the right of individual petition, the international effects of the Convention are not on that account negligible, since it is still possible for another Contracting State to make an inter-State application. The cases brought by Greece against the United Kingdom in the Cyprus affair, and by Austria against Italy in the *Fundres/Pfunders case* prove that, even without the optional clauses of Articles 25 and 46, the ratification of the Convention by those countries which have not yet done so is desirable, I would say necessary.

Throughout the three days of the Conference we have followed, step by step, the life of the Convention in the internal legal systems of the Contracting States. Yet, in addition to the direct effects which have been described to us, the Convention also has indirect effects in internal law which could form the subject of a study as interesting as it would be useful. Already at the Strasbourg Colloquy, Professor Henri Rolin stressed the indirect influence of the Convention. He pointed out how careful a State was not to be found 'guilty' by the Commission or the Court, by taking, on its own initiative if need be, the appropriate measures.

Mr Rolin referred to the *De Becker case* in which the Belgian Parliament, at the proposal of the Government, amended Article 123 *sexies* of the Criminal Code, on which the Commission had expressed its opinion and which had been sent to the Court for a decision. He also recalled that in the Cyprus affair the British Government had abrogated, on its own initiative, certain Ordinances which had been attacked by the Greek Government even before the Commission had expressed its opinion. To these two examples quoted by Mr Rolin we might today add the cases of Pataki and others in which, following contacts between the Austrian Government and the Commission, the Austrian Parliament approved the amendment of Article 294 of the Code of Criminal Procedure. These cases do not only prove the influence of the Convention on national authorities, they show—and this is to the credit of our Governments—how our Convention operates in our democratic institutions.

This observation leads me to wonder whether, in the interest of the Contracting States themselves, it would not be advisable to strengthen these indirect and, to a certain extent, preventive effects of the Convention by systematising them. Doubtless it is not unusual for a Government to screen a Bill dealing with human rights in the light of the provisions of the Convention and the case-law of the Commission and Court before presenting it to Parliament. But such an examination is not yet systematically organised. Consequently I should like to draw your attention to a very happy initiative taken recently by the

Turkish Parliament at the suggestion of a former member of the Commission, Mr Nihat Erim: a 'Human Rights Group' has been formed in Turkey for the purpose of examining all Bills and proposals for laws in the light of the provisions of the Convention.

It has become customary to emphasise that one of the merits of the Convention is that it does not take account of either the nationality of its beneficiaries or the principle of reciprocity which is normally the very basis of all intercourse between men and States. To my mind, we should lay more stress on this special and original aspect of the Convention. Indeed, as the frontiers of the Contracting States are opened to the nationals of countries which are not members of the Council of Europe and to their investment capital, the 'users' of the machinery for protection introduced by the Convention will tend more and more to come from the ranks of these new arrivals. Thus, if we look at the statistics for 1964, we see that the Commission was seised of applications submitted by Americans, Algerians, Hungarians, Israelis, Jordanians, Poles, Russians, Czechs, Yugoslavs and also stateless persons. It would be extremely regrettable, and would amount to a false conception of the spirit of the Convention, if the problem of inequalities between the Contracting Parties were to arise again or if the reciprocity clause were invoked. The fact that René Cassin is President of the European Court and that Swiss and Maltese judges are also members demonstrates the community spirit which inspired the authors of our Convention. Obviously we would like the commitments to be equal and the obligations identical, and we sincerely hope that the eighteen Member States of the Council will ratify the Convention, accept the right of individual petition and recognise the compulsory jurisdiction of the Court. But the acceptance of the optional clauses by some must not condition the attitude of the others, for that would eventually compromise what has already been achieved.

One writer, Mr Pierre Duclos, recently stressed the fact that a new legal category was gradually coming into being on our continent: the European. Indeed, thanks to the combined effects of the Community Treaties and of our Convention, amongst other factors, the European is beginning to take on a legal character similar to that of a national citizen. I wonder, however, whether, thanks to the application of our Convention which knows no frontiers, the non-European is not also acquiring a true status which is legally protected in the Contracting States. Since dreams are not prohibited, might one perhaps ask whether the day will soon come when every non-European who reaches the frontiers of that part of Europe comprised in the Council will be given a document telling him what rights he will enjoy on territory which is nevertheless foreign to him?

Doubtless we have here a possible field of action for an International Institute of Human Rights, the need for which several of you—and I should like to thank you for it—have stressed. Perhaps the plan I had the honour to submit a long while ago was premature; perhaps it can be taken up again and altered in the light of our work. I sincerely hope so.

Ladies and Gentlemen, I think you have reached the end of your labours. The teaching of human rights is, in my opinion, more necessary than ever. These rights must not be a bone of contention between countries with different conceptions and different political or economic systems. The knowledge of human rights ought not to separate States and human beings, but bring them closer together.

Speaking only a few days ago in Strasbourg at the inauguration of the Human Rights Building,—and I am happy to stress the fact that today in Strasbourg there is a building dedicated to human rights— I said:

shaped by the great spiritual forces of our time, the Convention bears the stamp of universality. Its lesson is that there are not two forms of justice, one for individuals and another for States. Nor are there two ethics, one national and one international, for Justice cannot hold more than one set of scales.

Inspired by your work and remembering what the Chancellor, Dr Klaus, said at the opening session of this Conference, allow me to add today: humanity is a single unit. There must not be several types of justice for several categories of men.

F. SCHWIND

Thank you very much indeed, Mr Secretary-General, for your excellent and very moving speech. Your task was a difficult one, but you have managed to combine very felicitously the history of the Convention with the results of our discussions, adding ideas of a quite personal nature which are all the more valuable as they come from such an eminent specialist. Your speech was further evidence of the expertise and breadth of vision which we know that you possess.

Before closing our last session, I should like, on behalf of my Faculty and of its Dean, who is with us here today, to thank all those who have contributed towards the success of this Conference. We thank the officials of the Council of Europe, the Secretary-General and particularly the Deputy Secretary-General, who have placed at our disposal their experience, their skill and their industry, which have been of inestimable value to us all.

We offer our most sincere thanks to the Austrian Government.

The Federal Chancellor has been good enough to honour our Conference with his presence; his inaugural address was of great value because it showed the importance which a statesman responsible for the future of his people attaches to a subject of an academic character. The Minister for Foreign Affairs had to attend a meeting of the United Nations General Assembly and was unable to be with us in person, but he has repeatedly given proof of his personal interest in our work. The Minister of Education has, despite serious budgetary difficulties, provided us with the funds needed to hold the Conference and we thank him for it. But the foundation of the whole Conference was the work of scholars from all over Europe who kindly accepted our invitation to come to Vienna. This is not the time to pass judgment on the importance and significance of our work; we are sure, however, that it will provide the basis for further progress in the application of the Convention on Human Rights.

Our thanks are also due to the authorities who kindly gave receptions in the historic buildings of our beautiful city and thus created the atmosphere of friendship and mutual understanding which is so conducive to the success of learned discussions.

We thank very sincerely the officials of the Federal Chancellery and the Secretariat of the Conference: first and foremost, the Director-General, my eminent friend, Baron Loebenstein, who directed the secretariat and was always able to solve any difficulty which arose in his usual elegant manner.

We thank Dr Vasak very sincerely for his untiring efforts. He provided the Conference with the benefit of his experience and applied his tact to a number of delicate matters requiring a diplomatic touch.

My French vocabulary is too limited to pay tribute to the work of Dr Pahr. What he has done was quite contrary to the European Convention on Human Rights, in particular Article 8, for his right to respect for his private and family life was flagrantly violated.

I hope, Ladies and Gentlemen, that, with the advantage of the fine weather, you have had a pleasant stay in our capital and that you will visit it again. I wish you a safe journey home and thank you once more for your help, your attention and your presence.

APPENDIX

List of Participants

PROFESSOR MUAMMER AKSOY, *Professor of Law, Cebeci-Ankara, Turkey*
DR WALTER ANTONIOLLI, *President of the Constitutional Court, Vienna, Austria*
MR GEORGES ARONSTEIN, *President of the Belgian League for the Defence of the Rights of Man, Brussels, Belgium*
DR ILHAN ARSEL, *Professor of Law, Bakirköy–Istanbul, Turkey*
PROFESSOR KADER ASMAL, *Lecturer in Law, Trinity College, Dublin, Ireland*
MME LOUISE AYNARD, *Paris 6e, France*
MR G. BALLADORE-PALLIERI, *Judge on the European Court of Human Rights, Professor of International Law, Milan, Italy*
DR T. BALTA, *Professor of Public Law, Member of the European Commission of Human Rights, Ankara, Turkey*
MR ROGER BÄR, *Attaché in the Legal Section, Federal Political Department, Berne, Switzerland*
DR GERHARD BEBR, *Counsellor in the Legal Department of the European Executives (E.E.C.), Brussels, Belgium*
DR HANS BECK, *Attorney, Vienna, Austria*
DR MAHMUT BELIK, *Professor in the Faculty of Law, Istanbul, Turkey*
MR PETER BENENSON, *President of the International Executive, Amnesty International, London, England*
DR RUDOLF BERNHARDT, *University Professor, Frankfurt-am-Main, Federal Republic of Germany*
DR WILHELM BERTRAM, *Ministerial Counsellor, Ministry of Justice, Member of the Committee of Experts on Human Rights of the Council of Europe, Bonn, Federal Republic of Germany*
MR ANDRÉ BLONDEL, *Professor in the Faculty of Law, Dijon, France*
MR MENNO J. VAN EMDE BOAS, *Lecturer in Public International Law, Leyden, Netherlands*
DR KURT BRACKMANN, *President of a Chamber in the Federal Court for Social Affairs, Kassel, Federal Republic of Germany*
DR HEINRICH BRÖLL, *Hofrat in the Supreme Court, Vienna, Austria*
DR JOHANN W. BRÜGEL, *Freelance writer, London, England*
MR JACQUES DE BRUYN, *Delegate of the World Veterans' Federation, Brussels, Belgium*
MR THOMAS BUERGENTHAL, *Professor of Law, State University of New York, Buffalo, N.Y., U.S.A.*
MR FRANCESCO CAPOTORTI, *Professor of International Law, University of Bari, Italy*
MR MIGUEL CASTRILLO, *Lecturer in International Law, Oviedo, Spain*
MRS ANNAR CASSAM, *London, England*
MR EDIP CELIK, *Professor of Law, University of Istanbul, Turkey*

The Hon. MR JUSTICE J. J. CREMONA, *Judge on the European Court of Human Rights, Vice-President of the Constitutional Court and Court of Appeal, Malta*

FATHER M. B. CROWE, *University Lecturer in Philosophy, University College Dublin, Ireland*

DR FRITZ CZERWENKA, *Lawyer, Vienna, Austria*

MME ERICA DAIS, *Attorney, Athens, Greece*

MR JACQUES DEHAUSSY, *Dean of the Faculty of Law, University of Dijon, France*

MR NIHAT DINC, *Permanent Representative of Turkey to the Council of Europe, Strasbourg, France*

PROFESSOR KARL DOEHRING, *Member of the Max Planck Institute, Heidelberg, Federal Republic of Germany*

DR HANS DRECHLER, *Director, Federal Ministry of Justice, Vienna, Austria*

MR MARC-ANDRÉ EISSEN, *Deputy Secretary of the European Commission of Human Rights, Council of Europe, Strasbourg, France*

MR KJELL ELIASSEN, *Counsellor, Ministry of Foreign Affairs, Member of the Committee of Experts on Human Rights of the Council of Europe, Oslo, Norway*

MR GEORG-HEINRICH ELKMANN, *St Gallen, Switzerland*

PROFESSOR FELIX ERMACORA, *Member of the European Commission of Human Rights, Professor of Law, Vienna, Austria*

MR BÜLENT NURI ESEN, *Professor of Law, Ankara, Turkey*

MR W. V. J. EVANS, *Deputy Legal Adviser, Foreign Office, London, England*

MR GUY FEUER, *Professor of Law, University of Strasbourg, Strasbourg, France*

DR KARL FIRSCHING, *Judge on the Court of Appeal, University lecturer, Munich, Federal Republic of Germany*

DR CARL-AUGUST FLEISCHHAUER, *Counsellor, Member of the Committee of Experts on Human Rights of the Council of Europe, Bonn, Federal Republic of Germany*

DR ISI FOIGHEL, *Professor, Copenhagen, Denmark*

PROFESSOR W. J. GANSHOF VAN DER MEERSCH, *Premier Avocat Général à la Cour de Cassation, President of the Institute of European Studies, Brussels, Belgium*

MR MICHEL GAUDET, *Director General of the Legal Service of the European Executives (E.E.C.), Brussels, Belgium*

MR FRANÇOIS GOERENS, *Avocat Général, Luxembourg*

MR F. GOLDIE, *Assistant Professor, Loyola University School of Law, Los Angeles, U.S.A.*

DR HERIBERT GOLSONG, *Registrar of the European Court of Human Rights, Council of Europe, Strasbourg, France*

MR ANTHONY GOMREE, *Magistrate at the Ministry of Justice, Member of the Committee of Experts on Human Rights of the Council of Europe, Brussels, Belgium*

DR WILLFRIED GREDLER, *Permanent Representative of the Austrian Federal Republic to the Council of Europe, Strasbourg, France*

DR THEODOR GRUBER, *Secretariat of the European Commission of Human Rights, Strasbourg, France*

DR WALTHER J. HABSCHEID, *Professor at the University of Würzburg, Würzburg, Federal Republic of Germany*

DR RUDOLF HARTMANN, *Hofrat on the Supreme Court, Vienna, Austria*

MR PAUL-EMILE HEIM, *Member of the Secretariat-General of the Council of Europe, Strasbourg, France*

DR PAUL HEMPEL, *former Director-General in the Ministry of Social Affairs, Vienna, Austria*

MR GUY HERAUD, *Professor of Law, University of Strasbourg, Strasbourg, France*

SIR SAMUEL HOARE, *Chairman of the Committee of Experts on Human Rights of the Council of Europe, London, England*

DR HANS HUBER, *Professor in the Law Faculty, University of Berne, Switzerland*

DR ERNST JAHODA, *Attorney, Delegate of the International Federation of the Rights of Man, Vienna, Austria*

MR PAUL JAQUET, *Professor in the Faculty of Law, Nancy, France*

MR PETER EMIL JUCHLI, *St Gallen, Switzerland*

MR BLAISE JUNOD, *Assistant in the Faculty of Law, La Chaux-de-Fonds, Switzerland*

MR MÜNCI KAPANI, *Professor of Public Law, Ankara, Turkey*

DR RUDOLF KIRCHSCHLÄGER, *Chef de Cabinet of the Minister for Foreign Affairs, Vienna, Austria*

DR HANS KLECATSKY, *Professor at Innsbruck University, Innsbruck, Austria*

DR KARL KLEE, *Ministerial Counsellor, Palace of Justice, Vienna, Austria*

DR PAUL KLEINKNECHT, *Judge on the District Court, Stuttgart, Federal Republic of Germany*

MR ALFRED KOBZINA, *Parlamentsrat, Vienna, Austria*

DR GÜNTHER KUNST, *Public Attorney, Vienna, Austria*

MR JEAN-FLAVIEN LALIVE, *Attorney at the Geneva Bar, Geneva, Switzerland*

MR VASSILIOS LAMBADARIOS, *Professor, Secretary-General of the Institute of International Law, Athens, Greece*

DR FRIEDRICH LEHNE, *Hofrat at the Federal Administrative Court, Vienna, Austria*

MR PETER LEUPRECHT, *Secretary of the Legal Committee of the Assembly of the Council of Europe, Strasbourg, France*

MR DENIS LEVY, *Professor in the Faculty of Law, Director of the Political Science Department of the Centre of European Studies, University of Nancy, France*

DR VIKTOR LIEBSCHER, *Public Attorney, Vienna, Austria*

MR JOSEPH LINTON, *Consultant on International Affairs, World Jewish Congress, London, England*

MISS FRANCES LIVINGSTONE, *Research Assistant, British Institute of International and Comparative Law, London, England*

DR EDWIN LOEBENSTEIN, *Head of Section in the Federal Chancellery, Vienna, Austria*

MR ÅGE LORENZEN, *President of the Supreme Court of Denmark, Copenhagen, Denmark*

PROFESSOR ANTONIO DE LUNA, *Spanish Ambassador, Vienna, Austria*

MR SEÁN MACBRIDE, *Secretary-General of the International Commission of Jurists, Geneva, Switzerland*

MR IAIN C. MACGIBBON, *Law Teacher, Department of Public International Law, University of Edinburgh, Scotland*

DR RUDOLF MACHACEK, *Attorney, Secretary-General of the Austrian Commission of Jurists, Vienna, Austria*

PROFESSOR ANDREW MARTIN, Q.C., *Law Commissioner, London, England*

MR JEAN MASQUELIN, *Counsellor of State, Brussels, Belgium*

MR ANGELO DE MATTIA, *Judge on the Italian Supreme Court, Bologna, Italy*

MR THEODOR MAYER-MALY, *Professor in the Law Faculty of the University of Cologne, Federal Republic of Germany*

MR A. B. MCNULTY, *Secretary of the European Commission of Human Rights, Council of Europe, Strasbourg, France*

DR ERWIN MELICHAR, *Professor at Vienna University, Austria*

MR PIERRE MERTENS, *Research Assistant, University of Brussels, Belgium*

MR HANS MICHELSEN, *Attorney-General, Oslo, Norway*

DR HERBERT MIEHSLER, *University Lecturer, Vienna, Austria*

MR MARIO MIELE, *Professor of Internationl Law, Rome, Italy*

MRS C. MOLANPHY, *Freedom Through Law, New York, United States*

DR JOHANN MOKRE, *Professor at the University of Graz, Austria*

MR EUGÈNE MULLER, *Government Attaché, Member of the Committee of Experts on Human Rights of the Council of Europe, Ministry of Justice, Luxembourg*

DR ERIK NETTEL, *Ministerialsecretar, Federal Ministry for Foreign Affairs, Vienna, Austria*

MR ANDREAS O'KEEFE, *Judge of the Supreme Court, Dublin, Ireland*

MR SELCUK ÖZCELIK, *Professor of Constitutional Law, University of Istanbul, Turkey*

DR WILLIBALD PAHR, *Member of the Constitutional Service of the Federal Chancellery, Member of the Committee of Experts on Human Rights of the Council of Europe, Vienna, Austria*

MR PIETRO PASCALINO, *Rome, Italy*

MR FRANS DE PAUW DE VEEN, *Professor in the University of Brussels, Belgium*

MR GUSTAF PETRÉN, *Judge, Swedish Secretary-General of the Nordic Council, Stockholm, Sweden*

MR STURE PETRÉN, *President of the Svea Court of Appeal, President of the European Commission of Human Rights, Stockholm, Sweden*

DR RUDOLF PETZ, *University Lecturer, Graz, Austria*

DR HERBERT PETZOLD, *Rechtsreferendar, Gütersloh, Federal Republic of Germany*

DR HELFRIED PFEIFER, *University Professor, Vienna, Austria*

MR ALLAN PHILIP, *Professor, Copenhagen, Denmark*

MR JEAN PICTET, *Director of the International Committee of the Red Cross, Geneva, Switzerland*

MR NICOLA PICARDI, *Magistrate, Ministry of Justice, Rome, Italy*
MR ROGER PINTO, *Professor at the Faculty of Law, Paris, France*
DR FELICIAN PRILL, *Permanent Representative of the Federal Republic of Germany to the Council of Europe, Strasbourg, France*
DR W. F. PRINS, *Professor at Utrecht University, Netherlands*
MR HANS-GÜNTHER RABIGER, *Rechtsreferendar, Northeim, Federal Republic of Germany*
MR CHARLES VAN REEPINGHEN, *Royal Commissioner on Law Reform, Brussels, Belgium*
MR ERIK RISBJØRN, *Member of the Committee of Experts on Human Rights of the Council of Europe, Copenhagen, Denmark*
DR A. H. ROBERTSON, *Head of the Directorate of Human Rights of the Council of Europe, Strasbourg, France*
MLLE JACQUELINE ROCHETTE, *Paris, France*
MR KERSTEN ROGGE, *Secretariat of the European Commission of Human Rights, Strasbourg, France*
DR WILHELM ROSENZWEIG, *Member of the Federal Constitutional Court, Vienna, Austria*
MR DAVID RUZIE, *Professor in the University of Clermont, France*
MR CLAUDE DE SAINT-PHALLE, *Freedom Through Law, New York, U.S.A.*
MR MARC SAND, *Directorate of Human Rights, Council of Europe, Strasbourg, France*
MR JEAN-PIERRE SAULEAU, *Law student, Laval, France*
MR BAHRI SAVCI, *Professor in the Faculty of Political Science, University of Ankara, Ankara, Turkey*
DR ULRICH SCHEUNER, *Professor in the University of Bonn, Federal Republic of Germany*
DR HANS SCHIMA, *Professor in the Law Faculty, University of Vienna, Austria*
DR GEORG SCHRÖDER, *Judge on the Federal Labour Court, Kassel, Federal Republic of Germany*
DR F. SCHWIND, *former Dean of the Law Faculty, University of Vienna, Austria*
MR EGON SCHWELB, *Professor, Yale Law School, New Haven, Conn., U.S.A.*
DR IGNAZ SEIDL-HOHENVELDERN, *Professor in the University of Cologne, Federal Republic of Germany*
MR ANGELO PIERO SERENI, *Professor of International Law, Rome, Italy*
MR LOUIS B. SOHN, *Bemis Professor of International Law, Harvard University Law School, Cambridge, Mass., U.S.A.*
MR MAX SØRENSEN, *Member of the European Commission of Human Rights, Professor in the University of Aarhus, Denmark*
DR HANS SPANNER, *University Professor, Munich, Federal Republic of Germany*
MR SILVIO TAVOLARO, *President of the Italian Supreme Court, Rome, Italy*
MR HENRI THEVENAZ, *Professor at the Faculty of Law, Neuchâtel, Switzerland*
MISS P. J. TIGLER DE LANGE, *Research Assistant at the Europa-Institute, Leyden, Netherlands*

Dr János Tóth, *International Commission of Jurists, Geneva, Switzerland*
Mr Ulf Underland, *First Secretary, Royal Norwegian Embassy, Vienna, Austria*
Mr Josef Unger, *Professor of Law, University of Birmingham, England*
Mr M. H. Van Hoogstraten, *Secretary-General of the Conference on Private International Law, The Hague, Netherlands*
Dr C. W. Van Santen, *Member of the Committee of Experts on Human Rights of the Council of Europe, The Hague, Netherlands*
Mr A. T. Vanwelkenhuyzen, *Director of the Inter-University Centre of Public Law, Brussels, Belgium*
Mr Karel Vasak, *Directorate of Human Rights, Council of Europe, Strasbourg, France*
Mr Phédon Vegleris, *Member of the Committee of Experts on Human Rights of the Council of Europe, Professor at the University of Athens, Greece*
Mr Jacques Velu, *Procureur du Roi, Brussels, Belgium*
Dr Alfred Verdross, *Judge on the European Court of Human Rights, Emeritus Professor of the University of Vienna, Austria*
Mr Michel Virally, *Professor at the Faculty of Law, Geneva, Switzerland*
Mr Michel Waelbroeck, *Director of Legal Research, Institute of European Studies, Brussels, Belgium*
Dr Robert Walter, *Professor in the University of Graz, Austria*
Mr Mogens Warberg, *Permanent Representative of Denmark to the Council of Europe, Ministry of Foreign Affairs, Copenhagen, Denmark*
Mr Gustav Otto Warburg, *Director, UN Liaison Office, B'nai B'rith International Council, Geneva, Switzerland*
Mr Gordon L. Weil, *Deputy Official Spokesman, E.E.C. Commission, Brussels, Belgium*
Dr Hans Weiler, *Ministerial Counsellor, Vienna, Austria*
Dr Paul Weis, *Director, Legal Division, Office of the High Commissioner for Refugees, Geneva, Switzerland*
Dr Günther Winkler, *Dean of the Law Faculty, University of Vienna, Austria*
Mr Terje Wold, *Judge on the European Court of Human Rights, Supreme Court of Norway, Oslo, Norway*
Dr Karl Zemanek, *University Professor, Vienna, Austria*

Index

administrative proceedings, 208ff, 212; fair trial in, 188ff, 197
Aerial Incident case, 293
Africa, 324; regional conventions, 337f, 341; Organisation of African Unity, 331, 341
African Congress of Jurists, 331; Convention of Human Rights, 337
aliens: expulsion, 206, 211, 240f, 248, 364; internment, 160; political activity, 258f; protection, 218, 258f, 267
Ambatielos case, 138n, 292
America: regional conventions, 333f; Central, 337; Latin, 336f; South, 337
American: Inter-American Commission on Human Rights, 335; Inter-American Convention on Human Rights (Santiago draft), 331, 334, 336, 356; Organisation of American States, 330; — Conferences at Bogota, 334, at Santiago, 334; Organisation of Central American States, 331, 335
American Law Institute: restatement of Foreign Relations Law of U.S., 146
Amnesty International, 292, 340
Anzilotti, D., 47
apartheid, 144
appeal procedure, 207
Arab League, 330, 339
arbitration, 128, 131ff, 145, 147, 174; Convention on Recognition of Foreign Arbitral Awards, 145
arrest, rights under, 154ff, 160–5
Asia: regional conventions, 338f, 341
association, freedom of, 88, 91, 311; Convention on, 310; Fact-finding Conciliation Commission on, 296, 311
Asylum case, 292
asylum, right of, 346–52, 359ff, 365; Declaration on, 360
Aurore case, 132n
Austria, 15, 34, 53, 60, 95, 100, 102, 208f, 215, 229, 231, 233, 238, 240,

278; v. *Italy*, 107, 136ff, 172n, 177ff, 184ff
Azikiwe, Dr, 337
Azmi, —, 356

B against Ireland, 110n
Bakaert, H., 129
Bangkok, 338
Barcelona Traction, Light and Power Co Ltd case, 134n
Bavarian: Administrative Court, 252; Appeals Court, 189; High Court, 240
Beaufort, Father, 186
Beccaria, — 203
Belgium, 16, 41, 52, 102, 215, 229, 233, 238, 254; Court of Cassation, 132f; linguistic disputes, 148, 249, 262; Supreme Court, 168
Bentham, Jeremy, 290
Bill of Rights, British, 325
binding conventions, 147
Boeckmans case, 68, 126, 139n, 147
Brazilian Loans case, 235n
British Commonwealth, 325, 331, 339
Broda, Dr, 363
Brussels: future Conference, 371

Cambier, C., 133
Cameroun case, 293
Canada, 325; Bill of Rights, 354
Capitant, Henri, 97
Capotorti, F., 323
Cassin, René, 379
CENTO, 331
Central American Convention on Human Rights, 335f
centralisation of non-governmental organisations, 296, 318, 327
Chaumont, Professor, 45, 124n
Chorzow Factory case, 235n
church influence in promoting human rights, 327
civil and political rights, 93, 215; *see also* U.N. Draft Covenants on Human Rights
Civil Liberties Union, 292
civil proceedings, fair trial in, 173

389

Collective Bargaining, Convention on, 310
Colombia, Greater, 337
Colonialism, Declaration against, 147
COMECON countries, 358
Commission of Human Rights, European, and public interest, 99f, 112ff; applications by Contracting Parties, 105ff; — by individuals and non-governmental organisations, 108ff; — by nationals of non-member states, 109, 379; — inadmissible, 111; — procedure simplification, 150, 364; — procedure slowness, 344; — recognition of competence to examine (Art. 25), 33, 52–3, 56, 111, 117ff, 134ff, 343f, 346, 358; conciliation, 123ff, 149; decisions, xiv, 199; — not legal precedents, 270; decision on 'competent court', 155ff; — on *ordre public*, 100; — in Nielsen case, 153; duty before Court of Human Rights, 113; *ex officio* examination of complaints, 114f; hearings *in camera*, 374; immunities of members, 30; interpretation of reservations, 37; — of fair trial, 172, 174ff; — of trial within reasonable time, 163; Plenary Commission, 364; role of, 112f; rules of procedure, 111n, 113
Committee of Experts, 365; views on conciliation, 125
Committee of Ministers, 45, 51, 53; and conciliation, 123; competence regarding violations of Convention, 117; decisions, 233f, 365
Communist Party of U.S. v. *Subversive Activities Control Board*, 256n
communities of states, 8f
compensation, 124, 126f, 149, 165, 211
'competent court', 155f
complaint procedures, international, 296f
compulsion to change domestic legislation, 52
conciliation, 52, 123ff, 128, 149
Conference of Senior Officials, 20, 45
Congo, 315
Consultative Assembly, 45, 46n
contractual obligations (employees'), 270
Convention of Human Rights: accession by non-European states, 353–5;

— by U.S.A., 355, 357, 362; breaches of, 100, 281; collective enforcement, 106, 119; effectiveness, 342–6; First International Conference, xi; ignorance about, 283, 343ff; influence on U.N. jurisprudence, 287; interaction with bilateral agreements between Contracting Parties, 88f; — with European Communities, 371; — with international agreements, 84ff, 370f; List of Decisions of National Courts relating to, 266; political purpose, 345f; precedence over national rules, 52f, 102, 275; publications, 284; publicity, 283, 327, 345, 374; ratification and constitutional status, 34ff, 41ff, 55, 62, 68, 102ff, 228, 324, 377ff; reservations, 35, 37, 44, 95, 118f; self-executing nature, 44ff, 56, 62, 64, 101ff, 230f, 368; seminars on, 345; signatories, 228; text, authentic and original, 44, 54, 69f; uniform interpretation, 33, 223ff, 236f, 275, 281f, 287, 365;
and municipal law and national courts, 65, 69, 94, 101f, 134ff, 227, 228ff, 234ff, 238f, 264ff, 278ff, 367, 369, 372, 378; as binding international law, 221; in rules of law, 47ff, 55, 68;
'optional clauses' Art. 25 and 46, 378f; Art. 2, 239; Art. 3, 240ff, 267; Art. 4, 242ff; Art. 5, 154–70, 204 *passim*; Art. 6, 131ff, 171–94, 207 *passim*; Art. 7, 245ff, 268; Art. 8, 247ff, 266, 270; Art. 9, 253ff; Art. 10, 258ff; Art. 11, 260ff; Art. 12, 250ff; Art. 13, 194–7, 201 *passim*; Art. 15, 262f; Art. 16, 258ff; Art. 17, 262f; Art. 18, 262f; Art. 19, 112f; Art. 62, 127ff; Protocols: First, 86, 116, 119, 249; Second, 135n; Third, 123; Fourth, 116, 119, 364; additional, 364f
Costa Rica, 306, 312
Council of Europe, 2, 4, 95; Secretary-General, 54, 56, 101, 375; seminars, 345; Statute, 86, 90, 103
Court of Human Rights, European, xi, 28, 199; advisory opinions on interpretation of Convention, 44, 365; binding decisions, 233f; cases brought by Contracting Parties, 105;

Court of Human Rights—*continued;* decision in *Lawless case,* 152; different legal opinion from Commission, 53; direct individual application, 39; discontinuance of cases, 115f, 126; *ex officio* examination of cases, 115; immunities of members, 30; implementation of Convention, 51ff; President, 379; recognition of compulsory jurisdiction (Art. 46), 117ff, 134ff, 324, 343f, 346, 358; role, 112f; Rules, 115f

court proceedings, fairness in, 171ff, 188ff; rights of individual in, 151ff

courts, access to, 88, 91

criminal: defendant, specific rights, 176f, 179, 191ff; law procedures on minor offences, 129f; proceedings, fair trial in, 171

cultural and social rights, 215

Cyprus, 30, 122, 228, 278, 355, 370, 378

Czechoslovakia, 241

Dabin, Professor, 128

Da Costa et al v. *Netherlands Taxation Authorities,* 28n

death penalty, 239

de Becker case, 52, 54, 116, 122n, 224n, 233n, 259, 293, 365, 378

Declaration of the Rights of Man 1789, 214

declarations: implementation of, 320; on human rights, 315ff

defendant's rights: information on charges, 179; preparation of defence, 179f; right to counsel, 181, 192; examination of witnesses, 183, 192f; assistance of interpreter, 187

Dehousse, Fernand, 19

de la Torre case, 292

Denmark, 102, 228

deportation, 159f, 165

derogation from conflicting international agreements, 93, 95; from obligations, 26, 54, 119, 370; in time of war or emergency, 59, 120ff

detention in an asylum, 189; on suspicion, 152f; pending trial, 162f, 166ff; — relation to probable sentence, 169, 205, 211; permissible, 154ff; preventive, 170; rights of persons in, 160f, 162 *passim,* 179, 205

Deutsche Gesellschaft für Völkerrecht, 13n

dignity of the human person, 38f

diplomatic protection, 106

discontinuance of cases, 115f, 126

discrimination, prohibition of, 261f; I.L.O. Discrimination (Employment) Convention, 309

Dominican Republic, 315, 335, 336, 356

Duclos, Pierre, 379

Dunshirn v. *Austria,* 53, 172, 173n

Dupuy, R. J., 109f, 124

Echterhölter, —, 57f

ECOSOC, Economic and Social Council, 292f; reporting system, 295f

economic, social and cultural rights, 93; Draft Covenant on, 296; *see also* U.N. Draft Covenants on Human Rights

education, freedom of, 88, 91, 250; *see* UNESCO Convention on Discrimination in Education

effective remedy, right of, 51, 54, 68, 210; Commission interpretation of, 194; national courts interpretation of, 134, 196; exhaustion of domestic remedies, 141ff, 269

Egypt, 241, 313

Ehrlich, Stanislaw, 301

Eissen, M.-A., 113

elections, free, 101

El Erian, 356

emergency, derogation in, 59, 120ff

equality of arms, 172, 190, 207, 293

Ermacora, F., 187, 363

ESCS, 92

Establishment, European Convention on, 87

EURATOM, 92, 135n

Europe: regional conventions, 333; unification, 367

Europe, Eastern: exclusion of international implementation, 303, 306; human rights in, 299ff, 333; law reform, 301f, 358; peaceful co-existence policy, 304ff; trends in international law, 305

'European' as a legal character, 5, 379

European Committee on Crime Problems, 370

European Communities, 18, 46, 94; judicial bodies of, 92

European Economic Community: Court of Justice, 24, 43, 224f; Treaty, 19, 24, 27–8, 95, 135n, 223, 232
European Parliament, 19
European Social Charter, 365f
extradition, 159f, 240f; European Convention on, 349, 360

family life, protection of, 247ff
Fawcett, J. E. S., 289–99, 313f, 316, 323, 327
Fiji, 291
Fitzmaurice, —, 76, 78
Flaminio Costa v. *E.N.E.L.*, 19n
Foster and Elain v. *Neilson*, 23
France, 16, 95, 278; non-ratification of Convention, 92, 94, 228, 286, 322
friendly settlement, 123ff, 149, 205
Fuji v. *State of California*, 221n
Fyfe, Sir David Maxwell, 45, 121n

Ganshof van der Meersch, 320, 371
Genocide Convention, 305f, 308
Germany, East: immigrants from, 240; sentences imposed in, 155, 240
Germany, Federal Republic of, 15f, 102, 155, 215, 229 *passim*; Basic Law, 38f, 57ff; compatibility of Criminal Code with Convention, 140f; retrospective punishment, 245ff
Glaser et al v. *Austria*, 172n
Golsong, H., 92, 363
Greece, 16, 170, 230, 258; *against United Kingdom*, 116, 122
Greek-Turkish exchange of population, 12n, 50n
Guardianship of Infants Convention case, 292
Guggenheim, P., 277
Guieyesse case, 132n
Guradze, Heinz, 56–9

Haussmann, D., 64n
High Commissioner (European), 149
High Commissioner for Human Rights; for Refugees: *see* United Nations
Hinsley, F. H., 290n
Hoare, Sir Samuel, 45, 323
homosexuality, 239, 247
Hopfinger v. *Austria*, 53, 173n, 181n, 184n

human rights: before Commission and Court, 114ff; declarations on, 315ff; disputes, international judicial settlement of, 292ff; divergent concepts of, 324; High Commissioner for, *see* United Nations; inalienable under Convention, 59f; in Eastern Europe, 299ff; in national law, 54, 214ff; in international conventions, 294ff, 308ff; in international law, 218ff; protection, need for independent judiciary, 331f; —, universal, 289ff, 323ff, 328; publicity for, 289ff; regional commissioners, 299, 318; regional groupings for protection, 326, 328; research on, 40; restrictive clauses on, 119, 262f; under United Nations, 307–17; victim of violation of, 109f
Hungary, 302; refugees, 351

Iceland, 102, 228, 261
incorporation, doctrine of, 56f, 63
India, 339
individuals: application to Commission, 108ff; inadmissible applications by, 111; judicial protection of, 25, 209; petitions in United Nations, 324; rights, acquisition of, 66f; — in court proceedings, 151ff; — in international law, 31ff, 219; — in national law, 31ff; — of petition (Art. 25), xi, 29, 65, 70, 310, 319, 321f; *see also* Commission, recognition of competence to examine applications
information, freedom of, Convention, 310; Convention on International Right of Correction, 310
innocence, presumption of, 171, 177ff, 191
institutional guarantees (Central Europe), 216
Interhandel case, 143n
International Court of Justice: advisory opinion on cases, 292f, 295; Statute, 57, 222
international court with compulsory jurisdiction (proposed), 40
International Institute for Unification of Private Law, 280n
International Institute of Human Rights (proposed), 371, 380
international judicial bodies, 92

International Labour Organisation, Commissions and Conventions, 220, 221n, 279f, 296, 309; reporting system and complaint procedures, 295f
international law, implementation, 50f; primacy of, 49ff
International Law Commission, 74ff
international research centre on human rights (proposed), 40
international treaties, conflicts between, 72–96; significance in national law, 22ff
interpreter, assistance of, 143, 187, 194
intervention on behalf of an individual not a national, 106
Ireland, 14, 102, 121f, 228
Israel, 313
Italy, 16, 42, 100, 102, 200ff, 215, 230
Iversen case, 242n, 244n

Jescheck, —, 268n
judges, competence of, 206; obligation to protect rights of accused, 187, 207
judgment of I.L.O. Administrative Tribunal on Complaints against UNESCO, 293
judicial protection against sovereign power, 209
Jurists: African Congress of, 331; Commission of African, 338; Congress of South-East Asian and Pacific, 338; International Commission of, 292, 298
jurists' views, divergence of Anglo-Saxon and Continental, 206, 208, 212
jus gentium, 217, 222
justice, deferment of, 210

Kaufmann, Erich, 56
Kelsen, Hans, 40, 48, 63
Kiss, A. C., 106
Klaus, Josef, 1–3, 363
Klein, —, 58f
Krishnaswami, —, 305

labour, compulsory, 242ff; ad hoc Committee on Forced, 296; I.L.O. agreements on Abolition of Forced, 91, 95, 309
labour relations, 310
Lagos, Law of, 337
language: disputes in Belgium, 249, 262; of Convention, variance in

texts, 54, 188; of information to arrested persons, 161, 179
Lannung, H., 106
Laswell, H. D., 305
Lausanne Convention, 12
Lauterpacht, H., 304
Lawless case, 112f, 122, 152, 157, 161, 166, 170, 225, 236n, 238n, 262f, 293, 365
Law of Treaties, 74, 76f; and *l'ordre public international*, 146
League of Nations, 218
lectures on Convention, 285
legal aid system, 364
liberty, deprivation of, 154ff; right to, 204f
life, security of, 239
Ligue Belge des Droits de l'Homme, 292
Locke, John, 214
Loebenstein, E., 62, 363, 381
Lukács, György, 302
Lukié, Radomir, 301
Luxembourg, 16, 18, 41, 102, 229, 278

MacBride, Séan, 298n, 306
MacMillan, Harold, 104
McNulty, A. B., 363
Malik, —, 356
Malta, 95, 228; Bill of Rights, 325f
marriage, protection of, 216, 247ff; right to, 148, 250ff, 268
Marshall, Chief Justice, 23
Matznetter v. *Austria*, 164n, 189n
Mavromatis case, 106n
mediation, 128
Meyer-Lindenberg, 57, 59
migrant workers, 148
Ministère public, 112ff
minorities, 323; Sub-Commission on Protection of, 305
minors, detention of, 158f, 165
Mixed Commission and Arbitral Tribunal, 218
Modinos, Polys, 353–80
monism, radical and moderate, 49, 67f
movement, freedom of, 145, 364
Movchan, A. V., 303
Muuls, —, 45

Nassinowsky, —, 306
national courts, and Art. 5 of Convention, 166ff; and Art. 6 of Convention, 188ff, 207; application of

national courts—*continued;*
  Convention *ex officio,* 134ff; List of
  Decisions relating to Convention,
  266
national law: obligation to conform
  with Convention, 51, 53, 55, 71, 233,
  264ff, 275f; obligation to implement international treaties, 11ff,
  13ff, 29f, 63
nationality, 309; of applicants to
  Commission, 109, 379
NATO, 330
Natural Resources, Declaration on
  Sovereignty over, 147
Netherlands, 16, 41, 102, 149, 215,
  229, 238, 243, 249, 251, 261, 278;
  religious freedom in, 254ff
Neumeister v. *Austria,* 158, 161, 163n,
  164n, 189n
Nielsen case, 153, 172n, 180
Nigeria, 355
Nihat Erim, 379
Nipperdey, —, 270
non-governmental organisations: ap-
  plications to Commission, 108ff;
  centralisation of, 296, 318, 327
Norway, 46, 102, 228, 233, 243
Norwegian Loans case, 235n
Nottebohm case, 106n, 235n
Nuremburg Clause (Austrian Civil
  Code), 60

Ofner v. *Austria,* 53, 173n, 181n, 184n
ombudsman, 149f, 210; international,
  298, 318, 324, 375
opinion, freedom of, 259
Oppenheim, L., 75n, 76
optional clauses in Convention (Art.
  25 and 46), 378f; *see also* Commission, recognition of competence
  to examine applications; and Court
  of Human Rights, recognition of
  compulsory jurisdiction
ordre public, xiii, 97–143, 144 *passim;*
  and the Convention, 103ff; *européen,*
  148; in international law, 98ff; in
  municipal law, 97f
Outer Space, Declaration of Legal
  Principles governing activities of
  States in use of, 147

Pahr, W., 363, 381
Panama–U.S.A. dispute, 150
Panevezys-Saldutiskis case, 106n

Pataki v. *Austria,* 53, 172, 173n
peaceful co-existence, 304ff
Perassi, —, 45
perjury, 30, 242, 365
Permanent Court of Justice, 12, 50n,
  219
Permanent Mandates Commission,
  295
petitions: *see* individuals; and Commission, applications to
Pigorsch, —, 58
Pinto, Roger, 361
Poland, 333
political: refugees, 241; rights, 215,
  272
Pope John XXIII, 327
Prague Faculty of Law: Socialist
  charter of human rights, 333
Press, freedom of, 215f, 260; publicity
  for human rights, 290, 327
property, rights of, 216, 260f, 271
'public action', 107
public order, 144; policy, 144f
punishment by fines, 129f; degrading,
  240, 267; retrospective, 245ff; 'sleeping hard', 114, 240

racial discrimination, 309; Declaration on, 147, 291, 309
refugees, 88, 309f, 347ff; Convention
  on Status of, 88, 91, 321, 348; High
  Commissioner for, *see* United
  Nations
regional commissioners, 314
regional organisation for human rights,
  330, 355f, 359, 362, 376
religious: discrimination, 309; freedom, 254ff; Intolerance, Convention on Elimination of, 291, 309
remedies, exhaustion of domestic,
  141ff, 269
renunciation of the exercise of rights,
  131ff, 147, 148
reporting systems, 295
Rhine, Central Commission for Navigation of, 92
Rhodesia, 291
Robertson, A. H., 363
Rolin, Henri, 45, 99, 101n, 106n, 107,
  110, 111n, 112, 115, 121n, 125n, 378
Romashin, P. S., 301f
Rotterdam, High Court, 206
Rousseau, J. J., 214
Rumania, 302

Saar, 92
Saarbrücken, Court of Appeals, 168
Santiago Draft, 331, 334f, 336, 356
Scales v. *U.S.A.*, 256n
Scandinavian countries, and Conven-
    tion, 14, 150; *see also* Denmark,
    Iceland, Norway, Sweden
Schelb, Professor, 323
Scheuner, Ulrich, 38
Schwind, F. 363, 380–1
SEATO, 331, 338
Secretary-General of the Council of
    Europe: information on implement-
    ation of Convention, 54, 56, 101
self-determination, right of, 291
self-executing treaty concept, 23f, 43f,
    46
sentence, indeterminate, in German
    penal law, 157n
Serbian Loans case, 106n
Slavery Convention of 1926, 90; Con-
    vention on Abolition of Slavery, 91,
    308
'sleeping hard' punishment, 114, 240
Smithers, Peter, 2, 3–6
Soblen case, 279, 361
social and cultural rights, 215
socialist legal system, rights in, 301
    passim
Sohn, L. B., 316, 319
Sørensen, Max, 323
South Africa, 144, 314
South West Africa case, 293
Soviet Academy of Sciences, Institute
    of State and Law, 301
Soviet treatise on international pro-
    tection of human rights, 303; policy
    concerning human rights, 304
Sperduti, Professor, 138n
Stalev, Jivko, 301
Stateless Persons, Convention on
    Status of, 91; Convention on Reduc-
    tion of Statelessness, 309
Stögmüller v. *Austria*, 158, 163n
Strasbourg Colloquy, 92, 106, 115
study courses on Convention, 283;
    on human rights, 283f; on United
    Nations, 292
Sub-Commission (of Commission of
    Human Rights), 123, 127; abolition
    of, 364
Sweden, 102, 228, 248
Switzerland, 16, 95, 215, 228, 277f
Szabó, Imre, 301

tape-recordings, unauthorised, 266
*Teaching about the European Conven-
    tion in Universities*, 283
Teitgen, P. H., 104
thought, freedom of, 253ff
treaties, uniform interpretation of
    international, 27f
Treaty of Friendship, Trade and
    Navigation between Italy and Ger-
    many, 89
Treaty of Peace, 90
Treaty of Versailles, 95
trial: exclusion of public, 171; right
    to fair, 153f, 164, 170, 207; within
    reasonable time, 161ff, 166f
tribunal, public hearing by inde-
    pendent, 131ff
Triepel, H., 47
Trusteeship Council, 295
truth drug, 203
Tunkin, G. I., 303f
Turkey, and Convention, 16, 102, 121,
    149f, 239; Chair of Human Rights,
    358; Human Rights Group, Parlia-
    mentary, 379; incorporation of
    international agreements, 278; *see
    also* Greek-Turkish exchange of
    population

UNESCO: Convention on Discrimina-
    tion in Education, 91, 291, 296, 309;
    reporting system and complaint
    procedures, 295f
United Kingdom, 14, 102, 121f, 228
United Nations (U.N.): Charter, 49,
    219; —, human rights in, 99f; Com-
    mission of Human Rights, 121, 311;
    Draft Covenants on Human Rights,
    85, 91ff, 121, 145, 290f, 292, 296,
    310, 316; High Commissioner for
    Human Rights (proposed), 297ff,
    306, 312ff, 318, 321f, 326, 356, 375;
    High Commissioner for Refugees,
    298, 312, 318, 321f, 326; investiga-
    tions of violations of rights, 314f;
    regional organisations, 330; report-
    ing system 315f; seminars on human
    rights, 315; Specialised Agencies,
    87; Yearbooks on Human Rights,
    292
United States of America, 15; acces-
    sion to Convention, 355, 357, 362;
    detention of vagrants, 159; State
    Commissions on human rights,

United States of America—*continued;*
297; State Declarations of Funda-
mental Freedoms, 214; U.S.A.-
Panama dispute, 150
Universal Declaration of Human
Rights, 40, 66, 86, 99f, 146f, 216,
219ff, 287, 290, 358f
Uruguay, 297
U.S.S.R., 300 ff; basic rights in draft
Constitution, 302

vagrancy, 159
van Gend and Loos case, 25n
Vasak, Karel, 111, 141, 363, 381
Velu, Jacques, 121
Verdross, Alfred, 40
Vergin, —, 45
Verri, —, 203
Vienna: School of Law, 95; Univer-
sity of, 1
Vietnam, South, 314
von Weber, H., 268n
Vyshinsky, Andréi, 300, 303

Waldock, Sir C. H. M., 112, 323
war: derogation in, and public emergency, 59, 120ff; Convention on
Settlement of Matters Arising out
of, 370
Warsaw Colloquium of International
Association of Legal Science, 300f

Wäsche, —, 59
Weis, Paul, 323
Wemhoff v. *Federal Republic of Germany*, 163n, 181n
Wiebringhaus, H., 141n
Winkler, Günther, 4, 6–10, 363
witnesses, privileges and immunities,
365; right to call and examine, 183,
192f, 207
women, status and nationality of, 90;
Convention on Political Rights of,
309; Convention on Nationality of
Married, 309

X against Austria, 110n, 114n, 115n
X against Belgium, 114n
X against Federal Republic of Germany,
108n, 110n, 114n, 115n
*X, Y and Z against Federal Republic of
Germany*, 110n
X against Ireland, 108, 122n
X against Netherlands, 114n
X against Norway, 108

*Yearbook of the European Convention
on Human Rights*, xiv
Yugoslavia, 302f

Zemanek, Professor, 323
Zoernsch v. *Waldock and McNulty*, 30